POLITICS AND ECONOMICS OF LATIN AMERICA

POLITICS AND ECONOMICS OF LATIN AMERICA

FRANK COLUMBUS
(EDITOR)

Nova Science Publishers, Inc.
Huntington, New York

Senior Editors: Susan Boriotti and Donna Dennis
Office Manager: Annette Hellinger
Graphics: Wanda Serrano
Information Editor: Tatiana Shohov
Book Production: Cathy DeGregory, Kay Seymour, Jennifer Vogt and Lynette Van Helden
Circulation: Ave Maria Gonzalez, Ron Hedges, Andre Tillman

Library of Congress Cataloging-in-Publication Data
Available upon request.
Includes bibliographical references and index.
ISBN 1-56072-884-1

227 Main Street, Suite 100
Huntington, New York 11743
Tele. 631-424-6682 Fax 631-424-4666
e-mail: Novascience@earthlink.net
Web Site: http://www.nexusworld.com/nova

Printed in the United States of America

CONTENTS

PREFACE

This series is intended to provide a forum for substantial research contributions dealing with current political and economic developments in Latin America. The papers have been selected for their quality, relevance and timeliness. The coherence of each book rests in its fit within the larger framework of the series and its goals.

Chapter 1

POLITICAL DETERMINANTS AND ECONOMIC EFFECTS OF BANK PRIVATIZATION IN ARGENTINA

George R.G. Clarke and Robert Cull*

The World Bank

Washington, DC

1. INTRODUCTION

In 1991, facing the specter of hyperinflation, the Argentine government decided to implement a far-reaching and radical reform. The Argentine currency was pegged to the US dollar and the Central Bank was required to fully back domestic currency with international reserves. Implementation of this reform, which was known as the Convertibility Plan, had a significant effect on the Argentine economy. Inflation fell dramatically, macroeconomic stability returned, and a massive inflow of foreign investment resulted in several years of rapid economic growth.

The economic boom that followed the implementation of the Convertibility Plan ended in December 1994.[1] Spooked by devaluation in Mexico, and concerned about growing fiscal imbalances and the upcoming presidential elections, investors started to seriously question Argentina's commitment to convertibility. Anticipating devaluation, foreign investors and local consumers scrambled to convert pesos into dollars, causing a drop in international reserves. Under the currency board arrangement, this translated

---

* Respectively, Economist, Development Research Group – Public Economics, The World Bank and Economist, Development Research Group – Finance, The World Bank. We would like to thank Stefan Alber and Paul Levy for helpful comments and suggestions. For providing data and many helpful discussions we are indebted to Javier Bolzico, Andrew Powell, Gabriel Caracciolo, Maria Hernandez, Andrea Molinari, Laura D'Amato, Juan Barale, Horacio Fernandez, and Jorge Lombardi of the Central Bank of Argentina; Rogelio Frigerio, Alejandro Caldarelli, and Enrique Scala of the Fondo Fiduciario; and Raul Benitez and David Rosenblatt of the World Bank. All remaining errors are ours. The findings, interpretations, and conclusions expressed in this paper are entirely those of the authors and do not necessarily represent the view of the World Bank, its Executive Directors, or the countries they represent

[1] See World Bank (1998) for a discussion of the Convertibility Plan and its impact on the financial sector.

directly into a reduction in the domestic monetary base, which, in turn, resulted in nervous depositors withdrawing deposits from many poorly performing domestic banks.

Faced with an imminent banking crisis, and with convertibility preventing the Central Bank from acting as a lender of last resort, the Argentine government took immediate action. It negotiated a relief package with the World Bank, International Monetary Fund and the Inter-American Development Bank, and the Central Bank reduced reserve requirements to increase liquidity. Although these actions succeeded in ending the crisis, it became clear that the government would have to strengthen the banking system if it wanted to stop future currency crises from becoming banking crises. To accomplish this, the government took steps to improve regulation, strengthen supervision, and allow increased foreign entry into the sector. In addition, since many publicly owned provincial banks had suffered large deposit losses during the crisis, privatization of poorly performing public banks became an immediate priority.

It was hoped that privatization of these banks would accomplish at least three goals. First, privatizing the provincial banks was supposed to remove a fiscal burden from the provincial governments. Since the Convertibility Plan prevented the Central Bank from acting as a lender of last resort, the provincial governments would ultimately be responsible for reimbursing depositors in the case of provincial bank failure. Even if failure did not occur, the poor performance of the provincial banks threatened to impose a significant fiscal burden on the provinces – in 1995, provincial bank losses averaged over three percent of provincial revenues. Clarke and Cull (1999) show that privatization does appear to have had a positive impact in this respect – the fiscal benefits of privatization appear far greater than the immediate costs.

Second, it was hoped that privatization would improve bank performance and reduce the risk that provincial bank failure would lead to future banking crises. In this paper, we assess the effect of privatization on provincial bank performance. Although the post-privatization period has been short, and some of the privatized banks have subsequently faced problems, the initial evidence appears to be encouraging – especially given the instability in the Argentine banking system since the crisis occurred. In general, provincial banks that were privatized appear to have restructured more than provincial banks that were not and, in many cases, portfolio quality and net worth have not declined substantially since privatization. However, the banks remain heavily reliant on service contracts with the provincial governments and the transition to commercial banking has not been easy.

Finally, it was hoped that privatization would improve overall sector performance. Although the provincial banks were small on a national scale, they often dominated local markets. It was hoped that privatization would increase competition and improve the allocation of credit in the provinces. In Section 4, we assess the effect of privatization on other banks in the sector. We find preliminary evidence that strongly suggests that privatization increased competition and reduced sector concentration. This suggests that the benefits of privatization might have extended beyond the immediate impact on the performance of the individual privatized banks.

2. POLITICAL DETERMINANTS OF PRIVATIZATION

At the beginning of the 1990s, all Argentine provinces owned at least one bank (twenty provinces owned only one and three provinces owned two).[2] Many of these publicly owned banks were created in the 1950s and 1960s – although some were older – and served as development banks, provided credit to favored sectors, and helped the provincial governments to finance their operations.[3] Because the provincial banks' existence was dictated in provincial laws or constitutions, provincial governments had to pass new or amend existing laws before the banks could be privatized. Consequently, the national government could not privatize the banks without the consent of provincial policymakers.

2.1 Behavior and Performance of the Provincial Banks in the 1980s and Early 1990s

Over time, the provincial governments and the provincial banks developed a complicated relationship, with the provincial banks receiving many benefits and providing many services to the provincial governments. For example, the provincial governments would deposit tax revenues in non-interest bearing accounts in the provincial banks. However, in return, the provincial banks provided unremunerated services such as tax collection, maintained inefficient branch networks to provide banking services in remote areas, and expanded employment inefficiently to create jobs. The provincial banks also provided loans to favored enterprises and individuals at below market interest rates and would be "lenient in their collection policies" (World Bank, 1990a, p. 79).

The most important service that the provincial banks provided was to finance the provincial governments' deficits at subsidized rates. Although, in theory, provincial laws often restricted how much the provinces could borrow from the banks, these limits were ignored or sidestepped. For example, provincial banks would often agree to lend to one another, would accept provincial bonds at below market interest rates, and would discount payment orders issued by the provincial governments (World Bank, 1990a, p. 78). In 1990, more than 60 percent of the provincial governments' deficits were financed through the public provincial banks, over 20 percent were financed through other public banks, with most of the remainder being financed through arrears to suppliers and workers.[4]

The provincial banks' relationships with the provincial governments meant that the Central Bank could not regulate the provincial banks as closely as it regulated private banks. Because many important policies were dictated in provincial laws or constitutions,

---

[2] An additional bank was jointly owned by several provinces and several private sector entities.

[3] Some of the provincial banks are considerably older, with a few dating from the Nineteenth Century. Most notably, the *Banco de la Provincia de Buenos Aires* is the oldest surviving commercial bank in Argentina.

[4] Dillinger and Webb (1999, p. 6) and World Bank (1993, p. 125).

the Central Bank's regulatory powers were limited (World Bank, 1994a, p. 10). For example, because provincial laws restricted the closure or merger of the provincial banks, the Central Bank would find it difficult to reorganize or liquidate a provincial bank that was illiquid or insolvent.[5]

Despite the benefits of public ownership and loose regulation, the public provincial banks were performing poorly by the mid-1980s. There were several reasons for this. First, the banks tended to be overstaffed. In 1988, public banks (including national and municipal banks) accounted for 56 percent of banking sector employment but only 45 percent of deposits (World Bank, 1990b). Further, the banks had very poor quality loan portfolios. By June 1991, nearly 50 percent of loans by public provincial banks were non-performing, compared to about 6 percent of loans for the 10 largest private banks (see **Figure 1**). Finally, many of the banks were losing money. For example, in the first six months of 1991, profits were negative for 13 of the 26 banks and total losses exceeded $62 million (in 1995 US $).

Figure 1: Non-performing loans as percent of total loans, June 1991.

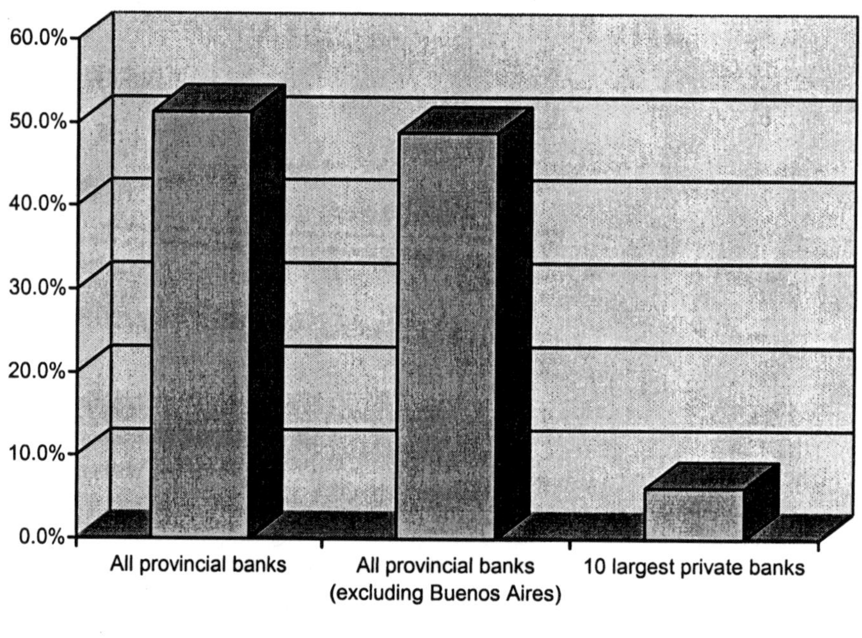

Data Source: Central Bank of the Republic of Argentina.
Note: Data excluding Buenos Aires excludes loans by *Banco de la Provincia de Buenos Aires.*

[5] World Bank (1990b, p. 139) notes "the Central Bank has considerable difficulty regulating publicly owned provincial banks, especially the banks owned by provincial governments." For example, in September 1987, the Central Bank held only 0.8 percent of the deposits of the provincial and municipal banks (excluding Banco de la Provincia de Buenos Aires) as forced investments or reserves. In contrast, 73.1 percent of the deposits of domestic private banks and 67.1 percent of the deposits of foreign private banks were forced investments or reserves (World Bank, 1990b, p. 142).

The poor performance of the public banks made it progressively harder for them to attract deposits. Between the end of 1985 and the end of 1988, total deposits in public banks fell from 117 billion Australes to 86 billion Australes, while deposits in private banks rose from 83 billion Australes to 101 billion Australes. The provinces' continued need to finance their deficits led the provincial banks to increasingly rely upon Central Bank rediscounts for funds. By March 1987, rediscount credits from the Central Bank reached 65.7 percent of deposits in provincial banks (World Bank, 1990b, p. 129). After a small drop in 1988, due to the Central Bank limiting several banks' access to rediscounts, they continued to grow.

The heavy reliance upon Central Bank rediscounts affected the provinces in several ways. First, it created tension between the provinces and the Central Bank. Although the Central Bank tried repeatedly to end or limit the provincial banks' access to this credit, political pressure usually forced it to abandon these attempts. Second, the increased use of Central Bank rediscounts amplified the Central Bank's exposure to provincial bank failure. Despite the Central Bank's limited ability to regulate the provincial banks, it faced substantial losses in the case of failure further reducing its incentives to deal forcefully with insolvent provincial banks. By pushing the cost of failure onto the Central Bank, it also reduced the provincial governments' incentives to force the banks to behave responsibly and to expend valuable resources monitoring bank behavior. Finally, access to funds from the Central Bank allowed the provinces to indirectly monetize their deficits. In federal systems, where the cost of inflation is borne by all provinces but the benefit of increased expenditures (or reduced taxes) goes to a single province, each province had a strong incentive to do this.

2.2 Macroeconomic Crisis and the Implementation of the Convertibility Plan

Irresponsible behavior by all levels of the public sector eventually began to affect macroeconomic conditions. After fourteen years when inflation was greater than 90 percent, and after several failed stabilization attempts, Argentina was finally faced with hyperinflation at the end of the 1980s. In 1989, inflation reached 3,079 percent and stayed at 2,314 in 1990 (World Bank, 1993). Although there were many contributing factors, most observers agreed that the main problem was weak public institutions, which resulted in high deficits and a heavy reliance on the inflation tax to finance the gap in public finances.[6] Although the fiscal problems of the provincial governments and their reliance upon borrowing from the provincial banks was not the only problem, the mismatch between provincial revenues and expenditures was certainly a contributing factor (see Figure 2). Between 1985 and 1991, provincial expenditures exceeded revenues (excluding transfers from the federal government) by more than the consolidated public sector deficit in four years of seven years. Further, even including transfers, provincial deficits were 10 percent of the public sector deficit in 1989, 68

[6] See, for example, World Bank (1993) for a discussion of the economic problems in the late 1980s and early 1990s.

percent in 1990 and over 100 percent in 1991. Therefore, the provincial government's problems appear to have contributed to the crisis in public finance and, ultimately, to hyperinflation.

After a failed conventional attempt at stabilization, the Peronist Menem administration, which had come to power in July 1989, introduced a radical reform, popularly known as the Convertibility Plan. The April 1991 Convertibility Law, which pegged the Argentine peso to the U.S. dollar and forced the Central Bank to restrict the monetary base to the dollar value of international reserves, was the most important part of the Convertibility Plan. To support the Convertibility Law, Congress approved a new Charter for the Central Bank in September 1992. The Charter prevented the Central Bank from guaranteeing commercial bank deposits, prevented the Central Bank from taking on any new financial assets, and restricted Central Bank credit to commercial banks to liquidity rediscounts for a period of fifteen days.

Figure 2: Fiscal balance in Argentina, 1983-1991.

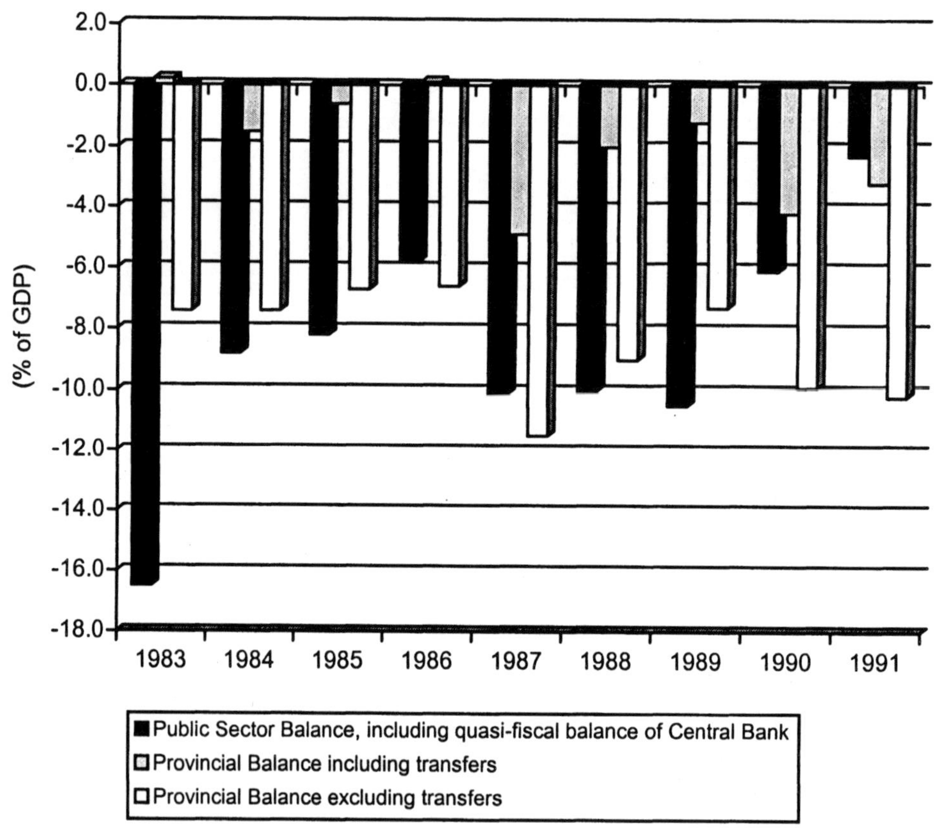

Source: World Bank (1993)
Note: Fiscal deficits are negative and surpluses are positive.

This effectively ended the provincial governments' ability of using the provincial banks to provide cheap and easy access to financing (Dillinger and Webb, 1999; Alston and Gallo, 2000). These new laws affected the provincial governments in several ways:

> "First, the charter dictated that the central bank could not take any new domestic assets. This meant that the provinces could no longer count on the central bank to rediscount loans by provincial banks to provincial governments, ending their access to seigniorage and the inflation tax. Second, the charter prohibited the central bank from guaranteeing bank deposits. Then provincial banks had to rely on depositor confidence to maintain liquidity. Both measures reduced the central bank's role as a lender of last resort and hardened the budget constraint on provinces, limiting their ability to borrow (indirectly) from the central bank or from depositors." (Dillinger and Webb, 1999, p.16)

Although these provisions did not explicitly prevent the provincial governments from borrowing from the provincial banks, it substantially increased the cost of doing so. Because they could no longer rely upon the Central Bank for bailouts, the changes meant that the provinces would have to bail out depositors from their own resources in the case of bank failure. In this way, by decreasing the benefits associated with owning a bank and increasing the risk, the Convertibility Plan made owning a poorly performing bank significantly less attractive than it had been before.

2.3 Provincial Bank Privatization and the Tequila Crisis

Ending access to Central Bank rediscounts had a modest initial impact on bank ownership. In November 1991, the provincial government of Corrientes passed a law authorizing the privatization of *Banco de Corrientes*. Over the next three years, several more provinces passed laws or decrees authorizing the privatization of their provincial banks. By the end of 1994, when the "Tequila Crisis" hit Argentina, seven provinces had passed laws authorizing the privatization of their provincial banks and either the bidding or the entire transaction was complete in five cases.[7]

Although the law changes increased the extent to which the provinces bore the costs associated with poor bank performance, the benefits of public ownership were not eliminated. For example, although the Central Bank slowly tightened the regulation of public banks, it remained looser than the regulation of private banks. Even by 1994, problems with reported portfolio quality and low provisioning meant that the reported capital of many provincial banks was thought to be overstated (World Bank, 1994b, p. 8). Further, until March 1994, reserve requirements were lower for public banks. Consequently, the provincial banks could continue to provide unremunerated services such as tax collection and employment creation and, although to a lesser degree than

[7] According to Burdisso et al (1998), a law authorizing the privatization of the Banco de San Luis was passed in early 1989, although the transaction was not completed until August 1996. In 1991, the provincial bank in La Rioja, the *Banco de la Rioja*, was closed by the Central Bank. After being reorganized, the privatization of the *Nuevo Banco de la Rioja* was authorized in August 1993. Dates for privatization laws were provided by the Fondo Fiduciario or from Burdisso et al (1998).

before, provincial politicians could still use the banks to direct credit to favored enterprises. Further, although other regulatory changes significantly restricted provincial bank lending to public sector entities, including to the provincial governments, this lending was not eliminated immediately.[8]

Several additional external factors might have also contributed to the slow pace of privatization. The success of the Convertibility Plan resulted in an economic boom and a rapid inflow of foreign capital into the Argentine banking system. Alston and Gallo (2000) suggest that this resulted in the provincial banks receiving a massive inflow of capital from both depositors and other banks and argue that this allowed many provincial banks to avoid bankruptcy and privatization.

The strong economic conditions had two other effects that also reduced the provinces need to privatize. First, although the provincial banks performed poorly relative to private banks, losses were relatively modest between 1991 and 1994 (see **Figure 3**). In 1991, the provincial banks (excluding the Banco de la Provincia de Buenos Aires, which was profitable) lost about US $116 million (in 1995 prices), less than one percent of provincial revenue (see **Figure 3**).[9] Total profits became positive in 1992, before becoming negative again in 1993 and 1994. Second, economic growth resulted in a rapid increase in provincial revenues, which grew over 60 percent between 1991 and 1994 in real terms. This, in turn, reduced fiscal pressure on the provinces and made bank privatization less urgent. Although provincial bank losses reached US $184 million (in 1995 prices) in 1994, revenue growth meant this was only 1.1 percent of revenue.

In summary, institutional changes enacted in the early 1990s increased the cost that the provinces had to pay for politically motivated lending, overstaffing and financing provincial deficits (Alston and Gallo, 2000; Dillinger and Webb, 1999). However, the economic boom that followed the implementation of the Convertibility Plan gave the provinces some breathing room. Fast credit growth, modest bank losses and rapidly expanding government revenues meant that the provinces were not forced to sell the provincial banks immediately. Consequently, less than one-third of the provinces passed laws to authorize bank privatization despite pressure from the federal government to do so.

In December 1994, the devaluation of the Mexican peso led to an attack on the Argentine peso. Anticipating a possible devaluation, customers began to withdraw dollar-denominated deposits from Argentine banks, which led to a run on all deposits in weak banks, including those in most public provincial banks. Other than *Banco de la Provincia*

[8] General restrictions on the maximum exposure to single lenders, especially affiliated lenders, restricted the amount that the provincial banks could lend to the provincial governments (Dillinger and Webb, 1999, p. 6). Further, specific provisions prevented the provincial banks from lending more to provincial public-sector entities than they had in equity and public deposits. Over time, both regulation and the enforcement of regulation became considerably tighter. In particular, bank lending to the non-financial public sector were subsequently prohibited, except for the purchase of public bonds and in a few other specific cases (see, Central Bank of the Republic of Argentina, 2000).

[9] Throughout much of the discussion, we will omit the *Banco de le Provincia de Buenos Aires*. Historically, this bank has substantially outperformed other provincial banks. A full discussion of the unique position of this bank and why it *appeared* to perform better than the other public provincial banks is beyond the scope of this paper.

de Buenos Aires, which gained deposits, nearly all public provincial banks had lost more than 14 percent of deposits, and several had lost more than 25 percent, by March 1995. In general, the worst performing banks suffered the greatest deposit flight (Clarke and Cull, 1999). The dramatic loss of liquidity facing the public banks highlighted the risks associated with owning poorly performing banks and the weaknesses inherent in public ownership (Clarke and Cull, 1998, 1999).

Although the Convertibility Law severely restricted the Central Bank's ability to respond to the crisis, it quickly took some steps to limit the damage caused by the sudden loss of liquidity.[10] However, the crisis still brought Argentina's post-Convertibility boom to a sudden stop. This, in turn, led to a collapse in provincial revenues, which fell 6 percent in real terms in 1995, and to a dramatic increase in bank losses, which increased over 200 percent (see **Figure 3**). Without a lender of last resort, the provinces found themselves facing a substantial cost, at a time when revenues were dropping precipitously. In response, many provinces began to reconsider the benefits of provincial bank privatization. In the first half of 1995, seven additional provinces passed laws or decrees authorizing privatization (see, Burdisso et al. 1998).

Figure 3: Half year operating profits of provincial banks (Jun 91-Dec 95).

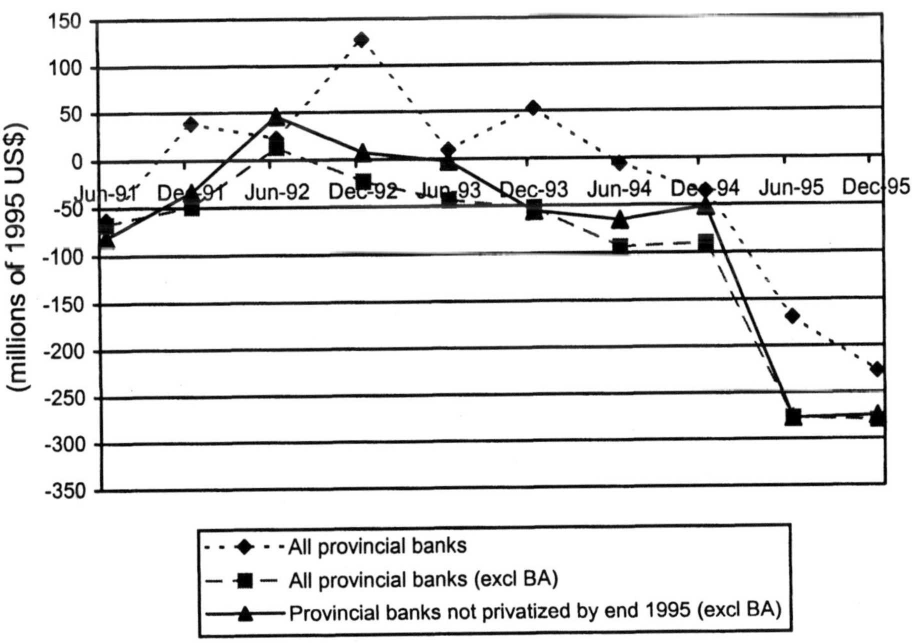

Data Source: Central Bank of the Republic of Argentina.
Note: Data excluding BA excludes Profits from *Banco de la Provincia de Buenos Aires*.

[10] In particular, it lowered reserve requirements and put a $1 billion safety net in place (Alston and Gallo, 2000).

In contrast to the provincial governments, who could still benefit in some ways from public ownership of the provincial banks, the Menem administration was firmly committed to privatization for both ideological and practical reasons. The success of the Convertibility Plan in ending inflation, which had been running at over 90 percent for the 1980s, before accelerating into hyperinflation at the end of the decade, was the administration's main achievement. Systematic bank failure, which would have led to calls for a bailout, would make it harder to remain committed to convertibility and would have therefore threatened the Menem Administration's main success. This made provincial bank privatization, which – along with strengthening of supervision and regulation, and reducing barriers to foreign entry – was seen as an integral step towards improving bank sector performance, vitally important to the Administration.

Therefore, the Administration took several additional steps to encourage the provincial governments to privatize. First, it signaled that it would continue to tighten regulation and supervision of publicly owned banks, further reducing the benefits of public ownership. Second, with the assistance of the World Bank and the Inter-American Development Bank, the administration created the Fondo Fiduciario, a federal agency that would extend loans to help the provinces privatize the provincial banks. Since provinces were only eligible to receive loans from the Fondo Fiduciario after they had privatized their banks, there was no risk that they would use the funds to re-capitalize the banks while retaining ownership.

The Fondo Fiduciario allowed the provinces to split the public provincial banks into two parts before privatization – a healthy bank to be privatized and a residual entity that contained non-viable assets. Recovery of the non-viable assets in the residual entity would not be quick enough, or on such advantageous terms, to cover all residual liabilities. Since the provinces would have to cover many short-term obligations immediately, loans from the Fondo Fiduciario gave the provinces a way to convert the short-term liabilities into long-term loans. This meant that the purchaser of the privatized bank did not have to assume ownership of all pre-privatization assets and liabilities and the province was able to receive a positive (although nominal) price for the bank.

From a political perspective, financing obligations in this way was presumably beneficial, as the yearly loan payments due to the Fondo Fiduciario are less eye-catching than the short-term obligation payments would have been. More practically, the provinces likely could not have afforded to pay off the short-term obligations immediately – the disbursement from the Fondo Fiduciario was over 10 percent of 1995 provincial revenues in all but four cases (see Table 1). It is also unlikely that many private sector banks would have been willing to assume the provincial banks' entire non-performing portfolios and matching liabilities in the midst of a banking crisis. This suggests that some provinces either would have failed to privatize their banks or would have failed to meet some of their short-term obligations. Since 44 percent of the short-term obligations retired with Fondo Fiduciario funds were to the Central Bank and 20 percent were to the publicly owned *Banco de la Nación de Argentina*, this would have been costly (see Table 1).

With this new incentive, and an uncertain liability hanging over their heads, many additional provinces decided to privatize their banks. Of the twenty-seven provincial banks, almost half had been privatized by the end of 1997, and several other privatizations had been authorized but not completed. Alston and Gallo (2000) argue that the institutional changes associated with Convertibility Plan, combined with the Tequila crisis, which would have forced many of the provincial banks to go bankrupt, were the primary factors that affected privatization decisions. In contrast, they argue that the Fondo Fiduciario mainly served to reduce the pain to creditors and to save the political lives of provincial politicians.

Table 1: Fondo Fiduciario Assistance and Liabilities Retired with Fondo Fiduciario

Bank	Total Disbursement from FFDP	Disbursement (as % of 1995 revenues)	Type of Liability Retired with Loan Proceeds			
			Debts to BCRA	Debts to BNA	Compensation to Personnel	Other Debts
Chaco	78	11.1%	78	0	0	0
Entre Ríos	78	7.2%	45.3	0	9.9	22.8
Formosa	80	14.8%	32.2	37.7	0	10.1
Jujuy	50	9.8%	21.7	7.1	19.2	2
Mendoza*	260	25.1%	169	91	0	0
Mendoza	*160*	*15.5%*	*89.7*	*70.3*	*0*	*0*
Prevision Social	*100*	*9.7%*	*79.3*	*20.7*	*0*	*0*
Misiones	78	13.6%	20.2	47.6	0	10.2
Río Negro	80	14.8%	32.2	11.5	3.9	26.7
Salta	50	6.9%	16.7	9.5	9.2	14.7
San Juan	78	14.7%	43.7	34.3	0	0
San Luis	50	11.6%	21	0	7.4	21.7
Santa Cruz	80	14.8%	0	0	0	80
Santa Fe	160	14.9%	19.8	0	16.1	124.1
Santiago del Estero	48	7.9%	4.7	0	1.3	42.1
Tucumán	80	10.3%	53.6	18.1	7.7	0.7
Total	**1250**	**12.9%**	**574.8**	**265.7**	**80.7**	**389.3**
% of Total			**44%**	**20%**	**6%**	**30%**

Data Source: FFDP and World Bank
* Includes both provincial banks owned by the province of Mendoza

However, by making privatization more attractive to provincial policymakers by reducing the immediate pain associated with privatization, the creation of the Fondo Fiduciario might have had a substantial impact on privatization decisions. Since the Tequila crisis and the creation of the Fondo Fiduciario roughly coincided – as discussed earlier, the Fondo Fiduciario was created to exploit a perceived window of opportunity for privatization – it is difficult, if not impossible, to assess whether the existence of the Fondo Fiduciario affected privatization decisions. However, some evidence suggests that it might have. Clarke and Cull (1998, 2000a), which econometrically assesses the likelihood of provincial bank privatization for each province in Argentina, find the probability of privatization increased significantly following the Tequila crisis. Since they control for the effect of bank performance and provincial finances on privatization decisions, this suggests that the crisis increased the likelihood of privatization for reasons other than through the effect it had on bank performance and government finances. This suggests that institutional changes, such as tighter regulation and supervision following the crisis or the creation of the Fondo Fiduciario, did affect privatization decisions.[11]

3. The Impact of Privatization on Bank Performance

As noted in the previous section, provincial bank privatization was intended to satisfy several goals. The provincial governments, which after the implementation of the Convertibility Plan found themselves responsible for the recapitalization of poorly performing banks, wanted to rid themselves of a potentially large drain upon their finances. Although the public banks could still provide them with limited political services, tightened regulation reduced the degree to which they could use the banks to finance their deficits or provide investment funds for public enterprises. Faced with large potential liabilities and reduced benefits, many provincial policymakers concluded that the cost of financing the public provincial banks' losses was greater than the benefits of continued public ownership. Privatization appears to been considerably less costly than continued public ownership. Clarke and Cull (1999) show that the fiscal benefits of privatization far exceeded the costs under a wide range of different assumptions.

In addition to reducing the drain upon provincial finances, the Central Bank and Federal government hoped that privatization would improve bank and sector performance. In the absence of a lender of last resort, the weak performance of the public provincial banks could threaten the viability of the Argentine banking system and, ultimately, the Convertibility Plan itself. In this section of the paper, we assess preliminary evidence on whether this goal was achieved and discuss reasons for differences in post-privatization performance of the privatized provincial banks. In the next section, we discuss the impact of privatization on other banks involved in the provincial banking sectors.

3.1 The Method of Privatization

One of the reasons that provincial bank privatization in Argentina is interesting is the method of privatization. Although the individual cases varied, the basic strategy was to first place attractive assets in the privatized bank and then to match those assets with

[11] Another possibility is that the performance measures included in the econometric analysis (net worth over liabilities and share of the banks' portfolios that were non-performing) do not adequately capture all aspects of performance that affected privatization decisions. In particular, the loss of liquidity due to the Tequila crisis might not be adequately captured by these performance variables (Clarke and Cull, 1998).

liabilities, up to the point that the privatized bank's net worth met Argentina's prudential standards. As discussed in the previous section, the remaining assets and liabilities were then transferred into a residual entity. The main determinant of the size of the residual entity was, therefore, the attractiveness of the public provincial bank's assets.

Table 2 shows the size of the privatized and residual entities for the fifteen completed provincial privatizations that relied on Fondo Fiduciario assistance. The most striking feature is the size of the residual entities. The province managed to transfer more than half of pre-privatization assets to the purchaser in only four of the fifteen cases for which data are available, and one of these, Entre Rios, is somewhat misleading. Both Entre Rios and Chaco had nearly finalized their privatizations before the Fondo Fiduciario became operational. To provide fiscal relief to the early privatizers, these provinces were allowed to enter the program after the fact. Because most details of the transactions had already been worked out, neither transaction was typical of those that followed. In particular, Entre Rios transferred all pre-privatization assets to the purchaser and later used Fondo Fiduciario assistance to guarantee some of them.

Table 2: Sizes of Privatized and Residual Entities

Bank	Privatized Entity		Residual Entity		% Transferred to Private Owner	
	Assets (million pesos)	Liabilities (million pesos)	Assets (million pesos)	Liabilities (million pesos)	Assets (million pesos)	Liabilities (million pesos)
Chaco	42.9	34.5	245.3	233.1	15%	13%
Entre Ríos	425.5	414.5	0.0	0.0	100%	100%
Formosa	26.5	11.5	135.7	244.9	16%	4%
Misiones	67.2	57.8	133.9	340.8	33%	14%
Río Negro	59.4	47.4	379.2	402.6	14%	11%
Salta	42.9	41.0	70.0	68.4	38%	37%
Tucumán	66.9	56.9	261.7	262.9	20%	18%
San Luis	38.6	38.6	29.7	81.8	56%	32%
Santiago del. Estero	43.8	43.5	199.6	227.3	18%	16%
San Juan	173.9	158.9	78.6	175.3	69%	48%
Mendoza*	335.1	326.9	666.6	666.6	33%	33%
Prevision Social	62.9	41.0	292.1	292.1	18%	12%
Jujuy	35.7	33.7	206.9	218.7	15%	13%
Santa Fe	--	--	--	--	--	--
Santa Cruz	157.9	142.9	37.7	126.9	81%	53%

Data Source: FFDP.

* Province also refinanced some (less than ten percent) of residual assets. Refinancing is not included in the recovery figures presented here.

Although the negotiations were principally over the assets and liabilities that the purchaser would assume, other factors also featured. Although price was an important issue, it was not usually the main focus of negotiations and, consequently, prices were generally low compared to the face value of the assets transferred to the privatized bank (see Table 3). Non-price factors also featured in most of the negotiations. To overcome opposition to privatization, the provincial governments used the negotiations to obtain concessions designed to compensate two important groups of stakeholders – workers and residents of (mainly rural) areas who might find it difficult to obtain other banking services. They did this by restricting layoffs, compensating laid off workers, and forcing the new buyers to maintain branches in certain areas (see Table 4).[12] These contract provisions strongly suggest that the political buyoffs present in other privatizations were also evident in Argentina.[13]

Table 3: Characteristics of Purchasers of Privatized Entities

Privatization	Principal Buyer	Price Paid (million pesos)	Characteristics of Principal Buyer on Date of Purchase*		
			Assets (million pesos)	Return on Assets	Return on Equity
Chaco (94)	Patricios	6.3	200.9	0.3%	2.5%
Entre Rios (94)	Institucional	15.1	131.7	0.5%	4.1%
Formosa (95)	Patricios	9.3	383.9	0.0%	0.1%
Misiones (95)	Macro	9.1	310.0	-0.4%	-1.3%
Rio Negro (96)	Mildesa	10.2	145.2	0.2%	0.9%
Salta (96)	Macro	7.9	254.0	0.4%	1.6%
Tucumán (96)	Comafi	10.3	281.7	0.2%	1.7%
San Luis (96)	Exprinter	12.4	398.0	-0.3%	-4.5%
Santiago del Estero (96)	Florencia	6.7	551.6	-1.6%	-9.8%
San Juan (96)	Piano	11.5	134.2	0.3%	1.9%
Mendoza (96)	República	20.1	1163.6	1.4%	11.4%
Prevision Social (96)	República	8.2	1163.6	1.4%	11.4%
Jujuy (98)	Macro	12.3	504.9	2.0%	12.2%
Santa Fe (98)	Gn Negocio	57.2	644.5	0.9%	9.9%
Santa Cruz (98)	San Juan	10.5	319.6	2.1%	55.2%
Banking Sector:					
1994			78132.5	--	--
1995			93560.0	-0.0%	-0.2%
1996			108342.0	0.6%	4.4%
1997			131935.7	0.7%	5.9%
1998**			157618.3	0.7%	6.1%

Data Source: Central Bank of the Republic of Argentina.

* Figures are for last complete quarter before purchase of the provincial bank.

** Figures through July 1998.

---

[12] The issues discussed in this paragraph are analyzed in Clarke and Cull (2000b).

[13] See, for example, Shleifer and Treisman's (2000) discussion of how political considerations affected the design of Russia's privatization program.

Table 4: Terms of the Provincial Bank Privatizations

Province	Branching	Employees	Duration of Banking Service Contracts	Portfolio Guarantees
Chaco (6/94)	Maintain service	Keep at least 715 workers	20 years	None
Entre Ríos (12/94)	Maintain service, closures require approval	Up to 700 (of 1500) early voluntary retirement	7 years	Up to $26 million maximum
Formosa (9/95)	Maintain service	--	10 years	35% recovered residual assets
Misiones (12/95)	--	No dismissals in first six months; <30% of workforce after	5 years	Up to $16 million maximum
Río Negro* (2/96)	--	--	10 years	Up to 80% of portfolio or $50 million
Salta (3/96)	Maintain similar geographic coverage	--	10 years	None
Tucumán (3/96)	Maintain service	Workforce <= 200 at transfer	10 years	Up to $32 million
San Luis (5/96)	Maintain service	--	10 years	$16 million deposit from province, up to 5 years
Santiago del Estero (7/96)	Maintain service	Job re-training program, >= 1 yr.	10 years	None
San Juan (7/96)	Maintain similar geographic coverage	--	10 years	None
Mendoza (7/96)	Maintain all branches	Keep at least 600 workers	5 years	Can substitute privatized assets for residual assets, up to $20 million
Mendoza (Prevision Social) (7/96)	Maintain all branches	Keep at least 500 workers	5 years	Can substitute privatized assets for residual assets, up to $10 million
Jujuy** (1/98)	Maintain all branches	Keep at least 170 workers	10 years	Fund created w/ 35% recovered residual assets
Santa Fe (5/98)	Maintain service in all branches or through paid representatives	Keep at least 1500 workers	5 years	Up to $43 million guaranteed by a bond
Santa Cruz (6/98)	Not available	Not available	Not available	Not available

Data Source: Fondo Fiduciario para el Desarollo Provincial (FFDP)

*Rio Negro – Portfolio guarantees and flexibility with respect to the object of sale were modifications to original pliego. Pliegos were initial announcements by the provinces of the proposed terms of sale. ** Jujuy – The original pliego was altered to allow for a higher share of capital to be transferred to the new owner, less stringent restrictions regarding firing, and slightly more generous guarantees.

To pass low-quality assets to private purchasers while imposing branching and labor restrictions would have been difficult, or even impossible, without concessions on other dimensions. The contracts often included important concessions, including asset guarantees and service contracts, which provided compensation for banking services provided to the provinces. The service contracts, under which the private owners coordinated the payments activities of the provincial government, varied in length from five to twenty years (see Table 4). In interviews, the new private owners confirmed that the contracts were of vital importance, as an abnormally high share of the privatized banks' income is generated from services.

In addition, many provinces guaranteed a share of the assets transferred to the privatized bank (see Table 4). These guarantees took several different forms. In six cases, the province guaranteed assets either up to a fixed limit or up to a certain share of the total assets acquired. In two cases, private owners were able to substitute assets from the residual entity for privatized assets during a trial period and in another, the buyer could shift low-quality assets to the residual entity for a period following privatization. Finally, in two cases the guarantee was set as a fraction of the residual assets recovered. Since the owner of the privatized entity was also charged with managing the residual entity, the idea was to increase incentives to recover residual assets. Only three cases did not guarantee the privatized asset portfolio at all.

3.2 Characteristics of the Banks that Bought the Privatized Banks

The previous discussion makes it clear that the provincial banks were not particularly attractive acquisition targets – they had been losing money over an extended period and the quality of their assets was low. In addition, the banks were small and their asset portfolios were poorly diversified (at least, geographically). Because the strongest banks were unwilling to purchase the poorly performing provincial banks, the purchasing banks tended to be small and poorly performing themselves (see Table 3). In most cases, the provincial banks were bought by banks with return on assets (ROA) and equity (ROE) below the sector average (see Table 3).[14] Table 5, which presents comparisons between the buyers and the provincial banks that they acquired, provides a detailed description of the purchasers as of the first quarter of 1995. In many cases, the purchasers acquired banks that were larger than they were and in some cases, the targets were more then 2.5 times the size of the acquirer. The purchase of a provincial bank, therefore, appears to have been an important growth opportunity for the acquirers.

[14] Jujuy and Santa Cruz are somewhat misleading because both were bought by former provincial banks (Jujuy by Banco Macro-Misiones and Santa Cruz by Banco San Juan).

Table 5: Acquisition/Purchaser Comparisons, First Quarter, 1995

Bank Privatized (Buyer)	Balance Sheet (millions pesos) Assets	Liabilities	Performance Net Worth	% of portfolio non-performing	Income from services as % of total
Chaco	87	76	13.8	0.0	49.7
Patricio	320	276	16.0	11.6	50.6
Entre Rios	314	303	3.6	58.9	30.7
Institut	123	105	16.7	9.8	23.2
Formosa	346	287	20.4	42.7	47.5
Patricio	276	276	16.0	11.6	50.6
Misiones	523	495	5.7	13.7	17.9
Macro	190	130	46.4	13.4	4.4
Rio Negro	381	341	11.8	60.4	21.4
Mildesa	145	104	39.3	1.1	7.6
Salta	141	114	23.4	91.8	7.4
Macro	190	130	46.4	13.4	4.4
Tucumán	444	331	34.2	53.1	16.8
Comafi	248	212	16.7	11.9	4.9
San Luis	102	93	9.3	22.0	19.9
Exprinter	186	156	19.1	19.9	2.6
Santiago del Estero	77	76	1.0	94.1	43.8
Florencia	81	67	21.7	12.3	16.3
San Juan	335	366	-8.4	29.9	25.2
Piano	113	95	19.3	8.0	21.7
Mendoza	1106	952	16.2	58.0	11.9
República	691	592	16.7	5.1	2.9
Prevision Social	629	555	13.3	28.3	19.7
República	691	592	16.7	5.1	2.9
Jujuy	145	126	14.9	53.0	29.5
Macro	190	129	46.4	13.4	4.4
Santa Fe	846	688	23.0	56.0	31.0
General de Negocios	431	395	9.1	9.7	23.6
St Cruz	335	327	11.9	54.9	23.4
San Juan	366	366	-8.4	29.9	25.2
Average Privatized Bank	367	323	15.4	46.7	26.5
Buyer	281	240	22.2	11.8	15.6

Data Source: Central Bank of the Republic of Argentina.

Note: Comparisons for Chaco are misleading because the privatization transaction was complete by the first quarter of 1995 and, therefore, the residual bank had already been formed.

Provincial banks also offered their acquirers an opportunity to break into a new line of business. Many of the acquirers were "mayoristas" or wholesale banks. Interviews with directors of Macro (which acquired and later merged with Misiones) and Mildesa (which acquired and later merged with Rio Negro) indicated that the wholesale banking business was drying up as foreign entry increased competition. Many felt that they needed to break into retail banking to survive, and the provincial banks offered them a useful way of doing this. Although their ROA and ROE was below the sector average, their net worth was higher and their percent of bad credit was much lower than the provincial banks they acquired. The transactions, therefore, clearly placed the provincial banks in hands that were more capable.

3.3 Post-Privatization Performance

Although several privatized banks had problems following privatization, given the remarkable consolidation that followed the Tequila crisis, and recognizing that both the provincial and the purchasing banks were relatively weak, it would be surprising if this were not the case.[15] In general, the performances of the provincial banks improved following privatization and privatized banks have restructured more successfully than provincial banks that were not privatized. As noted earlier, the provincial banks tended to be overstaffed and their lending was heavily directed towards the public sector. By the end of 1998, the privatized banks had reduced their workforces more successfully, despite the restrictions on layoffs, and lent less to the public sector than provincial banks that had not been privatized (see Table 6).

In most cases, the privatized banks grew rapidly in terms of assets, liabilities, loans, and deposits. This growth was most pronounced for the earliest privatizers (cohorts one and two in Table 7). Average asset growth for the earliest (cohort one) privatizers was 32% per year, compared to an average rate of 19.2% for the whole banking sector. The second group (cohort two) has grown at an average annual rate of 38%, compared to 19% for the system.[16] Although the late privatizers (cohort three) have grown more slowly, this is largely due to Mendoza and Prevision Social. These banks were involved in lengthy disputes between the province and the private buyer, which led to delays and adjustments in the residual and privatized portfolios. For three other banks in the third cohort, Tucumán, San Luis, and San Juan, assets have grown between 28-42% per year, well above the system's 21% growth rate. A fourth bank, Santiago del Estero, has experienced above average growth in loans but not in assets, liabilities, or deposits.

[15] Before the Tequila crisis, there were over 200 banks operating in Argentina. By June 1997, only 141 were still operating.

Table 6: Lending to the public sector and change in employment (Q3 1998)

	% Public (Q3 1998)	Change in Employment (July 1995- September 1998)
Public Provincial Banks	**9.43%**	**-5.45%****
Banco de la Provincia de Tierra del Fuego	2.04%	7.20%
Banco de Chubut	42.61%	-19.06%
Banco de La Pampa	0.01%	30.02%
Banco de Neuquen	5.05%	13.52%
Banco de la Provincia de Buenos Aires	16.57%	-4.73%
Banco de la Provincia de Cordoba	5.67%	-19.33%
Banco de Social Cordoba	3.00%	-34.55%
Banco Santafesino de Inversion	0.46%	-16.67%
Privatized Provincial Banks +	**6.15%**	**-34.12%****
Banco de Catamarca	0.21%	24.70%
Banco de Entre Rios ++++	9.33%	-15.18%
Banco de Formosa	15.80%	-45.99%
Banco de Jujuy	0.00%	-61.41%
Banco de Rio Negro	4.41%	-35.17%
Banco de Salta	0.15%	-5.73%
Banco de San Juan	3.23%	-32.11%
Banco de Santiago del Estero	8.23%	-37.84%
Banco del Tucumán	11.25%	-50.40%
Banco San Luis	0.07%	-41.23%
Nuevo Banco de La Rioja	0.00%	----
Nuevo Banco del Chaco S.A.++++	0.18%	-13.01%
Banco Macro Misiones ++	19.82%	-32.84%
Banco de Mendoza +++	0.31%	-55.98%

Data Source: Central Bank of the Republic of Argentina.

** Test of null hypothesis that the two means are the same is rejected at a 5% level

+ Excludes Banco de Santa Fe and Banco de Santa Cruz, because post-privatization data were not available.

++ Includes employees of Banco Macro, which was merged with Banco de Misiones after privatization.

+++ Includes assets and employees of both Social de Mendoza and Banco de Mendoza, which were merged after privatization.

++++ Data for Nuevo Banco del Chaco S.A is pre-privitization data.

[16] The disparities in reported growth rates for the entire banking system are due to the slightly different periods over which each of the three cohorts have operated as private banks.

Table 7: Post Privatization Performance

Bank	Years Since Privatization	Basic Balance Sheet (millions pesos)					Performance			
		Assets	Liabilities	Loans	Deposits	Net Worth	% of portfolio non-performing	Return on Assets	Return on Equity	Percent of income from services
Chaco	1	87	76	35	33	13.7	0.0	1.1	8.9	49.7
Chaco	2	140	160	53	85	-12.4	22.1	0.4	--	38.5
Chaco	3	196	181	80	129	8.6	24.0	0.7	8.2	45.5
Chaco	4	298	278	156	211	7.2	7.0	0.3	3.8	32.5
Entre Rios	1	520	482	432	288	7.8	32.8	0.5	6.3	20.5
Entre Rios	2	656	610	450	500	7.5	26.4	0.4	5.5	25.5
Entre Rios	3	744	687	500	583	8.2	23.3	0.3	4.6	27.3
Entre Rios	4	750	691	406	567	8.4	27.9	0.2	2.7	31.8
***% change* Cohort 1**		**32**	**36**	**32**	**60**					
Formosa	1	100	126	17	98	-20.8	0.0	-2.7	--	16.9
Formosa	2	141	124	71	99	13.9	2.5	0.5	3.8	9.1
Formosa	3	133	113	49	77	17.8	6.9	0.5	3.5	46.0
Misiones	1	125	112	65	81	11.8	17.0	1.7	16.6	58.8
Misiones	2	170	151	112	126	12.3	71.2	1.4	13.0	53.9
Misiones	3	*580	*507	*442	*359	14.5	34.7	0.6	4.9	26.5
Rio Negro	1	159	147	83	71	8.2	27.4	0.0	-0.1	51.3
Rio Negro	2	*366	*321	*234	*205	14.1	8.9	0.0	-0.3	42.0
Rio Negro	3	*422	*373	*266	*244	13.0	4.5	0.3	2.2	37.7
Salta	1	140	132	49	85	6.0	0.1	1.0	17.8	71.1
Salta	2	277	261	189	215	6.3	0.1	1.5	25.4	40.3
Salta	3	328	304	213	253	8.1	0.5	0.6	7.4	46.1
***% change* Cohort 2**		**38**	**28**	**131**	**41**					
Tucumán	1	120	108	54	80	11.3	0.6	1.2	11.8	60.5
Tucumán	2	154	139	90	112	10.7	0.6	1.3	13.3	50.2
San Luis	1	72	125	90	97	-42.0	71.6	-0.3	--	42.7
San Luis	2	102	96	59	75	5.8	46.2	-0.1	-2.5	41.8
Santiago del Estero	1	272	263	39	107	3.4	2.7	0.5	16.7	47.8
Santiago del Estero	2	236	225	59	127	4.9	8.5	0.0	-0.1	47.4

Mendoza	1	465	429	36	322	8.4	23.6	-1.4	-17.5	53.8
Mendoza	2	440	422	34	337	4.1	27.0	-1.0	-24.2	40.8
Prevision Social	1	374	334	50	233	11.7	21.7	-0.4	-4.1	32.4
Prevision Social	2	368	318	47	244	15.7	22.5	-0.3	-2.4	25.6
San Juan	1	231	215	48	152	7.5	1.9	0.1	2.0	42.3
San Juan	2	296	274	40	195	7.8	3.6	0.5	6.6	34.9
***% change* Cohort 3**		**13**	**2**	**9**	**12**					

Data Source: Central Bank of the Republic of Argentina.

* Acquirer merged with privatized entity. Figures are for the merged bank. These observations are excluded from the reported growth rates in assets, liabilities, loans, and deposits.

Signs of growing pains were, however, evident. As the equity and asset base of the new banks increased, their ROA and ROE figures tended to decline. One could argue that these were initially abnormally high due to the heavy reliance on service income and their low levels of assets and equity. Although the time-series in Table 7 is too short to yield firm conclusions, as these banks begin to generate a higher share of income from lending, it is hoped that their ROA and ROE figures will stabilize.

In most cases, net worth and portfolio quality have not deteriorated substantially since privatization. The exceptions are again instructive. Entre Rios, which failed to create a residual entity, started with a relatively high percentage of bad credits that it has been unable to reduce. Chaco, which also entered the FFDP program late, started out without any non-performing loans, only to see the figure jump to 24% within two years, suggesting that purchasers and the province did not create an ideal privatized entity. Although the percentage of the portfolio that was non-performing later declined, the 1998 failure of its major shareholder, Patricios, suggest that this privatization is different from the others. Unfortunately, Patricios was also the major shareholder in Formosa, although its (Formosa's) performance statistics were not as dire as those of Chaco were.

Among the remaining cases, however, things are more encouraging. In those cases where initial levels of bad credit levels were relatively high, there has been substantial post-privatization decline (Misiones, Rio Negro, and San Luis). In those cases where the privatized entity started with close to no bad credit, the figure has increased slightly, but not dramatically, and the ratio of net worth to total liabilities has typically improved. The slight increase in bad credit likely reflects the difficulties associated with forging a lending business. The transition from a typical provincial bank portfolio has followed a predictable pattern – in most cases, there was a substantial reduction in credit to the financial and public sectors. The largest growth category has been personal lending. Interviews with owners of the privatized banks indicate that this lending is less risky than other types, because as bankers to the province, they assumed many payments systems responsibilities, including payments to public employees. Payments for many types of personal loans are automatically deducted from the accounts of the public employees.

Growth in other, less secure, types of lending is much slower. Owners indicated that it requires time to build up a solid lending clientele among businesses, especially since many of the new owners have little experience in this area. The long-term sustainability of the new banks likely depends heavily on the success of the transition, especially if the service contracts are not renewed.

The privatized entities continued to generate a disproportionate share of income through services due, largely, to the service contracts with the provinces. In fact, during the period just after privatization, most privatized banks received more that 40% of their income from services (Table 7). This, no doubt, reflects the initial dislocation associated with creating a commercially oriented lending business largely from scratch. Most privatized entities have experienced gradual declines in service income shares since their inception, although the levels remain above those of the old provincial banks. The service contracts remain key to the survival of the privatized entities, and their renewal represents an important concern for the new managers.

4. Effect of Privatization on the Provincial Banking Sector

In the first quarter of 1995, most public banks accounted for less than 1%, and only *Banco de la Provincia de Buenos Aires* accounted for more than 5%, of total national lending.[17] Despite their small share of national lending, the provincial banks often dominated local banking markets, with many banks accounting for over forty-five percent of sector lending (see Table 8). The provincial banks' size relative to local markets could affect other banks operating in the provinces in at least two ways. First, public ownership might affect concentration. For example, since the public banks do not necessarily have to maximize profits, they might be larger (or smaller) than is optimal, increasing (or reducing) market concentration. Since banking markets are essentially local, privatization of the public provincial banks might affect concentration and, in so doing, affect the degree of competition.[18] Second, even if privatization has little effect on local market concentration, it might affect sector performance in other ways. For example, lending by the public provincial banks was primarily focused on financing the provincial governments' deficits and providing politically motivated loans to supporters of the ruling party. If the privatized banks redirect lending towards commercial, rather than political, goals, effective competition might increase even if concentration is unaffected. This section of the paper looks at the effect of privatization on concentration and on lending by other private and public banks.

[17] Data for 1995 is used because data on individual bank lending at the provincial level is not available before this time.

[18] Gilbert (1984, p. 629) argues that concentration in local markets is the correct measure of concentration in banking studies. Burdisso and D'Amato (1999) use provincial level data to construct measures of local market power and concentration for Argentina.

Table 8: Loans by public provincial banks in provinces where privatization was not complete.

	% of Loans in Province	% of Loans in Nation
Formosa**	69.65%	0.47%
La Pampa	66.66%	0.59%
Santiago del Estero**	65.08%	0.46%
Santa Cruz**	56.05%	0.30%
Tierra de Fuego	55.23%	0.26%
Misiones**	52.57%	0.46%
San Juan**	49.89%	0.45%
Salta**	48.29%	0.71%
Mendoza**	45.76%	1.93%
Jujuy**	45.67%	0.19%
Cordoba	45.44%	3.47%
Catamarca	44.37%	0.13%
Rio Negro**	44.13%	0.57%
San Luis**	31.32%	0.11%
Neuquen	27.98%	0.32%
Chubut	23.37%	0.17%
Tucumán**	18.40%	0.28%
Santa Fe**	16.18%	0.98%
Buenos Aires (including federal capital district)	14.64%	9.74%

Source: Central Bank of the Republic of Argentina.
* Data is for first quarter of 1995. ** Privatized by the end of 1998.

4.1 The Theoretical Relationship Between Concentration and Sector Performance

A large empirical literature has studied whether there is any evidence that market concentration affects either bank profits or interest rates, primarily using local-level data from the United States. Based upon a survey of nearly fifty studies of banking in the United States, Gilbert (1984, p. 644) concludes:

> "Estimates of the influence of market structure on measures of bank performance are highly variable among these studies. The studies that use the most appropriate measures of bank performance and the best estimation procedures find significant influences of market structure on bank performance measures, with hypothesized signs, more consistently than the other studies."

In a recent paper, using quarterly data from between 1996 and 1998 for the twenty largest banks in Argentina, Burdisso and D'Amato (1999) find that market concentration is significantly correlated with bank profitability.

There are several plausible explanations for a positive correlation between market concentration and profits.[19] The most direct explanation, which is known as the *structure-conduct-performance hypothesis*, is that banks operating in highly concentrated markets are able to collude, setting interest rates above the competitive level.[20] Under this hypothesis, all banks, large and small, operating in concentrated markets charge above market interest rates, increasing profitability for them all. Consequently, small banks (as well as large one) operating in highly concentrated markets are able to make excess profits.

A related hypothesis, the *relative market power hypothesis*, suggests that the positive correlation between market concentration and bank profitability might not be the direct result of collusion between different banks. Under this hypothesis, product differentiation, perhaps due to location or advertising, allows banks that are large relative to the local market to exercise market power when setting interest rates. This results in an indirect relationship between market concentration and bank profitability. On average, a greater number of large banks operate in concentrated markets (i.e., a market is concentrated because many large banks operate there) and since large banks, which can exercise market power, are more profitable, market share and profitability are correlated. The main difference between the *structure-conduct-performance* and *relative market power* hypotheses is that concentration affects the profitability of small banks under the first hypothesis, but not under the second.

Several studies, including Berger (1995), have tested whether empirical evidence supports the *relative market power* or the *structure-conduct-performance* hypothesis by including measures of both market concentration and market share in their analysis. Berger (1995, p. 416) notes that studies of banking in the United States have generally found that coefficients on measures of market concentration become statistically insignificant once measures of market share are included in the analysis. This supports the *relative market power* hypothesis over the *structure-conduct-performance* hypothesis for banks in the United States. However, Burdisso and D'Amato (1999) find for

[19] See Berger (1995) for a recent discussion of the effect of market power on bank performance and possible reasons for the relationship.

[20] One criticism of the structure performance hypothesis is that if banks were able to charge above market interest rates and there were no significant barriers to entry, then new banks should enter these markets. Consequently, market structure, which is determined by industry characteristics that affect barriers to entry, does not determine competition (Gilbert, 1984; Baumol, Panzar and Willig, 1982). However, the banking market in Argentina might not be a good approximation of a 'contestable market', since entry is not free and exit might be costly – violating two criteria for contestable markets (see Baumol, 1982). Before 1993, banks operating in Argentina could enter or open new branches only by purchasing existing branches or banks (World Bank, 1994b, p. 24). Therefore, the threat of entry was probably not significant. Although these restrictions were lifted in December 1993, Central Bank approval was still required before new banks could enter and before existing banks could open new branches. Rozenwurcel and Bleger (1998, p. 389) suggest that the Central Bank continued to forbid existing banks from opening new branches to encourage stronger banks to help rehabilitate banks facing liquidity/solvency problems following the Tequila Crisis. According to sources at the Central Bank, entry and branching policy has since become relatively liberal, at least for well-performing banks.

Argentinean banks that the coefficient on market share is statistically insignificant, while the coefficient on market concentration is highly significant. This supports the *structure-conduct-performance* hypothesis rather than the *relative market power* hypothesis in Argentina.

Although a positive correlation between market share and profitability might suggest that banks with large market shares could exploit market power to raise interest rates and earn excess profit, there are other plausible reasons for a positive correlation. Banks with lower costs, either due to scale efficiencies (scale efficiency version of the *efficient-structure* hypothesis) or due to better management or technology (X-efficiency version of the *efficient-structure* hypothesis), will have higher profits than their less efficient competitors (Berger, 1995). Further, under these hypotheses, the more efficient banks are able to exploit their greater efficiency to gain market share (Demsetz, 1973). Consequently, more efficient banks are both more profitable and have higher market share, resulting in a spurious correlation between profitability and market share.

If profitability and market share are only correlated because efficient, more profitable banks are relatively larger, then the coefficient on market share will become statistically insignificant when measures of efficiency are added to the profitability regression (Berger, 1995). When Berger (1995) adds measures of scale- and X-efficiency to profitability regressions for banks in the United States, the coefficient on market share remains statistically significant and positive and the coefficient on X-efficiency is also statistically significant and positive.[21] These results suggest that although X-efficiency affects profitability, market share also affects profitability. Berger (1995, p. 416) notes that this is consistent with the *relative market power* hypothesis. In contrast, in a similar study for the 20 largest banks in Argentina, Burdisso and D'Amato (1999) find that measures of X-efficiency are negatively related to profits. They suggest that this might be because the most efficient banks operate in the most developed, and competitive, markets (e.g., in Buenos Aires), while the less efficient banks operate in the more underdeveloped, and less competitive, provinces.

4.2 Effect of Bank Privatization on Market Concentration in Argentina

4.2.1 Model Specification

In this section of the paper, we look at the effect of bank privatization on total lending, concentration of lending and lending by each class of bank (the provincial bank, private banks and other public banks). We are interested in how privatization immediately impacts lending and in how privatization affects lending in the medium-term. The three main variables of interest are:

1. A dummy variable that takes the value one in each period following the initial transfer of assets to the residual entities and the subsequent revaluing of the provincial banks' portfolios. Since loans transferred to the residual entity are

[21] Berger's (1995) results do not support the scale-efficiency version of the efficient markets hypothesis.

removed from all measures of lending in the province, lending by the provincial bank and total lending drop when assets are transferred to the residual entity.

2. A dummy variable that takes the value one each quarter after the new private owners took control of the provincial banks. In several cases, the private owners did not take control until several periods after the initial transfer of assets to the residual entity. At this time, an additional drop in assets appears to occur in several cases. This dummy variable, therefore, represents a one-time shift in the size of the lending portfolio that takes place when the private owners took control of the provincial bank. The additional reduction in the assets of the provincial banks at this time was probably either due to more assets being transferred to the residual bank or due to an additional revaluing of the portfolio. The sum of the two dummy variables represents the immediate impact of privatization on each of the lending variables.
3. A trend variable indicating the number of periods since the new private owners took control of privatized provincial bank. This indicates the evolution of lending following privatization. For example, it will tell us whether lending grew at a faster or slower rate.[22]

All regressions include time dummies to proxy for overall trends in lending due to macroeconomic events (e.g., the Tequila crisis) and changes in regulation and supervision that affect all banks. We also include provincial GDP and population to control for the size and wealth of the province. Finally, we use regression techniques that control for other provincial level variables that are (roughly) constant over the period being studied. The data is quarterly data from 1995 until 1997. Table 9 presents results from fixed-effects regressions that include provincial level dummy variables.[23] Including fixed effects means that we are essentially looking at how privatization affects lending in each province relative to lending in that province before privatization.[24]

---

[22] In some specifications, we also included an additional trend indicating that the residual entity had been formed but that the private owners had not yet taken control. This variable was not statistically significant in any model specification and did not affect other results. Therefore, we did not include it in the regressions presented in Table 9.

[23] For comparison, we also ran regressions of the first-differences of lending on the first-differences on the independent variables. Except where noted in the text, results using this method are very similar. As a final robustness check, we also ran random effects estimation. All results were virtually identical to the results shown in Table 9. However, using a Hausman (1978) test, we rejected the random effects specification in favor of the fixed effects specification in two of the six cases. Results from these regressions are available from the authors upon request.

[24] See Hsiao (1986) for a description of fixed-effects regression analysis.

Table 9: Effect of privatization on bank loans (fixed effects model)

Dependent Variable (all dependent variables are natural logs)	(1) **Loans by provincial banks**	(2) **Total loans**	(3) **Loans by private banks** (excluding privatized banks)	(4) **Loans by private banks** (including privatized banks)	(5) **Loans by public banks** (excluding provincial banks)	(6) **Herfindahl's Index**
Number of Observations	230	230	230	230	230	230
Fixed time effects	*Included*	*Included*	*Included*	*Included*	*Included*	*Included*
Fixed state effects	*Included*	*Included*	*Included*	*Included*	*Included*	*Included*
Assets transferred to residual entity	-1.1154***	-0.3712***	0.0540	0.2587**	0.0371*	-0.1193***
(t-statistic)	(-5.90)	(-6.74)	(1.00)	(2.54)	(1.82)	(-7.17)
Private owners took control of privatized bank	-0.6285***	-0.1422**	-0.0529	0.1481	-0.0312	-0.0096
(t-statistic)	(-3.24)	(-2.51)	(-0.95)	(1.42)	(-1.49)	(-0.56)
Periods since owners took control of privatized bank	0.0965***	0.0102	-0.0263***	0.0188	0.0051**	0.0014
(t-statistic)	(4.24)	(1.54)	(-4.03)	(1.53)	(2.09)	(0.69)
Natural Log of ***Provincial GDP***	-0.1570	-0.1079	0.4599***	0.3543	-0.1748***	-0.0581
(t-statistic)	(-0.33)	(-0.77)	(3.34)	(1.37)	(-3.38)	(-1.38)
Natural Log of ***Provincial Population***	2.9581	0.3419	-2.3910***	0.2236	-1.2146***	0.5733
(t-statistic)	(1.13)	(0.45)	(-3.18)	(0.16)	(-4.29)	(2.48)
R-Squared	0.54	0.68	0.71	0.83	0.85	0.47
Test that all fixed effects are equal	17.36	85.44***	166.35	33.62	621.74	42.40
(p-value)	(0.00)	(0.00)	(0.00)	(0.00)	(0.00)	(0.00)

* Significant at 10% level
** Significant at 5% level
*** Significant at 1% level.

4.2.2 Effect of Privatization on Lending by the Provincial Banks

As discussed in the previous subsection, on average, only about 29 percent of the public provincial bank's loans were transferred to the privatized bank at the time of privatization (see Column 1 in Table 9). The remainder of the assets, which remained in the provinces' hands, was transferred to a 'residual entity'. Since the loans that were transferred to the residual entity are no longer included in the bank's portfolio, this leads to a large drop in the provincial bank's loan portfolio at the time of privatization. Further, since loans transferred to the residual entity are no longer included in total loans, it also leads to a large drop in this variable. Two dummy variables are included, one representing the initial revaluation/transfer of assets to the residual entity and the second representing the additional revaluation/transfer of assets when the new private owner's took control of the provincial bank. The two statistically significant negative coefficients on the two dummy variables represent the large negative growth rates when the residual entity was created and the private owners took control (see Table 9).[25]

After the new private owners took control, the provincial banks' loan portfolios grew approximately 10 percentage points faster per quarter than they did before privatization (see Table 9). At this rate of growth, a provincial bank that retained 30 percent of its assets would take about three years to regain its former size. Since the data covers only two and a half years, and since most privatizations were completed in late 1995 or 1996, it is unclear whether this fast growth will be sustained long enough for the banks to attain their pre-privatization size. However, even if this does not occur, the rapid growth following privatization suggests that the privatized banks are likely to become large relative to the provincial banking sectors.

If, as predicted by the *relative-market-size* hypothesis, large banks are able to exploit their large size to gain market power, then the large size of the privatized provincial banks might be a potential concern. Although the public provincial banks dominated the local banking markets (see Table 8), similar sized private banks might behave quite differently than public banks. Most notably, there is little evidence that the public provincial banks successfully used their large size to earn excess profits. In fact, as noted above, the public provincial banks tended to lose large amounts. However, there are several reasons to doubt the privatized banks will exploit market power more successfully than the public banks did. First, although the public banks did not appear to be exploiting market power to make excess profit, they could have used market power in other ways. Most notably, they might have used their relative size to become overstaffed or to make politically motivated loans. The high administrative costs and poor quality loan portfolios of the public banks, relative to the largest private banks, is certainly consistent with this (see, Clarke and Cull, 1999). Consequently, despite their poor performance, it is still possible that the public banks were exploiting market power. In fact, since the public banks had access to cheap investable funds from the public sector, they might have found it easier to exploit their large size than a similar sized private bank would have. Second, although evidence from the United States appears to weakly support the *relative market power* hypothesis (see Berger, 1995), Burdisso and D'Amato (1999) found that Argentinean banks appeared unable to do the same. In summary, there is little evidence either that the privatized provincial banks will be able to use their large size to gain market power or that they would behave more opportunistically than a similar sized public bank would.

4.2.3 Effect of Privatization on Total Sector Lending

Due to the transfer of assets to the residual entities and revaluing of the provincial banks assets, total loans contracted considerably when the residual entities were created and when the new private owners took control of the privatized provincial banks. Sector loans shrunk by 37 percent in the quarter that the residual entity was created and by an

[25] Note that all growth rates are exponential growth rates (i.e., growth rate at time 0 = natural log of loans in period t – natural log of loans in period t-1). Consequently, negative growth rates can exceed –100 percent.

additional 14 percent in the quarter that the private owners took control of the privatized bank (see column 2 in Table 9).

There is little evidence that total loans grew much faster following privatization of the provincial bank, despite the rapid growth of the provincial banks. Although the point estimate suggests that total lending grew one percentage point faster each quarter following privatization, the point estimate is statistically insignificant at conventional levels (see column 2 in Table 9). Given the low point estimate, it would take over twelve years of faster growth to make up for the large decrease in loans at the time of privatization.

The effect of the contraction of lending in provinces that privatized depends, in large part, on the economic value of the provincial banks' lending before privatization. For example, one justification for public ownership of banks is that publicly owned banks might be able to resolve market failures in provincial credit markets. If the provincial banks focused their lending to sectors, such as creditworthy agricultural producers or small and medium-sized enterprises, that private banks failed to serve, then the contraction might be harmful. In practice, this does not seem to be the case. Rather than serving under-served sectors to resolve market failures, most observers suggest that a significant part of lending by the provincial banks was to provincial governments and public enterprises or was politically based.[26] This is further demonstrated by the large non-performing loan portfolios held by the provincial banks relative to private banks (see **Figure 1**). Consequently, to the extent that lending by the provincial banks was economically inefficient, the overall contraction in lending might not be costly.

4.2.4 Effect of Privatization on Lending by other Private Banks

Privatization increased total loans by private banks by reclassifying loans by the provincial bank as loans by private banks (see column 4 in Table 9). However, even if privatization had an immediate impact on the behavior of other private banks (i.e., private banks other than the privatized provincial banks), it would take some time before privatization affected the other banks' loan portfolios. Therefore, it is not surprising that privatization did not have an immediate impact on loans by other private banks (see column 3 in Table 9).

Following privatization, quarterly growth of loans by other private banks in the province slowed by nearly three percentage points following privatization of the provincial banks (see column 3 in Table 9). As noted earlier, loans by the privatized banks grew quickly following privatization, making the net effect on growth of loans by private banks (including the privatized provincial banks) close to zero (see column 4 in Table 9).[27] In summary, because the provincial banks' loans were classified as private following privatization, total loans by private banks increased upon privatization. However, growth of lending by other private banks (i.e., excluding the privatized banks) actually slowed following privatization of the provincial bank. In contrast, growth

---

[26] See, for example, Alston and Gallo (1999, p. 2), Burdisso et al. (1998, p. 10) and World Bank (1994b, p. 7).

[27] Although the point estimate of the coefficient on the trend is positive in the regression including loans by the privatized banks as loans by private banks, it is statistically insignificant at conventional levels.

lending by all private banks (i.e., including lending by the privatized provincial bank) was similar before and after privatization, due to fast expansion by the privatized bank (see Column 4 in Table 9).

Interpreting these results takes some degree of care. One reasonable interpretation of the slower growth by other private banks following privatization is that they now found themselves in competition with the privatized provincial banks. Whereas the public provincial banks' lending decisions had been based on political criteria, the privatized banks' decisions were based on commercial criteria. This might have brought the privatized bank into competition with the other private banks, which, in response, reduced their lending. For example, if the privatized banks were more efficient than other private banks, the *efficient structures* hypothesis predicts that they might take advantage of the disequilibrium caused by privatization to expand at the expense of other private banks. However, there are reasons to question this interpretation of events. Most notably, as discussed in the previous section, the banks that purchased the privatized provincial banks were mostly wholesale banks that were performing relatively poorly (see Table 3). Although it is possible that they stole market share from even less efficient private competitors, another interpretation is that provisions in the privatization contracts (e.g., restrictions on layoffs and branch closings) made it difficult for them to contract their lending. Consequently, they might have been forced to increase lending to maintain their workforces and networks of branches. Since the new loans were based on commercial, rather than political, criteria this brought them into competition with other private banks, reducing the profitability of new lending. Since other private banks had fewer restrictions preventing them from downsizing, they responded to lower profitability by reducing the size of their operations. Consequently, although increased competition might have improved sector efficiency, contract provisions in the privatization contracts might have meant that the most efficient banks failed to increase market share. Analyzing bank-by-bank data might make it possible to assess whether this is the case and is an important topic for future research.

4.2.5 Effect of Lending on Lending by other Public Banks

Since privatization of the provincial bank does not immediately impact existing loans by other (non-provincial) public banks, the transfer of assets to the residual entity should not have an immediate impact on lending by other public banks. The empirical results are broadly consistent with this. Although the coefficient on the first dummy variable is statistically significant at a 10 percent level (see column 5 in Table 9), the sum of the two dummies is very close to zero. Lending by other public banks appears to have grown faster following privatization. The coefficient on the trend variable is positive and statistically significant (at a 5 percent significance level). This result, however, does not hold when first differencing, rather than the inclusion of fixed provincial dummies, is used to remove the influence of persistent province-level effects, suggesting that the result is not highly robust.

One plausible explanation for this is that the public provincial banks might have had functions that broadly overlapped with the functions of other public banks. For example, most of the provincial banks were created to serve the development needs of the province, to finance provincial governments and provincially owned public enterprises (e.g., utilities). Following privatization, the privatized banks behaved more like other private banks (see previous subsection).[28] To the extent that lending under public ownership was similar to lending by national and municipal banks, this might have created an opportunity for these banks to increase their lending in provinces that had privatized.

Increased lending by other public banks might reduce the benefits associated with privatization. However, the magnitude of the change is quite small – loans by other public banks grew only 0.5 percent faster per quarter following provincial bank privatization. Even with the faster growth of other public banks that was observed post-privatization, it would take 37 years before they were the other public banks were the same size as the public and provincial banks would have been without privatization. Since the short-term growth observed immediately after provincial bank privatization is unlikely to persist for this long, it seems likely that total state-owned banks has been permanently reduced by privatization.

4.2.6 Effect of Privatization on Lending on Sector Concentration

The changes in the provincial banking sector following privatization – the contraction of lending by private banks, the expansion of other public banks and the reduced size of the provincial banks has the potential to affect sector concentration. In this section of the paper, we look at the effect of privatization on sector concentration using a standard measure of industrial concentration, Herfindahl's index (H_p):

$$H_p = \sum_{i=1}^{n} s_{ip}$$

where H_p is concentration in lending in province p and s_{ip} is the share of total loans in province p made by bank i. H_p ranges between zero and one. Higher numbers indicate greater concentration, with one indicating that all loans are held by a single bank.

In the first quarter on 1995, Herfindahl's index ranged between 0.05 in Buenos Aires (including the Federal Capital district) and 0.52 in Formosa. In general, concentration was higher in smaller and poorer provinces.[29] In the first quarter of 1995 – the first period for which data is available – the mean level of Herfindahl's index was 0.26, with a standard deviation of 0.13, among the provinces that had not started the privatization process.

The creation of the residual bank led to an immediate reduction in concentration. The transfer of assets from the provincial bank to the residual entity reduced the size of the provincial bank significantly and, given the large size of the provincial banks relative to

[28] Evidence on the sectoral distribution of the banks' lending portfolios is also consistent with this (Clarke and Cull, 1999).

[29] In provinces that had not started the privatization process by the first quarter of 1995, the correlation between concentration and per capital GDP was –0.16 and the correlation between concentration and population was –0.50.

the provincial banking sector, resulted in concentration falling. The effect is large in economic terms – on average, privatization led to a 0.12 point drop in Herfindahl's index (see column 6 in Table 9). This is close to one standard deviation of the difference across provinces before privatization.

Despite the rapid growth of the privatized provincial banks' portfolios, on average, concentration did not seem to increase significantly in the period following privatization. The parameter of the trend variable is statistically insignificant and small. Based upon the point estimates of the parameters in column 6 of Table 9, it would take over twenty years for concentration to reach the level it was at before privatization. Since the short-term trend in concentration is unlikely to persist, it seems likely that concentration has been reduced even in the long-term.

The *structure-conduct-performance* hypothesis suggests that a drop in concentration might have a significant effect on sector efficiency. Although U.S. evidence does not support this hypothesis once market power is controlled for (see, for example, Berger, 1995), Burdisso and D'Amato (1999) find that banks are less efficient and more profitable in concentrated markets in Argentina. Consequently, the drop in concentration associated with privatization might have a significant positive effect on overall sector efficiency and might reduce the potential for banks to make excess profits.

5. Conclusion

Although the Argentine experience with bank privatization was generally positive, there were many problems. For example, attracting potential buyers was difficult, since the provincial banks were among the least attractive banks in a sector recovering from crisis. Consequently, the provincial governments were forced to sell to small wholesale banks with little experience in retail banking. In addition, the governments had to make significant concessions, including long contracts guaranteeing that the privatized banks can continue to provide post-privatization banking services to the governments, guaranteeing parts of the portfolios, and removing non-performing loans (and matching liabilities). In return, however, provincial politicians often restricted layoffs and branch closings. Accommodations to both purchaser and province were costly, and a strong case can be made that these transactions could not have been completed without the fiscal resources provided by the Fondo Fiduciario.

The ultimate question is whether these funds were put to good use. Although the post-privatization period has been short, initial indications are that bank performance has improved in most provinces. Moreover, the provinces with post-privatization difficulties have tended to be those that were not fully part of the Fondo Fiduciario program. It is also clear, however, that the privatized banks rely on their service contracts with the provinces to generate a high share of their income, and that the transition to commercial lending is proving difficult for many of them.

In addition to improving individual bank performance, there is preliminary evidence that privatization also improved sector performance. Privatization appears to have reduced sector concentration, which might improve efficiency and performance for all banks.[30] In addition, lending by other private banks appears to have contracted in those provinces where privatization has taken place. One interpretation of this is that the privatized banks, which are now making loans based upon commercial criteria, are now in competition with existing private banks. The most notable problem is that total sector lending seems to have contracted in provinces that have privatized. If the provincial banks were successfully solving market failures – for example, by providing credit to small and medium enterprises – the drop in lending might be a concern. However, most public provincial bank lending before privatization was directed towards inefficient state-owned enterprises and the provincial governments. Consequently, the drop in total credit might not be a major concern. However, this suggests that a more detailed analysis of the effect of privatization on lending to small and medium enterprises would be useful.

In summary, the early evidence suggests that privatization has improved both bank and sector performance. Given the importance of bank stability in countries with currency boards, this is no small feat. Further, even if the observed improvements are not sustainable – and this will be uncertain for some time to come – at the very least, these transactions have lifted a fiscal burden from the provinces.

6. References

1. Alston, Lee J. and Andrés Gallo, 2000. "Evolution and Revolution in the Argentine Banking System under Convertibility: The Roles of Crises and Path Dependence." *Mimeo*, University of Illinois, Champaign-Urbana IL.
2. Anderson, T.W. and Cheng Hsiao, 1981. "Estimation of Dynamic Models with Error Components." *Journal of the American Statistical Association* **76**, 598-606.
3. Anderson, T.W. and Cheng Hsiao, 1982. "Formulation and estimation of dynamic models using panel data." *Journal of Econometrics* **18**, 47-82.
4. Baumol, William J., 1982. "Contestable Markets: An Uprising in the Theory of Industry Structure." *American Economic Review* **72** (1), 1-15.
5. Baumol, William J., John C. Panzar, and Robert D. Willig, 1982. *Contestable Markets and the Theory of Industry Structure*. Harcourt Brace Jovanovich, San Diego CA.
6. Berger, Allen N., 1995. "The Profit-Structure Relationship in Banking – Tests of Market-Power and Efficient Hypotheses." *Journal of Money, Credit and Banking* **27** (2), 404-431.
7. Burdisso, Tamara, and Laura D'Amato, 1999. "Prudential Regulations, Restructuring and Competition: The Case of the Argentine Banking Industry." *Banco Central de la Republica Argentina Working Paper 10*, Buenos Aires, Argentina.

[30] See Burdisso and D'Amato (1999) for evidence on the effect of sector concentration on bank performance and profitability in Argentina.

8. Burdisso, Tamara, Laura D'Amato, and Andrea Molinari, 1998. "The Bank Privatization Process in Argentina: Towards a More Efficient Banking System?" *Banco Central de la Republica Argentina Working Paper 4*, Buenos Aires, Argentina.
9. Central Bank of the Republic of Argentina, 2000. "Main Features of the Regulatory Framework of the Argentine Financial System." *Central Bank of the Republic of Argentina*, Buenos Aires, Argentina.
10. Clarke, George R.G., and Robert Cull, 1998. "The Political Economy of Privatization: An Empirical Analysis of Bank Privatization in Argentina." World *Bank Policy Research Working Paper 1962*, World Bank, Washington, DC.
11. Clarke, George R.G., and Robert Cull, 1999. "Why Privatize? The Case of Argentina's Public Provincial Banks." *World Development* **27** (5), 867-888.
12. Clarke, George R.G., and Robert Cull, 2000a. "Getting to Yes: Privatizing Banks in Argentina." *Mimeo*, World Bank, Washington DC.
13. Clarke, George R.G., and Robert Cull, 2000b. "How Politicians Privatize Banks." *Mimeo*, World Bank, Washington DC.
14. Demsetz, Harold, 1973. "Industry Structure, Market Rivalry, and Public Policy." *Journal of Law and Economics* **16** (1), 1-9.
15. Dillinger, William, and Steven B. Webb, 1999. "Fiscal Management in Federal Democracies: Argentina and Brazil." *Policy Research Working Paper 2121*, World Bank, Washington DC.
16. Gilbert, Alton R., 1984. "Bank Market Structure and Competition: A Survey." *Journal of Money, Credit and Banking* **16** (4, Part 2), 617-645.
17. Hausman, Jerry, 1978. "Specification Tests in Econometrics." *Econometrica* **46** (6), 1251-1271.
18. Hsiao, Cheng, 1986. *Analysis of Panel Data*. Cambridge University Press, Cambridge, UK.
19. Rozenwurcel, Guillermo and Leonardo Bleger, 1998. "Argentina's Banking Sector in the Nineties: From Financial Deepening to Systematic Crisis." *World Economy* **21** (3), 369-396.
20. Shleifer, Andrei and Daniel Treisman, 2000. *Without a Map*. The MIT Press, Cambridge MA.
21. World Bank, 1990a. *Argentina: Provincial Government Finances*. World Bank, Washington DC.
22. World Bank, 1990b. *Argentina: Reforms for Price Stability and Growth*. World Bank, Washington DC.
23. World Bank, 1993. *Argentina: From Insolvency to Growth*. World Bank, Washington DC.
24. World Bank, 1994a. *Argentina. Staff Appraisal Report: Capital Market Development Project*. World Bank, Washington DC.
25. World Bank, 1994b. *Argentina: Capital Markets Study*. World Bank, Washington DC.
26. World Bank, 1998. *Argentina Financial Sector Review*. World Bank, Washington DC.

Chapter 2

ON EQUITY ISSUES IN EDUCATION IN THE ANGLOPHONE CARIBBEAN COUNTRIES

John Gafar
C.W. Post Campus
Long Island University
Greenvale, N.Y

ABSTRACT

The evidence shows that primary school level has the largest share of school enrollment in the English speaking Caribbean countries, but, a disproportionate share of public expenditure went to higher education. The poor benefit primarily from primary education, while the non-poor are the principal beneficiaries of higher education. Public expenditure on higher education is regressive, and upper income groups should bear a greater share of the economic cost for higher education. The evidence shows, that performance of the educational system, as measured by pass rates at the 11+ and CXC examinations, is rather low. This is a manifestation of the poor performance of primary education, and there is need for the state to emphasize and provide good primary education, and improve the quality of the All-Age schools that the poor predominantly attend. The evidence shows that the level of education is correlated with the level of earnings, unemployment, and poverty. Finally, the evidence shows that free education does not mean free education for all classes, and that expenditures on higher education by the state is a subsidy to the upper incomes.

1. INTRODUCTION

The primary goal of economic development in any society is the improvement in the quality of life and human welfare. Both the neoclassical models of economic growth, and the new endogenous growth models, emphasize human resource accumulation as an important factor in the growth process.[1] The development of human resources in any nation determines largely the character and dynamism of its economic, social and cultural development.

The English speaking Caribbean countries (referred to loosely as the Caribbean region or countries in this paper) have historically committed themselves to providing some minimum level of education and health services, which they consider as basic human needs. The Caribbean countries have all justified social spending on equity grounds, and as a method of income redistribution.[2] The thinking in the Caribbean is that deepening the education process (to wit, providing free higher and tertiary education) is not only egalitarian, but it will benefit the poor.[3] In this paper we hope to provide some empirical evidence to demonstrate that public expenditures on higher education do not benefit each income group equally, and that public expenditures on higher education amount to a subsidization of the higher income groups. But, here we need to place the deepening of education in post-colonial Caribbean in some historical perspective in order to acknowledge the role of higher education. Caribbean governments viewed the establishment of an indigenous regional university as important to provide the cadre of professionals to facilitate economic development. In fact, many of these governments found it too expensive to send their students abroad (U.K., Canada and U.S.A.) on scholarships to be trained. This was the argument advanced by the Government of Guyana when it chose to opt out from the University of the West Indies and established its own national university.

Despite economic progress in the Caribbean, poverty remains the main challenge to development.[4] The principal asset that the poor possesses is their labor time. Emphasis on education helps to contribute to growth and improvement in human welfare by increasing the productivity of labor. An educated person is better able to participate more fully and

---

[1] See Behrman (1993) for a discussion of the role of education in economic growth.

[2] Jimenez (1986) provides an empirical analysis of the equity issues involved in health and education expenditures for developing countries.

[3] The socialist governments of Burnham in Guyana and Michael Manley in Jamaica experimented with free university education. The political left, who are drawn from the intelligentsia, professional class and academy, applauded this as a progressive policy. With deep economic recession in the 1980s, these countries have had to abandon free university education, and imposed fees below economic cost. In the English Caribbean, primary education is compulsory and free, and secondary education is generally free. Under socialism, Guyana had a state control educational system, private secondary schools were taken over by the state. The *Sunday Chronicle*, June 14, 1998 reports that the Guyana government is now allowing the private sector to run its own schools, and the Catholic Church is set to re-enter the education sector. There is a rush from parents to enroll their children in the Catholic-run schools. But this does not come cheaply. Tuition costs for nursery education have been set at G$20,000 (G$150 = US$1) per term, G$35,000 for the primary school, and G$55,000 for secondary school. The minimum wages in 1997 were G$8804 per month. The poor will not be able to send their children to the Catholic-run schools, The *Chronicle* reports that the public education is not without difficulties, that there is little sympathy for public education, and that the "public school system is perceived as an adversary of pious homes." This is the view in the region. Public education in the Caribbean is under attack for its failure to teach the 3R's, and for the declining moral values among students. There is a crisis in public education in the Caribbean, and reforms are needed. Part of the problem is the state monopoly of the Ministry of Education, the protection of teachers' tenure, and the power of the teachers' unions.

[4] World Bank (1997 p.I). For a discussion of the poverty situation in the Caribbean, see Gafar (1998a; 1998b) and World Bank (1996).

gainfully in the economy; and she is also better equipped to acquire and use information and new technologies, and be competitive in the rapidly changing global economy.

The World Bank's highly influential policy publication, *World Development Report (WDR) 1990*, reported that a study of the determinants of real GDP for 58 countries during 1960-85 reveal (after controlling for other factors), that an increase of one year in average years of education may lead to a 3 percent increase in GDP.[5] Behrman (1993) reported that for Latin America, one year more of schooling will lead to a 0.35 percent increase in per capita GNP, 0.85 percent in manufacturing earnings, and 0.20 percent decrease in population growth.[6] *World Development Report 1990* (p.80) further noted that farmers in Africa who completed four years of schooling (UNESCO has maintained that four years of schooling is the minimum needed to achieve literacy), produce on average about 8 percent more than farmers who are illiterate.

The empirical evidence for the Caribbean region, and for other developing countries, strongly suggests that increases in educational attainment improve an individual's productivity, earnings and well being; and in the case of females, increased educational attainment correlates with lower fertility, infant and maternal mortality rates, and improved nutritional status.[7] There is a link between educational attainment, unemployment and poverty for the Caribbean region, as this paper will demonstrate.[8] An individual's educational attainment is largely influenced by historical, sociological, cultural, familial and communal resources; by one's access to educational and financial resources; by externalities (i.e. whether an individual is located in the rural or urban area); and by public policy.[9] The development strategy that the Caribbean countries adopted in the post-independence era, meant that there was an urban bias associated with the allocation of economic, social and educational resources.

The purpose of this paper is to explore some of the equity issues in education for the Anglophone Caribbean countries. The principal argument of this paper is that there exists a highly unequal distribution of public expenditures on education in favor of higher education. And, more importantly, the statistical evidence amassed in this paper shows that higher education in the Caribbean tend to benefit the higher income groups in these societies, while the children from poorer families basically receive only a primary education. This therefore added, rather than helped to reduce the poverty levels and the inequality in the Caribbean region. The structure of this paper is as follows: Section I

---

[5] World Bank (1990, Box 5.2, p.80). The influence of the World Bank's publications and research on this paper is tremendous and obvious, and we acknowledge our debts fully. We wish to acknowledge our debt to the World Bank for making some of its unpublished reports available. The data used in this paper rely on the IDB (Inter American Development Bank) and the World Bank, because other Caribbean data are not available. Because the World Bank findings are not readily available, bringing them together should benefit students and policy makers.

[6] The econometric evidence is summarized in Behrman (1993, Appendix Table 1, p.241).

[7] See especially the econometric results of Behrman (1993, Appendix Tables 1 and 2), and World Bank (1993a, p.60). On the need to emphasize female education, consult Dreze and Sen (1995, Chapters 6 and 7).

[8] For the evidence relating to the incidence of poverty in the Caribbean, see Gafar (1998a; 1998b).

[9] Hillary Clinton's thesis that "it takes a village" to educate a child has more than a ring of truth to it. Children of the poor have little or no access to financial resources for education; and, the poor, particularly the rural poor have to commute farther to schools than children in the urban areas. And, since transport costs to school are borne by the children, the rural-urban inequities are heightened.

provides a brief overview of the educational system. Section II examines the distribution of enrollment and public expenditures by level of education. The allocation of resources to education will be discussed in Section III. Section IV provides some estimates of the costs and returns to education. Section V discusses the relationship between education, unemployment, and poverty. The issue of whether an expansion of educational opportunities would lead to an improvement in the distribution of income, we are not able to explore, because of the lack of appropriate longitudinal data sets needed for such an exercise. And, finally, the paper ends with some concluding observations.

2. Overview of the Educational System

The educational system in the Anglophone Caribbean countries covers a wide range of services, ranging from pre-school to university level. The educational base consists of: pre-school and primary education, secondary education, and tertiary education. It should be noted that parents bear a significant burden: most of the costs of pre-school, plus uniforms, textbooks, supplies, and transportation for primary and secondary students. For poor families, these costs are considerable. Primary and secondary education are almost entirely financed by the central budget, and education policy and decision making are under the control of the appropriate Ministry of Education (a bureaucratic state monopoly). Salaries of teachers are determined by the Ministry of Education; and teachers have permanent positions. Teachers are generally accountable only to the Ministry of Education, and not to the users (students, parents and local community) of the educational services. This structure makes it possible for teachers to shirk or be inefficient, thereby leading to the classic principal-agent problem. There is need for the educational system to be more accountable and responsive to the local community needs; and teachers and schools ought to be held accountable for student performance. Private schooling in the Caribbean is predominantly pre-school, some secondary, and tertiary; and most private schooling facilities are urban based. In Trinidad and Tobago approximately 21 percent of the poor children in the age group 3-4 years attend pre-school compared to 59 percent for children of higher incomes, because the poor are unable to finance tuition and other expenses (books, lunch, uniforms etc.) associated with early childhood education.[10] The poor in the Caribbean are heavily concentrated in the rural areas;[11] they tend to have more children than the wealthier households; they live in unsatisfactory, overcrowded conditions and lack proper housing, access to potable water, adequate sanitation facilities, and other basic services that affect a child's learning process.

The English Caribbean speaking countries in 1900 had enrollment rates at the primary level higher than in all countries in the world except for Western Europe,

[10] For an analysis of the survey of living conditions for Trinidad and Tobago, see World Bank (1995a, 1996).

[11] While the casual observer may observe significant amounts of poverty in inner city areas, for example Lavantille, in Port-of-Spain, Trinidad; Trench Town, in Kingston, Jamaica; New Orleans, in Bridgetown, Barbados the statistics summarized in World Bank (1996, Table 4 p.160) indicate that poverty is predominantly rural. Gafar (1998b) discusses this.

Canada, U.S.A., Australia and New Zealand (World Bank 1992, p.57). But while primary education is compulsory in the Caribbean, children of the lowest income group do not have the same access to primary education as the children of higher income groups.[12] In Jamaica, for example, the attendance rate at primary level in 1991 was 72 percent, but, in the rural areas where poverty is pervasive it was 50 percent (World Bank 1994a, p.63). And, in Trinidad and Tobago, at the primary level approximately only 68 percent of the poor had access to textbooks, compared to 95% of the higher-income students (World Bank 1995a, p.44). An important input in the educational process is teacher quality, and in Guyana in the poorer and rural areas 76 percent and 90 percent of primary school and secondary school teachers were unqualified and untrained (World Bank 1993b, p.223). John Simmons (1974, p.31) points out that children from the higher-income groups who begin primary school are better nourished, better cared for, and have been exposed to cognitive and non-cognitive skills (by having pre-school training), compared with children of the poor. Once a student enters the primary level, promotion is generally not automatic from one grade to the next, but is based on tests and performance. The higher-income children have little or no difficulty in moving from one grade to the next. The poor often fail their tests and have to repeat the grade, creating among the poor the psychology of the failure syndrome. Repeating grades by the poor often lead to high drop out rates (wastage rates) at the primary school level, but there is little justification for social promotion and lowering of standards.

Students at the primary level gain access to the selective public secondary schools by passing the 11 plus (11+) competitive Common Entrance Examination (CEE). While admission to secondary schools is based on merit (11+ examination), and this can be justified on efficiency grounds, there are serious equity issues involved. The number of secondary school places is limited and are rationed by the 11+ examination. Higher income families are at a distinct advantage since they are able to spend more on books, pre-school education, nutrition, health and private tutoring which make it possible for their children to gain access to better quality secondary schools (which are located in the urban centers). The common practice in Guyana is to stream students at an early age and assign the best teachers to prepare the ablest students for the 11 plus examination; the weakest students, who are predominantly from the poor and need more help, are at a disadvantage.

The proportion of primary school graduates who 'pass' the common entrance examination to enter the traditional secondary schools is rather low: Guyana 33 percent and Jamaica 24 percent (World Bank 1992, p.84). The Planning Institute of Jamaica (1995) reports that in the 1993/94 school year, 54,942 students took the common entrance examination of which 91 percent of the students were from the public primary schools, and 9 percent from private prep schools that children of the higher incomes attend. The number of secondary school places awarded was 13,459 (i.e. 25 percent of the entrants were selected). Fifty four percent of private prep students who took the CEE were successful, while only 22% of the public school students succeeded. Those students who do not secure a secondary school place remain in the All Age Schools, the quality of

[12] This point has been made by Jimenez (1986).

which is rather low. The World Bank (1996, p.135) underscored the fact that in the case of Jamaica, in 1992, nearly 73 percent of the poorest students attended the academically inferior All Age schools; that the All Age schools received the lowest budgetary allocation; and that about one half of the students who completed the 9th grade in the All Age schools were functionally illiterate. This situation is similar in Guyana where almost one half of the poorest students attend the comprehensive All Age school, while only 8 percent of the poorest student attend the selective secondary schools (World Bank 1994b, p.70).

Secondary school instruction in the Caribbean is designed to allow students to satisfy the Caribbean Examination Council (CXC) requirements, and to a lesser degree the General Certificate of Education (G.C.E.) Ordinary Level (O' Level) and advanced Level (A' Level) administered by U.K. examination boards (namely University of London, and Oxford and Cambridge Universities).[13] Tertiary education comprise of technical and vocational education, teacher training, and university level training etc. The two principal regional universities are the University of the West Indies (UWI) and the University of Guyana (UG). These two regional universities are state funded; policies are established by the government; and students pay fees that are below economic cost. Apart from these two regional universities, there are other colleges, for example the University of Technology in Jamaica, the Caribbean Union College in Trinidad, and several recent schools many of which are linked to American tertiary institutions, or religious denominations.

3. Enrollment and Recurrent Public Expenditures by Levels of Education

Table 1 presents the percentage distribution of enrollment and recurrent government expenditures by levels of education.

The data on enrollment in Table 1 represent the average enrollment for those years, during the period 1980-89, that the World Bank (1992) reported. Examination of the statistics indicate that primary school enrollment range from 52% to 63% of total enrollment, while the share of tertiary enrollment range from a low of 2 percent in Guyana to a high of nearly 7 percent in Barbados. However, recurrent expenditures do not represent the total expenditures on education by the public sector, since capital expenditures are excluded. The statistics contained in *Human Development Report* 1997 [see UNDP 1997, Statistical Appendix 1997, Table 15 p.180] for the period 1990-94 indicate that public expenditure on primary and secondary education as a percent of total public expenditures on education at all levels averaged 75 percent for Barbados, 62 percent for Jamaica, and 72 percent for Trinidad and Tobago. On the other hand, higher education which accounts for 2 to 7 percent of total school enrollment captured 19

[13] The CXC, the regional examination board replaced the G.C.E. exams administered by U.K. examination boards some 25 years ago.

percent of total public education expenditures in Barbados, 22 percent in Jamaica, and 13 percent in Trinidad and Tobago.

Table 1: Distribution of Enrollment and Government Recurrent Expenditures by Level of Education

Country	Enrollment				Recurrent Expenditure (%)		
	Primary	Secondary	Tertiary	Total	Primary	Secondary	Tertiary
Barbados	33,209 (51.8)	26,591 (41.6)	4,250 (6.6)	64,050 (100.0)	N.A.	N.A.	N.A.
Guyana	118,595 (61.4)	70,989 (36.7)	3,650 (1.9)	193,234 (100.0)	64.5	28.9	6.5
Jamaica	343,403 (57.2)	244,832 (40.7)	12,500 (2.1)	600,795 (100.0)	38.5	40.2	23.2
Trinidad and Tobago	165,897 (62.9)	90,589 (34.3)	7,350 (2.8)	263,836 (100.0)	45.5	33.3	21.2

Source: Computed from data contained in World Bank, *Access, Quality and Efficiency in Caribbean Education* 1992, Tables 4.3, 5.1 and 6.1. The enrollment data represent the average for those years during the period 1980-89 for which there were reported data. The expenditure data were taken from Table 2.5 of the World Bank's study. The figures in parentheses denote percentages. N.A. = not available.

A determining factor which affects the distributional impact of public expenditures on education is the efficiency of the educational system. One way of examining the efficiency of the educational system is to determine the probabilities of students making it through the ladder. Table 2 provides some estimates of the chances (based on historical data) of students achieving different education levels for each of 100 primary school entrants.

A number of observations need noting from an analysis of Table 2. First, at least 80 percent of all primary school entrants complete primary school. Compared to a number of developing countries in Africa and Asia, this is an impressive achievement. Second, at least 70 percent of the initial primary school entrants go on to obtain some secondary (All Age and Secondary schools) education. However, the completion rate at the secondary level varies from a low of 26 percent in Guyana to a high of 65 percent in Trinidad and Tobago. This suggests that drop out rates at the secondary level are indeed high. Third, the data reveal an extremely small percent of the students passing 4+ CXC subjects: it varies from a low of 2 percent in Guyana to a high of 8 percent in Barbados of the initial students who entered the primary level. And, if passing 4+ CXC subjects is used as a rough proxy of success (since at least 4+ CXC subjects are needed for employment in the civil service or for entry to colleges), the data in Table 2 suggest the need for significant improvements in secondary level education. And, finally the information in Table 2 indicates that only a small minority of the students (from 2 to 3 percent) who entered the primary level ultimately end up entering a Caribbean university.

Table 2: Probabilities of Different Levels of Educational Attainment for Some English Speaking Caribbean Countries

	Barbados	Guyana	Jamaica	Trinidad
a) Enter Primary I	100	100	100	100
Complete Primary	100	80	85	100
b) Enter Post Primary (e.g. All Age)	4	54	32	23
c) Enter Secondary	96	26	53	70
Complete Secondary	n.a.	26	53	65
Pass CXC English	n.a.	3	8	24
Pass CXC Math	n.a.	3	7	19
Pass 4+ CXC subjects	8	2	3	5
d) Take GCE A'Levels	5	n.a.	3	7
Pass 2+ A'Levels	n.a.	n.a.	n.a.	2
e) Enter other Tertiary	42	6	7	10
f) Enter Caribbean University	3	2	2	3

Notes: n.a. = not available

Source: Taken from World Bank, *Access, Quality and Efficiency in Caribbean Education*, Report No. 9753-CRG, 1992, Table 3.1, p.45.

4. Resource Allocation

The allocation of public expenditures on education reflects the importance that Caribbean governments attach to public education. Table 3 presents total public expenditure on education as a share of GNP and total government expenditures for some Caribbean countries.

The data in Table 3 indicate that on average the Anglophone Caribbean countries spend approximately 5 percent of their GNP on education, compared to less than 2 percent for the other Caribbean countries. The statistics indicate that between 1980 and 1990 public expenditure on education as a percent of total expenditures declined across all countries. This is due largely to the economic decline in the 1980s. External shocks (declining terms of trade), mounting foreign debt problems, and inappropriate domestic policies were responsible for the economic decline in the 1980s.[14] As a consequence, the Caribbean countries have had to implement adjustment programs which require fiscal austerity, elimination of subsidies, and reductions in public expenditures. Health, education and other social spending became easy targets for reductions in the era of IMF austerity, since the poor, who depend on the social services, do not have the political muscle to prevent any reductions in the social services budget.

Table 3: Total Public Expenditures on Education as a Percent of Total Government Expenditures and GNP for some Caribbean Countries

	Total Public Educational Expenditures as a Percent of:			
Country	GNP		Government Expenditure	
	1980	1990	1980	1990
Barbados	6.50	7.50	20.50	18.60
Guyana	9.70	4.70	14.00	9.00*
Jamaica	7.00	6.20	13.00	12.90
Trinidad and Tobago	4.00	3.60	11.50	10.30
Non-English Caribbean Countries				
Dominican Republic	2.20	1.70	16.00	9.00
Haiti	1.50	1.80	14.90	20.00

Notes: n.a. = not available
* denotes for 1988, and taken from World Bank, *Access, Quality and Efficiency in Caribbean Education*, 1992, Table 2.1, p.24.
Source: Inter American Development Bank, *Economic and Social Progress in Latin America 1996 Report*, Appendix, Table 2, p.332.

The Inter-American Development Bank (1996) noted that in 1990 the industrial economies spent 5.7 percent of their GNP on education, the Latin American and Caribbean countries 4.3 percent, East Asia 4.1 percent, South Asia 4.1 percent, Other Asia (including China) 3.5 percent, and Sub-Saharan Africa 4.3 percent. And, by income groups, the high income countries spent 5.2 percent and the low income countries 3.6 percent.

5. Costs and Returns to Education

There is, in the literature, some criticism regarding the "disproportionate" per pupil costs (expenditures) of education by education level.[15] Table 4 summarizes the recurrent education expenditures by unit cost according to educational level, and GDP per-capita income.

[14] Gafar (1996a) provides an analysis of the effects of domestic and external factors on the performance of Caribbean countries.

[15] On this point and other issues of the economics of education, see Todaro (1996, Chap. 11), from which this paper draws freely.

Table 4: Recurrent Government Education Expenditures by Unit Cost Per Level and Per Capita GDP (US$)

Country	Unit Cost (1990 US$) [1]				GDP per Capita (1990 US$) [2]	
	Primary	Secondary	Tertiary	University	1990	1995
Barbados	672	913	1,200	n.a.	6,657	6,580
Guyana	26	54	146	858	471	722
Jamaica	101	257	639	5,138	1,633	1,637
Trinidad and Tobago	596	811	n.a.	10,510	4,259	4,369

Notes; (1) Taken from World Bank, *Access, Quality and Efficiency in Caribbean Education*, p.27, Table 2.5. Unit Cost is the average recurrent government education expenditures per pupil enrolled in each level.

(2) Taken from IDB, *Education and Social Progress in Latin America 1996 Report*, Table B.2 p.359.

(3) n.a. = not available.

The unit cost is derived by taking the average recurrent government education expenditures per pupil enrolled in each level. At the primary level, the average unit cost varies from US$26 in Guyana to US$672 in Barbados. The effective unit cost at the primary level is much higher, if adjustments are made for drop-outs. At the secondary level, the average unit cost ranges from US$54 in Guyana to US$913 in Barbados. The average unit cost of university education varies from US$858 in Guyana to US$10,510 in Trinidad. The unit cost of university education is approximately 2.5 times the 1990 level of per capita GDP in the Caribbean countries. There are two explanations for the high average unit cost of university education. First, in order for Caribbean universities to attract and retain faculty they must of necessity pay competitive salaries. And, second, because of the shortage of higher educated personnel in these societies, higher education which is fairly labor intensive activity, tends to be more costly than it would otherwise be. How does the unit cost ratios in the Caribbean compare with other developing and developed countries? Table 5 presents a comparative analysis of the unit cost of the Caribbean, with that for some developed and developing countries.

The data in Table 5 suggest that the ratio of secondary unit cost to primary unit cost in the Caribbean varies from 1.4 to 2.5, compared to 6.6 for the developed countries. In the case of higher (university) versus primary education, the data suggest that the equivalent cost of educating one university student in terms of the primary level is 18 for Trinidad and Tobago, 33 for Guyana, and 51 for Jamaica. This clearly suggests that the Caribbean countries spend a large proportion of their educational budget on a small proportion of middle and upper income students enrolled in higher education.

Table 5: Ratios of Unit Costs by Education Level

Countries	Relative Cost [2]	
	Secondary Versus Primary	**Higher Versus Primary**
Barbados	1.4	n.a.
Guyana	2.1	33.0
Jamaica	2.5	50.9
Trinidad	1.4	17.6
Groups of Countries [1]		
United States, Great Britain, New Zealand	6.6	17.6
Malaysia, Ghana, South Korea, Kenya, Uganda, Nigeria, India	11.9	87.9

Notes: (1) The groups of countries are contained in Michael Todaro, *Economic Development* 6th ed., Addison-Wesley Pub. Co. 1996, Table 11.2. The data reported in Todaro Table 11.2 is reprinted from George Psacharopoulos, *The Returns to Education: An International Comparison*, Elsevier, Amsterdam, 1973, Table 8.2.
(2) Based on Table 4 for the Caribbean countries.

The empirical evidence in the literature suggests that the relative earnings of secondary versus primary education in the developed countries is 1.4 to 1 compared to 2.4 to 1 for the developing countries; and the relative earnings of higher versus primary education is 2.4 to 1 in the developed countries, and, for the developing countries it is 64 to one.[16] But, since the average cost of higher/primary education in the developing countries is about 87.9, the data clearly suggest that, from an equity perspective, higher education may be over-funded.

There has been considerable effort, most notably by the World Bank economist George Psacharopoulos, to estimate private and social rates of returns for education. This is important in any discussion of the equity-productivity trade off relating to schooling. Estimates of the returns on education for each Caribbean country are not readily available, however, as illustrative evidence of the magnitudes of the rates of return involved, Table 6 summarizes the returns to education by level, and region.

Private rates of return reflect the expected returns to the individual excluding the opportunity costs (income, tuition etc.) of the education. Social rates of return, which matter for policy making, are adjusted for government expenditures on education, but they do not take into account various externalities (for example, abilities and traits of students). Calculations of returns implicitly assume, as Bhagwati (1973) pointed out, that for any level of the education ladder it is the same for each class of the social structure, and this is not true. The poor do not have access to educational financing. Moreover, capital markets are imperfect, incomplete and segmented, and there is imperfect information. Absent these methodological and statistical limitations, the data in Table 6 reveal the following: First, private returns are higher than social returns. Second, primary education reflects the highest private and social returns world wide. Third, social rates of return for secondary and higher education are very close. Fourth, there is considerable difference between private returns and social returns on higher education. If public subsidies tend to increase with the level of education, this will be regressive. The evidence reported by Psacharopoulos (1994, Table 2) suggests that private and social returns at all levels of the education ladder decline with the level of a country's per capita income. Psacharopoulos (1994) reported that the rates of return for females in Latin America and the Caribbean exceed those of males by one percentage point. For Jamaica, Psacharopoulos (1993) reported that at the primary level the private rates of return are 20.4 percent and the social returns are 17.7 percent; at the secondary level the private returns are 15.7 percent and the social returns are 7.9 percent; the overall returns on education for males is 12.3 percent and 21.5 percent for women; and the returns to education in employment in the private sector are 24.9 percent compared to 16.0 percent in the public sector. In a competitive economy returns for each level of education ought to be equalized. The lower returns at the higher level suggests an overallocation of resources to higher education.

Table 6: Returns to Education by Level (percent), and Region

Country	Social Rate of Return			Private Rate of Return		
	Primary	Secondary	Higher	Primary	Secondary	Higher
Developing						
Sub-Saharan Africa	24.3	18.2	11.2	41.3	26.6	27.8
Asia	19.9	13.3	11.7	39.0	18.9	19.9
Latin America and Caribbean	17.9	12.8	12.3	26.2	16.8	19.7
Developed	14.4	10.2	8.7	21.7	12.4	12.3
World	18.4	13.1	10.9	29.1	18.1	20.3

Source: George Psacharopoulos, "Returns to Investment in Education", *World Development*, Vol. 22, 1994, pp.1325-1343, Table I.

Employing a Mincerian earnings function, and controlling for such factors as gender, ethnicity, experience, and education, The World Bank (1995a, p.100) reported that, in the case of Trinidad and Tobago, returns to education are positive with each year of education increasing earnings close to 13 percent for males, and 14 percent for females. The Mincerian rate of earnings for years of schooling for both sexes in Jamaica is 7.2 percent. (Psacharopoulos, 1993). These results clearly show that more education leads to higher incomes, and perhaps widening income inequality. Behrman (1993) has seriously challenged the estimates of the returns on education (years of schooling) because of the failure to control for educational quality. According to Behrman the estimates of returns on primary education are substantially overstated; and if adjustments are made for

[16] See Todaro (1996, Chapt. 11).

quality, third world countries might be better off on productivity grounds in deepening secondary education, rather than extending primary education.

Behrman has suggested that third world countries might improve productivity gains by upgrading existing schools and spending the resources on fewer students, rather than spending the resources broadly and thinly on more students and on low quality primary schools. But, this has serious equity issues, since it is the middle and high income groups who are the principal beneficiaries of secondary and higher education, as the next section will establish.

6. EDUCATION, INEQUALITY AND POVERTY

The census data provide information on the educational attainment (stock) of the population 5 years and over. Details of the educational attainment for the latest census of Jamaica and Trinidad and Tobago are summarized in Table 7.

Table 7: Population by Sex and Highest Level of Education Attainment in Jamaica and Trinidad and Tobago (percent)

Country	Primary and Below	Secondary	University	Other	Not Stated	Total
Jamaica (1991 census) [1]						
Male	67.4	27.3	1.3	0.6	3.4	100.0
Female	62.7	31.7	1.3	0.9	3.4	100.0
Both Sexes	65.0	29.5	1.3	0.8	3.4	100.0
Trinidad andTobago (1990 census) [2]						
Male	57.6	37.6	2.5	0.9	1.4	100.0
Female	56.7	39.1	1.8	1.1	1.3	100.0
Both Sexes	57.2	38.4	2.1	1.0	1.3	100.0

Sources: (1) Author's calculations based on Statistical Institute of Jamaica, *Statistical Abstract 1995*, Table 3.1.

(2) Author's calculations based on Central Statistical Office, *Annual Statistical Digest 1994/95*, Trinidad and Tobago, Table 56.

The evidence in Table 8 reveals two broad conclusions. First, approximately 1.3 percent of the population in Jamaica and 2.1 percent in Trinidad and Tobago have a university education (indicating that there is a shortage of qualified technical, professional and managerial personnel in the Caribbean). Second, the evidence suggests that there is no gender problem regarding educational attainment of females in Jamaica and Trinidad and Tobago. While the information in Table 7 provides a measure of the educational stock in the Caribbean, the data do not tell the story regarding the educational attainment of the various classes (poor, middle income, and upper income). The surveys of living conditions conducted jointly by the government statistical agencies and The World Bank provide an insight to the educational attainment of the various income groups, to wit, the bottom 20 percent etc. The results of the surveys of living conditions are summarized in several World Bank reports, which form the basis for this section.[17] Table 8 provides details regarding the highest educational attainment of the head of households for Guyana, Jamaica, and Trinidad and Tobago.

Table 8: Highest Educational Level of Head of Households in Selected Caribbean Countries

Country	Highest Educational Level	Quintile Group (Income Group)					
		Q1	Q2	Q3	Q4	Q5	Total
Guyana	Primary	90.0	83.5	77.6	76.7	55.5	74.6
	Secondary	10.0	15.3	20.5	21.5	36.0	22.2
	Tertiary	0.0	1.2	1.9	1.8	8.5	3.2
Jamaica	Primary	59.6	51.0	49.9	45.0	31.2	44.5
	Secondary	40.4	48.0	48.6	52.5	52.6	50.9
	Tertiary	0.0	1.0	1.5	2.5	11.8	4.6
Trinidad and Tobago	Primary	78.0	76.0	74.0	62.0	46.0	64.0
	Secondary	22.0	23.0	26.0	35.0	42.3	32.0
	Tertiary	0.5	1.0	0.4	0.4	12.0	4.0

SOURCE: World Bank, *Caribbean Countries Poverty Reduction and Human Resource Development in the Caribbean*, Report No. 15342-LAC, 1996; Statistical Appendix, Table 5. For example, Q1 refers to the bottom 20 percent of the expenditure (income) distribution, while Q5 refers to the top 20 percent of the income distribution. Moreover, Q1 plus Q2 represent the bottom 40 percent of the income distribution.

The evidence in Table 8 shows that most of the poor (lowest quintile) just have a basic primary education. The summary data do not distinguish the educational levels between rural and urban areas. The World Bank (1994a, pp.60-61) noted that educational levels in Jamaica are highest in Kingston (capital) and lowest in rural areas. This is largely due to the urban bias associated with economic, educational and social policies. The World Bank also noted that for Jamaica, there is a positive correlation between education levels and consumption levels. Since the disparity in consumption (welfare) between rural and urban areas is due in part to education, improvements in the provision of quality public education in the rural areas would benefit the poor. Approximately 10 percent of the poor in Guyana have some secondary education, compared to 22 percent in Trinidad and 40 percent in Jamaica. Students in Jamaica are enrolled in secondary education programs in both the traditional secondary schools and the All Age schools. The World Bank (1996, p.24) has reported that about one half of the students of the secondary level All Age schools (that the poor basically attend) are functionally illiterate.

[17] We do not have access to the survey of living conditions data, and this explains our reliance and debt on the World Bank reports. The findings of the World Bank are scattered in various reports, and are not readily available. The Bhagwati (1973) influence on this section should be obvious to those familiar with Bhagwati's contributions to the literature.

There is evidence to suggest that functional literacy rates in Jamaica have fallen in recent years due in part to economic recession, education budget cuts, instability of the family, and the emigration of qualified teachers. Janet Brown (1998, p.219) makes the point of declining functional literacy rates in Jamaica as follows:

> "A 1989 Ministry of Education survey of grade six students showed rates of functional literacy among girls of 89 percent down to 63 percent, depending on the type and location of schools. The levels for boys ranged from a high of 67 percent to a low of 37 percent for functional literacy for rural all-age schools. The rural all-age schools have the highest concentration of the country's poorest children. Thus, an intolerably high percentage of Jamaica's children, most of them poor, leave primary school without even basic literacy, much less preparation for further education or training to later be able to support self and family."

Recent estimates for Guyana suggest that 89 percent of the out-of-school youths are functionally illiterate, hence, the literacy rates data published by the international institutions (UNESCO, UNDP and World Bank) for developing countries, must be viewed with circumspection.[18] There is need to upgrade the quality of the All-Age schools in the Caribbean so that the poor can benefit. Declining education quality spells disaster for the ability of the poor to be gainfully employed, to escape poverty, and to be competitive in the global economy. Much of Asia's economic growth can be explained by the accumulation of human capital (education, health, and nutrition). The World Bank (1993c, p.52) reported that primary education is "by far the largest single contributor to HPAEs' [High performing Asian economies] predicted growth rates." In the case of Japan 58 percent of the predicted growth is due to primary school enrollment, and for Thailand the figure is 87 percent. (World Bank 1993c, p.52). The World Bank further noted that education is the principal factor responsible for growth between Sub-Saharan African and the Asian countries.

The statistical evidence in Table 8 unambiguously reveals that it is the upper income households who are better educated. In many Caribbean and developing countries the urban middle class and the wealthy are extremely powerful; they are economically and politically well-connected, and they aggressively use their influence to shape policies for their benefit; the poor, it must be emphasized, are concerned with day to day survival, and are unorganized to leverage benefits from the state.

Education plays an important role in the allocation of jobs in the labor market. One view is that education and training bear directly on a worker's productivity. Another view is that education achievements convey useful information regarding workers' ability, quality and motivation, and higher education acts as a "filter" or "screening device" in the labor market. In the modern sector, credentials and certification play an important role in determining the allocation of jobs and salaries. And this has had the effect of people with secondary education bidding and obtaining jobs that just require literacy (Bhagwati, 1973). Any policy of linking jobs on the basis of certification, not

[18] The functional illiteracy statistics are in Gafar (1998b).

performance, means that the poor are at a disadvantage, and such education-job link can result in widening income inequalities.

Table 9 documents the unemployment rates by consumption (income) quintiles for Guyana, Jamaica, and Trinidad and Tobago.

Table 9: Unemployment Rate by Consumption Quintile in Guyana, Jamaica, and Trinidad and Tobago

Country	Quintiles					
	Q1	Q2	Q3	Q4	Q5	Total
1. Guyana [1]	12.7	11.8	11.7	10.9	8.8	11.1
2. Jamaica (All) [2]	9.3	15.6	14.3	15.3	9.2	n.a.
Kingston	20.0	22.0	14.0	12.0	6.0	n.a.
Rural Areas	8.0	13.0	12.0	17.0	13.0	n.a.
3. Trinidad and Tobago [1]	36.2	32.6	21.0	16.3	10.3	20.8

Sources: (1) World Bank, *Caribbean Countries Poverty Reduction and Human Resource Development in the Caribbean*, 1996, Statistical Appendix, Table 7.

(2) World Bank, *Jamaica: A Strategy for Growth and Poverty Reduction, Country Economic Memorandum*, 1994, Table 2.5

The statistical evidence in Table 9 indicates that in Guyana and Trinidad and Tobago, the unemployment rates are highest for the poor. The data for Jamaica indicate that the unemployment rate for the rural poor is the lowest. Bhagwati (1973) has provided an explanation for this apparent paradox. According to Bhagwati, the rural poor do not have the "capacity" to hold out for better paying jobs, and they are forced to take whatever comes first. Gafar (1997) has reported that under economic liberalization there has been an increase in the informalization of the labor market in Jamaica. It is the poor who primarily seek employment in the informal sector, and since wages in the informal sector are much lower than those prevailing in the formal sector, this has aggravated poverty, and suggests a rise in income inequality. The data in Tables 8 and 9 clearly establish the link between educational level and unemployment rate. Workers with lower levels of education (training) are more likely to be unemployed and poor, as the data in Tables 8 and 9 suggest. Evidence on unemployment rates by level of education is only available for Trinidad and Tobago. According to the World Bank (1995a, Statistical Appendix Table 15) the unemployment rate for holders of a university degree is: males 2.1 percent and females 0.0 percent; with no degree: males 22.0 percent, and for females 28.5 percent; with school leaving (primary) certificate: males 17.9 percent and females 16.2 percent. There is a direct relationship between level of education attainment and earnings, as the data in Table 10 for Trinidad and Tobago illustrate.

Table 10: Monthly Earnings by Level of Education Attainment in Trinidad and Tobago ($TT)

Education Level	Male	Female
No degree	1270	788
CXC Basic	877	872
G.C.E. O'L (3-4 subjects)	1698	1307
G.C.E. O'L (5+ subjects)	2790	1956
G.C.E. A'L (1-2 subjects)	2011	2690
Diploma	2859	2740
Degree	5746	3531
Other	1600	1352
Total	**1750**	**1500**

Notes: TT$5.80 is approximately equal to US$1.00.
Source: World Bank, *Trinidad and Tobago Poverty and Unemployment in an Oil Based Economy*, 1995 Statistical Appendix Table 61.

Two broad conclusions can be drawn from an examination of Table 10. First, women with comparable educational attainment earn less than men. Second, workers with university degrees earn approximately 4.5 times more than those with no university degree. This suggests that public subsidies for university education may be difficult to justify. Children of upper income families tend to have more schooling than children of the poor, hence, public funding of higher education is a subsidy to the upper income families which can lead to widening income inequalities. Policy makers in both the developed and developing countries are concerned with the gap between the skilled and unskilled workers because of its implications for income inequality. Consider the case of Jamaica. The data reported by Gafar (1997, Table 9) show that the ratio of earnings of skilled/unskilled in Jamaica in 1986 was 1.4, but this rose to 2.7 in 1993. In Guyana, the ratio of the salary of a graduate teacher to the minimum wages increased from 2.8 in 1992 to 3.4 in 1997. Passell (1998) has reported that since the 1970s the gap in wages between skilled and unskilled workers in the U.S. increased considerably. Passell noted that the median wage of workers with only a high school diploma in the U.S. fell by 6 percent between 1980 to 1996, while the earnings of college graduates rose by 12 percent. Passell also noted that in 1982 workers in the top one tenth of the labor force earned 3.95 times for workers in the bottom tenth, but, by 1996 the gap widened to 4.72 times. The widening gap between the earnings of the skilled (educated) and unskilled in both Guyana and Jamaica, is consistent with what is happening in developed countries.

We now examine the relationship between the level of education attainment and poverty, as measured by the head count index, for Trinidad and Tobago. The head count index is the proportion of the population living below the poverty line, defined by The World Bank as US$1.56 per day at 1992 prices. Table 11 presents the details.

Table 11: Education Level and Poverty by Head of Households in Trinidad and Tobago, 1992

Highest Education Level	Share of Total (%)	Poverty Head Count Index (%)
No education	5.5	28.6
Primary	74.1	25.4
Junior Secondary	7.4	28.6
Secondary	12.2	12.5
Post-Secondary	0.6	2.8
Other	0.2	2.0
Overall	100.0	21.2

SOURCE: World Bank, *Trinidad and Tobago Poverty and Unemployment in an Oil Based Economy*, Report No. 14382-TR, 1995, Statistical Appendix Table 4 p.127.

The data in Table 11 demonstrate that there is an inverse relationship between the magnitude of poverty and years of schooling (education). Together with broad based economic growth, that is labor absorbing, improvements in education represent the best chance for the poor to escape poverty.

The central question is: Which socio-economic class is the principal beneficiary of public expenditures in education? Professor Bhagwati (1973, p.24) advanced the following hypothesis:

> "For each class in education, the State (in capitalist LDCs) will subsidize the cost of education; the benefits of these subsidies will accrue disproportionately less to the poorer groups at each level of education; the higher the educational level being considered, the higher will be the average income-level of the groups to which the students belong; and the rate of government subsidization to higher education will be greater than to primary education."

What the Bhagwati hypothesis tells us is that public expenditures on education will reflect class structure, and that higher income groups will benefit more. The evidence amassed in this paper on private and social rates of returns, earnings by level of education, and the level of education and poverty clearly support this proposition. A more direct test of the hypothesis is to examine the incidence of public spending on education. Table 12 presents the quintiles shares of beneficiaries of public education spending in Guyana, Jamaica, and Trinidad and Tobago.

Table 12: Quintiles Shares of Beneficiaries of Public Education Spending in Guyana, Jamaica and Trinidad and Tobago

Country	Expenditure Item	Quintile Group				
		Q1	Q2	Q3	Q4	Q5
Guyana	*Education*					
	Primary	28.9	24.9	18.5	19.0	8.6
	Secondary	15.7	24.0	22.0	23.5	14.8
	Post Secondary	7.7	12.5	28.0	19.4	32.5
	Meal at School	23.4	27.1	19.7	21.0	8.8
	Free Textbooks	25.6	24.5	22.9	16.4	10.7
Jamaica	*Education*					
	Primary	31.0	26.8	20.6	15.4	6.2
	Secondary	10.2	14.8	24.8	29.9	20.4
	Technical/Vocational	6.2	31.0	22.1	28.9	11.7
Trinidad and Tobago	*Education*					
	Primary	30.9	24.0	22.2	15.6	7.3
	Junior Secondary	29.1	23.3	22.4	19.3	5.8
	Secondary	17.7	19.6	27.5	20.4	14.9
	University/Technical	4.1	9.3	13.6	36.3	36.7
	School Feeding	43.1	27.3	15.2	10.6	3.8
	Free Textbooks	19.6	13.6	17.4	27.4	21.9

SOURCE: World Bank, Caribbean Countries Poverty Reduction and Human Resource Development in the Caribbean, 1996, Statistical Appendix Tables 32, 34 and 36.

The evidence in Table 12 indicates that public expenditures on primary education and school feeding programs are well targeted, since the poor benefit greatly. The same is true for public expenditures on health care. The statistics indicate that the top 40 percent of the income distribution benefit significantly from public expenditures on post-secondary and university education, and this is highly regressive. Behrman (1996, Table 5.1, p.181) has summarized the percentage of government higher education subsidies received by the upper 20 percent of the income distribution and the lower 40 percent of the income group. In the case of Colombia the top 20 percent of the income group received 76 percent of the higher education government subsidies, while the lower 40 percent of the income group received 2 percent of the higher education subsidies; for Colombia the top 20 percent of the income profile received 60 percent of the higher education subsidies while the bottom 40 percent of the income distribution just got 6 percent; and in the case of Chile the upper 20 percent of the income distribution received 54 percent of the higher education subsidies while the lower 40 percent of the income group received 12 percent. Commenting on who gets schooling subsidies in the Latin American and Caribbean region, Behrman (1996, p.180) writes:

> "There are additional policy concerns at the tertiary and advanced schooling levels. In much of the region, for instance, the per capita subsidies to tertiary schooling have been very large relative to subsidies to lower schooling levels, and have mainly benefitted the upper and middle classes......the nature and the rationale for these subsidies need to be addressed."

It can be argued that public subsidies on higher education are needed to obtain the scientific, engineering, management, and medical skills that the region needs for economic development and to be competitive in the global economy. Moreover, the externalities associated with higher education (to wit, research) may partly justify subsidies on higher education. It appears, from a cursory examination of the data in Table 12 that public expenditures on education in the Caribbean have become an instrument for the State to dole out subsidies to the higher-income groups. In terms of political economy, the search for an explanation is compelling. Professor Bhagwati (1973, p.24) provides the following explanation:

> "The benefits can be handed out to elite groups by the State without disaffection if they are handled via the educational system which, in principle, at least, is open to all classes and and castes [and races] and therefore conceals effectively its inegalitarian impact."

There is need, on equity and efficiency grounds, for some aggressive full cost recovery programs to be instituted at the post secondary level. The World Bank (1996, p.24) noted that 76 percent of the emigrants from Guyana had secondary or post secondary education, and less than 10 percent of the migrants from Guyana were from the poor households. In the case of Jamaica, the World Bank [1994a, p.61] pointed out that in the 1980s, 18 percent of those who migrated from Jamaica were classified as "professional, technical and related fields" and 27 percent were "skilled" workers, and this represents a serious brain drain and capital outflows from the Caribbean countries, which is exacerbated in part, by the bias in U.S. immigration laws towards skilled and technical immigrants.

7. Conclusion

The main conclusions of this paper are the following. First, primary school level has the largest share of enrollment, but, a disproportionately higher share of public education expenditures went to higher education. The drop out rates are highest at the primary level. Second, the poor have less years of schooling; about 80 percent of the poor have just a primary education. Most of the poor live in rural areas, and rural schools have high student-teacher ratios, and rural schools are excessively staffed with unqualified and untrained teachers. Third, the performance of the educational system, as measured by pass rates at CXC examinations etc., is rather low, only few students (not the poor) make it through the education ladder. This is a manifestation of the abysmal performance of primary education in the region. There is need for the state to provide good primary education, and improve the quality of the All-Age schools that the poor predominantly attend, if the poor would have any chance to escape the vicious cycle of poverty and hopelessness. Fourth, the data indicate no gender problem regarding female educational attainment, but, for comparable educational levels females earn less than men. The data suggest that earnings are directly related to the level of educational attainment, and that unemployment and poverty vary inversely with the level of education. Improvements in the level of education for the poor is a way to increase their employment opportunities, and thus providing a means for the poor to escape poverty. Fifth, the evidence shows that the poor benefit substantially from primary education and school feeding programs, and there should be a reallocation of the education budget in these areas. The upper income groups are the principal beneficiaries of higher education, and this is regressive. Free education does not mean free education for all classes. The upper income groups should pay more of the economic cost for secondary and higher education, and the poorer groups should be subsidized. Sixth, the empirical evidence shows that the returns at the primary level are the highest, suggesting that quality primary education should be emphasized.

National testing at the primary level may help to maintain and raise standards. Finally, on equity grounds, the poor need more access to preschool, school feeding, school materials and transportation; they should be given the opportunity to attend better schools; and the education dollar will be better spent improving the All-Age schools that the poor mainly attend and extending primary education, rather than funding higher education thereby doling out subsidies to the urban middle income families, the wealthy, and the ruling class.

8. References

1. Behrman, J.R., "Investing in Human Resources" in Inter-American Development Bank, *Economic and Social Progress in Latin America 1993 Report*, Washington, D.C., Inter-American Development Bank, 1993.
2. Behrman, J.R., *Human Resources in Latin America and the Caribbean*, Washington, D.C., Inter-America Development Bank 1996.
3. Bhagwati, J., "Education, class structure and income equality," *World Development*, Vol. 1, No. 5, 1973 pp.21-35.
4. Brown, J., "Comment" in Shadid Javed Burki, Sri-Ram Aiyer and Rudolf Hommes, eds. *Annual World Bank Conference on Development in Latin America and the Caribbean 1996: Poverty and Inequality*, Washington: D.C. The World Bank,1998, pp.218-220.
5. Central Statistical Office, *Annual Statistical Digest 1994/95*, Port of Spain, Trinidad and Tobago, 1997.
6. Dreze, J. and Sen A., *India: Economic Development and Social Opportunity*, Delhi, Oxford University Press, 1995.
7. Gafar, J., "Macroeconomic Performance and External Shocks on Small, Open Economies: The Caribbean Experience," *The Journal of Developing Areas*, Vol. 30, No. 3, 1996a, pp.341-360.

8. Gafar, J., "Guyana: From Cooperative Socialism to Economic Liberalization and Growth: 1976-1994," *The Journal of Developing Areas*, Vol. 31, No. 1, 1996b pp. 41-74.
9. Gafar, J., "Structural Adjustment and the Labour Market in Jamaica," *Canadian Journal of Development Studies*, Vol. XVIII, No.2, 1997, pp.239-261.
10. Gafar, J., "Growth, Inequality and Poverty in Selected Latin American Countries with Emphasis on Guyana," *Journal of Latin American Studies* Vol. 30 1998a, pp.591-617.
11. Gafar, J., "Poverty, Income Growth, and Inequality in Some Caribbean Countries: *The Journal of Developing Areas* Vol. 32, 1998b, pp.467-490.
12. Inter-American Development Bank, *Economic and Social Progress in Latin America 1993 Report*, Washington, D.C., Inter-American Development Bank, 1993.
13. Inter-American Development Bank, *Economic and Social Progress in Latin America 1996 Report*, Washington, D.C., Inter-American Development Bank, 1996.
14. Jimenez, E., "The Public Subsidization of Education and Health in Developing Countries: A Review of Equity and Efficiency," *The World Bank Research Observer*, Vol. 1 No. 1, 1986 pp.111-129.
15. Kershaw, S., "To Speak The Same Language: Schools seek path for Caribbean kids." *Newsday*; Queens, N.Y., Newsday Inc., Vol. 58, No. 313, Sunday July 12, 1998.
16. Passell, P., "Benefits Dwindle Along With Wages For The Unskilled," *The New York Times*, June 14, 1998.
17. Planning Institute of Jamaica, *Economic And Social Survey: Jamaica 1994*, Planning Institute of Jamaica, Kingston, Jamaica, 1995.
18. Psacharopoulos, G., *Returns to Education: An International Comparison*, San Francisco: Elsevier, 1973.
19. Psacharopoulos, G., "*Returns to Investment in Education: A Global Update*," Working Papers WPS 1067, The World Bank, 1993.
20. Psacharopoulos, G., "Returns to Investment in Education: A Global Update," *World Development*,Vol. 22, No.9, 1994, pp.1325-1343.
21. Schiefelbein, E., "Education Reform in Latin America and the Caribbean: An Agenda for Action," in Burki, S.; S. Edwards and Aiyer, S. eds. *Annual World Bank Conference on Development in Latin America and the Caribbean 1995*; Washington, D.C.; The World Bank, 1997.
22. Simmons, J., *Education, Poverty, and Development*, Bank Staff Working Paper No. 188, The World Bank, 1974.
23. Statistical Institute of Jamaica, *Statistical Abstract 1995*, Statistical Institute of Jamaica, Kingston, Jamaica, 1996.
24. Todaro, M., *Economic Development*, 6th ed., New York, Addison-Wesley Pub. Co. 1996.
25. United Nations Development Programme, *Human Development Report 1997*, New York, Oxford University Press for UNDP, 1997.

26. World Bank, *World Development Report 1990, Poverty*, N.Y., Oxford University Press for the World Bank, 1990.
27. World Bank, *World Development 1991 - The Challenge of Development*, N.Y., Oxford University Press for the World Bank, 1991.
28. World Bank, Access, Quality and Efficiency in Caribbean Education. A Regional Study, Report No. 9753-CRG, The World Bank, 1992.
29. World Bank, Caribbean Region: Current Economic Situation, Regional Issues, and Capital Flows, Washington, D.C., The World Bank, 1993a.
30. World Bank, *Guyana: Public Sector Review*, Washington, D.C., The World Bank, 1993b.
31. World Bank, *The East Asian Miracle*, New York: Oxford University Press published for The World Bank, 1993c.
32. World Bank, Jamaica: A Strategy for Growth and Poverty Reduction. Country Economic Memorandum. Report No. 12702-JM, Washington, D.C., The World Bank, 1994a.
33. World Bank, *Guyana: Strategies for Reducing Poverty*, Report No. 12861-GUA, Washington, D.C., The World Bank, 1994b.
34. World Bank, *Trinidad and Tobago Poverty and Unemployment in an Oil Based Economy*. Report No. 14382-TR, Washington, D.C., The World Bank 1995a.
35. World Bank, *World Development Report 1995. Workers in an Integrating World*, N.Y. Oxford University Press for The World Bank, 1995b.
36. World Bank, Caribbean Countries Poverty Reduction and Human Resource Development in the Caribbean. Report No. 15342-LAC, Washington, D.C., The World Bank, 1996.

Chapter 3

POVERTY: MEASURES, DIMENSIONS AND SOME STRATEGIES FOR POVERTY REDUCTION IN THE CARIBBEAN

John Gafar
C.W. Post Campus
Long Island University
Greenvale, N.Y

ABSTRACT

This paper briefly traces the development of poverty studies, and discusses some of the statistical measures of poverty; it surveys the evidence of poverty world-wide providing illustrative country examples to underscore the depth and magnitude of human poverty; and, finally, the paper discusses poverty strategies applicable for the Caribbean countries. The paper ends with some concluding comments and observations regarding ethnic conflicts and ethnic poverty that is creating a chasm in Guyana, a problem that development economics need to address.

1. INTRODUCTION

Adam Smith (1776), in the *Wealth of Nations* wrote:

"No society can surely be flourishing and happy, of which by far the greater part of the numbers are poor and miserable." [Quoted in Todaro (1997) p.137]

Two centuries later, notwithstanding the phenomenal economic and scientific progress in the world, the poor still constitute the greater part of society. The eminent Columbia University economist, Professor Jagdish Bhagwati titled chapter one of his book, *The Economics of Underdeveloped Countries*, "Poverty and income distribution". The opening paragraph of Professor Bhagwati's (1966) book reads as follows:

> "The world we live in presents a picture of appalling contrasts. While few countries are immensely prosperous nearly two-thirds of the population of the world subsists on substandard incomes. Illiteracy, bad housing, lack of medical care and malnutrition are prevalent throughout most of Asia, Africa, the Middle East and Latin America. These facts can no longer be ignored. Indeed they have come to dominate intellectual thought and political action to an unprecedented degree in our time." (p.9)

Then, as now, Bhagwati's characterization of the nature of poverty in developing countries, some thirty years ago, is true, except for one fact, it is no longer two thirds of mankind, but 80 percent or more who subsist on sub-standard incomes.

The Nobel Committee awarded Professor Amartya Sen the 1988 Nobel prize in economics for his work on poverty, social choice theory and welfare distributions. Professor Sen has argued that the construction of theoretically sound indexes to measure welfare and poverty must satisfy well defined theoretical properties, and that any aggregation rule must be transitive and complete, Pareto compatible, independent, etc.[1] This article does not intend to follow this approach. This discussion is much more mundane, pedestrian, applied and social science oriented. Firstly, this paper provides an explanation for poverty and hunger, and then traces rather superficially the importance and historical evolution of poverty studies. Secondly, there is a brief discussion of how poverty is measured, and the distinction between absolute and relative poverty is drawn. A brief reference to the Human Development Index (HDI) and the Human Poverty Index (HPI) to measure the depth and dimension of poverty will then follow.[2] Thirdly, the paper surveys the empirical evidence of the depth and magnitude of human poverty world-wide, and provides several illustrative cases. Fourthly, the paper discusses poverty strategies applicable to the Caribbean region in particular, and to the third world countries in general. The paper ends with some concluding observations regarding the volatile issue of ethnic conflicts and ethnic poverty that is creating a chasm in Guyana, and threatening national disintegration. The issues of ethnic conflicts (as we witness conflicts ravaging Europe, the African continent and elsewhere) is a matter that needs to be part of the study of development economics.

2. Explanation and Historical Development

Professor Gary Becker, a University of Chicago economists and a winner of the 1992 Nobel prize in economics, commenting on the Nobel prize awarded Professor Sen remarked:

---

[1] See Amartya Sen and James Foster (1997). Much of the theoretical aspects of this paper is influenced by this important publication, and I acknowledge my debts fully.

[2] The reader should consult the Technical Notes of *Human Development Report* 1990 and 1977. Anyone familiar with *Human Development Report* will notice its imprint on this paper.

> "Economics isn't simply about finance and financial markets. Understanding poverty surely has to rank among the most important issues that economists study."[3]

A single mother from Guyana defines poverty in these terms:

> "Poverty is hunger, loneliness, nowhere to go when the day is over, deprivation, discrimination, abuse and illiteracy" [Human Development Report (HDR) 1977, p.18]

A slum dweller from Philippines notes with exasperation:

> "Poverty is the squatter mother whose hut has been torn down by government for reasons she cannot understand." [Human Development Report 1977, p.18]

The foregoing quotes and observations, in one way or the other, define the parameters and correlates of poverty. Professor A.K. Sen has provided the most persuasive explanation for famines, hunger and poverty. In his address given at the award ceremony in Turin for the second Senator Giovanni Agnelli International Prize, Professor Sen advanced the following proposition:

> "In explaining famines, we have to look not primarily at the total food supply (though it is one influence among many), but at the "entitlements" of vulnerable groups, i.e., the owner- ship rights over food that these groups can establish. We have to concentrate, therefore, on the economic and political changes that rob particular occupation groups of their ability to command food. For example, the development of extensive unemployment leading to widespread inability to earn an income, or a severe rise in food prices vis-à-vis wages, or a sharp fall in the price of products that craftsmen make, can lead to widespread starvation.
>
> In view of this diagnosis it is not surprising that the policy of supplementing people's incomes (e.g. through offering public employment, with wages being paid to the destitute people who seek work) can be one of the most effective ways of preventing famines. This is, in fact, how famines have been systematically prevented in India since independence.
>
> Whenever large occupational groups have lost their earning power (e.g. when agricultural workers have become unemployed because of a severe drought or flood), the lost purchasing abilities of the affected population have been to a considerable extent regenerated through the provision of public employment at a wage."

Even though India had enacted the Famine Codes of 1880, Professor Sen asked the following question: Why, then, did famines in India continue to occur right up to 1943, but not after independence in 1947? Sen provides the following perceptive analysis:

> "I have tried to argue elsewhere that the big difference has been made by the plural, democratic nature of post-independence India. With a relatively free press, with periodic elections and with active opposition parties, no government can escape severe penalty if it delays preventive measures and permits a real famine to occur. That threat keeps governments on their toes....

[3] Michael M. Phillips and Tristan Mabry, "Student of World's 'Miserable' Wins Nobel", *The Wall Street Journal* October 15, 1998, B1.

> The contrast is sharp, not only in pre-independence India, but also with many countries in sub-Saharan Africa in which the governments do not have to worry about threats from opposition parties and in which newspapers are far from free. The Chinese famine of 1958-61, in which between twenty three and thirty million died, was partly caused by the continuation of disastrous government policies, and that in turn was possible because of the non-democratic nature of the Chinese polity. For three years, notwithstanding intense famine conditions, official policies were not officially reversed. The government did not feel threatened; there were no opposition parties; no newspaper criticized the public policies. In fact, for the most part, the famine was not even mentioned at all in the controlled press, despite the carnage that was taking place across the country. Indeed, in the terrible history of famines in the world, it is hard to find a case in which a famine has occurred in a country with a free press and an active opposition within a democratic system."

The measurement of poverty goes back to more than a hundred years. Professor A.B. Atkinson (1987), and *Human Development Report 1990* (Technical Notes) provide a useful survey of the attempts to measure poverty, and from which this paper borrows quite liberally. The earliest studies on poverty were undertaken in the 18th century in England, since the King had to provide estimates of the number of paupers. Sir F.M. Eden, *The State of the Poor* (1797) provides materials on family budgets. Booth (1892-7) and Rowtree (1901) are the truly early scientific studies that attempted to measure poverty. Booth's 9 volumes, *Life and Labour of the People of London* provide first hand observations of his attempts to measure the extent of poverty in London. Using the street as his unit of analysis, Booth was able to capture and construct his "celebrated" poverty maps of London. Rowtree's (1901) *Poverty* was intended to document and compare the situation in the county of York, with the evidence that Booth had accumulated for London. But Rowtree's study represents a significant methodological departure from that of Booth, in that Rowtree was concerned with individual family incomes, and he developed a poverty standard based on nutritional and other requirements. It was left to the famous economic statistician A.L. Bowley (1913) to pioneer the use of survey methods and sampling techniques to the study of poverty. Bowley used a one in twenty random sample of working class households in Reading to study poverty.[4] In the case of the United States, Professor Atkinson reminds us that the first attempt at defining a poverty line was in 1904, when attempts were made to measure "the minimum comfort" based on budgets for New York City. But it was not until the 1960s that the issue and measurement of poverty dominated the policy agenda in the United States. Harrington's (1962) *The Other America* and Galbraith's (1958) *The Affluent Society* struck America's moral conscience and the need to deal with the issues of fairness, equity and poverty; just as Mrydal's (1944) *An American Dilemma* (a study that explained the disadvantaged position of Afro-Americans). Mrydal's (1968) monumental study, *Asian Drama: An Inquiry into the Poverty of Nations* is compelling reading for anyone interested in poverty issues.

[4] The estimates obtained from a properly drawn sample can be robust, and they are much more cost effective to produce compared to census taking.

A central methodological issue in poverty studies is whether poverty should be expressed and discussed in absolute or relative terms.[5] An absolute measure of poverty is generally expressed to reflect some biological or physiological needs, but this is invariably difficult, if not impracticable to measure. Absolute poverty is generally based on some level of basic needs. A relative measure of poverty depends on circumstances, such as the disparities between the rich and poor in that society or community. In essence, poverty is concerned with the absolute standard of living of that part of society, to wit, the poor, and their ability to attain some minimal standard of living.

3. Absolute Poverty

Estimates of poverty need to be specified in absolute terms if it is to be fixed across time and space. [*HDR 1990*, p.106] This absolutist measure of poverty is based on the notion of "subsistence", a concept that is fraught with measurement problems.

In the empirical literature, in order to arrive at some measure of subsistence, a minimum calorie intake is specified. Once the level of calories specified it is then converted into a consumption basket, which should be culture specific. After the consumption basket is obtained, it is then priced, at market prices, in order to establish the poverty line. In the 1960s the Indian Planning Commission used 2,250 calories as the minimum, while the Anglophone Caribbean countries, using epimedicological studies, have established a benchmark of 2,400 calories.[6] In studies done by ECLAC for Latin America, the commodity basket has been adjusted to satisfy the calorie intake (by age, sex, activity and health status). This specification is an improvement over delineating a common threshold minimum calorie intake. The consumption basket omits non-food items needed for subsistence, hence, an adjustment must be made for non-food items. The standard approach is to multiply the amount of money needed to buy the food basket by the Engel coefficient. The Engel coefficient is taken as the reciprocal of the ratio of food expenditure to total expenditure. By Engel's law, the food ratio is higher for the poor than that of the non-poor. If the reciprocal of the food ratio of the poorest is taken as the Engel law, this would tend to lower the poverty line, and thus the percentage of the poor.

Any poverty line, once established, has to be adjusted for changes in time and inflation. A crude method is to index the poverty line to the consumer price index or to the price index of food. There are three problems associated with this approach. First, there is the assumption of a common, constant calorie intake which may be unrelated to an individual's personal circumstance over time. Second, any poverty line re-calculated over time for price changes should allow for substitution between foodstuffs as relative prices and taste change over time, hence, necessitating re-computing the Engel coefficient. And, finally, the assumption of a common calorie intake leads to the well-known aggregation problem. In many poor countries, and in some cultures, (and I am

[5] The discussion between absolute and relative poverty is based on the various Technical Notes in *Human Development Report*.

[6] For the Caribbean data, see World Bank (1996b).

familiar with the East Indians in Guyana), it is not uncommon for women to ensure that the males are well-fed (most East Indian women in the rural areas would only eat after the males finished). This is to ensure that the males have the energy to work on the farms. Because of scarcities, the consumption levels and health of poor women and girls tend to be below the minimum calorie intake. In short, there are intrahousehold inequalities in consumption and health care.

4. Relative Poverty

The relativist approach to poverty defines "requirements" not merely in terms of subsistence, but what is needed to satisfy a "full" life e.g. education, long life, fully employed etc. [see *HDR 1990*, p.107]. Poverty, in this context, is viewed in terms of inequality. One method of defining poverty is to take the poverty threshold as some measure of the median income. *Human Development Report 1998* (*HDR 1998*), arbitrarily took 50 percent of the median income in the industrial countries as the poverty benchmark for the industrial countries. In arriving at the poverty line in developing countries, consumption expenditures, rather than incomes, are used for the following reasons:[7]

(1) There are problems relating to income estimation, particularly, the incomes of the informal sector and the self employed. Then there are problems with valuation of non-traded goods; and estimating transfers or income remittances from abroad. Many Caribbean economies are "barrel economies", they depend heavily on the supplies and gifts shipped by relatives abroad, particularly from the U.S.
(2) Consumption, as a measure of welfare is more robust than incomes, since respondents are more likely to provide reliable estimates of expenditures; income is always subject to under-reporting; and
(3) Consumption is a better measure of long-run welfare, since people cannot save or borrow to maintain consumption levels.

5. Statistical Measures of Poverty

There are various measures of poverty, the one frequently used is the head-count index or ratio, which is simply a fraction of the population below the poverty line.[8] One problem with the head-count index is that it fails to capture the extent to which individual incomes (expenditures) fall below the poverty line, and it is insensitive to transfers of incomes within the poverty population. Any measure of poverty must be sensitive to the depth and intensity of poverty, and it should indicate an increase of poverty if there is some transfer of income from someone who is very poor to someone who is less poor.

---

[7] These arguments are contained in Gafar (1998a) and World Bank (1994).
[8] This section is based on the exposition in Sen and Foster (1997), and Psacharopoulos et al (1997).

The head-count ratio does not capture this, if the transfer of incomes from the very poor to the less poor does not push any of the less poor over the poverty line.

Building on the work of Sen (1976); Foster, Greer and Thorbecke (1984) developed a class of indices that meet these requirements. Referred to in the literature, as the FGT class of measures, they are defined as [see Sen and Foster (1997)]:

$$P_\alpha = [\sum_{i=1}^{q} z^\alpha]/n \tag{1}$$

where

n = number of individuals in the population

q = number of individuals with an income less than the poverty line.

k = poverty line

y_i = income of individual i

$Z_i = (k-y_i)/k$ is the nomalised variable

α = degree of poverty aversion.

The FGT is the summation of the percentage gap between the income of each individual of the poverty line, raised to the power which reflects the degree of poverty aversion [see Psacharopoulos et al, 1997].

Case 1: If $\alpha = 0$, this implies no interest in the intensity of poverty, and the index reduces to the head-count index (ratio):

$$P_o = H \tag{2}$$

where H is the head-count ratio. Most studies on poverty concentrate on the head-count ratio, because of its case of computation and simplicity.

Case 2: If $\alpha = 1$, the index reduces to the poverty gap index:

$$P_I = HI \tag{3}$$

where I is the income gap ratio.

The poverty gap measure is an improvement on the head-count index, since it is sensitive to the depth of poverty, and it is not only dependent on the number of persons below the poverty line, but also on how far they are on average below the poverty line. However, the poverty gap measure is still insensitive to transfers within poverty population, (provided that the transfers do not take any individuals out of the poverty population), since such transfers within the poverty population would leave the average income of the poor unchanged [see Sen and Foster 1997, and Pscharopoulos et al, 1997].

Case 3: If $\alpha = 2$ or higher, then $P\alpha$ will be distributionally sensitive. If $\alpha = 2$ we have

$$P_2 = H[\mathbf{I}^2 + (1-\mathbf{I})^2 C_p^2] \tag{4}$$

where C_P of variation among the poor. Sen and Foster (1997, p.179 footnote 101) point out that the relationship of P_2 with the coefficient of variation ensures that P_2 satisfies the transfer property axiom. Sen and Foster also point out that the FGT measures satisfy the properties of symmetry, replication invariance, scale invariance, the focus axiom, and also continuity. Sen and Foster (1997, pp.179-180) noted that all indices with α greater than one satisfy the weak and strong forms of the transfer axiom. The $P\alpha$ indexes are also decomposable, since a population comprising of n individuals can be divided into m mutually exclusive sub-groups (for example by ethnicity, sex, geographical region etc.). In view of this property, the over-all FGT poverty measure is a weighted average of the various sub-groups.[9]

6. Human Development Index (HDI) and Human Poverty Index (HPI)

The head count index is income based. Poverty is manifested in hunger, illiteracy, lack of good health, deprivation, exclusion, lack of gainful employment etc. Human development is concerned with enlarging choices needed for a long, healthy and productive life, to enjoy a decent standard of living, freedom and self respect [see *Human Development Report 1977 (HDR 1977)* p.15]. Because of the limitations of income to capture the pervasiveness of poverty, UNDP developed the Human Development Index (HDI). The HDI focuses on three essential elements of well-being, to wit, longevity, knowledge and a decent standard of living. For longevity, life expectancy at birth is crude approximation, since life expectancy reflects improvements in health, sanitation and nutrition. In the case of knowledge, literacy rates represent access to education; while per capita income is the most readily available indicator to proxy a decent standard of living. But the presence of non-traded goods and exchange rate distortions make per capita income at nominal prices not particularly useful, hence, UNDP used PPP$US to correct for these distortions. The HDI is the simple average of the life expectancy index, educational attainment index, and the adjusted real per capita income (at PPP$US) index.

In 1997 UNDP developed the Human Poverty Index (HPI) for 78 developing countries [see *HDR 1997*]. The HPI concentrates on three essential dimensions in human life, already captured in HDI. The HPI is based on three essentials of deprivation. First, there is the deprivation in longevity and this is measured by the percentage of people not expected to live to 40. Second, there is the deprivation in knowledge and this is measured by the percentage of people who are illiterate. And, third, there is the deprivation of a decent standard of living, and this is a simple average of three variables i.e. the percentage of people without access to water, the percentage of people without access to health services, and the percentage of moderately and severely underweight children. The HPI is an average of the deprivation in longevity, the deprivation in knowledge, and the deprivation of a decent standard of living.

[9] Head count ratios for Caribbean countries are contained in World Bank (1996b) and Gafar (1999c). Detailed head count ratios for Guyana are in Gafar (1998a) and World Bank (1994).

7. EMPIRICAL ESTIMATES OF POVERTY

In order to obtain poverty estimates that allowed for cross country comparison, the World Bank, *World Development Report 1990 (WDR 1990)*, arbitrarily chose a US$1 per person a day as the poverty line. Purchasing power parity (PPP) indices at 1985 prices were used to convert the US$1 per person per day standard into local currency. Estimates of the population living below US$1 a day in developing countries and transitional economies for 1987, 1990 and 1993 are summarized in Table 1. The head count index is the population below the poverty line of US$1 a day per person. The poverty gap index is the average distance below the poverty line (zero to the non poor) expressed as a percentage of the poverty line. The data in Table 1 may differ from other estimates of poverty since in Latin America, for example, a US$2 per day per person is often used (World Bank 1996a). In Europe and Central Asia, other studies use a poverty line of US$4 a day to capture the effects of higher levels of incomes. And, China's official poverty line is approximately US$0.60 per person a day. The data in Table 1 and other available statistics reveal the following:

(a) About 1.3 billion people live on incomes less than US$1 a day. More than a quarter of the world's population live in poverty

(b) South Asia has the most people affected by poverty: 515 million. Together, South Asia, East Asia and Pacific have more than 960 million of the 1.3 billion people who are poor. More than 44 million Russians, or 30 percent of the population, live below the poverty line at a per capita income US$32 a month. Poverty in Russia rose from 31 million in 1997 to 44.3 million in September 1998, because of the 9.9 percent contraction of GDP between 1997-1998.[10] The evidence shows that poverty in Russia (similar to the experiences in the third world) is more likely to affect women and those who do not finish high school; and that younger workers between the ages of 18 and 54 are likely to be poor because they have no supplemental income (to wit, pensions, disability benefits and other benefits that are available to employed workers). The statistics also indicate that about two million children in Russia lack families; about one third of these children live in orphanages, and the rest live in the street. After leaving orphanages, one in three of these children become alcoholic, and 10 percent commit suicide after one year on their own; and about 10 million Russian school-age children never attend school (*New York Times*, November 19, 1998). The situation in Russia grimly reflects the conditions of many third world countries ravaged by prolonged economic crises.

(c) The economic meltdown in Asia has resulted in more than 17 million Indonesians falling below the poverty line of US$1 a day per person and 60 million more below US$2 a day. The economic crisis in Indonesia is also one of about affordable food. Mark Landler, "Living for Rice, Begging for Rice", *The New York Times*, September 7, 1998, p.A6 describes the human situation in Indonesia in these terms:

[10] *The New York Times*, Tuesday, October 20, 1998 p.A8.

"It has become a ritual whenever a delivery truck arrives at the Cipinang rice market here. Young men clamor onto the truck to unload the sacks of rice, while women and children huddle next to the loading dock with crude brooms and dustpans.
As the sacks are hauled into a dimly lighted warehouse, the women swiftly sweep up any grains that spill out. They methodically sift out gravel, sand and cigarette butts, pour the brown rice into plastic bags, then scurry to wait for the next delivery..............Food riots have already erupted in eastern Java........Rice currently sells at the market for 17 cents a pound, more than double the Government's target price. For a family of five to buy 22 pounds of rice per capita each month, it would cost $18.70. About 40 percent of Indonesia's families earn less than that, meaning that nearly half the population cannot afford even a minimum supply of rice."

TABLE 1: Population Living Below US$1 a Day in Developing and Transitional Economies, 1987-1993.

Region	Number of Poor (millions)			Headcount Index (P0) (Percent)			Poverty Gap (P1) (Percent)		
	1987	1990	1993	1987	1990	1993	1987	1990	1993
East Asia and the Pacific	464.0	468.2	445.8	28.2	28.5	26.0	8.3	8.0	7.8
(excluding China)	(109.2)	(89.3)	(73.5)	(23.2)	(17.6)	(13.7)	(3.8)	(3.1)	(3.1)
Eastern Europe and Central Asia	2.2	n.a.	14.5	0.6	n.a.	3.5	0.2	n.a.	1.1
Latin America and the Caribbean	91.2	101.0	109.5	22.0	23.0	23.5	8.2	9.0	9.1
Middle East and North Africa	10.3	10.4	10.7	4.7	4.3	4.1	0.9	0.7	0.6
South Asia	478.9	480.4	514.7	45.4	43.0	43.1	14.1	12.3	12.6
Sub-Saharan Africa	179.6	201.2	218.6	38.5	39.3	39.1	14.4	14.5	15.3
Total	1227.1	n.a	1313.9	30.1	n.a	29.4	9.5	n.a.	9.2
Total (excluding Europe and Central Asia)	1224.9	1261.2	1299.3	33.3	32.9	31.8	10.8	10.3	10.5

Source: World Bank, *Poverty Reduction and the World Bank: Progress and Challenges in the 1990s*; (World Bank, Washington, D.C., 1996a; Table 1.2, p.4); n.a. = not available.

The financial crisis in Indonesia has resulted in widespread unemployment, a loss of purchasing power by the poor, and increased poverty. The President of The World Bank, Mr. James D. Wolfensohn, in his October 6, 1998 address to the Board of Governors entitled "The Other Crisis", said it best and succinctly, of the human costs of the Asian economic crisis:

"The mother in Mindanao, pulling her child out of school, haunted by the fear that he will never return. The family in Korea, with a mid-size scrap metal business, made destitute through lack of credit. The father in Jakarta, paying a money lender three times in interest what he can make that day, falling deeper and deeper into debt. Not knowing how he will ever work himself free. The child in Bangkok, now condemned to work the streets, a child no longer....
Today, while we talk of financial crisis..........a million children will now not return to school..........Today, while we talk of financial crisis - across the world, 1.3 billion people live on less than $1 a day; 3 billion live on under $2 a day; 1.3 billion have no access to clean water; 3 billion have no access to sanitation; 2 billion have no access to

power..............The poor cannot wait until we wake up - too late - to the fact that the human crisis affects us all........The child on the streets of Bangkok needs to go back to school. The mother in the slums of Calcutta needs to survive through childbirth. The father in the village in Mali needs to be able to see beyond today."

The foregoing statements by the President of the World Bank, clearly depict the desperation, hopelessness, and the plight of the poor that economic recessions and natural disasters inflect on the poor. Recently, hurricane Mitch left more than 9,000 dead in Honduras and Nicaragua, 1.5 million homeless, and more than 70 percent of the agricultural production destroyed. The poor are mostly engaged in agricultural activities. But it was the working class, particularly the rural poor and the urban poor living in the shanty towns who bore the brunt of the disaster because of inadequate, if not non-existent infrastructures. Many of the poor who had no information of the gravity of the natural disaster remained in their houses, instead of going out to investigate conditions, and a number of them who lived on the hill-sides got buried alive with the avalanche of mud, as they tried to outrun the flow of mud. This demonstrates that without reliable information, markets do not work well, disasters happen, and the poor suffer, since the non-poor who can afford it will seek the information and avoid the risks. *World Development Report 1998* (p.72) makes it very clear that information is the "lifeblood of every economy", it helps to reduce uncertainty, establish and enforce standards, to the benefit of all. And since information is costly to develop, but cheap to share, the state should ensure there is a constant flow of reliable information to enable the poor to make better decisions that will improve their lot.

(d) Sub-Saharan Africa and South Asia have the highest poverty (head count) rates. (Table 1)

(e) children are especially vulnerable - they suffer from malnutrition and illnesses. Some 160 million children in the third world are moderately or severely malnourished. (See *HDR 1997*).

(f) Poverty offers a breeding ground for the spread of HIV/AIDS. In Latin America and the Caribbean, the HIV/AIDS cases are concentrated in the urban slums; over 94 percent of the world's known HIV/AIDS cases are in the developing countries, with Sub-Saharan Africa having the greatest concentration. In Bostswana, the hardest hit country in Sub-Saharan Africa, life expectancy which was 61 years only five years ago has dropped to 47 and is expected to drop to 41 between 2000 and 2005. And in Guyana, life expectancy in 1998 was 64 years and this was expected to rise to 68 years (without AIDS) in 2010, but given the HIV/AIDS pandemic life expectancy is now estimated to fall to 50 years in 2010. It is estimated that in 1998 the HIV/AIDS pandemic has increased child mortality rate by 100% in Guyana and Kenya and by 150% in Zimbabwe (*HDR 1998*, p.15); and also child orphans. Poverty will rise since the HIV/AIDS infected workers would be unable to be engaged in productive activities, and also because third world health budgets cannot afford the US$15,000 a year protease inhibitor "cocktails" to prolong the life of an infected AIDS patient. Estimates by the World Bank suggest that the cost of one AIDS dosage is sufficient to keep 400 children in school (*New York Times*, November 15, 1998). The damage that the AIDS epidemic will do to the poor is easy to illustrate. For example, the typical breadwinner in Africa has around 10 dependents, and there are (apart from South Africa) no welfare systems. The death of a child (much less that of the breadwinner) is a financial burden because funeral expenses mean that the family may have to sell land or cattle (capital) or take the healthy child out of school (*New York Times*, November 15, 1998). The AIDS epidemic in Africa (similiar to the 14 century Black Death) affects the profitability of companies in several ways: absenteeism for funerals, medical and death expenses, and the costs of recruiting and training new workers. A massive safe sex public education campaign, and a concerted program of distribution of free condoms are essential prerequisites to deal with the AIDS crisis. For the poor in the third world (or for that matter anywhere), if the choice is one between the purchase of food to feed the family or the purchase of condoms for safe sex, usually the choice will be made against the purchase and use of condoms, nothwithstanding the risks.

(g) Nearly 1/3 of the people in third world countries are not expected to survive to age 40, mostly in Sub-Saharan Africa due to the HIV/AIDS pandemic, and this will place more children in poverty because of the early death of their parents. (*HDR 1997*).

(h) Nearly 1 billion people are illiterate. Most studies have shown a negative correlation between poverty and the level of education. (*HDR 1996*, p.20).

(i) Women are disproportionately poor. They are burdened by the strains of work, child care, caring for the family, and they tend to suffer from malnutrition, which explains why they die from childbirth. In China, women who are 35 years and over are more likely to be laid off. In her *New York Times* article captioned: "In China, Over 35+ Female = Unemployable", Elisabeth Rosenthal writes:

> "As China struggles to convert to a market economy, closing and shrinking state-owned industries, women over 35 bore the brunt of the pain; they are far more likely to be laid off and far less likely to find a new job than any other group........
> But they suffer, too, from outright discrimination and deeply held cultural biases about the limited abilities of women, particularly women over 35. Such biases have free play in a country where want ads often specify sex - not to mention height, age and body characteristics..............Companies are even more reluctant to hire women over 35 since, in China, they tend to bear full responsibility for both child care and elder care...." [*New York Times*, October 13, 1998]

As Burns (1998) noted the status of women in India is even more troubling, relegating women who are widowed to certain poverty. The reason for this is the custom of Hindi brides' marrying into their husbands' families and cutting ties with their own family. Indian parents, who view their daughters as a liability or financial burden, arrange childhood marriages. Once a woman is widowed she is unwanted again, and is forced in many cases to become unpaid servants for her in-laws, or left to work the streets. And even though laws have been enacted in India to protect widows' rights to inheritance, these laws are not enforced. Many of their (widows) husbands' families, wanting to keep property intact, often force the widows' to remarry back into the family. There are nearly 33 million unwelcomed widows who are driven to poverty. There is need to reduce the gender inequality that women world-wide experience in order to reduce human misery.

(j) Unemployment rates are highest among the poor; for the age group 15-24 years at least 75% in Haiti are unemployed. The poorest 40% of households get less than 15% of total incomes. Inequality is pervasive in poor countries, particularly in Latin America (see Gafar 1998a). In Latin America the top 5% income earners get more than 1/3 of total incomes, and control nearly 70% of total wealth.

(k) Of the more than 4.4 billion people in developing countries (i.e. approximately 80% of the world's population) nearly 3/5 lack basic sanitation; 1/3 have no access to clean water; 1/4 do not have adequate housing; 1/5 have no access to modern health services; and 1/5 do not have enough dietary energy and protein. (*HDR 1998*, p.2).

(l) Poverty is highly correlated with landlessness in South Asia, Southern Africa and Latin America (*World Development 1990*). Many of the poor have some access to fragmented and small plots of land, but without ownership rights which are important requisites for risk taking in a market economy. In Brazil, the top 2% landowners control 60% of the arable land, while the bottom 70% of rural households are landless or just about landless. (*HDR 1998*, p.22).

(m) Households with the lowest incomes tend to be large. The decision by the poor to have many children is not irrational, since mortality rates for children of the poor are high, and, then there is the need to have some surviving children to take care of the old parents (since social assistance for the elderly in developing countries is minimal at best, if not non-existent).

(n) Poverty is predominantly rural, and most of the poor are engaged in agriculture on small plots of land. (*WDR 1990*). In recent years urban poverty and the growth of shanty towns and favellas are on the rise. In Brazil in 1985, 75 percent of the poor worked in the informal sector (*WDR 1990*). Many of the urban poor may be full-time beggars, garbage sifters, prostitutes (a source for the AIDS infection) or pickpockets. In China urban poverty is on the rise due in part to the prevailing financial crisis, and the liberalization process. In a *New York Times* article captioned "Poverty Spreads, and Deepens, in China's Cities", Elisabcth Rosenthal writes:

> "The number of city dwellers living in poverty is now growing rapidly in China. A decade ago this group was virtually non-existent. Today, Chinese researchers estimate, anywhere from 12 million to more than 22 million urban residents - out of an urban population of 200 million - live in "absolute poverty", meaning that they cannot afford basic food, clothing or shelter. These urban poor are distinct from the large number of poor migrants from the country-side, who come to cities in search of work but are not counted as residents..........Under the old planned economy, nearly all Chinese who lived in cities were assigned to governmental "work units" which guaranteed them a place to live as well as subsidizing food staples, medical care, pensions and often schooling for their children. Under this system, living standards of urban residents rose steadily, en masse, throughout the 1980s......
> The circumstances that lead to poverty are diverse: a family's bread-winner loses a job; an elderly parent gets sick, requiring extensive unreimbursed medical treatment; a state factory stops paying retirement benefits, or once-free or low-cost housing ends up in the private market and becomes unaffordable". (*The New York Times*, October 4, 1998)

The situation in China reflects the objective reality for the third world, as the streets of Calcutta, Bombay, Manila, Mexico City, Caracas and Lagos will attest. Urban economies in third world countries cannot absorb all the rural poor as urban infrastructures are inadequate. Cairo (Egypt) built for around 2 million now has over 10 million; and this is true world-wide. In Latin America and the Caribbean 22% of the people in Panama City were poor in 1983, 64% of the people in Guatemala City in 1983, 45% of the people of Santiago, Chile, in 1985 [See *HDR 1998*, p.86]; and 46% in Jamaica (Gafar, 1998c).

Concomitant with the rise in urban poverty is the widespread growth of urban violence in the ghettos, as anyone familiar with Kingston, Jamaica would know. Crime, prostitution, violence and illegal drugs are all part of the urban sub-culture that the poor have to confront daily.

(o) Nearly 60 to 70 percent of the expenditures of the poor go for food, compared to around 10 percent in the advanced countries. [*WDR 1990*].

(p) Poverty is correlated with race and ethnicity. Indigenous peoples in Guyana (Gafar 1998a); Bolivia, Ecuador, Australia, Guatemala, Mexico and Peru are disproportionately poor (*WDR 1990*). In the United States, the over-all poverty rate in 1996 was 13.3 percent, for African-Americans 28.4 percent, and for Hispanic Americans 27.1 percent.[11]

(q) *Human Development Report 1998* states that globally, the 20 percent of the world people who are in the industrial countries account for nearly 86 percent of the world's incomes. This glaring inequality in the distribution of the world's incomes is also manifested in other forms. For example, the richest fifth (industrial world) consume 45 percent of all meat and fish (the poor fifth 5 percent), and 58 percent of total energy (the poorest fifth less than 5 percent). To demonstrate the inequality of incomes, a fundamental question in any discussion of poverty issues, is the status of the ultra-rich. According to *Human Development Report 1998*, the world's 225 richest people have a combined wealth of over US$1 trillion, equal to the annual income of 47 percent of the world's people (i.e. 2.5 billion people). The three richest people have assets that exceed the combined GDP of the 48 least developed countries. The wealth of the 32 richest people exceeds the total GDP of South Asia. The assets of the 84 richest exceed the GDP of China, the most populous country, with 1.2 billion people. It is against this background, that notwithstanding the increases in third world countries' incomes and food supplies due to the Green Revolution, the gains in life expectancy, and the near eradication of yellow fever, there is need to improve the welfare of the poor; and that solutions to the financial crisis ravaging the third world economies should not be aimed exclusively at improving the health of international banks (indeed there are moral hazard questions involved), while ignoring the human pain of the poor, the down-trodden, the

[11] A family of four in the U.S. was classified as poor if it had cash income of less than $16,400 in 1997. The threshold for a family of three was $12,802. Income, as officially defined, does not include capital gains, health insurance or Government benefits like foodstamps, Medicaid etc. [See Robert Pear, "Black and Hispanic Poverty Falls, Reducing Overall Rate for Nations", *The New York Times*, September 25, 1998 p.A25].

faceless and the voiceless, the hungry, the orphaned child, the old and the destitute, the miserable and the politically unrepresented.

8. ESTIMATES OF THE HUMAN POVERTY INDEX

Estimates of the Human Poverty Index (HPI) were computed by UNDP for 78 developing countries that have adequate data [*HDR 1997*, p.20]. The HPI, as noted before, deals with deprivation in three essential elements, namely, longevity, knowledge and a decent standard of living. The HPI ranking for some countries are summarized in Table 2. The HDI shows how far a country has to go to attain an average of 85 years, provide education for all, and achieve a decent standard of living. The maximum possible HDI value is one, and the difference between one and the reported HDI value, shows a country's short-fall in HDI. In 1994 the average HDI value for high human development countries was 0.907; 0.667 for medium human development countries, and 0.403 for low human development countries.

Table 2: HDI and HPI for some Developing Countries

Countries	Human Development Index (HDI)	Human Poverty Index (HPI) 1994	HPI Rank (%)	HPI Rank Rank Minus HDI Rank	HPI Rank Minus $1-a-day Poverty Rank
Trinidad & Tobago	0.880	4.1	1	-4	n.a
Cuba	0.723	5.1	2	-18	n.a
Costa Rica	0.889	6.6	5	2	-15
Mexico	0.853	10.9	7	-1	-9
Jamaica	0.736	12.1	12	-6	1
China	0.626	17.5	18	-11	-12
Dominican Rep.	0.718	18.3	20	-1	-5
Kenya	0.463	26.1	32	-14	-13
Algeria	0.737	28.6	37	20	21
Egypt	0.614	34.8	44	14	15
India	0.446	36.8	47	-2	n.a.
Nigeria	0.393	41.6	54	3	9
Haiti	0.338	46.2	61	-3	n.a.
Pakistan	0.445	46.8	64	14	11
Sierra Leone	0.176	59.2	77	-1	n.a.
Niger	0.193	66.0	78	2	3

Note: n.a. = not available. The maximum value for HDI is one. HDI and $1-a-day poverty ranks were calculated for the 78 developing countries that the HPI was calculated for. A negative number indicates that the HPI rank is better than the other, a positive the opposite.

Source: UNDP, *Human Development Report 1997*, p.21.

The data in Table 2 show that Trinidad and Tobago, and Cuba have an HPI value of less than 10 percent. This means that these countries have reduced human poverty where it affects less than 10 percent of the population; while Haiti has an HPI of 46.4 percent.

What is the difference between HDI and HPI? According to *Human Development Report 1998* (p.25) the HDI measures progress in a country as a whole; while HPI measures the extent of deprivation; i.e. the proportion of the society who are left out of progress. *Human Development Report 1998* (p.26) noted that while Egypt and Pakistan have reduced their income poverty to less than 15 percent, the human poverty in these countries are much higher, to wit 34.8% and 46.8% respectively. The HPI also shows progress that may not be revealed in the head count ratio of poverty, since head count ratio is based only on income.

9. Strategies for Poverty Alleviation in the Caribbean

In conclusion, I now outline some strategies to deal with poverty based on my experience with some of the Caribbean countries. A popular view in the 1960s and 1970s in the Caribbean and elsewhere, (particularly among the dependency school and the black power movement) was the clamour for structural changes, implying that state-run development was needed to alleviate poverty. Fidel Castro's authoritarian Marxist model was championed by the political left (Michael Manley in Jamaica; Cheddi Jagan and Forbes Burnham in Guyana; Maurice Bishop in Grenada; and academics at the regional universities) as the way forward, notwithstanding the obvious inefficiencies, economic decline and repression, and the massive Cuban exodus that were/are associated with Castro's rule. In Guyana, the Forbes Burnham semi-dictatorship racist and fraudulent government proclaimed the attainment of the socialist revolution when it nationalized the key sectors of the economy; decreed a socialist constitution proclaiming that "[t]here shall be no exploitation of man by man", that land shall go to the tillers, and instituted "socialist" (bureaucratic) planning and controls. In pursuit of its "socialist" objectives, the Burnham government made the judiciary, civil service and other organs of the state subservient to its political will; there were human rights violations; censorship, and the leading newspaper was state controlled; elections were rigged and the government silenced some of its critics by force; the socialist constitution mandated which labor (party) union would represent public employees; and a labor law was passed in the 1980s regulating wages to the 1978 levels (which was later held to be unconstitutional). The state control of the economy and the non-democratic nature of the body polity meant economic collapse, financial bankruptcy, inflation, fiscal and trade deficits, burdening foreign debt, exodus of skilled people, and an increase in the head count index of poverty from 26% in 1980 to 43% in 1990. [Gafar 1998a]. One of the sad and damaging consequences of dirigisme and the exclusionary policies of the Burnham regime is that nearly a whole generation of Guyanese children were pulled out of school and are semi-illiterate. In particular, Indo-Guyanese parents pulled out their sons from school to be engaged in petty trades to supplement the families' incomes, simply because educated

Indo-Guyanese were predominantly discriminated against by the Burnham regime in securing public sector employment. [While white apartheid was under attack (even from Burnham) and crumbling in South Africa, the Guyanese people had to be subjected to Burnham's callous racist rule. Indeed, many Caribbean governments remained silent, not wanting to criticize a "brother". The recent legal ruling by Britain's highest court, that Augosto Pinochet, the former Chilean strongman, is not entitled to immunity for alleged human rights abuses is welcome news and should be vigorously implemented world-wide. The poor stands to benefit for prosecuting many of the world's tyrants]. With a collapsing economy, the minority government had no way else to turn, and at the urging of the IMF and World Bank, Guyana in 1988 implemented liberalization policies and free elections in 1992. These changes have resulted in openness, more freedom and economic growth. (Gafar 1996).

Michael Manley in Jamaica pursued a policy of democratic socialism (economic populism), controls and some state ownership. These policies were perceived by many Jamaicans, (most vocally by the middle class), to threaten the democratic process and the Jamaican way of life. Economic decline resulted, investment contracted, unemployment soared, capital flight ensued and skilled people emigrated (Gafar 1988). There is substantial anecdotal evidence to suggest that human misery and poverty increased under the period of democratic socialism. The Manley government was thrown out of office in 1980, and its socialist experiment abandoned in favor of market policies, liberalization, and deregulation. Since then, there has been some economic growth; increased employment but in the low productivity informal sectors; and a reduction in poverty rates (Gafar 1998c). The tendency of Caribbean governments, in response to economic crisis, is to resort to controlling activities, licensing, price controls, tariffs and quotas and over-valued exchange rates. These policies are urban biased and pro-industry; they encourage inefficiencies, rent seeking, corruption; and they stifle growth and employment and worsen poverty. Price controls on domestically produced foodstuffs is a tax on the rural farmer and a subsidy to the urban population; price controls on foodstuffs reduce agricultural production, exacerbate rural poverty and encourage the rural-urban migration. There is considerable scholarly evidence to demonstrate that the African food famines are the result of price distortions, suppression of incentives, and high rates of taxation. According to the World Bank (1998, p.48)

> "The combination of high explicit taxes and overvalued currencies contributed to alarming declines in Sub-Saharan Africa's agricultural growth rates: from an annual of 2.2 percent in 1965-73 to 1.0 percent in 1974-80 and 0.6 percent in 1981-85."

The data summarized by Gafar (1998b) indicate that the maximum implicit tax, as a result of distortions in the exchange rate in Guyana averaged around 66 percent between 1981-90, and this accounted for the reduction of agricultural output and exports. As Professor Bhagwati (1993, p.50) has correctly pointed out for India, the rush to bureaucratic control arises from two factors: "firstly, the inability of policy markets to trust markets, and its resulting distribution, when scarcities are acute; and secondly, the failure of policy makers to understand that markets will do a better job in resource allocation than central planning." Professor Pranab Bardhan (1990) has noted that markets impose discipline and encourage learning, cost and quality consciousness. The failed interventionist economic policies and poor economic management by the Burnham and Manley regimes have seriously hurt the poor, and have made it difficult to popularise and have any faith in left of center administrations and their programs. In contrast to Guyana and Jamaica, Barbados with less resources, but with a reverence for democratic rule, market oriented policies, openness, an independent judiciary and civil service, fiscal discipline, free and fair elections, freedom of the press, and a less threatening economic policy has the highest per capita GDP in the Caribbean, life expectancy of 76 years, an adult literacy rate of 97.4%, and an HDI value of 0.909 in 1995. [For the United States life expectancy at birth is 76.4 years, the adult literacy rate is 99% and an HDI of 0.943. See *HDR 1998*]. These three Caribbean experiences confirm Professor Sen's (1990) analysis and underline the importance of good governance, sound, credible and consistent macro-economic policies; the rule of law, inclusion and a policy of political moderation; the importance of free and fair elections, a free press and free markets in achieving economic growth and enabling improvements in human welfare. The poverty reducing strategy outlined in *World Development Report 1990* is still relevant today. This strategy consists of three basic elements: broad based economic growth; developing human capital of the poor; and the provision of social safety nets for the vulnerable groups (World Bank, 1996a). The evidence in the literature (Morley 1994, Bruno et al 1996) suggests that the elasticity of poverty (head count ratio) with respect to growth in mean incomes is around minus two, which clearly supports the proposition that growth is poverty reducing. But economic growth when it expands employment, productivity and the wages of the poor is a sure way to promote human development and poverty reduction, since the principal asset that the poor possesses is their labor. Gender equality is essential for empowering women, and for eradicating poverty. Women need equal rights and access to land, credit and job opportunities. The evidence shows that poverty and unemployment are directly related (Gafar 1998a, 1998c), and there is a positive correlation between unemployment and violence (Gafar 1988). The rates of urban violence, particularly in Kingston, Jamaica affects the poor in terms of health costs, loss of property, life and employment opportunities. Unemployment rates among Caribbean youths are extremely high, and this partly explains the increasing youth gang warfare, violence and youth poverty. Anecdotal evidence suggests an increase in child poverty, malnutrition and unwanted children in the Caribbean, due in part to recessions and the disintegration of the family. Macro-economic policies in the Caribbean should not only be market oriented, but they need to be credible, consistent and transparent; property rights need to be secured to enable risk taking (no more nationalizations); and the state should not indulge in activities that the private sector can do more efficiently. Macro-economic policies should also aim at keeping inflation low, and budget deficits manageable, since protracted budget deficits, financed by monetary accommodation are just inflationary, invariably leading to dollarization of the economy and capital flight. In essence, inflation is anti-growth. But reductions in fiscal deficits in the Caribbean come with the reality of slashing public employment, and this creates more poverty, and in the case of Guyana ethnic tensions and a national chasm. Indeed, the gospel of fiscal austerity is under attack and losing force in the left-of-center governments in Europe, precisely because of the added unemployment effect. Over-valued exchange rates in the Caribbean favor the import substituting industries and city dwellers at the expense of labor-intensive (agricultural) goods, and it is a tax on labor; hence, exchange rates need to be competitive. Openness and trade liberalization would force competition, innovation and the need for quality improvements, and would allow for resources to be allocated more efficiently, favoring the use of the abundant resource (i.e. labor). But there is a problem here. If the export sector is the user of a specific factor (land for cultivation or minerals i.e. bauxite), the increase in income arising from liberalization will accrue as rents, and the welfare gains will depend on who own the specific factor. Since the sugar estates in the Caribbean are more or less owned by the wealthy (the poor have small land holdings), then the wealthy stand to benefit substantially (a tax-subsidy program can be implemented). For many Caribbean countries exporting primary goods, the depressed state of world commodity prices is not encouraging news. Any strategy of poverty reduction must provide Caribbean countries more open and equitable access to markets in the industrial countries; renumerative prices for primary products (extension of Lome IV is important for the sugar and banana economies), and debt relief. External debt burden is a major development constraint for Guyana, Jamaica and many African countries. Debt payments contribute to increased poverty, since scarce foreign exchange is diverted from improving health, education and the physical infrastructure. There is need to increase the flow of aid to poor countries, since the United Nations (1998) has pointed out that official development assistance (ODA) has fallen to 0.25 percent of gross domestic product, the lowest level it has been since foreign aid was "institutionalized" with the Marshall Plan. An integrated rural development program in the Caribbean is essential to ameliorate poverty (since most of the poor are in rural areas); rural infrastructure needs improvement; land reforms are essential; and agricultural prices need liberalization, since farmers are responsive to price [John Gafar (1997) summarizes the econometric evidence of the supply of agriculture for the Caribbean].

James Wolfensohn (1998) has argued that any development framework must include good governance, transparency; voice; a well trained, properly paid civil service, and a commitment to fight corruption; a legal and a tax system that secure property rights, enforceability of contracts, compliance and efficiency; and a financial system that is transparent, modern, adequately and independently supervised and subject to recognized accounting and auditing procedures. This framework is essential for growth, and poverty reduction in the Caribbean region.

While economic growth remains the key to poverty reduction, savage capitalism needs to be supplemented with safety nets for the benefit of the poor and the miserable. Throughout the Caribbean the poor lack adequate access to employment, good education, health care and proper sanitation. And, if the poor manage to see a doctor at the ill-equipped public health clinics, they cannot afford to pay for medicines (which are imported). The literature shows that increasing the human capital of the poor (good education and better health) is important for growth. Early childhood development (for example, nutrition programs) can have lasting effects. The governments of the Caribbean countries need to provide quality primary education, since the private rates of return on education at the primary level are much higher; and basic health care that the poor benefit from. Education is important for giving "voice" to the poor, because as people learn, they become aware of their circumstance (*World Development Report 1998*, p.118). While state control of the economy in the Caribbean region and elsewhere have not eradicated poverty, the gospel of reliance on unfettered markets alone is not the solution either, because of imperfect information, incomplete markets, externalities and lack of public goods. Without reliable information, markets (for example, the labor market) do not work efficiently, and the state should be engaged in producing and sharing information. Caribbean governments need to provide more social safety nets for the sick, the old, the disabled and those in the poorest regions assume crucial importance. Short-term public works (building roads, canals, school repair) jobs to provide employment opportunities are recommended to deal with the high levels of unemployment. In formulating and designing safety nets and poverty programs to benefit the poor, Margaret Grosh (1995) underscored the fact that these programs must be evaluated in terms of administrative feasibility, political feasibility, collateral effects, targeting, and tailoring the solution to the problem. Any poverty program must satisfy some minimum level of administrative efficiency to make it workable. For example, consider food price subsidy programs, foodstuffs distribution programs, foodstamps or school feeding programs. In the case of food price subsidies, this can be achieved easily, the price of foodstuffs can be regulated leaving the implicit tax to be borne by the producers of foodstuffs, but this would result in loss production and a flight from agriculture. Food stamp programs require the selection of the beneficiaries, the distribution and the collection of the foodstamps. The choice of the beneficiaries can be costly, time consuming or open to nepotism and corruption; and some recipients can simply sell the foodstamps, thereby negating the objective of nutritional improvements. [In the U.S. the food stamp program is abused, some beneficiaries sell the foodstamps to purchase drugs]. School feeding programs are well targeted and easy to implement. Food commodity distribution programs at health clinics aimed at meeting the needs of pregnant and lactating women, and those of young children are administratively manageable, since it is easy to identify the beneficiaries. A living standards survey of households in Jamaica provide useful information about two programs designed to benefit the poor, viz. subsidies for basic foods, and food stamps for low income households. Health clinics were used to identify food stamp recipients. The survey revealed that the middle and upper income families were the main beneficiaries of food subsidies (as the poor did not have the ability to purchase the food). The survey found that food stamps targeted to the poor were more effective to reach the poor, and, more-over, since clinics were used, health problems were treated (see *World Development Report 1998*, p.119). But here is the policy dilemma: while the provision of large basic needs and properly targeted safety net programs are poverty ameliorating, all Caribbean governments do not have adequate resources to fund these programs for a sufficiently long period to reduce poverty significantly..

10. CONCLUSION: ETHNIC CONFLICTS AND GUYANA

In conclusion, I want to discuss an issue that policy makers need some articulation and guidance. It concerns the problem of ethnic conflicts and ethnic poverty. This issue is the most explosive one that Guyana faces, and how she chooses to confront it can either lead to national cohesion or disintegration. In a nutshell, Guyana's population is made up of 51 percent of East Indian descent (who support the Jagan PPP party), and 42 percent of African descent (who support the Burnham PNC party). Voting in Guyana is racially entrenched, and the PPP (given that the population growth of East Indians exceeds that of Afro-Guyanese) will always win any free and fair elections, but the PPP will not be able to govern, as the ethnic violence after the December 15, 1997 free and fair elections suggests. The reason is that the state apparatuses (army, civil service etc.) are all predominantly staffed by Afro-Guyanese during the Burnham racist rule. The army is more than 80 percent Afro-Guyanese dominated, and for every one Indo-Guyanese in the public sector (civil service, nurses, school teachers etc.) there are 2.8 Afro-Guyanese. Poverty rates for Afro-Guyanese are higher than that of Indo-Guyanese (Gafar, 1998a). There are discussions in Guyana to implement some form of ethnic balancing in the army, police and public sector, and some affirmative action program to address the problem of ethnic poverty in Guyana.

The experiences from Malaysia and India are worth noting. In Malaysia, as in Indonesia, the ethnic Chinese minority controls most of the private wealth, while the poor masses are concentrated among the majority Muslims. To ease ethnic tensions, Malaysia ten years ago ordered than any Chinese entrepreneur must give a 30 percent stake in the company to "native" Malay, known as "bumiputera", as the price for obtaining government contracts. This policy has led to deals and bribes, and as Bardhan (1996) points out, these deals are referred to as Ali-Baba combinations, Ali being the Muslim "bumiputera" front man in the business contract, and Baba the Chinese businessman. Ethnic Chinese in Malaysia and Indonesia have been targeted and made the scapegoats for the economic crisis, and many had to flee these two countries, even though they were born there.

India's Constitution of 1950 tried to erase lines of caste prejudice by expanding a system of "reservations" that guaranteed the untouchables 15 percent of all seats in Parliament, university places, civil service etc. This policy has led to the creation of multiplicity of castes and the permanent institutionalization of combustible caste prejudices (see Bearak, 1998). This would happen to Guyana if she travels this ethnic balancing or quota route. More-over, quotas once given to any ethnic group would open the floodgates for other minorities (based on religion or otherwise) to demand same. Indeed, the only immediate economic benefit that any race-based policy would produce would be growth of DNA industries trying to count ethnic characteristics! Enforced ethnic balancing in the civil service and security forces is an affront and an assault to incentives, professionalism, productivity and efficiency, and is nothing more than an "incestuous child" of the race myth. The problem is how would ethnic balancing be implemented. More bureaucracy, more intervention and controls. This is nothing more than institutionalizing the Burundi and Rwanda Hutu-Tutsi tribalism conflicts, which, as Howard French (1998) aptly titled, "Rwanda's Disease". Race based policies (similar to the infant industry argument used to justify the failed import substitution strategy) would lead to labor market distortions, stifling economic growth, dependency, resentment, red tape, corruption and may well affect the chances of the protected for upward mobility, and may well exacerbate poverty. Pro-growth policies; a political philosophy aimed at the median voter (moderation and pragmatism), political stability, empowerment, inclusion and voice; free and fair elections and acceptance of the will of the people, adherence to the rule of law, and a vigorous opposition and a free press; an open, competitive, merit based and a renumerative public sector employment policy; zero tolerance for corruption; independence of the judiciary; and policies that reward effort and promote savings and foreign investment are necessary conditions to create the environment conducive for growth and creating the framework to ease ethnic tensions and ethnic poverty, but whether they are sufficient, that's speculation.

11. Acknowledgement

This is a revised and expanded version of my *Ventures in Research* lecture that I delivered on October 19, 1998 to the C.W. Post Campus, Long Island University academic community. The section entitled "Strategies for Poverty Alleviation" was not delivered. I have benefited from several conversations I had with Dr. Udayan Roy, Dr. Donald Solar, Dr. Ralph Knopf, the participants of the lecture, and the encouragement of Dr. Paul Sherwin. All errors and interpretations are my responsibility.

12. References

1. Atkinson, A.B. (1987), "Poverty" in *The New Palgrave: A Dictionary of Economics* eds. John Eatwell, Murray Milgate and Peter Newman (New York: Macmillian Press).
2. Bardhan, P. (1990), "Symposium on the State of Economic Development", *Journal of Economic Perspectives* Vol. 4 No. 3 pp.3-7.
3. Bardhan, P. (1996), "Efficiency, Equity and Poverty Alleviation: Policy Issues in Less Developed Countries", *The Economic Journal* Vol. 106, (September) pp.1344-1356.
4. Bearak, B. (1998), "Caste Hate, and Murder, Outlast Indian Reforms", *The New York Times*, September 19, 1998 p.A.3.
5. Bhagwati, J. (1966), *The Economics of Underdeveloped Countries* (New York: World Univ. Press, McGraw Hill Book Co.).
6. Bhagwati, J. (1993), *India in Transition: Free the Economy* (New York: Oxford University Press).

7. Booth, C. (1892), *Life and Labour of the People of London*, 9 vols. (London: Macmillan).
8. Bowley, A.L. (1913), "Working class households in Reading", *Journal of the American Statistical Society* Vol. 76 (June), pp.672-701.
9. Bruno, M M. Ravallion and L. Squire (1996), *Equity and Growth in Developing Countries, Old and New Perspective on the Policy Issues*, Policy Working Papers 1563 (The World Bank: Washington, D.C.).
10. Burns, J. (1998), "Once Widowed in India, Twice Scorned", *The New York Times*, March 29, 1998, p.A.I.
11. Eden, Sir F. M. (1797), *The State of the Poor* (London: Cass.).
12. Foster, J., J. Greer, and E. Thorbecke (1984), "A Class of Decomposable Poverty Measures", *Econometrica*, Vol. 52 pp.761-765.
13. Foster, J. and A.K. Sen (1997), *On Economic Inequality* (New York: Oxford University Press).
14. French, H. (1998), "Congo Catches Rwanda's Disease", *The New York Times*, August 9, 1998, A.3.
15. Gafar, J. (1988), "Economic Growth and Economic Policy: Employment and Unemployment in Jamaica, 1972-1984," *The Journal of Developing Areas* Vol. 23, pp.63-84.
16. Gafar, J. (1996), "Guyana: From Cooperative Socialism to Economic Liberalization and Growth: 1976-1994", *The Journal of Developing Areas* Vol. 31, pp.41-74.
17. Gafar, J. (1997), "The supply response of aggregate agricultural output in Jamaica", *Agricultural Economics* Vol. 16, pp.205-217.
18. Gafar, J. (1998a), "Growth, Inequality and Poverty in Selected Latin American Countries with Emphasis on Guyana", *Journal of Latin America Studies* Vol. 30, pp.591- 617.
19. Gafar, J. (1998b), "Economic Policy and Growth: Agricultural Performance and the Rice Industry of Guyana", *Canadian Journal of Development Studies* Vol. XIX No. I pp. 153-174.
20. Gafar, J. (1998a), "Poverty, Income Growth, and Inequality in Some Caribbean Countries", *Journal of Developing Areas* Vol. 32, pp.467-490.
21. Galbraith, J.K. (1958), *The Affluent Society* (Boston: Houghton Mifflin).
22. Grosh, M. (1995), "Five Criteria for Choosing among Poverty Programs" in *Coping with Austerity, Poverty and Inequality in Latin America* ed. Nora Lustig (The Brookings Institution, Washington, D.C.).
23. Harrington, M. (1962), *The Other America* (New York: Macmillan).
24. Landler, M. (1998), "Living for Rice, Begging for Rice. Beyond Politics, Indonesia's Crisis Is About Affordable Food", *The New York Times*, September 7, 1998 p.A.5.
25. Morley, S. (1994), *Poverty and Inequality in Latin America: Past Evidence, Future Prospects* (Overseas Development Council, Washington, D.C.).
26. Mrydal, G. (1944), *An America Dilemma* (New York: Harper Paperback ed. 1964).
27. Mrydal, G. (1968), *Asian Drama: An Inquiry Into the Poverty of Nations* (New York: Twentieth Century Fund).

28. Pear, R. (1998), "Black and Hispanic Poverty Falls, Reducing Overall Rate for Nation", *The New York Times*, September 24, 1998, p.A.I.
29. Phillips, M. and T. Mabry (1998), "Student of World's 'Miserable' Wins Nobel", *The Wall Street Journal*, October 15, 1998, p.B1.
30. Psacharopoulos, G.; S. Morley, A. Fiszbein, H. Lee and B. Wood (1997), *Poverty and Income Distribution in Latin America. The Story of the 1980's*; World Bank Technical Paper No. 351 (The World Bank, Washington, D.C.).
31. Rosenthal, E. (1998), "Poverty Spreads, and Deepens, in China's Cities", *The New York Times*, October 4, 1998 p.3.
32. Rosenthal, E. (1998), "In China, Over 35+ Female=Unemployable", *The New York Times*, October 13, 1998, p.A.I.
33. Sen, A.K. (1976), "Poverty: An Ordinal Approach to Measurement", *Econometrica* Vol. 46, pp.437-446.
34. Sen, A. (1990), "Individual Freedom as a Social Commitment", *The New York Review of Books*, June 14, 1990 pp.49-53.
35. Todaro, M. (1997), *Economic Development* 6th ed. (New York: Longman).
36. United Nations (1998), "The Changing Face of Poverty 1998" (New York: United Nations Department of Public Information Newsletter October 1998).
37. UNDP (1990), *Human Development Report 1990* (New York: Oxford Univ. Press), and various issues referred as HDR (Year).
38. Wolfensohn, J. (1998), *The Other Crisis*. Address to the Board of Governors, World Bank (The World Bank, Washington, D.C.).
39. World Bank (1990), *World Development Report 1990* (New York: Oxford Univ. Press for the World Bank).
40. World Bank (1994), *Guyana. Strategies for Reducing Poverty*. Report No. 12861-GUA. (World Bank, Washington, D.C.).
41. World Bank (1996a), *Poverty Reduction and the World Bank. Progress and Challenges in the 1990s*. (The World Bank, Washington, D.C.).
42. World Bank (1996b), *Caribbean Countries Poverty Reduction and Human Resource Development in the Caribbean*, Report No. 15342-LAC (The World Bank, Washington, D.C.).
43. World Bank (1998), *World Development Report* 1998 (New York: Oxford Univ. Press for the World Bank), and various issues.

Chapter 4

ECONOMIC GROWTH AND CIVIL SOCIETY UNDER PINOCHET AND THATCHER: A POLITICAL ECONOMY ANALYSIS OF THE FREE-MARKET MODELS IN CHILE AND THE UNITED KINGDOM*

David E. Hojman†
University of Liverpool,
UK.

ABSTRACT

The Pinochet military regime in Chile in 1973-1990 and the Thatcher government in Britain in 1979-1990 represent the first attempts to implement coherent packages of free-market ('neoliberal') policies, which have now become fashionable all around the world. These policies included tough measures against inflation, market liberalization, lower taxes, a reduction in the economic role of the state, privatisation, and anti-union laws. Several authors have argued that the similarities between the Pinochet and Thatcher administrations were substantial. We look at the evidence and conclude that possibly the differences were more important than the similarities. The similarities were superficial whereas the differences were fundamental. The Pinochet regime intended to change the Chilean economy, politics, society, institutions and culture, in order to bring about fast economic growth and development along capitalist lines. To a large extent these aims were achieved. Margaret Thatcher intended to restore to the UK the leading role it had played in the world stage during Victorian times: to put the 'Great' back into 'Great Britain'. Although it may be early days for a definitive assessment, at least in some

* A previous version of this paper was presented to the Workshop on Civil Society and Political Economy in Latin America, Truman Institute, Hebrew University of Jerusalem, 22 December 1994. The present version has been thoroughly revised to take into account developments up to the third quarter of 2000. The author wishes to thank the Workshop organisers and participants (in particular Mario Sznajder and Luis Roniger) as well as Shanti Chakravarty and Arthur Thomas for their helpful comments. The Nuffield Foundation provided financial support for several research visits to Chile. This support is gratefully acknowledged.
† Department of Economics and Accounting, University of Liverpool, Eleanor Rathbone Building, Bedford Street South, L69 7ZA, UK. Fax: 44 (0) 151 794 3028. E-mail: JL33@liv.ac.uk

respects Mrs. Thatcher may have failed, possibly because her aims were far too ambitious, or even impossible to achieve. This paper is devoted to examine similarities and differences in objectives and outcomes.

1. INTRODUCTION

Free-market, open economy policies (FMOEP) are now being applied all around the world[1]. These neoliberal policies represent a worldwide anti-government revolution. However, when they were first introduced - by Chile in 1973 and Great Britain in 1979 - , FMOEP were seen by many observers as either intellectual curiosities or the product of unrepresentative and extreme ideologues. The Chilean and British neoliberal experiences are interesting not only for their pioneering nature, but also because of their different outcome: the former a success, the latter a 'failure'[2].

Some sectors of the British left used to attack the Thatcher government in the United Kingdom (1979-1990), by saying that the British and Chilean free-market regimes were exactly the same. This happened especially during the first half of the 1980s. In the less sophisticated versions of this form of criticism, the administrations headed by Margaret Thatcher and the Chilean military dictator, General Augusto Pinochet (1973-1990), were both 'extreme right-wing'. According to Barnes (1988, pp. 56-7), the two governments 'share the anti-statist, pro-free market monetarist prescriptions associated with the new orthodoxy/Chicago school of Milton Friedman and Friedrich von Hayek on the economic side, and the cold war, national security, right-wing populist rhetoric emphasising law and order, religion, race, family, chauvinism and anti-welfarism on the political side'[3].

These comparisons became less frequent after the mid 1980s. Until then, the Pinochet regime had been generally seen as a particularly ruthless military dictatorship, brutally attempting to impose an alien socio-economic system on a population and civil society cowed by massive human right abuses. But after 1985 the Chilean experiment was increasingly identified by international public opinion with economic success.

[1] See Hojman (1994, 1999a) for a discussion of FMOEP throughout Latin America.

[2] Although, as we will see, agreement on whether these experiments were 'successes' or 'failures' (or even on whether we should talk of a single 'Thatcher experiment') depends entirely on how their respective objectives are defined. For analyses of diverse aspects of the Pinochet model, see Fontaine (1988), Valdes (1989), Edwards and Edwards (1991), Hachette and Luders (1992), Wisecarver, ed. (1992), Hojman (1993a, 1995a), Bosworth, Dornbusch and Laban, eds. (1994) and Puryear (1994). Some key references on the Thatcher model are Jessop et al (1988), Skidelsky, ed. (1988), Smith (1988), Overbeek (1990), Haas and Knox, eds. (1991), Riddell (1991), Young (1991), Gilmour (1992), Letwin (1992), Thatcher (1993) and Gamble (1994). For comparisons between the models, see Barnes (1988), Gallagher (1992) and Thatcher (1994a, 1994b). Other useful references, either presenting more recent material or providing some historical context, are Hojman (1990, 1996, 1997, 1998, 2000a), Business Monitor International (1997, 1999), and Hiscock and Hojman (1997), for Chile; and Muller (1993), Marr (1996), Neil (1996), Tomlinson (1996) and Evans (1997), for the UK.

[3] Some readers may disagree with several aspects of this quotation. Among them, its attempt to attach the British FMOEP to Milton Friedman. Why should the British neoliberals need Friedman when they have Adam Smith, the 'founding father of political economy', on their side (Muller, 1993; Thatcher 1994a)? Moreover, it would be difficult to describe the 1987-1988 boom under Chancellor of the Exchequer Nigel Lawson - 'the Lawson boom' - as 'monetarist' (Smith, 1988; Cobham, 1994; Gamble, 1994), or any of the main ideologies linked to the Pinochet regime as 'populist' (Fontaine, 1988; Valdes, 1989; Hojman, 1993a).

Of course, the Pinochet and Thatcher regimes had in common the particular historical contexts in which they were born. The origins of both regimes can be found in highly special, unusual or 'abnormal' political circumstances: extreme class polarisation in Chile in the period 1970-1973, and substantial union militancy in Britain in 1977-1979. The British and Chilean governments actively collaborated during the Falklands war and its aftermath.

One of the arguments of the present paper is that the differences between the Pinochet and Thatcher regimes were much more important than the similarities between them. Moreover, and despite the harsh conditions under which it was imposed upon a mostly reluctant population, possibly the Pinochet model was more appropriate to the Chilean situation, than the Thatcher model (or its actual implementation, since in some areas the policy measures were very different from the theoretical model) ever was to the British case. On the other hand, the comparison may be unfair since the Thatcher objectives were more ambitious and difficult to achieve. It is true that both regimes used free markets in order to try to build a strong economy. But in the Chilean case this can be seen as a typical example of a strategy of modernisation and economic development in a Third World country. In contrast, Thatcherism in the UK intended to stop, and if possible reverse, economic decline in what had been less than a hundred years before the most powerful nation on earth. The objectives and characteristics of this attempt at going against the tide of history make Thatcherism unique.

In this sense, the present paper's emphasis on Chile's 'success' against Britain's 'failure' should be taken with great care. Chile's income per capita in the late 1990s was still only about fifty percent of Britain's (at purchasing power parities, PPP). Chile's Human Development Index (HDI) was about 95% of the UK's, but income in Chile is distributed much more unevenly, with negative consequences in terms of both efficiency and equity. In 1992, the Chairman of Chile's Central Bank warned local entrepreneurs against their tendency to see themselves as 'Asian tigers', suggesting that describing them as 'manic-deprcssive cats' would be more appropriate (Zahler, 1992).

The nature of the relationship between free-market economics and civil society in these two cases is not simple and straightforward. In Chile, economic success in the 1990s coexisted with a renaissance of civil society, but no direct or indirect causal relationship can be established unequivocally, in either direction, between a possible strengthening of civil society (to be defined in the next paragraph) and success of the FMOEP model. The same is true in the British case. Some Thatcherite policies may have led to at least a certain degree of antagonising and weakening of civil society, but no causal relationship, one way or the other, is apparent between this particular evolution of civil society in the UK, and 'failure' of the Thatcherite experiment.

Eisenstadt (1993, p.27) defines civil society as 'a relatively wide range of social sectors - such as family, segments and groups, voluntary associations and the like - which are independent of the State, or autonomous with respect to the state'. Other aspects that are important in Eisenstadt's definition are the existence of seemingly 'private', yet potentially autonomous public arenas, distinct from the state; and the presence of various associations that prevent society from becoming a shapeless mass. These sectors should be open, not embedded in more or less closed, or corporate settings; there should be a multiplicity or plurality of such sectors; and there should be autonomous access to the central political arena, and a degree of commitment to shared objectives.

The next section introduces some of the differences and similarities between the Pinochet and Thatcher models. Section 3 highlights the fact that similar policy measures may be hiding fundamental differences in the models' ultimate objectives. Given the unique nature of Thatcherism in contemporary history, Section 4 is devoted to discussing it in more detail. The differences in outcomes are examined in Section 5, and possible reasons for these differences in Section 6. Section 7 addresses what happened after the demise of the Pinochet and Thatcher regimes in 1990 and looks at the paradox that the application of FMOEP, and the eventual adoption of the model by the political centre and left, may have seriously damaged the right's electoral prospects in both cases. Sections 8 and 9 deal with the links between civil society and the free-market model in Chile and Britain, respectively. Finally, the main conclusions are summarised in Section 10.

2. Pinochet and Thatcher: Similarities and Differences

As previously mentioned, possibly one of the most visible (but superficial) similarities between the two regimes is that both were born under highly unusual circumstances: serious class polarisation in Chile and extreme union militancy in Britain. Political, commercial and diplomatic collaboration between the two governments was facilitated by ideological affinities, and then the Falklands conflict contributed to bring them even closer together.

According to Barnes (1988, p. 57):

> 'Obvious differences exist between the two monetarist experiments (e.g. economic structure, differing levels of repression, depth of privatisation, Chile's inferior position in the international economic order, etc). Nevertheless, so many similarities do exist that the drawing of parallels is useful. These include increased state control over the operation of trade unions and restrictions on the collective strength of the union movement; increased police powers and restrictions on the right to assembly; the maintenance of a permanent core of unemployed ... ; the existence of short-term unemployment schemes as a source of cheap labour; moves to bring the education system in line with the new economic order; the deliberate engineering of a slump (Britain 1980-82, Chile 1975-76) with which to rationalise the economy and prepare the ground for long-term economic and social restructuring; the increased opening of the economy to the international market and the penetration of foreign capital; the shift in favour of the finance and services sector to the detriment of manufacturing industry; the erosion of the welfare state and moves towards its privatisation ... '

In fact, Barnes was writing at a time when important changes were taking place (Edwards and Edwards, 1991; Wisecarver, 1992; Hojman, 1993a, 1994, 1995a, 1996; Bosworth et al, 1994; Marfan, 1994; Puryear, 1994). By the end of the 1980s, Chilean unemployment had fallen so much that the emergency employment schemes which had been in force until then had to be discontinued. The Chilean FMOEP had a detrimental effect on manufacturing only in the short term. The imposition of a low uniform tariff on imports proved extremely effective at increasing industrial productivity and competitiveness (Hojman, 1999b), and by the end of the 1980s the index of manufacturing output had reached its highest level ever. Exports, including higher value added ones, have been expanding at a fast rate. There was never a welfare state in Chile, let alone one comparable with the British welfare state before 1979 (Hiscock and Hojman, 1997). Educational policies in Chile and the UK were quite different both before and after FMOEP. Post-1970s educational policies possibly were significantly more successful (or less of a failure) in Chile. Educational and other policies in Chile survived the transition from a military regime to a democratically elected, civilian centre-left administration in 1990. Excessive police powers and anti-union legislation have been dismantled but FMOEP have been preserved. Further opening of the British economy to international trade was subjected to the constraints imposed by membership of the European Union, where openness to European partners was not always extended to the rest of the world.

A highly noticeable characteristic shared by the Pinochet and Thatcher models is that both governments took office under conditions of high inflation. For several years, both regimes attempted to stop inflation by using monetarist recipes, i.e. by keeping the rate of money supply expansion under tight control. They eventually succeeded, although at a rather high economic and social cost in terms of recession and unemployment.

3. Common Policies but Different Objectives

Both regimes aimed at building a strong economy, but even if some of the policies geared to this objective were the same, the ultimate aims were different. In addition to their anti-inflationary policy, other common features of the Pinochet and Thatcher regimes were their attempts at improving incentives, in particular by lowering taxes, and at reducing the size of the state through privatisation, their reliance on markets, and their campaigns against trade unions and organised labour. However, these common measures were addressed to different aims. In Chile these policies were inserted into a wider development model, a modernisation strategy geared towards releasing the whole productive potential of the economy for fast growth. The Chilean measures should be seen as part of a complete package which also included as fundamental aspects, educational reform and opening the economy to international trade and foreign investment. In short, the aim was to unleash a 'capitalist revolution'. In contrast, the Thatcher measures were directed at regaining Britain's former glory as a world power, 'to put the Great back into Great Britain' (Riddell, 1991; Young, 1991; Thatcher, 1993). Rather than a capitalist revolution, this is more akin to 'imperial restoration'. So, even if some (or many) of the measures implemented by Pinochet and Thatcher were the same, the objectives that these measures tried to achieve were substantially different. The Chilean effort was devoted to complete change, whereas at least partly the British policymakers were seeking 'restoration'.

There were other differences. The Thatcher efforts to reduce the size of government damaged the welfare state, an institution the British people were rightly proud of. In Chile there was not much of a welfare state to be damaged. Pinochet devolved some power to local authorities, in areas such as basic and secondary education, primary health care, and distribution of subsidies to the poor, although local authorities were not democratically elected until the 1990s. In contrast, in Britain many decisions were removed from the local level and concentrated in the hands of central government. As explained later, civil society in Chile and Britain tended to evolve in complex, but generally quite different ways[4].

The Pinochet regime was 'foundational' in the sense that it intended to change not only the economy but also politics, society and institutions. However, Chile was not the first country to introduce economic reforms in the context of a wider development model and modernisation strategy (see Kohli, 1994, for a discussion of Japan and Korea). In contrast, the main objectives of the Thatcher model are possibly unique. Never before in contemporary history had a government set itself these aims. The next section explores 'Thatcherism' in more detail.

4. The Many Faces (and Contradictions) of 'Thatcherism'

According to Smith (1988), the most convenient way of examining the economic objectives of Thatcherism is by dividing them into four groups. Moving gradually from macroeconomics to microeconomics, these objectives were: a) controlling and eventually eliminating inflation (i.e., the policies which were originally identified with monetarism); b) reducing the size of the public sector; c) using tax cuts to increase incentives and improve the supply side of the economy; and finally, d) curbing the power of trade unions and improving the efficiency of the labour market[5].

As we move away from the economy, the picture becomes more confused. There is a long list of often conflicting characteristics that, according to different observers, would contribute to define 'Thatcherism'. They include 'a meaningless label', with nothing new about its aims; 'a ragbag of ideas', plenty of plans, but no 'Big Plan'; an effort to make the rich richer, with 'greed' at the centre of everything; a series of pragmatic attempts at improving economic efficiency motivated by the desire to rescue capitalism; a dogmatic economic doctrine inspired in a golden age that probably never was; a drive for power, either personal or to enhance the glory of Britain ('Thatcherism-as-Gaullism'); a project for concentrating power in central government by destroying the autonomy of local authorities and powerful interest groups; a moral crusade, either in favour of old-fashioned discipline and against the permissive society, or alternatively, bent on

[4] Another interesting difference between Pinochet and Thatcher are their reactions when facing difficulties. The Chilean financial crisis of 1982-83 was dealt with largely by reversing the privatisation drive, whereas the London Stock Exchange crash in October 1987 was met by money supply expansion. A full discussion of these events is, however, beyond the scope of this paper.

[5] On Thatcherite economics, see also Matthews and Minford (1987), Jessop et al (1988, pp. 170-74), the chapters by Minford and by Hahn in Skidelsky, ed. (1988), Johnson (1991) and Minford (1991).

enlarging the freedom of individuals and uprooting traditional ways (Letwin, 1992). It is tempting to conclude that these multiple interpretations are contradictory, simply because Thatcherism itself was contradictory[6].

Letwin has added another possibility, namely that Thatcherism was about emphasising the 'vigorous virtues'. Individuals should be 'upright, self-sufficient, energetic, adventurous, independent-minded, loyal to friends, and robust against enemies' (p. 33). The ideal family would be one that both forms these individuals and helps them to succeed. The role of society should be to encourage this family. The 'vigorous virtues' are in opposition to 'softer' ones: 'kindness, humility, gentleness, sympathy, cheerfulness' (p. 33). In Letwin's interpretation, Thatcherism would be about the belief that ordinary Britons would prefer to see themselves as practitioners of the 'vigorous virtues', rather than as targets or receivers of the softer' ones. In particular, Britons would not like to be considered as invalids in need of government help or protection. However, Letwin admits that sometimes actual policymaking under Thatcher was largely in contradiction with achievement of the 'vigorous virtues'. For example, educational policies were often 'Bismarckian' rather than Thatcherite[7]. Other authors have also pointed out that Mrs. Thatcher herself was not always a Thatcherite (Desai, 1994; Evans, 1997). According to Gilmour, '... Thatcherite adherence to free-market dogma was itself subordinate to the imperative of keeping Margaret Thatcher in office' (Gilmour, 1992, p. 274).

That Thatcherism was about 'making the rich richer' is not a slander invented by Thatcher's enemies. Lord Joseph, widely acknowledged as the father of Thatcherism, and described by Mrs. Thatcher herself as 'my mentor', used to define the objective of Thatcherism as 'increasing the inequalities in order to provide incentives to motivate entrepreneurs and innovators and to facilitate trickle down effects towards those at the bottom of the economic and social pyramid' (Owen, 1994)[8]. Inequalities effectively increased (Goodman and Webb, 1994), as admitted in 1994 by Peter Lilley, a cabinet minister in John Major's government, with rather negative results: '... the dispersion of earning power has had unattractive social consequences: ... the break up of families, the growth of lone parenthood, and a growing welfare dependency. It may even play a part in explaining delinquency and crime' (quoted in *The Economist*, 7 January 1995, p. 24). Inequalities increased in three ways. A lower income tax helped the better off, as higher unemployment hurt the worst off. Additionally, the earnings gap before tax between high earners and low earners, among those in full employment, increased (Kellner, 1994). But this increase in inequalities, 'making the rich richer', may not have succeeded in

[6] This is why it may not make much sense to talk of a single 'Thatcher experiment'. 'Thatcherism can be viewed as ideology, style, mood, I-must-have-my-own-way, monarchism, nineteenth-century Liberalism, millenarian revivalism, right-wingery, a method of controversy, a set of moral values, statecraft ...' (Gilmour, 1992, p. 10). See also Jessop et al (1988).

[7] Successful encouragement of the 'vigorous virtues' by the family and by society depends on a) well-functioning markets being allowed to perform freely, and b) any instances of market failure being swiftly corrected.

[8] However, Joseph was well known for his willingness to offer striking oneliners, only to eventually change his mind. Statements along the lines of 'it is only recently that I have become a Conservative', or 'monetarism is not enough' should be seen either as an expression of Joseph's refreshing candour, or as proof that not even he understood what Thatcherism was all about, or as proof that Thatcherism was constantly in the making, or more likely as a combination of all of these.

improving the long-term trend in economic growth. Thatcherism 'succeeded' in its attempt at engineering a regressive change in the pattern of wealth and income distribution, and in the fact that this change has now acquired a more or less 'permanent' character. However, so far no substantive positive impact on the dynamism of the British economy has been observed as a result, beyond cyclical upswings such as the 1996-97 one, itself helped by pre-election expenditure and by the 'honeymoon' period following the Labour Party electoral victory in May 1997 (Labour's first victory in 18 years). On the other hand, despite the increase in inequality, the living standards and real expenditure in absolute terms of the poorest ten percent of the population have actually improved since 1979 (Adonis, 1995a; Neil, 1995a; Timmins, 1995).

5. The Most Important Difference: 'Success' and 'Failure'

Possibly the most crucial difference between the Pinochet and Thatcher regimes was that the former 'succeeded' whereas the latter 'failed'. After some years of difficulties, setbacks and fluctuations, by the late 1990s the Chilean model looked highly successful. In fact, it has been looking highly successful for more than a decade (Business Monitor International, 1997, 1999). Progress is being more or less systematically reported in areas such as economic growth, savings, investment, foreign trade, inflation, employment, real earnings, and poverty reduction (Hojman, 1995a, 1995b; 1999c; *The Economist*, several numbers; *Financial Times*, several numbers). The new democratic institutions seem increasingly solid and stable. Success in economics and in politics possibly reinforce each other.

Admittedly, not everything is perfect. Income distribution has not improved (Hojman, 1996, 2000a). The domestic currency has experienced substantial appreciation and the dynamism of agriculture has suffered. Faster economic expansion may have been prevented by rent seeking activities. The political and political economy conditions in Chile during the mid and late 1990s may not have been conducive to reaching the fastest possible rate of growth. However, at least some of these are pains provoked by fast growth. Things may be improving gradually (Hojman, 1995b). The prospects for the first decade of the 21st century and beyond may be brighter (Hojman, forthcoming). On the positive side, the fact that the dividing line between 'modernisers' and 'conservatives' cuts across each political party in the centre-left government coalition may be contributing to make civil society stronger, by encouraging new forms of association which are independent from these parties and the government. The 'foundational' attempts by the military regime to change the economy, politics and society severely damaged many old civil society institutions. However, civil society strengthened as the economy progressed in the second half of the 1980s, and this process accelerated after the democratic transition in 1990.

During its first two terms (1979-1987), the Thatcher government achieved some significant successes. Inflation (which had initially increased as a result of the shift from direct taxes to indirect taxes such as VAT) fell and most impartial observers became convinced that money supply control was ultimately more effective than incomes policies. The economy recovered, although this eventually proved to be no different from (and no more permanent than) previous upswings in the economic cycle. Some limited progress was made in extending freedom of choice to low income families, by allowing tenants to buy their local-authority-owned homes ('council houses'), and by eliminating the compulsory catchment areas of state schools in inner cities. Taxes fell, largely to the benefit of high income taxpayers. More recently, school league tables have been introduced, in order to publicize differences in performance and make comparisons with the competition possible. Universities have become more entrepreneurial, although there is no agreement among academics on whether this development is favourable or unfavourable[9].

The economy took many years to recover after the London Stock Exchange crash in October 1987 (reactions to the crash were suboptimal, because observers tended to misread the strength of the impact of the crash on the 'real' economy), the excessive cyclical swings following the Lawson boom, and the high interest rates required by membership of the European Exchange Rate Mechanism (ERM). Civil disobedience against the poll tax eventually became widespread[10]. Political support for the Tory government collapsed. As mentioned before, Thatcher 'succeeded' only if her aim was to make the rich richer, but 'failed' if her intention was to use this change in income and wealth distribution in order to increase the long-term trend of economic growth or 'to put the Great back into Great Britain'[11].

---

[9] Many of these successes refer to the public sector. There were not many similar successes to show in the private sector, despite the fact that the free-market model sees the private sector as the engine of the economy. Some privatised enterprises became successes, such as British Airways and British Telecom, but by contrast British Gas, a natural monopoly, only made the news because its chairman awarded himself spectacular pay increases, at the same time as the wages of its shop assistants were being reduced (*The Economist*, several numbers; *Financial Times*, several numbers). In any case, all of these are large firms, with at least some degree of oligopolistic power in their respective product markets. It is possible that the target of improving efficiency in the public sector was adopted as the top priority only as a second-best solution, after it was realised that a substantial increase in the dynamism of the private sector was extremely difficult to achieve. Maybe further privatisations of traditional public sector activities were prevented by politically powerful white-collar state employees, public servants and other middle income groups, and opposition from within the Tory Party. The privatisation of British Rail had to wait until the mid 1990s.

[10] The poll tax was introduced in 1989 to replace the old property-based local taxes (the 'rates'). It was a personal tax, with the same amount to be paid locally by every adult, although this amount changed from one local authority to the next. The poll tax was highly regressive and it made a large majority worse off. Many people, including some whose previous living standards had been reasonably above the poverty line, could not afford to pay it. The poll tax was a spectacular political mistake, especially considering that local government reform could have become a winner for Mrs. Thatcher. Lavish expenditure and nil or poor accountability make many local authorities extremely unpopular.

[11] The notion of 'failure' is however relative, in the sense that, by the beginning of 1995, access to consumer durables such as refrigerators, television sets, telephones, deep freezers, video recorders, or central heating and cars, was several times higher than for the previous generation (Macrae, 1995; Smith, 1995a). Employment creation was also expanding at a fast rate, although jobs felt less secure than before because the labour market had become more flexible (Segall, 1995). See Adonis (1995a), Neil (1995a) and Timmins (1995) for evidence of improving living standards among the poorest ten percent of the population since 1979.

6. Possible Explanations for the Different Outcomes

Some of the reasons put forward to explain the different outcomes of the Pinochet and Thatcher experiences are the different length of planning horizons (with this length being significantly greater under a military dictatorship), and the need to preserve democracy in the British case. However, a short planning horizon in Britain does not prevent the government from making the economic and political cycles coincide, by expanding the economy at the most convenient time and calling a general election at a moment of its own choice. Moreover, a working majority in the British Parliament is almost as powerful as an elected dictatorship, since, in contrast with other Western democracies, neither the second chamber nor the executive can successfully challenge majority decisions by the House of Commons. Other, more realistic reasons for the different outcomes are discussed in the following paragraphs[12].

The reader should be warned again that the Chilean picture may misleadingly look excessively positive and the British one, excessively negative. This is because the aspects being highlighted here are quite partial. They are included because they are related to the degrees of achievement by the Pinochet and Thatcher regimes, of their respective aims. But it would be a mistake to interpret the present discussion as indicating something else in terms of the general quality of life, or of other wider areas, in Chile and the UK.

Mrs. Thatcher did little in terms of modernising many traditional institutions, including the monarchy, the House of Lords, the 'first-past-the-post' electoral system, the educational system (from Oxford and Cambridge to inner city schools), the judicial system and the military, among others. In some cases, she may positively have done her best to strengthen some of these institutions. The old Labour Party itself, with its conservative - with a small 'c' - attachment to obsolete activities and practices, was another traditional institution, and therefore part of the problem, not of the solution. Regardless of whether we choose to see old institutions as ossified expressions of successful rent seeking in the past, or as indicators of possible returns of present and future rent seeking, the fact is that the survival of some old institutions may have prevented economic growth and discouraged the development of a dynamic, meritocratic and entrepreneurial society[13].

---

[12] Separate sections will be devoted to discussing the role of civil society in both cases. For more on the 'elected dictatorship' nature of British government during the 1980s, see Gilmour (1992), Chapter 8. It is possible that the Thatcher authoritarian style, observed by Gilmour at cabinet level, may not be an isolated phenomenon and just a product of Mrs. Thatcher's personal attitude, but rather a reflection of something else. Jessop et al (1988, p. 81) argue that an increasingly inadequate 'combination of parliamentary and corporatist modes of interest intermediation' has resulted in a gradually growing 'decisional autonomy of the state elite'. If this is true, it means that the 'elected dictatorship' nature of British government, and its manifestations at different levels, would be provoked by structural rather than personal or voluntaristic causes.

[13] 'The real failure of Thatcherism was its failure to understand that a market model could be safely imposed only if it was joined to a comprehensive social and political liberalism - the creation of a constitutional framework that fosters democratic forms of community to replace the old aristocratic intermediate bodies ... (O)ne section of British society was able to champion free-market ideas without for a moment assuming that it would ever be subject to the insecurities and risks inseparable from a more egalitarian and competitive social order ... Thatcherism was a monstrously unbalanced program ... in attending to market

Olson (1982) has argued that Britain is possibly the most characteristic contemporaneous example of a society which has enjoyed uninterrupted democratic government for generations, and no invasions by foreign powers. This may have led to the development and gradual strengthening of many special interest groups and distributional coalitions which eventually weakened the economy and undermined the potential for long-term growth.

There are several British institutions and practices, old and new, which are likely to have hindered economic growth (this list is not exhaustive nor does it follow any particular order). The electoral system, for example, may encourage extremism on both right and left. No realistic proposals for reforming the House of Lords have ever been put forward (Bogdanor, 1995). The government is protected by excessive secrecy, which in some cases may reach ridiculous and damaging proportions (Neil, 1995b). The privatised utilities are inadequately regulated (Helms, 1994; Rogaly, 1995; Taylor, 1995a, 1995b). Privatisation and deregulation were followed by a boom in 'quasi-autonomous non-governmental organisations' ('quangos'), which were filled by government appointees selected, not on their merits, but according to where their political sympathies lay (Mulgan, 1994; Adonis, 1995b; Blitz and Adonis, 1995). Until mid 1997, both Tory government and Labour opposition refused to admit the need for an independent Central Bank (Doyle and Weale, 1994). Antitrust policies and support for competition are timid by the standards of other advanced industrial democracies (Stelzer, 1995). Mass education has suffered from the inability or unwillingness of the authorities to see it as a fundamental aspect of investment in human capital (Snow, 1994; Neil, 1995c; Wooldridge, 1995). Some practices in the judicial system (such as the appointment of QCs) may be inefficient on economic grounds (Berlins, 1995). In local government, the contradiction between libertarian and authoritarian instincts in Mrs. Thatcher eventually solved itself in favour of the latter and of centralisation[14].

inefficiencies, trade union power and feather-bedding it failed to address larger issues of fairness ...' (Siedentop, 1995). '... (T)he contradiction between neoliberalism and the (Thatcher) government's attachment to privilege was revealed in its lack of interest in a radical reform of the state ... The notorious inefficiencies of British life, from the secretive and ineffectual system of state economic policymaking to the archaic systems of taxation, banking, and law, the insanely slow and costly system of real-estate conveyancing, and an educational system as spectacularly inadequate in its day as it had been in 1900 - such spheres were not objects of Mrs. Thatcher's concern. She distrusted the civil service, the universities and the BBC ... but ... stopped short of a radical assault on the structures on which the establishment's power rested ...' (Leys, 1983, pp. 94-95). Considering the limitations and contradictions of the actual application of the Thatcherite model to Britain (and Mrs. Thatcher's lack of enthusiasm for at least some aspects of British civil society, see Section 9), it is surprising that she sometimes mentioned the eighteenth century British-American revolutionary Tom Paine as one of her sources of inspiration (Eagleton, 1995; Pimlott, 1995; Rutherford, 1995). For the role of institutions in Latin American and Chilean history, see Hojman (2000b).

[14] Another traditional British practice which is unlikely to increase the economy's dynamism, regardless of its merits in other respects, is that of 'kicking someone upstairs'. This treatment is reserved for senior politicians, who are sent to the House of Lords, or for the managing director of a company, who may be appointed chairman of the board. In either case the objective is to get him or her out of the way, but keeping the appearance that the person thus 'promoted' is still making a useful contribution. This practice would be inconceivable in Pinochet's or post-Pinochet Chile. It is such a peculiar British institution that the English language expression 'kicking someone upstairs' cannot be translated into Spanish.

In Chile, some of the old institutions were weakened or eliminated by the left-wing government of Salvador Allende in 1970-1973, and others were destroyed after 1973 (even if some extremely negative institutions and practices such as rent seeking and corruption survived into the 1990s). In general, the Chilean efforts at modernisation during the 1970s and 1980s were largely successful. These efforts were applied not only in the economic arena, but also to social, institutional, political and administrative aspects.

Mrs. Thatcher experienced considerable opposition from within her own ranks, which at least sometimes she was unable or unwilling to neutralise. Many in the British Conservative Party and among its traditional allies were natural supporters of 'restoration' (not only of the Victorian empire, but also of many anachronistic, anti-meritocratic and anti-growth practices), rather than 'revolution'. These include paternalistic landowners, old-style 'one-nation' Tories, high ranking civil servants (the so-called 'Whitehall mandarins'), the Anglican Church and the professional associations. Some of the worst enemies of Thatcherism were precisely Thatcher's own supporters, or certain natural Tory voters. Some of the opposition to Thatcherism was on ethical grounds, but other was simply to protect old privileges[15]. A first hand account describes how 'the first Thatcher cabinet, with its complement of wets, dries, and those who were too intelligent, cautious, fearful or uncommitted to be either, was palpably not a happy and united body; probably, indeed, as Jim Prior has said, it was the most divided Conservative cabinet ever' (Gilmour, 1992, p. 4).

For obvious reasons, in Chile there was no opposition to the military dictatorship for many years. Policymaking gained from the input of a new class of highly qualified technocrats, most of whom were radical reformers (Fontaine, 1988; Valdes, 1989; Hojman, 1990, 1993a; Puryear, 1994). As mentioned before, the Pinochet regime was more of a foundational regime than Thatcher's. This was facilitated not only by a shared radical free-market ideology and by the presence of widely respected technocrats, but also by the fact that the actual policies being adopted were usually backed by the most powerful economic sectors and groups (Silva, 1993).

Mrs. Thatcher fundamentally compromised on Europe. She accepted (however reluctantly) the ERM and the Common Agricultural Policy (CAP), among other measures, against the advice of most of her own economists. Europe represents a genuine contradiction for the Tories, the source of a conflict between foreign investment and national sovereignty. Foreign investment is necessary for modernisation, but much of it will be forthcoming only if the UK becomes a base from where to export to Europe. In

[15] In this connection see Desai (1994) for evidence of disappointment in radical right-wing think-tanks. It is tempting to compare the opposition to Thatcherism amongst Tories and natural Tory voters during the 1980s, with the British Establishment's opposition to Churchill's firm stand against Nazi Germany in the 1930s. This is an interesting historical parallel since Churchill's position was unpopular among key sectors of the traditional British upper classes. However, Churchill persevered whereas Thatcher did not. Some may argue that this is a good example of Churchill's vision against Thatcher's myopia. Except that not only Thatcher, but also her Tory opponents were myopic. Among them, even the most lucid of 'one-nation' Tories had severe difficulties in seeing the anti-growth nature of some of the most anachronistic of traditional British institutions. According to Gilmour (1992, p. 241), those parts of British life 'most in need of ... Mrs. Thatcher's reforming zeal' were the tabloid press and newspaper ownership concentration.

the early 1990s the largest 'British' exporter of motor cars was Nissan, using plants in England under Japanese management (Rehder and Thompson, 1994). Thatcherites see the European Union as interventionist, protectionist and bureaucratic.

Chile is a member of the Asia-Pacific Economic Cooperation Forum (APEC) and may join Canada, the USA and Mexico in the North America Free Trade Agreement (NAFTA). In contrast with Europe, the most actively protectionist forces in APEC and NAFTA have been effectively neutralised, and Chilean membership would contribute to even faster expansion of Chile's international trade. Chile left the Andean Pact in the mid 1970s as a rejection of the Andean restrictions on foreign investment, and recently joined Mercosur as an 'associate' rather than a full member, to avoid a high common external tariff. Chilean policymakers prefer to engage in unilateral opening of the economy, rather than indulge in the protectionist practices that were typical of Latin America in the 1960s and 1970s (or in the complicated negotiations that inevitably must precede bilateral agreements).

Thatcherite policymaking may have suffered as a result of having been based on simplistic economics (Hahn, 1988). The real world is very different from the textbook market economy. In practice, policy options in the real world are not between the free market and central planning, but between different mixes of free markets coexisting with limited forms of government intervention. All successful experiences of growth and development since the mid and late nineteenth century, and especially more recently (from Scandinavia to Switzerland to East Asia), are combinations of free markets and government intervention, each combination being especially designed to fit a particular, individual country situation.

It is possible to point out a number of instances of insufficient, excessive, or misdirected government intervention in the UK after 1979: the European ERM; bus deregulation and the choice between rail and motorway (or between train and car), with insufficient attention being paid to negative externalities of pollution, contamination and crowding; fluctuating and incoherent policies towards higher education; the poll tax; privatisation of natural monopolies followed by inadequate regulation; excessive money supply expansion after the 1987 crash; and the inability or unwillingness to deal with corrupt practices among government politicians.

For Chile, a long list of policy mistakes could be equally compiled. However, some successful examples of government intervention may be more relevant to the present discussion. The privately-run pension funds (AFPs) made a significant contribution towards increasing the rate of domestic savings and avoiding excessive reliance on foreign capital. The exchange rate policy (a managed float within a narrow band until the late 1990s) encouraged exports and prevented excessive appreciation of the domestic currency and excessive short-term swings. The legal limitations on short-term foreign capital flows may have avoided excess volatility in foreign payments. Other success areas were the public-private mix in the financing of higher education, renegotiation of the external debt, and the import tariff policy (Hachette and Luders, 1992; Wisecarver, 1992; Hojman, 1993a, 1995b, 1999b, 1999c; Bosworth et al, 1994; Marfan, 1994).

Again, we must insist that both the list of Chilean failures and that of British successes are possibly long. But they are not as relevant to the questions under examination here. In Chile, one of the most serious weaknesses when applying the FMOEP model was the failure of successive regimes, from Pinochet to Lagos, to privatise the state-owned copper mines. However, although this failure may have hurt the coherence of the Chilean free-market effort, it did not fatally wound it.

7. Chile and Britain after 1990

Both the Pinochet and the Thatcher governments ended in 1990. After losing a plebiscite in 1988 on its possible continuation for a further eight-year period, the Chilean military regime had to call a general election in 1989. The leader of the opposition, Christian Democratic lawyer Patricio Aylwin, was elected President. In Britain, the opinion polls were suggesting that the Tory Party had lost so much popular support, that Labour was bound to win the general election, due in 1991 or 1992. The economy was in deep recession and instances of civil disobedience against the poll tax were becoming widespread. So the Conservative Members of Parliament (MPs) unceremoniously dumped Mrs. Thatcher and elected a new party leader, John Major.

However, despite these changes in government, free-market policies continued being applied in both countries. In Chile, the centre-left government coalition adopted the FMOEP model wholeheartedly, a process that was reinforced by the election of President Eduardo Frei, another Christian Democrat, in December 1993 (Hojman, 1993a, 1995a, 1995b). In Britain, the continuation of free-market policies by the Major government was not surprising, since John Major had been a member of the Thatcher cabinet for many years. What was more surprising was that the Labour Party in opposition pledged that, if elected (which effectively happened in May 1997), it would continue applying many Thatcherite policies. Labour has not reversed the privatisations, or the trade union laws, or the special advantages granted to private schools. Not only has Labour dropped its previous opposition to school league tables, designed to 'increase and inform parent choice', but it has also offered suggestions on how to improve on these league tables. The leader of the Labour Party sent his own sons to a school that 'opted out' of local authority control, taking advantage of a policy measure bitterly opposed by Labour in the not-too-distant past (Snow, 1994). Labour ditched its old policy of nationalisation (Clause Four), and its current stand against inflation is at least as tough as that of the Tories (Smith, 1995b; *The Economist*, several numbers).

Thus, the fate of the Pinochet and Thatcher models in the 1990s was a paradoxical one. In Chile, the Pinochet supporters suffered electoral defeat twice, in 1988 and 1989 (and again in 1993 and 1999), but this was followed by adoption of the free-market economic model by its political opponents. In the UK, a chain of election victories by Thatcher - 1979, 1983, 1987 - was followed by economic failure, and eventually personal and electoral defeat: personal defeat for Thatcher herself at the hands of her own MPs in 1990, and also defeat for the Tories in the 1997 general election. But the adoption of many of her policies by the Labour Party suggests that ultimately Thatcher may have won the economic argument. To some extent Pinochet and Thatcher may have repeated the feat of the Spanish medieval hero Cid Campeador, who allegedly continued winning military victories after his death.

This important similarity, among so many differences between the Pinochet and Thatcher experiences, points to the fact that FMOEP are being increasingly adopted by the political centre and left everywhere. In electoral terms, a centre-left political coalition which promises to carry out free-market economic policies is possibly an unbeatable combination. The long-term trend may be towards a natural, relaxed, spontaneous, and more or less permanent identification of FMOEP with centre-left and left politics. Eventually, and after the demise of Marxism-Leninism and Soviet-style socialism, FMOEP may be naturally more at home with the political centre and left, than with the political right. This is because any determined attempt at using FMOEP in order to protect traditional privilege, to defend the old system (in the sense of 'Ancient Regime') may be self-defeating, because of the high degree of dynamism of the economic and social processes that the FMOEP will set in motion. Conservatives - with a small 'c' - should stay away from FMOEP, because FMOEP are potentially revolutionary[16].

Unfortunately, the post-1997 British Labour Party (Tony Blair's 'New Labour' in government) may have inherited not only Thatcher's economic policies, but also at least some of her unwillingness to modernise the old-fashioned, anti-growth institutions of the traditional establishment, as witness the Blair government decision to preserve the special government funding for the elite universities, Oxford and Cambridge (Glennerster, 1997; Targett and Kampfner, 1997).

8. Chilean Civil Society and the Free-Market Model

Civil society is far from static. O'Donnell and Schmitter (1986) have identified four phases in the evolution of civil society before, during and after a military regime. The military coup destroys 'self-organised and autonomously defined political spaces' (p. 48). In some cases, during the authoritarian period 'something like a subterranean network of preexisting associations, unions movements, and parties persists behind the facade' (p. 55). The democratic transition is characterised by 'the resurgence of previous political parties or the formation of new ones, ... the sudden appearance of books and magazines, ... the conversion of older institutions, such as trade unions, professional associations, and universities, ... the emergence of grassroots organisations, ... the expression of ethical concerns by religious and spiritual groups, ... and so forth' (p. 49). But 'this popular upsurge is always ephemeral ... (Its) decline ... leaves many dashed hopes and frustrated actors; ... disenchantment ... is a persistent problem ...' (pp. 55-56).

Depending on our definition of 'civil society', the free-market model may allow less room for 'civil society' in the economic sphere, as compared with, for example,

---

[16] On adoption of FMOEP elsewhere in Latin America, see Espinal (1992), Weffort (1992) and Hojman (1994, 2000b). On the role of uncertainty in delaying FMOEP adoption, which after adoption are seen to benefit a majority of the population, see Fernandez and Rodrik (1991) and Rodrik (1993).

corporatism[17]. Many economic decisions are left to markets, rather than being taken or suggested by intermediate associations. However, in extreme and anti-democratic forms of corporatism such as fascism, these intermediate associations are not independent from the state. It would be misleading to present them as expressions of a healthy civil society. To some extent this is also true of associations such as trade unions in the typical populist Latin American experiences, or under the PRI in Mexico.

But we do not need to go back to the classic expressions of fascism or populism in order to find similar ambiguities. During the 1980s in Chile, all grassroots forms of opposition to the military regime were unequivocally part of a growing civil society (Hojman, 1993b; Oxhorn, 1995). Some of these grassroots organisms worked in close contact with the opposition political parties. However, after the democratic transition in 1990, many of these grassroots organisms were co-opted by the largest political parties in the new government coalition, Christian Democrats and Socialists (Hojman, 1993a; Lowden, 1995). By becoming instruments of the government parties, these grassroots movements lost their independence. This was especially worrying since Chilean political conditions in the 1990s were such that the centre-left coalition was likely to remain in office for a long time (Hojman, 1995b).

During the 1980s, and despite the attacks on Chilean civil society by the authoritarian regime, civil society may have been strengthened in at least two ways. Firstly, the military government devolved power to the local authorities ('municipalities') in areas such as education, health, social policy and others. Secondly, opposition to the Pinochet regime led to the creation and growth of many grassroots associations and non-government organisations (NGOs).

During the 1980s and the 1990s, but especially after the democratic renewal in 1990, new forms of autonomous associations have resulted from fast economic growth. For example, a powerful 'new social movement' has arisen among those interested in influencing exchange rate policy in order to keep the Chilean currency competitive in international markets. This 'new social movement' is formed by small and medium-size non-traditional exporters, and by producers of import-competing goods and services in agriculture, manufacturing, transport and communications, the financial sector, and so on. The substantial structural change (both economic and social) being provoked by fast economic growth represents a significant encouragement to the creation of autonomous associations in defence of particular interests. Furthermore, in the political sphere the cleavage between 'modernisers' and 'traditionalists' in the centre-left government coalition (which to a large extent overlaps with the distinction between supporters and opponents of free markets) cuts across every government party (Hojman, 1995b). This generates incentives to the establishment of informal links, groups and associations along lines quite different from those defined by narrow political party affiliation.

Among these mostly positive developments in Chilean civil society, a negative one after 1990 was that, as mentioned before, many grassroots organisms which had been autonomous from the state during the 1980s, were effectively 'deautonomised', i.e. 'taken

[17] This discussion of 'civil society' follows the definitions offered by Eisenstadt (1993) and Waisman (1994).

over' by members of the government parties, Christian Democrats and Socialists in particular. This also applies to many NGOs.

Because of the onslaught against civil society in the 1970s, and because of the multidimensional nature of civil society (Waisman, 1994), it is difficult to argue that Chilean civil society in the 1990s was stronger (or weaker) than in the 1960s. Maybe on balance the positive developments observed in recent years compensate for the steps backwards taken in the 1970s and 1980s. But because civil society growth is not unilinear, the comparison between the 1960s and the 1990s may be largely meaningless, since the old institutions (which disappeared in the 1970s) and the new institutions (which were born in the mid and late 1980s and more recently) are qualitatively different.

However, it seems clear that the current characteristics of civil society in Chile are largely functional to that country's free-market economic model, and that the operation of the model results in further favourable effects on civil society. The Chilean evidence is not sufficiently strong to confirm unambiguously that a dynamic market economy is a prerequisite of a healthy civil society (Brittan, 1993), but on the other hand it does not contradict this possibility. Nor does the Chilean case seem to be in contradiction with the Japanese and Korean development models, in which at least some forms of 'civil society' may have constituted an obstacle to economic growth (Kohli, 1994).

9. British Civil Society and the Thatcher Government

The Thatcher model attacked three aspects in particular of British civil society. First, several laws were passed against trade unions. Second, a number of responsibilities were taken away from local authorities in order to concentrate decision making in the hands of central government politicians or unelected officials. As previously mentioned, this was combined with an explosion in the number of both 'quangos' and Thatcherite (and after 1997 Blairite) appointments to them. And thirdly, the Thatcher government engaged in a deliberate attempt to distance itself from 'consensus politics' (Young, 1991; Gilmour, 1992), and to move away from the political centre. This Thatcher attitude may have been critical, since a degree of cohesion among diverse sectors and groups is possibly essential to a healthy civil society (Eisenstadt, 1993). This ideological stance by Thatcher further increased political polarisation, which was already high as a result of some particularly divisive economic policies and of the 'first-past-the-post' British electoral system. In Gilmour's view, 'the need to impose a free economy easily overrode the desirability of nurturing a plural society' (Gilmour, 1992, p. 274).

These Thatcher policies, if they did not seriously damage it, at least went against the grain of British civil society. They possibly tended to undermine a traditionally more cohesive British collective identity. A possible indication of this is the fact that politics and economics in Britain during the 1980s and the first half of the 1990s were overwhelmingly perceived by practically all key actors as zero-sum games. Maybe the Thatcher government should not be blamed for this characteristic, which could have been present in British political culture for a very long time. In any case, zero-sum views of politics and economics may have been especially harmful to the Thatcher objective of regaining for Britain her previous role and glory as a world power[18].

On the other hand, the Thatcher government's withdrawal from many aspects of welfare care and social work helped to further develop a particular aspect of British civil society. This withdrawal opened the field to a much enlarged role for mutual aid and for philanthropic and charity associations. In some cases, the government suspended its active participation in welfare activities, but it provided financial support for the voluntary sector to take over these activities. Both deliberately and by default, the Thatcher policies in this area contributed to restore welfare to something similar in structure (although much more expensive in terms of national resources) to what it had been during Victorian times[19].

As compared with the Pinochet model in Chile, the Thatcher model in Britain was less successful in achieving its main objectives. It is possible that the balance of direct and indirect effects of the Chilean free-market policies, both before and after 1990, could have encouraged, rather than antagonised and weakened civil society (except that the new institutions are qualitatively different from the old ones). In contrast, the balance of effects of free-market policies on British civil society may have been the opposite. However, it would be a mistake, or at least an oversimplification, to conclude that Thatcher 'failed' BECAUSE she went against civil society, and Pinochet 'succeeded' BECAUSE he did not (voluntarily or more likely involuntarily). It is in fact equally possible to argue the contrary case, namely that Thatcher 'failed' precisely because she did not get rid of those institutions which were disfunctional to her model's objectives (or were no longer functional, despite having been so fifty, a hundred or even two hundred years before).

---

[18] Further evidence of the British zero-sum view of politics under Thatcher is present in the conclusions to several studies of Thatcherism, with their emphasis on the 'lessons for the left' (Jessop et al, 1988; Overbeek, 1990; Desai, 1994; Gamble, 1994). Some erosion of British civil society, and further concentration of power at the top, may have structural roots. They may be the inevitable consequence of the twin crises of the parliamentary and corporatist channels of interest intermediation (as discussed by Jessop et al, 1988; see Note 12). In that case it would be inaccurate and unfair to blame Mrs. Thatcher's subjective attitudes. In Chile, these 'lessons for the left' may be redundant, since the political left, especially that outside the centre-left government coalition, electorally disappeared (Lowden, 1995). Zero-sum views of politics do not seem to prevail any longer in Chile, where, at least according to some authors, there has been a 'shift from a politics based heavily on emotion, ideology, populism and charisma to a politics based more on reason, analysis, pluralism and informed judgment' (Puryear, 1994, p. 167; see also Marfan, 1994).

[19] 'The voluntary sector would provide assistance for unexpected events such as death, funeral expenses, maternity costs, loss of income through unforeseen circumstance, special needs (e.g. special clothing or furniture), easy term loans and so forth ... There are indeed many other services which could be provided by mutual aid such as health care, leisure, education and even protection from crime ...' (Davies, 1991, p. 155). A critic could point out that the fact that Davies chooses to list 'maternity costs' amongst 'unexpected events' shows just how unrealistic and old fashioned this particular version of 'Thatcherism' is. See also Riddell (1991, pp. 132-33).

10. Some Conclusions

The key difference in fundamental objectives between Pinochet and Thatcher could be summarised as follows: in Chile, FMOEP were used to unleash a 'capitalist revolution', whereas in Britain, their purpose was to help with 'putting the *Great* back into *Great Britain*'. Given that Thatcher's objectives were much more ambitious and difficult to achieve than Pinochet's, maybe the comparison is unfair. But it is not irrelevant or unnecessary. The similarities between the two models are superficial and the differences, fundamental. After 1990 both models (or many aspects of them) were adopted by their respective political opponents. The Chilean and British cases suggest that civil society and FMOEP affect each other, but the nature of these interactions in each case depends on particular characteristics of individual civil societies, and on specific details of the free-market economic model being applied[20].

Because of uncertainty, supporters and opponents of FMOEP reform may not be the same before and after reform implementation (Fernandez and Rodrik, 1991; Rodrik, 1993). A possible way of looking at the Pinochet and Thatcher experiments is by examining both their respective 'original sins', and the weaknesses, compromises and 'betrayals' that affected these experiences. The root of the 'original sins' is that, even if these models were theoretically pure, they needed to be implemented in a real world which was (and is) politically impure. The 'original sin' of the Chilean FMOEP experiment was that the free markets were introduced by an authoritarian military regime. In Britain the 'original sin' of the FMOEP experiment (which otherwise could have acquired the character of a 'revolution') was that it was attempted by the party of 'restoration'. When assessing what went wrong, or the differences in outcomes, all these questions need to be examined. Whether the 'original sin' was overcome, how, and how serious these weaknesses, compromises and 'betrayals' were, may all be significant.

After implementation, FMOEP won new supporters in Chile, but lost old supporters in thc UK. In Chile, possibly the worst 'betrayal' was the failure to privatise the state-owned copper mines, whereas in Britain it was the preservation of traditional privilege[21]. In Chile, even if the 'worst betrayal' was never amended, at least the 'original sin' was

[20] The different fate of these two experiments could perhaps be summarised using Harrison's (1985, 1992) appeal to cultural stability and cultural change. Chilean political culture was changed by a series of shocks, starting with the worsening political confrontation and polarisation in the late 1960s and early 1970s, which was then followed by many years of a repressive authoritarian regime. In Harrison's conceptual framework, British political culture may not have been functional to the reversal of long-term economic decline. If the Thatcher 'revolution' intended to change this, there cannot be any doubt that it failed. Alternatively, it is possible to argue that what failed in the British case was that the system of price - and other - incentives which was required in order to bring forward economic change was never introduced. Rather than political culture, it would be a question of different vectors of relative prices. However, no vector of relative prices could have achieved success in the absence of favourable institutions.

[21] Of course, these 'betrayals' are only the most important ones for the present discussion. There were many other weaknesses, compromises and 'betrayals' in both cases. In Chile, many instances could be mentioned of inadequate response by the government to rent seeking attempts by traditional and industrial crop farmers, some industrialists and members of professional associations, or several activities in the tertiary (services) sectors. British examples are some aspects of the European policy, and arbitrary tax exemptions for mortgages, company cars and so on. On the preservation of traditional privilege in Britain, see also note 13.

overcome by the fact that the political centre and left eventually adopted FMOEP, thus ending the spurious association between military dictatorship and free markets. In Chile, overcoming the 'original sin' was compatible, or at least not incompatible with 'betrayal' in the copper sector. Strengthening of the FMOEP model was done without threatening the privileges of copper miners or state bureaucrats in the copper sector. Even in the hypothetical case that copper had been privatised, and the interests of copper miners and bureaucrats had been seriously hurt, still this would not have put the FMOEP model in Chile at risk. The original FMOEP supporters were completely different from, and eventually old and new supporters became much more powerful than, those social sectors and groups which would have been negatively affected by a hypothetical privatisation of copper.

In Britain the 'original sin' could not be overcome, and 'betrayal' of extremely damaging proportions was unavoidable, because some of Thatcher's own supporters were the worst enemies of change. Thatcher could not have 'revolutionised' British society, even if she had wanted to. This was a vicious circle. Thatcherism could not win new supporters, in addition to keeping its original ones, because it failed to deliver on its original promise. But the main reason why it failed to deliver was that its implementation was far from complete, and implementation was not completed because political support for Thatcherism (as opposed to political support for Mrs. Thatcher) was insufficient. Avoiding 'betrayal' would have required a ruthless and uncompromising attack on the traditional privileges of precisely the perpetrators of the 'original sin'. And this was politically impossible (and maybe Mrs. Thatcher did not want it).

Thatcherism was defeated by two contradictions that proved impossible to overcome. There was a contradiction between decentralised decision making based on the operation of markets, and an ever more intrusive and overwhelming central government. There was also a contradiction between the claims of a meritocratic society, and the preservation of inherited privilege. Moreover, Thatcherism may have been based on a misunderstanding, or an oversimplification of Adam Smith. Thatcher's (or her advisers') view of Smith's was limited to the role of the market in the optimal allocation of resources, but it ignored Smith's emphasis on the role of the market in achieving a well-ordered and civilised society. Whether British institutions will react positively to shocks such as the 1997 vote, or Scottish devolution, or the reassessment of the monarchy, remains to be seen.

However, to end on a more positive note, some of the Thatcherite economic reforms have been adopted by the Labour Party and as such they may have acquired a permanent character. A new consensus, with much more emphasis on free markets than before, has replaced the old consensus of the 1960s and early 1970s. It is still early to see the ultimate implications of some of the changes brought about by FMOEP in the UK, but at least in some areas it is possible that Mrs. Thatcher may eventually repeat the Cid Campeador's feat after all. A period of faster economic growth may be forthcoming, which will be presided over by governments which have a positive interest in the strengthening and renewal of British civil society.

11. References

1. Adonis, A. (1995a), Ground shifts under the great poverty debate, *Financial Times*, 26 May.
2. Adonis, A. (1995b), Funding for quangos has doubled under Tories, *Financial Times*, 7 February.
3. Barnes, J. (1988), Birds of a feather: Britain and Chile, in *The Thatcher Years: Britain and Latin America*, London, Latin American Bureau.
4. Berlins, M. (1995), A case of material excess, *The Guardian*, 18 April.
5. Blitz, J. and Adonis, A. (1995), Reform of quangos ruled out by government, *Financial Times*, 7 February.
6. Bogdanor, V. (1995), Why the Lords must face up to change, *Financial Times*, 8 June.
7. Bosworth, B.P., Dornbusch, R. and Laban, R., eds. (1994), *The Chilean Economy: Policy Lessons and Challenges*, Washington, The Brookings Institution.
8. Brittan, S. (1993), The government as a 'stationary bandit', *Financial Times*, 26 August.
9. Business Monitor International (1997), *Chile 1997: In A Class Of Its Own*, London, BMI.
10. Business Monitor International (1999), Chile 1999: Country Forecast Report with Forecasts through End-2001, London, BMI.
11. Cobham, D. (1994), The Lawson boom: excessive depreciation versus financial liberalisation, Department of Economics, University of St. Andrews, Discussion Paper Series No. 9411.
12. Davies, S. (1991), Beveridge revisited: new foundations for tomorrow's welfare, in R. Haas and O. Knox, eds., *Policies of Thatcherism: Thoughts from a London Think-tank*, New York, University Press of America.
13. Desai, R. (1994), Second-hand dealers in ideas: think-tanks and Thatcherite hegemony, *New Left Review*, 203, January/February, pp. 27-64.
14. Doyle, C. and Weale, M. (1994), 'Do we really want an independent Central Bank?, *Oxford Review of Economic Policy*, 10, 3, Autumn, pp. 61-77.
15. Eagleton, T. (1995), When revolution was reasonable, *The Guardian*, 18 April.
16. *The Economist*, several numbers.
17. Edwards, S. and Edwards, A.C. (1991*), Monetarism and Liberalisation: The Chilean Experiment*, Chicago, University of Chicago Press.
18. Eisenstadt, S.N. (1993), Civil society and democracy in Latin America: some comparative observations, *Estudios Interdisciplinarios de America Latina y el Caribe*, 4, 2, July-December, pp. 27-37.
19. Espinal, R. (1992), Development, neoliberalism and electoral politics in Latin America, *Development and Change*, 23, 4, October, pp. 27-48.
20. Evans, E.J. (1997), *Thatcher and Thatcherism*, London, Routledge.

21. Fernandez, R. and Rodrik, D. (1991), Resistance to reform: status quo bias in the presence of individual-specific uncertainty, *American Economic Review*, 81, 5, December, pp. 1146-55.
22. *Financial Times*, several numbers.
23. Fontaine, A. (1988), *Los economistas y el Presidente Pinochet*, Santiago, Zig-Zag.
24. Gallagher, D. (1992), Chile: la revolucion pendiente, in B.B. Levine, ed., *El desafio neoliberal: el fin del tercermundismo en America Latina*, Bogota, Norma.
25. Gamble, A. (1994), The Free Economy and the Strong State: The Politics of Thatcherism, London, Macmillan, Second Edition.
26. Gilmour, I. (1992), *Dancing with Dogma: Britain under Thatcherism*, London, Simon and Schuster.
27. Glennerster, H. (1997), Indefensible to a degree, *Financial Times*, 18-19 October.
28. Goodman, A. and Webb, S. (1994), For richer, for poorer: the changing distribution of income in the UK, 1961-91, *Fiscal Studies*, 15, 4, November, pp. 29-62.
29. Haas, R. and Knox, O., eds. (1991*), Policies of Thatcherism: Thoughts from a London Think-tank*, New York, University Press of America.
30. Hachette, D. and Luders, R. (1992), *La privatizacion en Chile*, San Francisco, CINDE.
31. Hahn, F. (1988), On market economies, in R. Skidelsky, ed., *Thatcherism*, London, Chatto and Windus.
32. Harrison, L.E. (1985), *Underdevelopment Is a State of Mind: The Latin American Case*, Lanham, MD, University Press of America.
33. Harrison, L.E. (1992), Who Prospers? How Cultural Values Shape Economic and Political Success, New York, Basic Books.
34. Helm, D. (1994), British utility regulation: theory, practice, and reform, *Oxford Review of Economic Policy*, 10, 3, Autumn, pp. 17-39.
35. Hiscock, J. and Hojman, D.E. (1997), Social policy in a fast-growing economy: the case of Chile, *Social Policy and Administration*, 31, 4, pp. 354-70.
36. Hojman, D.E. (1990), Chile after Pinochet: Aylwin's Christian Democrat economic policies for the nineties, *Bulletin of Latin American Research*, 9, 1, pp. 25-47.
37. Hojman, D.E. (1993a), Chile: The Political Economy of Development and Democracy in the 1990s, London, Macmillan.
38. Hojman, D.E. (1993b), Non-governmental organisations (NGOs) and the Chilean transition to democracy, *European Review of Latin American and Caribbean Studies*, 54, June, pp. 7-24.
39. Hojman, D.E. (1994), The political economy of recent conversions to market economics in Latin America, *Journal of Latin American Studies*, 26, 1, February, pp. 191-219.
40. Hojman, D.E., ed. (1995a), *Neoliberalism with a Human Face? The Politics and Economics of the Chilean Model*, University of Liverpool, Institute of Latin American Studies, Monograph Series No. 20.
41. Hojman, D.E. (1995b), Chile under Frei (again): the first Latin American tiger - or just another cat?, *Bulletin of Latin American Research*, 14, 2, May, pp. 127-42.

42. Hojman, D.E. (1996), Poverty and inequality in Chile: are democratic politics and neoliberal economics good for you?, *Journal of Inter-American Studies and World Affairs*, 38, 2-3, pp. 73-96.
43. Hojman, D.E. (1997), *El Mercurio*'s editorial page ('La Semana Economica') and neoliberal policymaking in today's Chile, in W. Fowler, ed., *Ideologies and Ideologues in Latin America*, Westport, Greenwood.
44. Hojman, D.E. (1998), Culture and the human factor in Chile's economic 'miracle', in S. Adjibolosoo, ed., *International Perspectives on the Human Factor in Economic Development*, Westport, Praeger.
45. Hojman, D.E. (1999a), Latin American and Caribbean economies: an introduction, in *Central America, South America and the Caribbean*, London, Europa Publications, Eighth Edition.
46. Hojman, D.E. (1999b), Industrialist support for free trade: a case of turkeys voting for Christmas?, Liverpool Research Papers in Economics, Finance and Accounting 9907, Economics Dept., University of Liverpool.
47. Hojman, D.E. (1999c), Economic policy and Latin American culture: is a virtuous circle possible?, *Journal of Latin American Studies*, 31, 1, February, pp. 167-190.
48. Hojman, D.E. (2000a), Inequality, growth, and political stability: can income mobility provide the answers?, in N. Birdsall and C. Graham, eds., *New Markets, New Opportunities? Economic and Social Mobility in a Changing World*, Washington DC, Brookings Institution / Carnegie Endowment.
49. Hojman, D.E. (2000b), Institutions and development in Latin America: a story of roving bandits, rent seekers, and neoliberals, Liverpool Research Papers in Economics, Finance and Accounting 0007, Economics Dept., University of Liverpool.
50. Hojman, D.E. (forthcoming), The political economy of Chile's fast economic growth: an Olsonian interpretation, *Public Choice*.
51. Jessop, B., Bonnett, K., Bromley, S. and Ling, T. (1988), *Thatcherism*, Oxford, Basil Blackwell.
52. Johnson, C. (1991), *The Economy under Mrs. Thatcher, 1979-1990*, Harmondsworth, Penguin.
53. Kellner, P. (1994), The day Peter Lilley told the truth about market forces, *Sunday Times*, 4 December.
54. Kohli, A. (1994), Where do high growth political economies come from? The Japanese lineage of Korea's 'developmental state', *World Development*, 22, 9, September, pp. 1269-93.
55. Letwin, S.R. (1992), *The Anatomy of Thatcherism*, London, Fontana.
56. Leys, C. (1983), *Politics in Britain: An Introduction*, London, Heinemann.
57. Lowden, P. (1995), What is left of the left in Chile?, in D.E. Hojman, ed., *Neoliberalism with a Human Face? The Politics and Economics of the Chilean Model*, University of Liverpool, Institute of Latin American Studies, Monograph Series No. 20.
58. Macrae, N. (1995), Gloomy forecasts, *Sunday Times*, 22 January.

59. Marfan, M. (1994), Chile, paper presented to the OECD-IDB Forum on Latin America's Perspectives, Paris, 4 November.
60. Marr, A. (1996), Ruling Britannia: The Failure and Future of British Democracy, Harmondsworth, Penguin.
61. Matthews, K. and Minford, P. (1987), Mrs. Thatcher's economic policies 1979-87 (and Discussion by S. Nickell and E. Helpman), *Economic Policy, A Special Report: The Conservative Revolution.*
62. Minford, P. (1991), *The Supply Side Revolution in Britain*, Aldershot, Edward Elgar.
63. Mulgan, G. (1994), Democratic dismissal, competition, and contestability among the quangos, *Oxford Review of Economic Policy*, 10, 3, Autumn, pp. 51-60.
64. Muller, J.Z. (1993), *Adam Smith in his Time and Ours*, Princeton, Princeton University Press.
65. Neil, A. (1995a), The poor may be richer but the underclass is growing, *Sunday Times*, 28 May.
66. Neil, A. (1995b), The spy who revealed the rot in the core of Britain, *Sunday Times*, 30 April.
67. Neil, A. (1995c), A bigger school vandal than Shirley Williams, *Sunday Times*, 11 June.
68. Neil, A. (1996), *Full Disclosure*, London, Macmillan.
69. O'Donnell, G. and Schmitter, P.C. (1986), Transitions from Authoritarian Rule: Tentative Conclusions about Uncertain Democracies, Baltimore, John Hopkins University Press.
70. Olson, M. (1982), *The Rise and Decline of Nations*, New Haven, Yale University Press.
71. Overbeek, H. (1990), Global Capitalism and National Decline: The Thatcher Decade in Perspective, London, Unwin Hyman.
72. Owen, I. (1994), Lord Joseph: the principal architect of Thatcherism (Obituary), *Financial Times*, 12 December.
73. Oxhorn, P.D. (1995), *Organising Civil Society*, University Park, Pennsylvania, Pennsylvania State University Press.
74. Pimlott, B. (1995), Early Islington man, *Independent on Sunday*, 16 April.
75. Puryear, J.M. (1994), *Thinking Politics: Intellectuals and Democracy in Chile*, 1973-1988, Baltimore, John Hopkins University Press.
76. Rehder, R.R. and Thompson, J.K. (1994), Nissan UK: the Japanese transplant beachhead in Europe, *Columbia Journal of World Business*, 29, 3, Fall, pp. 92-106.
77. Riddell, P. (1991), *The Thatcher Era: And its Legacy*, Oxford, Basil Blackwell.
78. Rodrik, D. (1993), The positive economics of policy reform, *American Economic Review*, 83, 2, May, pp. 356-61 (AEA Papers and Proceedings).
79. Rogaly, J. (1995), Twisting tales of rapacity, *Financial Times*, 7 February.
80. Rutherford, M. (1995), In pursuit of independence, *Financial Times*, 29-30 April.
81. Segall, A. (1995), Unemployment statistics fail to tell the whole story, *Daily Telegraph*, 21 January.

82. Siedentop, L. (1995), Grim future for UK's ancient regime, *Financial Times*, 13 January.
83. Silva, E. (1993), Capitalist coalitions, the state, and neoliberal economic restructuring: Chile, 1973-88, *World Politics*, 45, 4, July, pp. 526-59.
84. Skidelsky, R., ed. (1988), *Thatcherism*, London, Chatto and Windus.
85. Smith, D. (1988), *Mrs. Thatcher's Economics*, Oxford, Heinemann.
86. Smith, D. (1995a), We've never had it so good - so why do we moan?, *Sunday Times*, 22 January.
87. Smith, D. (1995b), Tougher than the Tories - and Blair means it, *Sunday Times*, 28 May.
88. Snow, J. (1994), In praise of hymns and homework, *The Guardian*, 6 December.
89. Stelzer, I. (1995), No competitiveness please, we' re British, *Sunday Times*, 4 June.
90. Targett, S. and Kampfner, J. (1997), Blair steps into Oxbridge funding row, *Financial Times*, 24 October.
91. Taylor, M.P. (1995a), 'Lemon' measure of the value of executives, *Financial Times*, 4-5 February.
92. Taylor, M.P. (1995b), It's lemons that leave sour taste, *Daily Post*, 9 February.
93. Thatcher, M. (1993), *The Downing Street Years*, London, Harper-Collins.
94. Thatcher, M. (1994a), Margaret Thatcher en el Centro de Estudios Publicos, *Estudios Publicos*, 55, Winter, pp. 65-80.
95. Thatcher, M. (1994b), Los retos del siglo XXI, *Estudios Publicos*, 55, Winter, pp. 315-28.
96. Timmins, N. (1995), Living standards have risen among poor, study claims, *The Independent*, 25 May.
97. Tomlinson, J. (1996), Inventing 'decline': the falling behind of the British economy in the postwar years, *Economic History Review*, 49, 4, pp. 731-57.
98. Valdes, J.G. (1989), *La Escuela de Chicago: Operacion Chile*, Buenos Aires, Grupo Zeta.
99. Waisman, C. (1994), Civil society and economic liberalisation in the Southern Cone, paper presented to the Workshop on Civil Society and Political Economy in Latin America, Truman Institute, Hebrew University of Jerusalem, 22 December.
100. Weffort, F.C. (1992), New democracies, which democracies?, The Latin American Programme, Woodrow Wilson International Centre for Scholars, Washington DC, No. 198.
101. Wisecarver, D.L., ed. (1992), *El modelo economico chileno*, Santiago, CINDE.
102. Wooldridge, A. (1995), Eton for all - but on merit, *Sunday Times*, 21 May.
103. Young, H. (1991), *One of Us: A Biography of Margaret Thatcher*, London, Macmillan, Second Edition.
104. Zahler, R. (1992), Reunion con los profesionales de medios de comunicacion, *Boletin Mensual del Banco Central de Chile*, 778, December, pp. 3185-90.

Chapter 5

FOREIGN DIRECT INVESTMENT IN CHILE: AN EMPIRICAL ANALYSIS

Miguel D. Ramirez
Trinity College
Hartford, CT

1. INTRODUCTION

As a new millennium dawns, foreign direct investment (FDI) undertaken by transnational corporations (TNCs) has become one of the motor forces in the process of economic and financial integration of the global economy. The surge in FDI flows in recent years can be appreciated by the following figures: Between 1985 and 1990 these flows averaged $142 billion on an annual basis, while during the 1990-98 period alone thcy averaged $340 billion, or two and one half times more.[1] The acceleration in FDI flows during the 1990s has also been accompanied by an increasing proportion of these funds directed to the developing nations, including the countries of Latin America and the Caribbean. Historically, most FDI flows have been sent to developed countries, but during the decade of the nineties the share of total FDI channeled to developing countries, particularly Asia and Latin America, rose from 15 percent in 1990 to 37.2 percent in 1997. Latin America's share of FDI flows to developing countries in 1997 stood at an impressive 40.3 percent, mainly confined to Argentina, Brazil, Chile and Mexico.[2]

The renewed increase in FDI flows to these countries, including Chile, has been due to the relatively successful implementation of macroeconomic stabilization measures and

[1] Data obtained from Economic Commission for Latin America and the Caribbean (ECLAC), *La Inversion Extranjera and America Latina y El Caribe.* Santiago, Chile: United Nations, 1998, Tables A.1-A.4, pp. 179-81; and ECLAC, *Foreign Investment in Latin America and the Caribbean--1999 Report.* Santiago, Chile: United Nations, 2000, p. 9.

[2] Ibid.

structural reform programs. These have taken the form of privatization and debt conversion programs, the liberalization of the tradeable sector, and the removal of overly restrictive FDI legislation concerning the repatriation of profits, prior authorization of investments, and sectoral restrictions such as local content and export requirements. The relative stability of the region and the adoption of outward-oriented, market-friendly policies has reassured both foreign and domestic investors in Latin America's commitment to market-based reforms. Whether this state of affairs is sustainable in the long run is one of the more important challenges facing the people of Latin America, particularly in the wake of severe economic and financial crises that buffeted the region during the decade of the nineties. Notwithstanding major setbacks such as the 1994-95 Mexican Peso crisis, the 1997-98 Asian economic debacle, and the 1999 Brazilian devaluation, it is evident that for Latin American countries in desperate need of long-term capital and technology, FDI flows will play a strategic role in their successful adoption of an outward-oriented model of economic growth and development.

In view of the above, this paper examines the evolution, rationale, and impact of FDI flows in one of the more important countries of Latin America: Chile. The selection of Chile is based, in part, on the fact that it is one of the earliest countries in the region to adopt and implement neoliberal reforms, albeit at great social and political cost; in fact, Chile started this process of economic and financial liberalization following the military coup of 1973 and, in recent years, it has further liberalized its FDI regime by modifying Decree Law 600 and its debt capitalization mechanism (Chapter XIX of the Central Bank's Compensation of International Exchange Regulations). FDI flows in the Chilean case have been mainly channeled to traditional sectors such as mining and energy sectors. However, during the nineties, a significant proportion of these funds have been channeled to export-oriented manufacturing operations or to non-traditional sectors using innovative technological processes and managerial techniques. An analysis of FDI flows to Chile during the decade of the nineties should therefore provide valuable insights into the major determinants of FDI and their potential economic and institutional impact, particularly the capacity of FDI to transfer up-to-date technology and managerial know-how as well as its long-term effect on labor productivity growth.

The paper is organized as follows: First, it develops a conceptual framework of analysis that identifies some of the major economic determinants of FDI. Next, the paper gives an overview of FDI flows to Chile in terms of their magnitude, composition, and sectoral destination. Third, it examines the policies and institutional mechanisms used by the Chilean government to attract FDI to key sectors of the economy. Following the lead of the endogenous growth literature, the fourth section of the paper develops a simple model which assesses FDI's potential impact on private capital formation and labor productivity growth. The fifth section presents an empirical counterpart to the theoretical model developed in the previous section and, using cointegration analysis, proceeds to assess the impact of changes in the stock of FDI on labor productivity during the 1960-97 period. The concluding section summarizes the major arguments and offers some policy prescriptions for attracting FDI into the region and enhancing its positive direct and indirect effects.

2. ECONOMIC DETERMINANTS OF FDI

Most of the literature examining the economic determinants of FDI, particularly its empirical component, has been focused on the developed nations. This is not surprising given that most FDI flows undertaken by transnational corporations (TNCs) are directed to goods and financial markets in developed countries. It also reflects the greater availability, reliability, and richness of the time series data for these countries, as well as the methodological consistency in the generation, collection, and presentation of the data.

When it comes to the developing nations, including the countries of Latin America and the Caribbean, empirical studies of the determinants of FDI flows, as well as their potential and actual economic effects, are more difficult to obtain given the paucity and inconsistency of the data and the greater economic and institutional/legal heterogeneity present in these countries. However, in recent years, a number of studies focusing on the determinants of FDI flows to developing countries have arisen as a result of the renewed surge in net flows to these countries beginning in the second half of the 1980s and the availability of reliable and methodologically consistent time series data for a number of countries, including the countries of Latin America in general, and Chile in particular.

From a conceptual standpoint, perhaps the most complete explanation of why firms undertake cross-border investments has been provided by John Dunning (1981; 1988). He argues that these investments provide firms with three major comparative advantages. First, the establishment of TNC subsidiaries gives the parent firms exclusive ownership rights over patents, trademarks, commercial secrets and production processes, thereby effectively denying access to both foreign and domestic competitors. Second, they generate for TNC affiliates locational advantages that arise from direct access to growing markets and lower unit labor costs, reduced transportation and communication costs, avoidance of tariffs and non-tariff barriers, and last but not least, direct access to raw materials and intermediate products that are indispensable for the production of certain goods. Finally, Dunning draws upon thc seminal work of Ronald Coase (1937) and points to the advantages TNCs derive from internalizing certain operations because utilizing market mechanisms are relatively more burdensome and costly. For instance, many TNCs would rather establish a subsidiary abroad and assume directly the contractual and administrative costs associated with research, development, production, and marketing of a given product or service, thereby avoiding the transaction costs associated with leasing licenses and securing patents to undertake production or hiring the services of advertizing agencies to market and distribute their products.

Another major set of reasons for why TNCs engage in cross-border movements-- and one which is directly related to Dunning's locational advantage hypothesis-- can be traced to the international trade literature developed by Bhagwati and Srinivasan (1983) and Grossman and Helpman (1991). They point to the allocative and dynamic efficiency gains that arise from cross-border investments when TNCs are faced with significant differences in relative costs structures due to factor productivity differentials and institutional differences across countries. Institutional differences are of particular interest to this study because they seem to play a very important role in either attracting or discouraging FDI flows to developing countries. For example, countries that exhibit a greater degree of political and macroeconomic stability, the existence of well-defined and enforceable property rights when it comes to the transfer of technology, liberal legislation governing the remittance of profits and dividends, and limited or non-existent local content or export requirements tend, on average, to attract greater flows of FDI. However, from the standpoint of the host country the very factors which act as an incentive for FDI flows in the short run may prove detrimental to long-term economic development if they lead to a net outflow of resources, few backward and forward linkages, and limited transfers of technology and managerial knowhow.

In addition, FDI flows are likely to be attracted to developing economies that pursue an outward-oriented, "market-friendly" strategy of economic development, such as Chile has since 1974. In this connection, the privatization of state-owned enterprises in Chile during the eighties and nineties played an important role in attracting FDI flows to leading sectors such as banking, steel, mining, and telecommunications. Government policy can also enhance the attractiveness of FDI flows by ensuring the adequate provision of economic and social infrastructure in the form of paved roads, ports, airfields, relatively cheap energy supplies, and a well-educated and disciplined work force. In fact, FDI flows may themselves act as an important catalyst in contracting out the provision of these quasi-public goods and services to the private sector (both foreign and domestic) as has already taken place in several countries, including Chile and Mexico (see ECLAC, 1998; World Bank 1994 Report; and Agosin, 1995).

Last but not least, changes in a country's exchange rate policy play a key role in altering its relative attractiveness to net FDI inflows. Economists, however, are not entirely of one mind when it comes to the optimal exchange rate strategy to pursue. Some researchers contend that a policy that keeps the real exchange rate undervalued relative to that of its key investment partners is, *ceteris paribus*, likely to enhance FDI flows because it artificially reduces the unit costs of the country's factors of production and thus enables investors to make a significantly larger investment in terms of the domestic currency.[3] Provided that no abrupt, repeated, and/or large devaluations of the domestic currency ensue, the larger investment increases the foreign investor's return in terms of the domestic currency and, possibly, foreign currency. Therefore, the amount of FDI should increase with a devaluation of the domestic currency after a reasonable lag (see Hansen, Hurwitz, and Madow, 1953).

Other investigators warn that, if after the initial devaluation, the domestic currency continues to exhibit volatility and/or a sharp fall in its real value, it will not only generate strong inflationary pressures in structurally dependent economies such as those of Latin America, but also considerable uncertainty among investors about the level at which the real exchange rate will eventually settle. The economic and political costs associated with a rapidly falling (and volatile) currency are likely to discourage FDI and may force the monetary authorities to adopt either a fixed or crawling peg system. Once the pendulum

[3] The surge of FDI into the *maquiladora* sector in Mexico following the 1994 peso devaluation provides support for this assessment of the impact of changes in the exchange rate on FDI flows. See ECLAC,

swings in the other direction, the currency may experience a period of real overvaluation which, on the positive side of the ledger, preserves the dollar value of the remittances of profits and dividends back to the parent company, but on the negative side--particularly if the overvaluation is large and persistent--contributes to rising current account deficits, distorted relative prices, and dwindling international reserves that leave the monetary authorities with no alternative but to undertake a massive real devaluation. Obviously, this sequence of events has been played out far too often in the Latin American context and is likely to act as a strong disincentive to FDI flows in the long run. In light of the above, a stable and credible exchange rate policy that ensures that the country's real exchange rate does not become distorted relative to that of its key trading and investment partners is, perhaps, the best strategy for ensuring an adequate and sustained level of FDI flows over the long haul.

3. Overview of FDI Flows to Chile during the 1990s

The onset and aftermath of the debt crisis resulted in an absolute decrease in net FDI inflows to Latin America and the Caribbean during the first half of the 1980s, after which they began to increase steadily during the second half of the 1980s and posted a dramatic upward surge during the decade of the 1990s. FDI flows to the countries of Latin American rose from $8.4 billion in 1990 to 76.7 billion in 1998, or more than a ninefold increase (ECLAC, 2000, Table 1.7). The strength of these flows is revealed by the fact that despite the serious economic downturn in Mexico in 1995, and the associated "Tequila effect" which reduced FDI inflows relative to 1994, they staged a remarkable recovery during the following three years, easily surpassing the pre-crisis levels. In absolute terms, the major recipients of FDI flows have been concentrated in a few major countries of the region, in order of importance of the cumulative level of inflows during the 1990-98 period, they are Brazil, Mexico, Argentina, Chile and Venezuela. In this connection, the major supplier of FDI flows to Latin America during the decade of the nineties (and historically) has been the United States followed, in order of importance, by Great Britain, Japan, Germany, and France (see ECLAC, 1998, pp. 37-38)

In relative terms, Table 1 shows that the major countries of Latin America, including Chile, have exhibited a consistently strong record of attracting FDI inflows during the decade of the 1990s, never falling below 1.5 percent of their countries' respective GDPs, and beginning in 1994, FDI inflows have averaged 5.4 percent in the case of Chile. From an economic standpoint, the importance of these inflows is more fully appreciated by focusing on their evolution relative to these countries' gross fixed capital formation. Table 2 shows that throughout the decade of the 1990s, and particularly after 1993, FDI flows now represent more than 15 percent of their countries' gross fixed capital formation, and in the case of Chile during 1996 and 1997, they even reached one quarter of gross fixed capital formation--the highest figure among the major countries of the

---

Economic Survey of Latin America and the Caribbean, 1996-97. Santiago, Chile: United Nations, 1997, pp. 256-257.

region, or for that matter, the developing world. Although these figures in and of themselves do not constitute *prima facie* evidence against the null hypothesis that FDI inflows have had a limited impact on the gross capital formation of the countries of Latin America, they do represent a radical departure from the historical experience of these countries with FDI flows, and if sustained at their present levels, they may indeed play a key role in fostering capital formation and economic growth in these countries.

Table 1. Part A. Latin America: FDI Flows as a Percentage of Gross Fixed Capital Formation, 1990-96.

Country	1990	1991	1992	1993	1994	1995	1996
Argentina	9.28	8.94	10.90	5.81	5.45	8.66	8.05
Brazil	1.13	1.23	2.46	1.41	2.83	3.85	8.72
Chile	8.34	7.21	7.50	7.22	14.56	12.11	25.71
Colombia	7.46	6.94	9.66	9.13	12.44	15.19	22.89
Ecuador	5.69	6.21	6.34	16.18	16.70	13.70	12.57
Mexico	5.61	8.72	7.12	7.14	16.44	16.56	15.73
Peru	0.11	0.09	1.59	6.84	22.75	12.23	22.42
Venezuela	6.57	19.64	4.97	3.10	8.46	10.17	20.03
Annual Total[a]	**3.94**	**5.52**	**5.80**	**4.79**	**8.93**	**8.89**	**12.76**

Source: ECLAC, *La Inversion Extranjera en America Latina y El Caribe.* Santiago, Chile: United Nations, 1998, p. 38. [a]Total also includes Bolivia, Paraguay and Uruguay.

Part B. Chile and Mexico: FDI Flows adjusted for the Remittance of Profits and Dividends as a Percentage of Gross Fixed Capital Formation, 1990-96.

Country	1990	1991	1992	1993	1994	1995	1996
Chile[b]	4.75	-1.66	-2.10	0.75	6.01	10.89	16.71
Mexico	0.73	4.19	3.35	3.07	11.18	7.95	8.02

Source: ECLAC, *Economic Survey of Latin America and the Caribbean, 1996-97.* Santiago, Chile: United Nations, Table VIII. 4, p. 126. [a] Latin America total includes twelve other countries. [b]A negative value indicates that profits and dividend payments exceeded FDI inflows for that year, thereby diverting resources away from fixed capital formation.

One way of measuring the net contribution of FDI to private capital formation is to deduct from these inflows the repatriation of profits and dividends to the parent companies, often residing in the U.S. for many of the countries in question. Critics of FDI have long argued that, instead of increasing the investable resources of the host nation, FDI flows represent a net drain on the country's scarce resources because they generate substantial reverse flows in the form of remittances of profits and dividends to the parent companies, as well as through the widespread practice of intra-firm transfer pricing (see Cypher and Dietz, 1997; and Plasschaert, 1994). Partial support for this contention can be gauged from the figures displayed in Table 3 (Part A). They reveal that during the decade of the nineties, remittances of profits and dividends by Latin America and the Caribbean to the developed countries more than doubled between 1990 and 1996, from $7.0 billion to $15.5 billion. Not surprisingly, the lion's share was accounted for by Argentina, Brazil, Chile, Colombia, and Mexico.

Table 2: Latin America: Accumulated Stock of FDI, 1990-96 (Millions of 1990 dollars)

	1990	1991	1992	1993	1994	1995	1996
Argentina	11 058	12 371	15 388	16 869	18 131	20 979	23 668
Brazil	104 557	96 040	91 996	88 021	83 323	84 190	89 897
Chile	12 332	11 700	11 627	11 716	12 281	13 243	16 099
Colombia	3 500	3 423	3 701	4 023	5 042	6 818	9 305
Mexico	37 132	38 271	40 004	41 784	48 318	53 600	58 480
Peru	-416	-384	-233	394	3 052	4 665	7 460
Venezuela	3 903	5 374	5 628	5 654	5 889	6 497	7 753
Latin America[a]	**175 597**	**170 351**	**171 896**	**172 777**	**180 857**	**195 630**	**219 203**

Source: ECLAC (1998). [a]Total also includes Bolivia, Ecuador, Paraguay, and Uruguay.

Table 3. Sectoral Distribution of FDI Flows in Mexico, 1980-1996. (Millions of dollars)

Year	Total	Industry	Services	Commerce	Mining	Agriculture
1980	1 622.6	1 285.7	131.3	118.0	86.7	0.9
1985	1 729.0	1 165.8	453.3	109.5	18.0	0.4
1986	2 424.2	1 918.9	323.1	151.2	30.8	0.2
1987	3 877.2	2 400.5	1 433.9	21.2	48.8	15.2
1988	3 157.1	1 020.0	1 877.4	246.8	24.9	12.0
1989	2 499.7	982.3	1 102.3	386.3	9.5	19.3
1990	3 722.4	1 192.9	2 203.1	171.4	93.9	61.1
1991	3 565.0	963.6	2 138.0	387.5	31.0	44.9
1992	3 599.6	1 100.8	1 700.0	750.9	8.6	39.3
1993	4 900.7	2 320.5	1 730.7	759.9	55.1	34.5
1994	10 158.8	5 878.9	2 929.5	1 239.6	102.9	7.9
1995	7 613.3	4 294.0	2 307.9	923.5	79.0	8.9
1996	5 646.1	3 196.9	1 834.4	526.4	65.5	22.9

Source: Instituto Nacional de Estadistica, Geografia e Informatica (INEGI), *Anuario Estadistico de los Estados Unidos Mexicanos*. Aguascalientes, Mexico: INEGI, 1998, Table 17.23, p. 500.

In the case of Chile the remittances of profits and dividends quadrupled between 1990 and 1996 from $335 million to $1.4 billion. Relative to the inflows of FDI during the 1990-96 period, Chile's remittances of profits and dividends averaged 51.2 percent of total FDI flows over the same period. If we subtract profits and dividends from FDI flows and express the net figure as a proportion of fixed capital formation, it is evident from part B of Table 3 that the net contribution of FDI inflows to gross fixed capital formation to Chile, although increasing in recent years, is far less than that advertised in Table 2. In fact, in the case of Chile it was even negative during the 1992-93 period. One final point. It is likely that the net contribution of FDI would be further reduced if we could accurately measure the amount of capital that leaves the region as a result of the widespread practice of intra-firm transfer pricing to avoid taxes and restrictions on the repatriation of profits (see Plasschaert, 1994).

However, economic theory suggests that rather than focus on the flows of FDI to the countries of Latin America, it is theoretically more appropriate to concentrate on the accumulated stock of FDI, because it is the latter that ultimately determines the marginal productivity of private capital (and labor). Table 4 shows that for the selected Latin American countries the stock of FDI in constant 1990 dollars rose from $175.6 billion in 1990 to $219.2 billion in 1996. In relative terms this represents a 25 percent increase in the stock of FDI of these countries, an increase which is far greater than that of the entire "lost decade" of the 1980s. Focusing on Chile, it can be seen that there was a rapid increase in the stock of FDI after 1993, reaching an impressive level of $58.5 billion by year-end 1996. Endogenous growth theory suggests that if this accumulation of capital in the form of FDI has generated substantial spillover benefits, both of an indirect and direct nature as explained in the previous section, then the long-term positive contribution of this surge in FDI during the decade of the 1990s cannot be adequately measured by focusing solely on flow variables.

Table 4: Latin America: Accumulated Stock of FDI, 1990-96
(Millions of 1990 dollars)

	1990	1991	1992	1993	1994	1995	1996
Argentina	11 058	12 371	15 388	16 869	18 131	20 979	23 668
Brazil	104 557	96 040	91 996	88 021	83 323	84 190	89 897
Chile	12 332	11 700	11 627	11 716	12 281	13 243	16 099
Colombia	3 500	3 423	3 701	4 023	5 042	6 818	9 305
Mexico	37 132	38 271	40 004	41 784	48 318	53 600	58 480
Peru	-416	-384	-233	394	3 052	4 665	7 460
Venezuela	3 903	5 374	5 628	5 654	5 889	6 497	7 753
Latin America[a]	**175 597**	**170 351**	**171 896**	**172 777**	**180 857**	**195 630**	**219 203**

Source: ECLAC, **Economic Survey of Latin America and the Caribbean, 1996-97.** Santiago, Chile: United Nations, 1998. [a]Total also includes Bolivia, Ecuador, Paraguay, and Uruguay.

Another (indirect) and admittedly crude way of assessing the potential spillover benefits of FDI inflows to Chile is to examine their sectorial distribution during the second half of the 1980s and the decade of the 1990s (see Agosin, 1995). By determining which sectors in these two countries have been net recipients of foreign direct investment, the potential positive spillover effects associated with the transfer of technology and managerial knowhow can be indirectly inferred. For example, if the sectors receiving the FDI inflows are traditional sectors using highly standardized technology with relatively few forward and backward linkages to the rest of the economy, then one may presume that these spillover effects are minimal, while if FDI flows are channeled to "greenfield" investments or to non-traditional sectors using innovative technological processes and managerial techniques, then one may infer that these positive spillover benefits are on an average greater.

Table 5 below shows that under the Chilean government's Decree Law 600 (to be discussed in Section III), a significant proportion of the surge in FDI to the country during the second half of the 1980s and the decade of the 1990s was directed to traditional sectors such as cooper mining. The table also suggests that beginning in 1993 a significant share was channeled to financial services and industrial sectors based on natural resources and oriented toward exports, such as cellulose and paper and fish and sea products. Although FDI flows authorized under Decree Law 600 have been, by and large, confined to traditional sectors such as cooper mining, Table 5 also shows that those authorized under Chapter XIX of the debt conversion program implemented in 1985 but discontinued after 1991, granted only limited access to the traditional mining sector and were primarily directed to priority sectors in industry with an outward orientation, such as cellulose and paper and non-traditional agricultural and sea products. Despite the Chilean's governments attempt to promote non-traditional sectors by imposing restrictions on investments in the mining sector, the amount of FDI flows channeled through both Chapter XIX and DL 600 during the 1987-95 period were primarily confined to mining and traditional industries such as textiles, leather, and footwear where the country's has a comparative advantage based on low unit labor costs and natural resources.

Having said this, during 1996-98 period there was a marked decline in the proportion of FDI channeled to the mining sector and a concomitant increase in the share allocated to manufacturing and financial services, particularly banking. The FDI flows destined to the manufacturing sector were primarily in the form of minority shares in leading industrial sectors, such as Coca-Cola's acquisition of a 6 percent share in the country's largest bottling company, *Embotelladora Andina.* By contrast, those flows directed to the financial services sector involved majority acquisitions such as Spain's Banco Santander's 51 percent stake in Banco Osorno for $500 million.[4] Whether this represents a break with the past remains to be seen, but the very preliminary evidence presented above seems to suggest that a large portion of the FDI attracted to Chile in recent years has been confined to production processes characterized by low value added, which,

[4] For further detail see ECLAC, op. cit., pp. 45-47.

obviously, does not bode well for the long-term sustainability of the Chilean economic model.

Table 5. Chile: Johansen Cointegration Test, 1960-1997.

A. Series: ln(Y), lnL, LnK_f, and lnK_p.
Test assumption: No deterministic trend in the data.

Eigenvalue	Likelihood Ratio	5% Critical Value	1% Critical Value	No. of CE(s)
0.727	94.014	62.99	70.05	None
0.548	48.487	42.44	48.45	At most 1
0.340	20.679	25.32	30.45	At most 2
0.160	6.110	12.25	16.26	At most 3

Normalized Cointegrating Vector; coefficients normalized on lnY in parenthesis.

Vector	ln(Y)	lnL	lnK_f	lnK_p	Constant
1.	1.000	-1.493	-0.486	-2.465	33.518
	(7.450)	(4.358)	(8.210)		

B. Series: ln(Y/L), lnL, lnK_f, and lnK_p.
Test assumption: No deterministic trend in the data.

Eigenvalue	Likelihood Ratio	5% Critical Value	1% Critical Value	No. of CE(s)
0.727	94.014	62.99	70.05	None
0.548	48.487	42.44	48.45	At most 1
0.340	20.679	25.32	30.45	At most 2
0.160	6.110	12.25	16.26	At most 3

Normalized Cointegrating Vector; coefficients normalized on ln(Y/L) in parenthesis.

Vector	ln(Y/L)	lnL	lnK_f	lnK_p	Constant
2.	1.000	0.493	-0.486	-2.465	33.518
	(2.882)	(4.358)	(8.210)		

Note: t-ratios are in parenthesis.

4. Neoliberal Reforms and FDI Legislation

The rapid increase of foreign direct investment flows into Latin America during the decade of the eighties and nineties has been stimulated by dramatic changes in the region's legal-institutional environment associated with the implementation of liberalization, privatization, and deregulation programs. In general, there has been a major liberalization in the restrictions governing the remittances of capital and profits, as well as the introduction of new laws that grant TNCs essentially the same benefits and responsibilities as domestic firms (viz., national treatment). For example, in most countries there are no restrictions on the repatriation of profits and dividends, corporate taxes have been reduced or replaced by value-added taxes, and the need for prior authorization has been either eliminated entirely or restricted to a few "priority" sectors such as oil in Mexico or copper mining in Chile.

In this respect as in others, Chile was one of the first countries of Latin America to liberalize its foreign investment regulations. Beginning in 1974, the Pinochet regime promulgated Decree Law 600 which eliminated taxes or time limits on the repatriation of profits and dividends, granted foreign investors free access to the domestic market and the formal foreign exchange market, and finally, guaranteed TNC subsidiaries unvarying tariff and value-added tax rates for a 10-year period (see Agosin, 1995, p. 13; and ECLAC, 1998,). Between 1987 and 1994 Chile received a total of over $7 billion in FDI inflows under Decree Law 600. Most of the FDI that entered through this decree for the period in questions was channeled to the mining sector (59.3%) followed by industry (15.8%), and financial services (11.4%). Chilean economist Manuel Agosin points out that although certain elements of this law have been changed in subsequent years, its main provisions have remained the same and it remains the main mechanism for governing foreign direct investment in Chile.

Another important mechanism for attracting FDI to the country was introduced in 1985 under Chapter XIX of the debt capitalization program established by the Central Bank. As indicated in the previous section, it assumed an important role in reducing the country's external debt during the 1986-91 period, as well as in attracting foreign capital for financially distressed firms reeling from the country's economic debacle following the 1981-82 debt crisis. The debt conversion program permitted foreign investors to buy Chilean external debt at a heavy discount in secondary markets and exchange it at face value for a claim or title issued by the Central Bank in domestic currency. The titles were then sold in the Chilean financial market or exchanged directly for stock certificates in government-approved enterprises. As opposed to Decree Law 600, there were time limits on the remittance of profits and capital as well as restrictions in the use of these titles for investment purposes in copper mining, but the implicit subsidy contained in the debt conversion program was so large that it more than offset the cost of these mild restrictions. In fact, critics of the program, such as Ricardo French-Davis (1990) and Patricio Meller (1993), contend that between 1985 and 1990 the implicit subsidy in the debt conversion program amounted to more than 46 percent of the total value of the investments undertaken. They also argue that many of these investments would have been made anyway, so that the Chapter XIX discount amounted to no more than a foreign exchange gift to investors.

In any event, Table 5 above shows that under this particular modality Chile's ability to attract FDI flows was relatively successful given that during the 1986-90 period the debt conversion mechanism was responsible for more than one-third of Chile's total FDI flows. The relative success of the program was not only confined to further stimulating FDI flows into the country, but as pointed out in the previous section, it also played an important role in channeling a significant proportion of these funds to high priority non-traditional sectors in agriculture, forestry and fishing, manufacturing, financial services, and mining.

In this connection, Agosin (1995) presents empirical results for a regression model that tries to explain the variation in FDI flows to Chile during the 1975-92 period. He finds that the level of real GDP in constant dollars (a proxy for market size) has a positive and statistically significant effect on FDI flows (coefficient = 0.02, t-ratio= 2.12), while the depreciation of the real exchange rate has a positive impact on FDI flows (coefficient=8.23, t-ratio=1.90). From an institutional standpoint, he finds that the adoption of the debt conversion program (Chapter XIX), proxied by a dummy variable, had a positive and statistically significant impact on FDI flows (coefficient= 0.04, t-ratio= 4.79). The variables included in the model, adjusted for degrees of freedom, explained about 89 percent of the variation in FDI flows to Chile, and the D.W. stat (=2.07) suggested that positive auto-correlation was not a major problem in the sample.[5]

The debt conversion program also played an important role in Chile's re-privatization process after 1985. According to Meller (1993), foreign investors were encouraged to use external debt paper to acquire shares in the privatized firms. As indicated above, this process was not only subsidized by the Chilean government, but also by a favorable exchange rate and the underpricing of shares of the traditional State-owned enterprises in telecommunications, the national airlines, electricity generation, and water and sanitation facilities. In total, between 1985 and 1991, the debt conversion program was responsible for close to 50 percent of foreign investment in the shares of privatized enterprises and, as pointed out above, it contributed to reducing significantly external debt. In this connection, the IFC (1996) reports that during the 1988-94 period FDI from privatization in Chile amounted to close to $400 million or 31 percent of total privatization revenues, and that it was directly involved in the privatization of 21 enterprises.[6]

[5] For further details see equation (1a), p. 121.

[6] For further details see Lawrence Bouton and Mariusz A. Sumlinski, **Trends in Private Investment in Developing Nations: Statistics for 1970-95.** Washington, D.C.: International Finance Corporation, 1996, pp. 6-12.

5. THE IMPACT OF FDI FLOWS ON ECONOMIC GROWTH AND DEVELOPMENT

In standard economic theory net FDI inflows to developing countries increase their stock of capital and technological knowhow which, in turn, raises the host country's labor productivity and incomes, a process that eventually translates into higher levels of output and potential tax revenues--the latter derived from taxing the foreign investment income generated by TNCs. However, FDI flows may have a negative effect on the growth prospects of a country if they give rise to substantial reverse flows in the form of remittances of profits and dividends and/or if the TNCs obtain substantial tax or other concessions from the host country. These negative effects would be further compounded if the expected positive spillover effects from the transfer of technology are minimized or eliminated because of overly restrictive intellectual property rights and/or prohibitive royalty payments and leasing fees charged by the TNCs for the use of these "intangibles."

Following the lead of De Mello (1997) and Barro (1995), the externality (positive or negative) associated with incorporating the stock of FDI can be explicitly modeled via an augmented Cobb-Douglas production function of the following form:

$$Y = A\, f\,[L, K_p\,, E] = A\, L^{\alpha}\, K^{\beta}\, E^{(1-\alpha-\beta)} \tag{1}$$

where Y is real output, K_p is the private capital stock, L is labor, and E refers to the externality generated by additions to the stock of FDI. α and β are the shares of domestic labor and private capital respectively, and A captures the efficiency of production. It is also assumed that α and β are less than one, such that there are diminishing returns to the labor and capital inputs.

The externality, E, can be represented by a Cobb -Douglas function of the type:

$$E = [L, K_p, K_f^{\gamma}]^{\theta} \tag{2}$$

where γ and θ are, respectively, the marginal and the intertemporal elasticities of substitution between private and foreign capital. Let $\gamma > 0$, such that a larger stock of FDI generates a positive externality to the economy. If $\theta > 0$, intertemporal complementarily prevails and, if $\theta < 0$, additions to the stock of FDI crowd out private capital over time and diminish the growth potential of the host country.

Combining equations (1) and (2), we obtain,

$$Y = A\, L^{\alpha+\theta(1-\alpha-\beta)}\, K_p^{\beta+\theta(1-\alpha-\beta)}\, K_f^{\gamma\theta(1-\alpha-\beta)} \tag{3}$$

A standard growth accounting equation can be derived by taking logarithms and time derivatives of equation (3) to generate the following dynamic production function:

$$g_y = g_A + [\alpha + \theta(1\text{-}\alpha\text{-}\beta)]g_L + [\beta + \theta(1\text{-}\alpha\text{-}\beta)]g_{Kp} + [\gamma\theta(1\text{-}\alpha\text{-}\beta)]g_{Kf} \tag{4}$$

where g_i is the growth rate of $i = Y, A, L, K_p$, and K_f. Equation (4) states that (provided γ and $\theta > 0$) additions to the stock of FDI will augment the elasticities of output with respect to labor and capital by a factor $\theta(1-\alpha - \beta)$.

6. Empirical Model and Results

In the estimation of equation (4) above, proxies are often used for variables such as the labor force and/or the stocks of private capital and FDI (see Aschauer, 1989 and 1990; Caceres, 1998; Calderon, 1988; Cardoso, 1993; Greene and Villanueva, 1991; Lin, 1994; Nazmi and Ramirez, 1997; Solimano, 1990). For example, population data is used rather than labor force data, or investment data (as a proportion of GDP) is substituted for capital stock data. Alexander (1994) has shown, however, that models using these proxies have to impose unduly restrictive assumptions (e.g., such as a fixed capital-output ratio) or unrealistic assumptions (a constant labor force participation rate) that generate both misspecified relationships and significant measurement errors. Part of the explanation for this common practice among researchers in the economic development field resides in the poor quality of existing data for private investment spending and/or the unavailability of labor force data and FDI flows over a sufficiently long period of time.

However, in the case of Chile we are fortunate to have now a sufficiently long (and official) time series data set (extending back to the decade of the sixties) for both private and public investment, as well as FDI flows. Using a perpetual inventory method, capital stock data can therefore be generated for the variables in question. Chile's National Institute of Statistics (INE) has also published official data on the labor force for the period under review. This study thus extends previous empirical work by estimating an empirical counterpart of the growth (labor productivity) model in equation (4) for the 1960-1997 period.

The most general formulation of the dynamic production function is given below,

$$\Delta y_t = \alpha + \beta_1 \Delta l_{t-i} + \beta_2 \Delta k_{pt-i} + \beta_3 \Delta k_{ft-i} + \beta_4 \Delta k_{gt-i} + \beta_5 D_1 + \beta_6 D_2 + \beta_7 D_3 + \beta_8 \Delta TOT + \epsilon \quad (9)$$

lower case letters denote natural logarithms, and Δ is the difference operator; y represents the natural log of real GDP (1977 pesos); l, as indicated above, refers to the natural log of the labor force; k_p, k_f and k_g denote, respectively, the natural log of the stocks of private capital, FDI capital, and public capital (1977 pesos); D_1 is a dummy variable that equals 1 for the crises years of 1973, 1975 and 1982-83 and 0 otherwise, while D_2 equals 1 for debt-led growth years of 1978-81; D_3 is set equal to 1 for the 1987-97 period (acceleration of real economic growth associated with the Chilean government's decision to pursue vigorously an outward-oriented strategy of economic development beginning in 1986-87); given the historical importance of copper exports in the Chilean economy, the regression also includes a terms of trade variable, ΔTOT, which is defined as the change in the terms of trade (in 1977 pesos) as a proportion of GDP. An increase in ΔTOT

denotes an improvement in Chile's terms of trade (see Ffrench-Davis and Munoz, 1992). Finally, ϵ is a normally distributed error term.

Economic data (including foreign direct investment) used in this study were obtained from official government sources such as the *Instituto Nacional de Estadisticas* (various issues) and the Banco Central de Chile, *Memoria Anual* (various issues).[7] Private and public investment data for Chile have been obtained from the International Finance Corporation, *Trends in Private Investment in Developing Countries: Statistics for 1970-95* [1996]. The relevant stock data was generated using a standard perpetual inventory model of the following form,

$$K_t = K_{t-1} + I_t - \delta K_{t-1} \tag{10}$$

where K_{t-1} is the stock of capital at time t-1, I_{t-1} is the flow of gross investment during period t, and δ is the rate at which the capital stock depreciates in period t-1. In this study the initial stocks of private (public) and foreign capital were estimated by aggregating over five years of gross investment (1956-1960), assuming an estimate of the rate of depreciation of 5 percent. To ensure the robustness of the econometric results, other estimates of the rate of depreciation were used (10 percent), as well as different estimates of the initial capital stock (e.g., summing over 4 and 6 years), but the results were not altered significantly.

The coefficients of equation (9) represent the annual percentage change in real GDP associated with a respective percentage change in the variables in question. The dependent variable in this study was estimated as a labor productivity growth equation by subtracting the percentage change in the labor force from the percentage change in GDP.[8] Defining the dependent variable in this manner reverses the expected sign of the labor variable because of diminishing returns to the labor input. The sign of β_1 is anticipated to be positive in the GDP growth rate formulation while, as indicated above, it is expected to be negative in the labor productivity growth specification. β_2 is expected to be positive, while the signs of β_3 and β_4 can be either positive or negative depending on whether accretions in the stocks of foreign and public capital, respectively, complement or substitute for private capital formation. The public capital stock variable was included as an argument because investments in economic infrastructure such as roads, bridges and ports are likely to increase the marginal productivity of both private domestic and foreign capital, thus stimulating economic growth and labor productivity.[9] β_5 is anticipated to

[7] Investment and FDI data was cross-checked with that found in the International Finance Corporation, *Trends in Private Investment in Developing Countries: Statistics for 1970-95* [1996] and no significant differences were discerned.

[8] In this study the coefficients on labor and private capital are neither constrained to sum to unity nor constrained to equal their factor shares because growth rate elasticities of the dynamic production function will only equal their factor shares if factor markets are perfectly competitive. This is an untenable assumption for a developing country such as the Chilean one. In addition, given that the public capital stock is included as an additional factor of production, it is not clear how its factor share should be estimated. For further detail see Coe and Moghadam (1993).

[9] There is now a vast literature that addresses the question of whether public investment enhances private investment and economic growth. The results have been mixed, with some researchers finding support for

have a negative sign for obvious reasons. β_6 is expected to be positive because of the high rates of economic growth associated with the short-lived lending boom of 1978-81. β_7 is also expected to have a positive sign because the average annual growth rate in Chile accelerated with the return of foreign direct investment and the expansion of exports during the 1988-94 period. Finally, β_8 is expected to have a positive sign because an improvement in the TOT variable, *ceteris paribus*, stimulates economic growth in an open economy such as Chilean one.[10]

Results

It is well established that (macro) time series data such as the ones used in this study tend to exhibit either a deterministic and/or stochastic time trend and are therefore non-stationary; i.e., the variables in question have means, variances, and covariances that are not time invariant. According to Engle and Granger (1987), the direct application of OLS or GLS to non-stationary data produces regressions that are misspecified or spurious in nature. These regressions tend to produce performance statistics that are inflated in nature, such as high R^2's and t-statistics, which often lead investigators to commit a high frequency of Type I errors (Granger and Newbold, 1974).[11] Consequently, this study tested the variables in question for a unit root (non-stationary) by using an Augmented Dickey-Fuller test (ADF) (Dickey-Fuller, 1981) with a constant and deterministic trend.

Table 6 (part A) below presents the results of running ADF test (one lag) on the variables in logarithmic form with a deterministic trend.[12] The results indicate that the null hypothesis of non-stationary cannot be rejected for any of the variables in level form with a deterministic trend, suggesting that the variables in question do not exhibit a deterministic time trend throughout the period under review. In other words, the common practice of detrending the data by a single trend line will not render the data in question stationary because the trend line itself may be shifting over time (see Wojciech and Deadman, 1997). When the ADF test is applied to these variables in first differences

---

the complementarity hypothesis (see Aschauer, 1989; Ram, 1986; and Ramirez, 2000), while others such as Sundaran and Tahkur (1980), Nazmi and Ramirez (1997), and Cruz and Teixeira (1999) report substitution of private investment by public investment.

[10] The government consumption variable was not included in the estimation because of the inherent difficulty in interpreting its potential impact on labor productivity. The difficulty resides in the fact that not only does it include human capital investments such as expenditures on health and education (which are likely to enhance labor productivity), but also a substantial portion is devoted to expenditures on public wages and salaries (which are likely to have a negative effect). The available data from the Central Bank of Chile is not sufficiently disaggregated to generate a human capital variable via the perpetual inventory model.

[11] This study estimated the labor productivity (and output) functions in level form and the results displayed very high R^2's and F statistics, as well as low D.W. statistics. These results are typical of spurious regressions. The results are available upon written request from the author.

[12] The order of the lag length was determined by applying both the Akaike Information Criterion (AIC) and the Schwartz Bayesian Criterion (SBC). Lower values for these performance statistics indicate a better fit to the data. Between the two criteria, the SBC is more reliable because the AIC is known to be biased towards choosing an over-specified model. For all the variables in this study, the ADF tests with one lag showed the lowest value for both the AIC and SBC criteria. The results are available from the author upon written request.

under the assumption of a constant and deterministic time trend, most of the variables become stationary at the five percent level of significance (and in one case at the 10 percent level).

Table 6. Part A: Chile: Unit Root Tests for Stationarity with constant and time trend, Sample Period 1960-97.

Variables	Levels	First Difference	5% Critical Value[1]	1% Critical Value
ln(Y)	-1.26	-3.92**	-3.54	-4.25
ln(Y/L)	-0.98	-3.83**	-3.54	-4.25
LnL	-1.31	-3.65**	-3.54	-4.25
LnK_f	-1.27	-3.67**	-3.54	-4.25
LnK_p	-2.48	-3.99**	-3.54	-4.25
lnK_g	-2.47	-2.91*	-3.54	-4.25
TOT	-2.21	-4.87***	-3.54	-4.25

[1]MacKinnon critical values for rejection of hypothesis of a unit root. *, **, and *** denote significance at the 10, 5 and 1 percent levels, respectively.

Part B. Chile: Unit Root Tests for Stationarity with constant only, Sample Period 1960-97.

Variables	Levels	First Difference	5% Critical Value[1]	1% Critical Value
ln(Y)	0.39	-3.83***	-2.95	-3.64
ln(Y/L)	-1.16	-3.72***	-2.95	-3.64
lnL	-0.29	-3.71***	-2.95	-3.64
lnK_f	0.85	-2.65*	-2.95	-3.64
lnK_p	0.67	-3.08**	-2.95	-3.64
lnK_g	-1.96	-3.87***	-2.95	-3.64
TOT	-1.64	-4.95***	-2.95	-3.64

[3]Same as above.

Table 6 (part B) also presents the results of running an ADF test (one lag) for the variables in both level and differenced form under the assumption of a stochastic trend only.[13] It can be readily seen that all the variables in level form are non-stationary; i.e., they appear to follow a random walk with (positive) drift (see Nelson and Plosser, 1982). In the case of first differences, however, the null hypothesis of non-stationarity is rejected

[13] A stochastic trend is one where the random component of the series itself, say variable x_t, contributes directly to the long run pattern of the series, either upward or downward. However, in the case of a deterministic trend the deviations from the non-stationary mean over time are quickly corrected. Thus, the former process is usually referred to as a random walk with drift, either positive or negative, and it is captured by including a constant in the DF or ADF tests. It is also possible for the variable in question to display both a stochastic and deterministic trend process over time. For further details see Charemza and Deadman, (1997, pp. 84-92).

for all variables (except one) at least at the 5 percent level.[14] Thus, the evidence presented above suggests that the variables in question follow primarily a stochastic trend as opposed to a deterministic one, although the possibility that for given sub-periods they follow a mixed process cannot be rejected.

Table 6a. Mexico: Error Correction Model; Dependent Variable is:(ΔlnY_t), 1963-95.

Variables	OLS Regressions					
	(1)	(2)	(3)	(4)	(5)	(6)
Constant	-0.09	-0.04	0.01	-0.04	-0.01	-0.05
	(-2.84)**	(-1.44)*	(0.34)	(-4.28)**	(-0.23)	(-2.83)**
ΔlnL_t	0.48	0.32	0.27	0.31	0.21	0.33
	(2.45)**	(3.32)**	(1.89)**	(1.98)**	(1.70)**	(2.83)**
ΔlnK_{ft-3}	---	---	0.06	---	---	---
			(1.95)**			
ΔlnK_{ft-4}	0.09	0.08	---	---	0.11	---
	(1.81)**	(1.73)**			(2.77)**	
ΔlnK_{ft-5}	---	---	---	0.11	---	0.13
				(2.27)**		(2.11)**
ΔlnK_{pt}	1.60	1.07	0.81	1.04	0.92	1.04
	(4.13)**	(4.42)**	(5.31)**	(6.37)**	(3.70)**	(5.46)**
ΔlnX_{t-1}	---	0.04	---	---	---	0.06
		(1.59)*				(1.93)**
ΔlnC_{gt-1}	---	---	---	---	-0.04	---
					(-1.43)*	
ECt_{t-1}	-0.73	-0.74	-0.65	-0.78	-0.53	-0.78
	(-2.20)**	(-5.65)**	(-6.56)**	(-7.44)**	(-6.02)**	(-6.95)**
DUM1	---	-0.04	-0.03	-0.03	-0.03	-0.04
		(-3.93)**	(-4.14)**	(-5.17)**	(-2.78)**	(-5.75)**
DUM2	---	0.05	0.06	0.06	0.06	0.05
		(4.30)**	(5.16)**	(4.56)**	(4.99)**	(3.94)**
T	---	-0.001	-0.001	---	---	---
		(-1.58)*	(-1.42)*			
Adj R^2	.68	.86	.83	.85	.84	.87
S.E.	0.03	0.02	0.02	0.02	0.02	0.01
D.W.	1.92	1.97	1.96	1.85	2.03	1.86
AR(1)	0.30	0.40*	0.25*	0.49*	---	0.51*

Note: same as in previous table.

[14] This study also performed unit root tests on the relevant variables using the Phillips-Perron (PP) test regression. The rationale for using this (nonparametric) procedure resides in the fact that, as opposed to the ADF test, it controls for higher-order serial correlation of unknown form. The results (available upon request) are consistent with those generated by the ADF test. See Phillips and Perron (1988) for further details.

Having shown that the variables are integrated of order one, I(1), it is necessary to determine whether there is at least one linear combination of these variables that is I(0). In other words, does there exist a stable and non-spurious (cointegrated) relationship among the regressors in each of the relevant specifications? This was done by using the cointegration method first proposed by Johansen (1988) and Johansen and Juselius (1990). The Johansen method was chosen over the one originally proposed by Engle and Granger (1987) because it is capable of determining the number of cointegrating vectors for any given number of non-stationary series (of the same order), its application is appropriate in the presence of more than two variables, and more important, Johansen (1988) has shown that the likelihood ratio tests used in this procedure (unlike the DF and ADF tests) have well-defined limiting distributions.

The presence of a cointegrating relationship among the selected variables in level form means that an error correction (EC) model can be estimated; viz., a model that combines both the short-run properties of economic relationships in first difference form as in equation (9) above, as well as the long-run information provided by the data in level form. EC models thus enable the researcher to estimate the speed of adjustment back to the long-run (stable) condition among the variables. In this connection, investigators who have applied OLS estimation techniques to different specifications of equations (4) or (8) above, without including the lagged residual of the cointegrating equation, have unwittingly ignored crucial information about the long-run production relationship--information which can only be extracted from the data in level form (see Engle and Granger, 1987).

Application of the Johansen procedure generated results (available upon request) which show that the null hypothesis of no cointegrating vector can be rejected at least at the one percent level, thus suggesting the presence of at least one cointegrating equation from which residuals (EC terms) can be obtained to measure the respective deviations between the current level of output (labor productivity) and the level based on the long-run relationship. .

The information provided by the L.R. tests was used to generate the EC models presented in Table 7 below. To conserve space, the table presents results only for the labor productivity growth rate relationship. The results suggest that the immediate impact of changes in the growth rate of the private capital stock are positive and statistically (and economically) significant, while contemporaneous changes in employment growth have a negative impact on the growth rate in labor productivity. The public capital stock variable also has a positive and statistically significant effect when lagged two to three periods. Turning to the foreign private capital stock variable, it can be seen that this variable has a positive and statistically significant effect when lagged four and five periods.[15] This result-- as well as the one for the public capital stock-- is not surprising because FDI-induced positive externalities in the form of a greater transfer of technology and managerial knowhow are likely to impact labor productivity with a considerable lag. The dummy variables in eqs. (2) -(5) have the anticipated signs and they are statistically significant, while, as expected, the change in the terms of trade effect (as a proportion of

[15] Again, the optimal order for the lag length was determined by using the AIC and SBC criteria.

GDP) has a positive and statistically significant effect. The relative fit and efficiency of the EC regressions is quite good and, as the theory predicts, the EC terms are negative and statistically significant, suggesting, as in equation (4), that a deviation from long-run labor productivity growth this period is corrected by about 33 percent in the next year. Finally, the results in Table 7 are robust to the exclusion and inclusion of the dummy variables.

Table 7. Chile: Error Correction Model; Dependent Variable is:($\Delta lnY_t - \Delta lnL_t$), 1960-97.

Variables	OLS Regressions				
	(1)	(2)	(3)	(4)	(5)
Constant	-6.57	-4.11	-7.00	-5.84	-6.21
	(-2.74)**	(-1.76)*	(-3.22)***	(-3.15)***	(-2.07)**
ΔlnL_t	-0.49	-0.43	-0.27	-0.36	-0.47
	(-2.07)**	(-2.44)**	(-1.70)*	(-2.56)**	(-1.85)**
ΔlnK_{ft-4}	---	---	---	---	0.15
					(1.67)*
ΔlnK_{ft-5}	0.16	0.16	0.17	0.12	---
	(2.59)**	(2.33)**	(2.59)**	(2.27)**	
ΔlnK_{pt}	0.77	0.51	0.55	0.55	---
	(5.75)***	(4.51)***	(4.62)***	(4.37)***	
ΔlnK_{gt-3}	---	---	---	---	0.66
					(2.10)**
ΔlnK_{gt-3}	0.43	0.55	0.74	0.49	---
	(2.42)**	(2.68)***	(4.39)***	(2.84)***	
Ect_{t-1}	-0.35	-0.28	-0.35	-0.33	-0.34
	(-4.19)***	(-2.33)**	(-2.13)**	(-3.97)***	(-4.41)***
DUM1	---	-5.46	-5.05	-4.23	-5.22
		(-2.54)**	(-2.39)**	(-2.32)**	(-3.27)***
DUM2	---	---	4.31	3.43	---
			(4.54)***	(3.81)***	
DUM3	---	---	---	2.11	---
				(2.19)**	
TOT	0.21	0.37	0.26	0.22	0.21
	(1.50)*	(1.98)**	(2.57)**	(2.18)**	(1.70)*
Adj R^2	.66	.79	.80	.84	.79
S.E.	4.10	3.44	3.28	2.98	3.29
D.W.	1.88	1.85	1.88	1.78	1.78
AR(1)	0.33*	0.36*	0.52**	0.35*	0.40**

Note: same as in previous table. The t-ratios are in parenthesis.

The EC models were also used to track the historical data on labor productivity growth in Chile. Table 8 below presents selected Theil inequality coefficients obtained from the historical simulations of the productivity growth equations. As can be seen from the Table, they are well below the threshold value of 0.3, e.g., 0.237 and 0.213 for equations (2) and (4), respectively (see Theil, 1966). Finally, Table 8 reveals that sensitivity analysis on the coefficients showed that changes in the initial or ending period did not alter the predictive power of the selected models (or, for that matter, any of the models run in this study). Figure 1, corresponding to equation (4) in Table 7, provides visual evidence of the models' ability to track the turning points in the actual series. (CLPGR) refers to the actual forecast and (CLPGRF) denotes the forecast.) It also highlights the Chilean economy's highly variable and, at best, modest increase in labor productivity for the period under review. Part of the explanation for this lackluster performance resides in the country's tumultuous economic and political history, particularly during the seventies and early eighties. However, beginning in 1985 and following the return to civilian rule, there is evidence of a modest upward trend in labor productivity, although it is too early to tell whether this represents a permanent break with the past.

Table 8. Chile: Forecast Evaluation for Error Correction Models.

	Equation (2)	**Equation (4)**
Sample: 1967 1997		
Root Mean Squared Error (RMS)	2.7886	2.5391
Mean Absolute Error (MAE)	2.2420	1.9359
Theil Inequality Coefficient (TIC)	0.2369	0.2136
Bias Proportion (BP)	0.0005	0.0001
Variance Proportion (VP)	0.0172	0.0094
Covariance Proportion (CP)	0.9822	0.9904
Sample: 1967 1991		
RMS	2.9627	2.7434
MAE	2.2292	2.1005
TIC	0.2482	0.2208
BP	0.0067	0.0066
VP	0.0736	0.0131
CP	0.9200	0.9801
Sample: 1970 1997		
RMS	2.6669	2.0032
MAE	2.0791	1.5017
TIC	0.2187	0.1610
BP	0.0114	0.0000
VP	0.0386	0.0210
CP	0.9501	0.9800

Note: Forecast evaluation estimates generated with EVIEWS 3.0.

Figure 1:

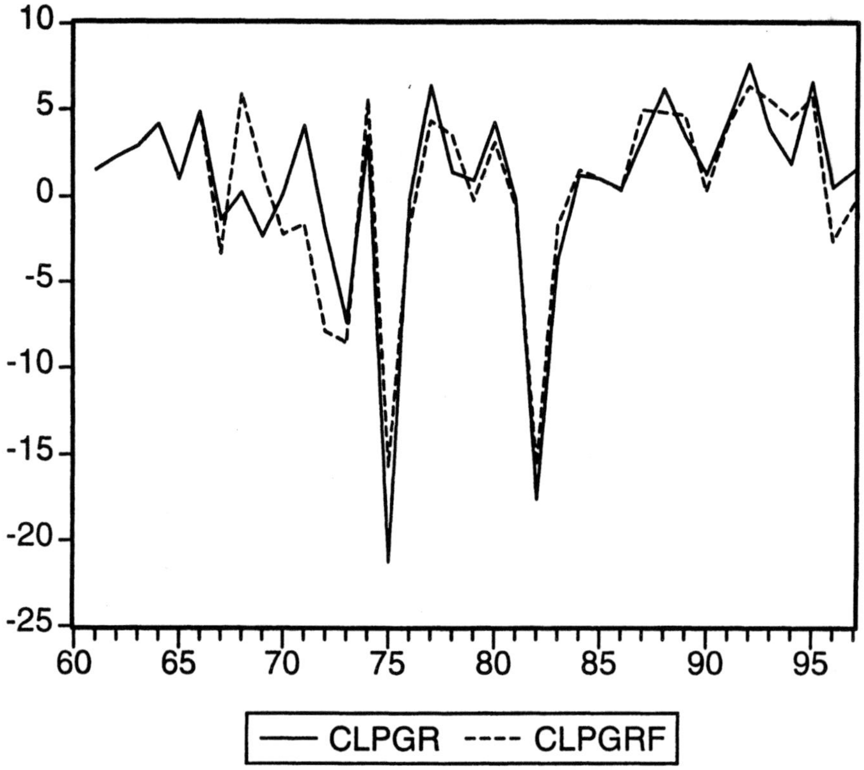

7. CONCLUSION

This paper analyzed the recent evolution, rationale, and impact of FDI flows in one of the leading countries of Latin America, Chile. It reviewed the relevant literature dealing with the major determinants of FDI, as well as examined the economic and institutional-legal channels through which FDI flows have affected key economic variables and sectors of the Chilean economy. Several major findings were presented. First, the descriptive evidence for Chile suggests that although FDI flows have been substantial during the second half of the eighties and nineties, particularly in relation to domestic capital formation, a large proportion of these funds have been directed to traditional sectors such as mining and agriculture where value added per worker is relatively low and the technology used is highly standardized and routine in nature. Although Chile has pursued policies to redirect FDI flows to high priority sectors in the tradable sector via the debt conversion program initiated in 1986 but discontinued in 1991, the (partial) evidence suggests that a significant proportion of FDI flows are not being channeled to innovative "greenfield" investments in the manufacturing sector where technological spillover effects are greater.

Second, the paper revealed that major institutional-legal changes such as the relaxation or elimination of restrictions on profit and capital remittances, the elimination of prior authorization of investments, and the opening of formerly "priority" sectors to foreign investors, has had the combined effect of vigorously stimulating FDI flows during 1986-97 period. The empirical evidence for Chile suggested that the Chapter XIX mechanism had a positive and statistically significant impact on FDI flows.

Third, the econometric results presented in Section VI indicate that there is a stable, non-spurious relationship between labor productivity growth and FDI flows during the 1960-97 period. The ECM estimates suggest that (lagged) FDI flows have had a positive and economically significant effect on labor productivity growth during the 1960-97 period. This is also the case with (lagged) public investment in roads, ports and bridges, as well as outward-oriented policies designed to capture the opportunities offered by the global marketplace, have had a positive impact on labor productivity growth. In essence, the results suggest that Chilean policymakers are anticipating that the (long-run) positive "spillover"effects associated with FDI in the form of "intangibles" such as the transfer of technology and managerial knowhow will offset the short-term costs associated with overly generous subsidies, lavish tax concessions, and the potential compromise of the national patrimony. Doubts about the eventual outcome of this "tradeoff" were presented in Section II where it was revealed that once the reverse flows of profits and capital are subtracted from the gross inflows of FDI into Chile and Mexico, the contribution of FDI to the financing of private capital formation is reduced dramatically. Moreover, if all the countries in the region engage in this form of "incentive competition" it may lead to a "beggar-thy-neighbor" effect as TNCs redistribute a fixed volume of FDI among the competing countries, and in so doing, capture for themselves the "lion's share" of the social benefits.

Finally, the paper argued that the macroeconomic context in which these policies are pursued is crucial in determining the volume and composition of FDI flows. FDI flows will be attracted to countries that implement complementary and credible macro policies that ensure sustainable rates of economic growth in a low inflationary environment. As indicated in Section I, it is very important for policy makers to avoid extensive overvaluation of the real exchange rate because not only does it discourage FDI flows into the "innovative" tradeable sector, but it also undermines the long-term stability of the real exchange rate, thereby discouraging FDI flows. In this regard, there is no question that over the past decade and a half Chile has been more successful than most countries in Latin America in implementing and maintaining fiscal, monetary, and exchange rate policies that accomplish these macro objectives.

8. References

1. Agosin, Manuel R., ed. 1995. *Foreign Direct Investment in Latin America.* Washington, D.C.: Inter-American Development Bank.
2. Aschauer, David A. 1989a. "Public Investment and Productivity Growth in the Group of Seven." *Economic Perspectives*, 13 (September/October): 17-25. 1990.

"Is Government Spending Stimulative?" *Contemporary Economic Policy*, 8 (October): 30-46.

3. Bouton, Lawrence and Mariusz A. Sumlinski. 1996. *Trends in Private Investment in Developing Nations: Statistics for 1970-95.* Washington, D.C. : International Finance Corporation.
4. Barro, Robert J. and Xavier Sala-i-Martin. 1995. *Economic Growth.* New York: McGraw-Hill, Inc.
5. Bosworth, Barry P. and Susan M.Collins. 1999, "Capital Flows to Developing Economies: Implications for Savings and Investment," *Brookings Papers on Economic Activity*, No. 1: 143-180.
6. Caceres, Luis R. 1997 "La Relacion de Largo Plazo Entre El Ahorro y la Inversion en La America Latina." *El Trimestre Economico*, LXIV, 3 (July-September): 305-317.
7. Calderon, Francisco. 1988. "La Inversion Privada en Mexico, 1970-1987." *CIDE: Documentos de Investigacion, Division de Economia*, 3 (September): 1-39.
8. Cardoso, Eliana. 1993. "Private Investment in Latin America." *Economic Development and Cultural Change*, 41 (July): 833-848.
9. Carrada-Bravo, Francisco. 1998. "Inversion Extranjera Directa e Industria Maquiladora en Mexico." *Comercio Exterior*, 48, 4 (April): 273-282.
10. Casar, J. 1993. "La Competitividad de La Industria Manufacturera Mexicana, 1980-1990." *El Trimestre Economico,* LX, 237 (January-March): 113-183.
11. Chanthunya, Charles L. and V. Murinde. 1998. *Trade Regime and Economic Growth*. Sydney: Ashgate, 1998.
12. Charemza, W.W. and D. F. Deadman. 1997. New Directions in Econometric Practice: General to specific Modelling, Cointegration and Vector Autoregression. Cheltenham, U.K.: Edward Elgar Publishers.
13. Coase, Ronald. "The Nature of the Firm," *Economica*, 4 (13), August 1937: 386-405.
14. Coe, David T. and R. Moghadam. 1993. "Capital and Trade as Engines of Growth in France." *IMF Staff Papers*, 40 (3): 542-561.
15. Cruz, Bruno de O. and J.R. Teixeira. 1999. "The Impact of Public Investment on Private Investment in Brazil, 1947-1990." *Cepal Review*, 67 (April): 75-84.
16. Cypher, James M. And James L. Dietz. 1997 *The Process of Economic Development*. New York: Routledge.
17. De Mello, Jr. Luiz R. 1997. "Foreign Direct Investment in Developing Countries and Growth: A Selective Survey." *Journal of Development Studies*, 34, 1 (October): 1-34.
18. ECLAC. Foreign Investment in Latin America and the Caribbean, 1999 Report. Santiago, Chile: United Nations, 2000.
19. ECLAC. La Inversion Extranjera en America Latina y El Caribe. Santiago, Chile: United Nations, 1998.
20. ECLAC. Economic Survey of Latin America and the Caribbean, 1996-97. Santiago, Chile: United Nations, 1997.

21. Dickey, D., and W. Fuller, 1979. "Likelihood Ratio Statistics for Autoregressive Time Series with a Unit Root." *Econometrica*, June: 1057-1072.
22. Dunning, John H. 1981. *International Production and the Multinational Enterprise.* Boston: Allen & Unwin, Publishers.
23. Dunning, John. H. 1988. *Explaining International Production.* London: Harper Collins.
24. Engle, R.F. and C.W.J. Granger. 1987. "Cointegration and Error Correction: Representation, Estimation, and Testing." *Econometrica* 55 (March): 251-76.
25. Feder, Gordon. 1983. "On Exports and Economic Growth." *Journal of Development Economics* 12: 59-73.
26. Glen, Jack D. and Mariusz A. Sumlinski. 1996. "Trends in Private Investment in Developing Countries: Statistics for 1970-1995." *Working P aper No. 31.* Washington, D.C.: International Finance Corporation.
27. Granger, C.W.J. and Newbold, P. 1974. "Spurious Regression in Econometrics." *Journal of Econometrics* 2: 111-120.
28. Green, Joshua and Delano Villanueva. 1991. "Private Investment in Developing Countries: An Empirical Analysis." *IMF Staff Papers*, 38, 1 (March 1991): 33-58.
29. Grossman, G.M. and E. Helpman. *Innovation and Growth in the Global Economy.* Cambridge, MA: The MIT Press, 1991.
30. Harris, Richard. 1995. Using Cointegration Analysis in Econometric Modelling. New York: Prentice-Hall.
31. Johansen, Soren. 1988. "Statistical Analysis of Cointegrating Vectors." *Journal of Economic Dynamics and Control*, 12 (June/September): 231-254.
32. Johansen, Soren and K. Juselius. 1990. "Maximum Likelihood Estimation and Inference on Cointegration with Applications to the Demand for Money." *Oxford Bulletin of Economics and Statistics,* 52 (May): 169-210.
33. Lin, A. Y. Steven. 1994. "Government Spending and Economic Growth." *Applied Economics*, 26: 83-84.
34. Moctezuma A. And A. Mungaray. 1997. "Subcontratacion Entre Maquiladoras y Pequenas Empresas en Mexico." *Comercio Exterior.* 47, 2 (February): 95-103.
35. Nazmi, Nader and M.D. Ramirez. 1997. "Public and Private Investment and Economic Growth in Mexico." *Contemporary Economic Policy*, 15 (January): 65-75.
36. Moschos, D. 1989. "Export Expansion, Growth, and the Level of Economic Development: An Empirical Analysis." *Journal of Development Economics*, 30: 93-102.
37. Nelson, C., and C. Plosser. 1982. "Trends and Random Walks in Macroeconomic Time Series: Some Empirical Evidence and Implications." *Journal of Monetary Economics,* 10, 1982: 139-162.
38. Phillips, P.C.B., and P. Perron, 1988. "Testing for a Unit Root in Time Series Regressions." *Biometrika*, 75 (June): 335-346.
39. Plasschaert, S. ed. 1994. Transnational Corporations: Transfer Pricing and Taxation. London: Routledge.

40. Ram, R. 1987. "Exports and Economic Growth in Developing Countries: Evidence From Time- series and Cross-section Data." *Economic Development and Cultural Change*, 36 (1): 51-72.
41. Ramirez, Miguel D., 2000. "Public Capital Formation and Labor Productivity Growth in Chile." *Contemporary Economic Policy*, 18 (April): 159-169.
42. Solimano, Andres. 1990. "Inversion Privada y Ajuste Macroeconomico: La Experiencia Chilena en la Decada del 80." *Coleccion Estudios CIEPLAN* No. 28 (Junio): 29-55.
43. Theil, H. 1966. *Applied Economic Forecasting.* Amsterdam: North-Holland.
44. Tyler, W.G. 1981. "Growth and Export Expansion in developing Countries: Some Empirical Evidence." *Journal of Development Economics, 9: 121-130.*
45. United Nations. 1988. World Investment Report 1988: Trends and Determinants. Switzerland: United Nations.
46. World Bank. World Development Report 1994: Infrastructure for Development. New York: Oxford University Press, 1994.

TRADE AND THE AMERICAS

Raymond J. Ahearn

MOST RECENT DEVELOPMENTS

By a vote of 309-110, the House on May 4, 2000, approved the conference report on H.R. 434 ("The Trade and Development Act of 2000"). Title II of the conference version (Trade Benefits for the Caribbean Basin) would extend duty-free and quota-free benefits to apparel made in CBI countries from U.S. yarn and fabric. The bill also provides trade preferences for apparel made with regional fabric under specified conditions. The Senate might vote on the conference bill as early as May 10.

Chile on August 10, 1999, proposed to start preliminary discussions on the negotiation of a bilateral free trade agreement with the United States. The U.S. government has remained divided on how to respond. Some agencies reportedly are concerned that a bilateral agreement could undermine U.S. multilateral objectives.

Negotiators working to create a Free Trade Area of the Americas agreed in July 1999 on a number of business facilitation measures to expedite the movement of the region's goods. The measures were approved at a November 3-4, 1999 meeting of FTAA ministers in Canada. The trade ministers also agreed at the meeting to instruct negotiators (through the Trade Negotiations Committee) to assemble the texts of the negotiating groups and to prepare a report for the next Ministerial meeting in April 2001. High-level political support, particularly from Brazil, remains less than overwhelming.

BACKGROUND AND ANALYSIS

Summit of the Americas: Trade Results

At the Summit of the Americas held December 9-11, 1994 in Miami, 34 hemispheric democracies agreed to create a "Free Trade Area of the Americas (FTAA)." Under the Declaration of Principles, the countries committed to "begin immediately" construction of the free trade area and to complete negotiations no later than the year 2005.

The Declaration stated that concrete progress toward the FTAA will occur before the close of the century. Based on the view that substantial progress towards economic integration in the hemisphere has already been made, the declaration called for building on "existing sub-regional and bilateral arrangements in order to broaden and deepen hemispheric economic integration and to bring the agreements together." At the same time, the declaration recognized the need to "remain cognizant" of the "wide differences in the levels of development and size of economies" in the Hemisphere in moving toward tighter economic integration.

The FTAA would have 34 members (Cuba is not included) with 850 million people. The population would be more than twice the 370 million of the now 15-nation European Union. The FTAA would also have a gross domestic product of more than $9 trillion, with the $7 trillion U.S. economy accounting for more than 75% of the total.

In the 5 years following the 1994 Miami Summit, Western Hemisphere trade ministers met five times under the FTAA process. The first meeting was held in Denver in June 1995; the second in Cartagena, Colombia in March 1996; the third in Belo Horizonte, Brazil in May 1997; the fourth in San Jose, Costa Rica in March 1998; and the fifth in Toronto, Canada in November 1999. The next ministerial meeting is scheduled to take place in Argentina in April 2001.

At the San Jose meeting, the 34 Ministers responsible for trade in the Hemisphere unanimously recommended that the Leaders formally launch the negotiation of the FTAA at the Second Summit of the Americas in Santiago. As provided by the San Jose Declaration, ministers agreed that negotiating groups are to achieve considerable progress by the year 2000, with a conclusion set for December 31, 2004. The San Jose Declaration also provided recommendations on the initial structure, objectives, venues, and principles of the negotiations.

Canada was designated as the Chair of the overall negotiating process for the initial 18 months (May 1, 1998-Oct. 31, 1999) and the United States and Brazil were named co-chairs during the final two years of the negotiations (November 1, 2002-December 31, 2004). As head ofboth the Ministerial and Trade Negotiations Committee (TNC), the Chair will provide overall direction and management to the negotiations.

The Ministers elected to establish nine initial negotiating groups, which cover all the tariff and non-tariff barrier issue areas identified by the Leaders at the Miami Summit of the Americas. These groups are market access, agriculture, services, government procurement, investment, intellectual property, subsidies, competition policy, and dispute settlement. In addition, the Ministers created two committees and a consultative group. A Committee on Electronic Commerce, comprised of both government and private sector experts, was established to make recommendations on how to increase and broaden the benefits to be derived from the electronic marketplace. A Committee on Civil Society was established to receive input at the hemispheric level from labor and environmental groups, and academic, consumer, and other non-governmental groups. And a Consultative Group on Smaller Economies was established to bring to the attention of the TNC the interests and concerns of the smaller economies.

The United States (Miami) will provide the venue for the negotiating groups and the administrative secretariat supporting those meeting during the first three years. The last four years of the negotiations will be held in Panama and Mexico.

The San Jose Declaration contains General Principles for the Negotiations, as well as General and Specific Objectives. In addition to transparency during the negotiations, the Ministers agreed that the FTAA should improve upon WTO rules and disciplines wherever possible and appropriate. This provision was an attempt to ensure that any final agreement will break down the most serious trade barriers in the region and provide a single set of rules for hemispheric trade. It was agreed that bilateral and sub-regional agreements such as NAFTA and Mercosur can coexist with the FTAA only to the extent that the rights and obligations under those agreements are not covered or go beyond those of the FTAA. It was also agreed that the negotiations will be a "single undertaking," in the sense that signatories to the final FTAA Agreement will have to accept all parts of it (i.e. cannot pick and choose among the obligations.)

At the Second Summit of the Americas, held in Chile in April 1998, President Clinton and 21 other presidents and 12 prime ministers of the Western Hemisphere agreed to begin the trade negotiations, and to make "concrete progress" toward the free trade goal by 2000. Nine working groups were established and meetings have been taking place since September 1998.

The most recent ministerial meeting, held in Toronto in November 1999, approved an FTAA declaration that instructs negotiators to assemble the texts provided by the negotiating groups for consideration at the next ministerial meeting, scheduled for April 2001 in Argentina. In addition to ordering the preparation of a limited draft agreement over the next 18 months, the ministers agreed to implement eight business facilitation measures beginning this year. The agreed measures focus mainly on streamlining and modernizing customs procedures in an effort to expedite trade in goods and services.

Vision of Free Trade in the Americas

The vision of free trade in the Americas was put forth initially by President Bush in June 1990. Proposed as the cornerstone of the Enterprise for the Americas Initiative (EAI), President Bush envisaged the creation of a " free trade system that links all of the Americas: North, Central, and South ... a free trade zone stretching from the port of Anchorage to the Tierra del Fuego" (the southern tip of Chile). The free trade vision was enthusiastically received in Latin America.

Bush Administration officials at the time emphasized that the goal of hemispheric free trade was long-term, and could take a decade or more to come to fruition. Moreover, the hemispheric free trade vision entailed a variable pattern of economic integration, perhaps involving a number of free trade agreements with individual countries or with the region's economic groupings. Given that the timing, terms, and actual dimensions of the proposal were uncertain, its main significance was an offer of a special relationship with the countries of the Western Hemisphere.

Since assuming office, President Clinton has strongly supported the hemispheric free trade concept. Both he and President Bush have viewed movement towards hemispheric economic integration as supportive of U.S. economic and political interests.

Initially, Clinton Administration efforts to clarify the process by which it would work toward creation of a hemispheric free trade area awaited the outcome of the congressional vote on NAFTA, a trade agreement that was touted as a first step in moving towards the vision of hemispheric free trade. Since NAFTA was approved in late 1993, the Administration restated its intention of negotiating a free trade agreement with Chile next, but declined from naming other specific countries as candidates for future free trade agreements.

The Summit of the Americas in Miami helped create a political consensus in the Administration to take further steps in moving towards hemispheric integration. In remarks delivered at the Summit, President Clinton hailed the proposal to build a free trade area from Alaska to Argentina as producing more jobs in the United States and improving the quality of life for residents of the Western Hemisphere.

Since Miami, the vision of hemispheric free trade has been promoted both by the formal negotiations held as a part of the FTAA process, and by the expansion of sub-regional groups and the proliferation of bilateral free trade agreements. Under the former approach, the trade ministers of the hemisphere laid the groundwork for the formal launching of the negotiations, which was agreed to at the Second Summit of the Americas in Santiago. Under the latter approach, Mercosur (the Southern Cone Common Market) has expanded and countries such as Chile and Mexico have negotiated bilateral free trade agreements. Lacking fast-track negotiating authority, the Clinton Administration has not been active under this process.

U.S. Interests and Concerns

Supporters view hemispheric integration as bolstering U.S. economic and political interests in a variety of ways. Movement towards freer markets is viewed as supportive of U.S. prosperity, while the strengthening of democratic regimes is viewed as supportive of U.S. values and security. Closer economic ties are also seen improving cooperation on a range of bilateral issues, including environmental concerns and anti-drug efforts.

In most general terms, a reciprocal reduction of trade barriers by two or more countries usually contributes to improved efficiency and higher living standards for both. As tariffs in Latin America are roughly four times higher than U.S. tariffs, supporters argue that the lowering of tariffs and other trade barriers should facilitate significant increases in U.S. exports.

Supporters point out that the Western Hemisphere has become the largest regional destination for U.S. exports of goods over the past three years. In 1998, the region accounted about 40% of total U.S. merchandise exports and nearly two-thirds of the increase in U.S. export growth worldwide.

Supporters also believe that a higher degree of economic integration should contribute to the consolidation of economic and political reforms that have taken place throughout the hemisphere. They maintain that the reforms have not only contributed to an improved economic performance in Latin America overall, but they have also made Latin America a more attractive setting for U.S. foreign investment. Similarly, they maintain that the stronger Latin America becomes economically, the more likely democratic institutions will continue to proliferate and deepen.

Opponents of an FTAA are concerned that hemispheric free trade would lead to the export of jobs that otherwise would be in the United States. Some critics believe that an FTAA will induce an outflow of American capital to take advantage of much lower wages and weak safety and environmental standards. Many opponents of the FTAA have argued that free trade with poorer countries will put pressure on the United States to lessen its workforce protections and environmental requirements.

Other critics are concerned that an FTAA will inevitably involve the United States in the instabilities, class tensions, and economic turmoil of many southern hemisphere societies. Some cite Mexico's financial crisis in 1995 as an example of potential costs. According to this view, costs include a deterioration in the U.S. trade balance, an increase in immigration pressures, and the need to extend a large amount of credit.

From a very different perspective, some opponents also argue that hemispheric free trade could undermine the achievement of a stronger and more open multilateral trading system. According to this perspective, regional free trade agreements that may weaken the multilateral trading system do not serve the interests of the United States because it has major commercial interests in all regions of the world — Asia, Europe, and North America, and Latin America.

Latin American Interests and Concerns

Over the last few years, Latin American nations have made considerable progress in implementing far-reaching trade reforms and opening their economies to outside competition. The prospects of hemispheric economic integration have spurred new sub- regional integration schemes and breathed life into sub-regional groups that had lost their stamina. Most importantly, the political commitment at the Miami Summit to create an FTAA by the year 2005 was a product largely of pressures from many of the countries in the region.

If the 1980s were Latin America's lost decade, the 1990s may be the catchup years. Since 1991, the economies of the region have averaged roughly 3.5% growth, up from 1.1% in the 1980s. Inflation has been reduced dramatically, averaging around 10% in recent years compared to 550% in 1990. And fiscal deficits are now approximately 2% of gross domestic product, compared to 9% in 1983.

One of the central aspects of the economic transformation of the region has been impressive market-oriented reforms and unilateral trade liberalization. This trend has been, in recent years, complemented by a surge of sub-regional integration efforts and growing hemispheric interdependence.

Since 1990, four sub-regional groups have made considerable progress breaking down intra-regional trade barriers. MERCOSUR, the Common Market of South, consists of Argentina, Brazil, Paraguay, and Uruguay and is the second largest preferential trading group in the Western Hemisphere. The Andean Community, consisting of Bolivia, Colombia, Ecuador, and Venezuela (Peru recently dropped out in 1997), currently is the third largest preferential trading group in the Western Hemisphere. Acting unilaterally as well as under the auspices of the Community (formerly the Andean Pact), individual members have liberalized their own trade and investment regimes in recent years. The Caribbean Community and Common Market (CARICOM), consisting of 13 English-speaking Caribbean nations, has agreed to implement a common external tariff over a period of six years, although members will be allowed to maintain their own non-tariff barriers. The Central American Common Market, (CACM), originally established in 1961, gained new stimulus after a 1990 summit of Central American Presidents. Within CACM, the Central American Group of four — El Salvador, Guatemala, Honduras, and Nicaragua—has taken measures to liberalize and harmonize their trade regimes. Other combinations and the deepening of sub-regional trade agreements are key factors in the economic turn-around. The Group of Three (G3) — consisting of Colombia, Mexico, and Venezuela — signed a free trade pact on June 13, 1994.

The likelihood of eventual hemispheric free trade could provide a further boost to the economies of the region. Hemisphere-wide free trade, according to a 1994 Institute for International Economics study, could boost the region's economic growth by an estimated

1.5% a year, which by 2002 would translate into an additional output of almost $300 billion a year. Needed inward investment flows would rise by an estimated $10 billion annually.

Most Latin American leaders generally support the establishment of a hemispheric free trade area, believing that an FTAA will help bring about greater prosperity, competition, and entrepreneurial activity. A number of critics, however, caution that the United States will benefit the most from the arrangement.

Similarly, many Latin Americans understand that negotiating a free trade agreement with the United States opens themselves to increased trade competition and potential U.S. involvement in such issues as environmental standards, workers' rights, and intellectual property rights protection. Some worry that as tariffs fall, the United States would increasingly resort to other procedural ways (such as the imposition of anti-dumping or countervailing duties) to protect its producers and workers. Consequently some nations might not be willing to move as quickly as others toward the goal of free trade. And others, such as Brazil, may attach greater importance and priority to the consolidation and strengthening of sub-regional trade groups before moving towards a hemispheric free trade area.

Beyond that, opposition to hemispheric free trade could grow if the region's unemployment and staggering poverty does not begin to decline. Despite the improvement in economic growth in the 1990s, unemployment has risen from around 5%-6% at the end of the 1980s to 8% in 1998. And the number of people living in poverty is about the same as in 1990. As a result, many workers and groups in these countries believe that the shift towards open markets and free trade has done little to improve their living standards, and that hemispheric free trade may only make things worse.

Policy Issues and Congressional Actions

Chile: Negotiating A Free Trade Agreement

Canada's Prime Minister Jean Chretien was widely quoted at the conclusion of the first Summit of the Americas on the invitation to Chile to join NAFTA: "For one year we have been the three amigos. Starting today, we will be the four amigos."

Accession negotiations were formally initiated on June 7, 1995 in Toronto, but they remained preliminary due to the fact that the Clinton Administration lacked fast- track negotiating authority. Chile elected not to negotiate on any "sensitive" issues unless fast track authority is renewed to cover the negotiations. Such authority allows the Administration to negotiate a trade agreement with assurances that the legislation implementing the agreement will be treated under special, expedited floor procedures. Differences between most House Democrats, on the one hand, and most Republicans, on the other hand, on the inclusion of labor and environmental objectives in future free trade agreements was a major obstacle to the renewal of fast- track in 1995, 1996, 1997, and again in 1998. The most recent attempt to pass a fast track bill occurred on September 25, 1998, when the House defeated H.R. 2621 by a vote of 180 to 243. In 1999, no comprehensive fast-track bills were reintroduced.

Both the Senate Finance and the House Ways and Means Committee fast-track bills, as well as the President's proposal of September 16, 1997, provided that a free trade agreement negotiated with Chile would be accorded fast-track legislative treatment. While NAFTA accession is the most likely form that any free trade agreement would take, a bilateral free trade agreement could also be accommodated under fast-track.

The significance of the inability of the Clinton Administration to carry through on its pledge to negotiate Chilean accession to NAFTA or to negotiate a bilateral free trade agreement is mostly political, not economic. In economic terms, NAFTA accession or a free trade agreement would unlikely have any demonstrable effect on the overall U.S. economy because trade between the two countries, although growing, is a minuscule percent of overall U.S. trade flows (approximately ½ of 1 percent). Chile ranks as the 28th most important market for U.S. exports worldwide, accounting for $3.0 billion in 1998. U.S. imports from Chile totaled $$2.1 billion in 1998, representing the 35th largest supplier. As a country of only 13 million people, with an economy the size of Dallas, and located some 4,000 miles from the United States, Chile is unlikely to become a major trading partner of the United States.

In political terms, the Clinton Administration's inability to carry through on its promise to achieve a free trade agreement with Chile has perhaps undermined its negotiating leverage in the context of the FTAA. The promise of Chilean accession to NAFTA, for some interest groups, was that NAFTA obligations and rules could be adopted to serve as the foundation for hemispheric integration. After Chile acceded, it was believed that other countries would be eager to join NAFTA when they were ready as well. Lacking fast-track, the Administration, however, arguably was forced to make a number of compromises concerning the objectives and structure of the FTAA negotiations as enunciated in the San Jose Declaration.

Despite the obvious set-backs and delays, the idea of free trade negotiations with Chile took an unexpected turn on August 10, 1999. On this day, Chile's Foreign Minister Juan Gabriel Valdes announced that Chile was prepared to start preliminary discussions on a bilateral FTA with the United States without fast-track negotiating authority in place. The United States termed the proposal "constructive" and "positive" at the October 5-6 meeting of the U.S.-Chile Joint Commission on Trade in Investment in Santiago, Chile. But no official decision has yet been made by the Administration on whether or how to proceed. Several agencies reportedly oppose the negotiation of a bilateral agreement with Chile on the grounds that it could undermine other U.S. multilateral or regional initiatives.

How To Deal with Caribbean Basin Countries

Ever since NAFTA was proposed in the early 1990s, Caribbean Basin leaders have expressed concern that Mexico's more preferential trading status would erode its own preferential access to the U.S. market as provided by the 1984 Caribbean Basin Economic Recovery Act (CBERA). At the Summit of the Americas, President Clinton and key legislators supported legislation to address the concerns of the CBERA countries. Legislation to prevent an erosion of the CBERA countries' preferential access to the U.S. market has been introduced in every Congress since 1993, but none have been enacted. In the 105th Congress, two different bills were reported out of the House Ways and Means Committee and the Senate Finance Committee, but neither received floor action. In the first session of the106th Congress, a number of proposals to enhance the trade preferences offered to the

CBERA countries were introduced in both chambers, and H.R. 434 passed the Senate by a vote of 76-19 on November 3, 1999 (for details, see below).

The CBERA, which is commonly referred to as the Caribbean Basin Initiative or CBI, was enacted in 1983 in an effort to bolster the economic development and political stability of this strategically important region. A key objective was to help these countries diversify their exports away from traditional agricultural and raw material based exports such as petroleum, sugar cane, coffee, cocoa, bananas, and aluminum ores.

The centerpiece of this U.S. government program is a unilateral, non-reciprocal, grant of duty-free or reduced duty access for certain Caribbean exports to the U.S. market. Most textiles and apparel, certain footwear, canned tuna, petroleum and petroleum derivatives, and certain watches are not eligible for any preferential treatment. The CBERA was amended by Caribbean Basin Economic Recovery Act of 1990, so-called CBI II. This act made the trade benefits permanent and included measures to promote tourism and establish a scholarship assistance program for the region.

Currently, 24 Caribbean, and Central and South American countries enjoy these trade preferences. (Four countries — Anguilla, Cayman Islands, Suriname, and Turks and Caicos Islands — are eligible to become a CBERA beneficiary country, but have not requested to be designated). Benefits under CBI are conditioned on various mandatory and discretionary conditions, including intellectual property rights protection, investment protection, improved market access for U.S. exports, and workers rights. In its 15-year history, CBERA has been popular with Caribbean exporters, and in recent years about one-fifth of overall U.S. imports from CBERA countries have entered the U.S. under CBERA preferential provisions.

In 1997, U.S. imports from CBERA countries amounted to $16.6 billion (or 1.9% of total U.S. imports), and total U.S. exports to CBERA countries totaled $17.8 billion (or 2.8% of total exports). The U.S. trade surplus with these countries totaled $1.2 billion in 1997, the eleventh consecutive year that the U.S. ran a trade surplus with the region.

In 1996, apparel was the most prominent U.S. import from the CBERA countries, constituting 42% of all U.S. imports. Traditional exports — petroleum, coffee, tea, fish, and sugar — comprised 21% of total imports, and vegetables and fruits 7%.

Although not eligible for CBERA trade preferences, apparel is also the fastest growing category of U.S. imports from CBERA countries. According to the U.S. International Trade Commission (U.S.I.T.C.), apparel imports grew from 5.5% of overall imports from the region in 1984 to 41% in 1996. From 1987-1996, apparel imports increased at a rate of 21%, the fastest increase among all foreign suppliers. About 80% of apparel imports from CBERA countries benefitted from reduced duties under a production-sharing provision of U.S. trade law (the 9802 provision of the Harmonized Tariff Schedule) which provides partial duty exemption for products assembled abroad of U.S. fabricated components. Shirts, trousers, underwear, and coats and jackets are the principal garments assembled under the production-sharing operations.

CBERA countries compete with one another and Mexico for assembly work from U.S. apparel firms. Since NAFTA went into effect in 1994, apparel assembled in Mexico from "fabric wholly formed and cut in the United States" enters free of duty and quota, but similar

CBERA garments are subject to a duty based on the value added offshore. This duty was estimated by the U.S.I.T.C. staff to be equivalent to a 6% ad valorem tariff in 1996. This alteration of the terms of competition arguably has been a factor in causing differential rates of increase in imports to the United States.

According the to the U.S.I.T.C., U.S. apparel imports from CBERA countries and Mexico both rose at around 26% from 1991-1993. However, apparel imports from CBERA countries grew by 15% per year from 1994-1996, while imports from Mexico increased by 44% per year.

Although Mexican apparel shipments to the United States are growing faster than CBERA shipment since NAFTA went into force, the CBERA countries are not losing market share. According the U.S.I.T.C., the CBERA share of leading U.S. imports of apparel increased from 13.1% in 1993 to 16.1% in 1996, while Mexico's share rose from 4.5% to 10.1% during the same period. Suppliers from the rest of the world incurred about a 10% decline in their share of the U.S. market in this post-NAFTA period.

These data have been used by both proponents and opponents of the so-called NAFTA parity or CBI enhancement legislation. Proponents have pointed to a declining rate of increase for CBERA countries' shipments of apparel to the United States, as well as the accelerated growth of Mexican shipments, as evidence that NAFTA has been a force for diverting trade (exports) from CBERA countries to Mexico. Opponents point to the fact that CBERA countries in the aggregate continue to gain a greater share of the U.S. apparel import market.

"NAFTA parity" or CBI enhancement bills introduced in Congress since 1993 have been premised, in part, on the notion that Mexico's more favorable tariff treatment under NAFTA would lead to a diversion of exports and investment, particularly in the textile and apparel sectors, from the CBERA region. To remedy potential trade and investment diversion, most bills have proposed extending NAFTA equivalent provisions to CBERA countries for products that did not enjoy equivalent preferential treatment under CBERA.

In the 106th Congress, the House on May 4, 2000, approved a conference report on H.R. 434 ("The Trade and Development Act of 2000) by a vote of 309-110. Title II of the conference version grants duty-free and quota-free benefits for apparel made in CBI countries from U.S. yarn and fabric. Additionally, the bill provides benefits for apparel made with regional fabric under specified conditions. The bill also requires that CBI countries implement strict Customs procedures to guard against transhipment. The Senate may vote on the conference report as early as May 10.

Movement Towards Hemispheric Free Trade

Since the 1994 Summit of the Americas, the goal of hemispheric free trade has been advanced by two different processes. The first process involves the expansion of sub-regional groupings such as MERCOSUR and the proliferation ofbilateral free trade agreements. Most all countries of the Western Hemisphere — except the United States— have been active in this process.

The second process involves the formal negotiations among 34 democratic countries of the hemisphere to create an FTAA. As described above, the March 1998 San Jose Declaration formulated a framework for the negotiations and the Leaders formally launched the FTAA negotiations during the second Summit meeting in Santiago in April 1998. And at the fifth hemispheric ministerial held in Canada in November 1999, ministers approved an FTAA declaration that sets goals for negotiators over the next 18 months and directs them to assemble the texts of all negotiating groups for consideration at the next ministerial meeting in Argentina in April 2001.

Assessments differ on whether this combined movement toward hemispheric free trade is "on-track" or "off-track." The former perspective maintains that a solid foundation and structure for FTAA negotiations has been agreed to and that on-going efforts to expand sub-regional groupings are accelerating hemispheric integration. The latter perspective holds that the United States, lacking fast-track authority, has been unable to provide the kind of leadership that is necessary to ensure that the FTAA negotiations proceed according to schedule or in a manner that is supportive of U.S. interests.

Those who see positive developments over the past two years point to the accomplishments of the San Jose Trade Ministerial and the Second Summit of the Americas in getting the FTAA negotiations off to an official start. While some critics doubt much progress can be made in the negotiations until the U.S. President obtains fast-track negotiating authority, others point to agreement on a range of business facilitation measures to date. These include temporary admission of certain goods related to business travelers, express shipments, simplified procedures for low value shipments, compatible data interchange systems, harmonized commodity description and coding system, hemispheric guide on customs procedures, codes of conduct for customs officials, and risk analysis/targeting methodology.

The "on-track" perspective also points to a continuing trend of greater market opening at both the bilateral and sub-regional level as contributing to an expansion of trade flows. In recent years, intra-hemispheric trade has been growing more rapidly than exports to the rest of the world. This trade growth, in turn, has bolstered the economic performance of the countries of the region and enabled Latin American leaders to negotiate with the United States more confidently, as well as to embrace the long-term goal of hemispheric free trade.

Those who judge that the process is "off-track" make several points. The first is that the United States, lacking fast-track authority, has not been able to promote its preferred approach (the expansion of NAFTA) to hemispheric integration. Instead it has been relegated to the sidelines as other countries and sub-regional groups have continued to reach preferential agreements. These agreements, in turn, are said to be discriminating against U.S. exports and making it more difficult to eventually negotiate a comprehensive, hemispheric free trade agreement. In the continuing absence of fast-track, this view also holds that the FTAA negotiations have lost momentum. These observers see the Toronto Ministerial declaration as a limited document, calling only for more discussions and compilations of draft texts.

These critics believe that a time-consuming and extended negotiation would provide Brazil, in particular, with significant advantages, not the least of which would be an opportunity to expand MERCOSUR into a larger South American trade bloc. Buttressed by the diplomatic support provided by a larger MERCOSUR, Brazil could be better positioned to negotiate with the United States from a position of strength. This is particularly important because Brazil wishes to extract from the United States concessions limiting Washington's use of unfair trade practices remedies (i.e., antidumping and countervailing duties) and to improve its access to the U.S. market for agricultural goods. In addition, because MERCOSUR currently protects a number of sectors (such as financial services, telecommunications, and automobiles), a longer period of time would provide these sectors with more leeway to adjust to increased import competition. The fact that the hemispheric trading partners remain at odds over the work programs of the nine negotiating groups, as well as the role labor and environmental considerations should play in the negotiations, play into the strategy of delay.

Public support for hemispheric free trade appears to be low both in the United States and in Latin America. Labor and environmental interest groups in the United States oppose free trade agreements that lack strong protections for basic labor and environmental standards. And many Latin American businesses and citizens fear the effects of greater exposure to the competitive pressures of large U.S. companies.

Extending the Andean Trade Preferences Act

The Andean Trade Preferences Act (ATPA) authorizes the President to grant certain unilateral preferential tariff benefits to Bolivia, Colombia, Ecuador, and Peru. The ATPA, which went into effect on December 4, 1991, will expire on December 4, 2001. Often referred to as the trade component of then President Bush's "war on drugs," the ATPA attempted to encourage the economic development of Andean countries and economic alternatives to drug production and trafficking.

The Andean countries have asked the United States to extend the program beyond its expiration date, to reduce the list of products excluded from tariff benefits, and to add Venezuela as a beneficiary country. In congressional testimony on February 22, 2000, before the Senate Caucus on International Narcotics Control and the Senate Finance Subcommittee on International Trade, Deputy U.S. Trade Representative Richard Fisher stated the Clinton Administration was prepared to example the request "very closely." Some Senators at the hearing indicated support for an early renewal of the program, saying it would show U.S. commitment to the region and help promote a favorable investment climate.

According to the Clinton Administration, the ATPA has been successful in encouraging a move away from narcotics trade to legitimate business in the region and in increasing U.S. exports. Since APTA was passed in 1991, the four Andean countries have increased their exports to the United States by about 80%. Products benefitting from ATPA tariff preferences include cut flowers from Colombia, Ecuador, and Bolivia; precious metals and jewelry from Colombia, Bolivia, and Peru; and fish and fish products from Ecuador.

CHRONOLOGY

05/04/00 — By a vote of 309-110, the House approved the conference report on H.R. 434, the Trade and Development Act of 2000. Title II expands trade preferences for Caribbean Basin exports of apparel products.

02/18/00 — Brazilian Foreign Minister Luiz Felipe Lampreia announced that Brazil is not going to commit to an FTAA until it sees what the final package is and whether the U.S. Congress will approve it.

11/3-4/99 — Hemispheric trade ministers agreed at a meeting in Toronto to instruct trade negotiators to assemble the texts of the negotiating groups and to prepare a report for the next ministerial, scheduled to be held in Argentina in April 2001.

11/03/99 — The Senate passed a bill (H.R. 434) by a vote of 76-19 that expands trade preferences for Caribbean Basin countries. The bill must be reconciled with a House-passed bill that addressed African trade preferences only.

10/7-8/99 — A U.S.-Chile Joint Commission on Trade and Investment met in Santiago to explore possible negotiations on a free trade agreement.

08/10/99 — Chile's Foreign Minister Juan Gabriel Valdes announced that Chile was ready to start preliminary work on a bilateral free trade agreement without U.S. fast-track negotiating authority in place.

07/28/99 — At a meeting of the Trade Negotiations Committee (TNC) of the FTAA, representatives of 27 countries reached agreement on nine business facilitation measures. The measures will be reviewed at the November 1999 ministerial summit in Canada.

06/22/99 — The Senate Finance Committee reported out a CBI bill, S. 1389 (Roth), by voice vote.

06/10/99 — The House Ways and Means Committee reported out a CBI bill, H.R. 984 (Crane), by voice vote.

05/18/99 — The Ways and Means Trade Subcommittee approved H.R. 984, the U.S.-Caribbean Trade Partnership Act, by voice vote without amendments.

03/04/99 — Congressman Philip Crane (R-Il) introduced the "United States-Caribbean Trade Partnership Act. Title I of the bill offers additional incentive for economic development in the region through enhancement of the CBI trade program.

02/04/99 — Senator Bob Graham (D-Fla) and nine other Senators introduced the "Caribbean Relief Act of 1999." The bill, S. 371, contains a proposal to enhance the trade benefits offered CBI countries.

01/26/99 — Senate Majority Leader Trent Lott stated that he intends to bring a Caribbean trade bill to the floor for a vote early this year.

09/25/98 — The House defeated H.R. 2621, a Republican leadership sponsored fast-track bill, by a vote of 180 to 243.

09/01/98 — The first negotiating sessions of working groups on market access and agriculture took place in Miami under the FTAA rubric.

06/11/98 — Commerce Secretary William Daley expressed doubts that the 2005 deadline for completion of the FTAA can be met given an enormous negotiating agenda and the large number of diverse economies involved in the process.

04/19/98 — 34 Leaders meeting at the second Summit of the Americas in Santiago, Chile agree to formally launch FTAA negotiations.

03/19/98 — Trade ministers meeting in San Jose, Costa Rica agree on the principles, objectives, and venues that will guide the FTAA negotiations.

11/04/97 — The House defeated by a vote of 234-182 the United States-Caribbean Trade Partnership Act (H.R. 2644).

10/09/97 — House Ways and Means Committee approves by voice vote a 14-month Caribbean Basin Trade Partnership bill (H.R. 2264).

10/01/97 — Senate Finance Committee approves by voice vote a 3-year Caribbean Trade Enhancement bill (S. 1278).

07/27/97 — Conferees on the budget-tax legislation deleted the House-passed NAFTA parity provision from the final bill.

06/26/97 — The House passed a budget reconciliation bill (HR 2014) that contained provisions to establish "NAFTA parity" for the Caribbean Basin Initiative beneficiary countries.

07/25/95 — Negotiations for Chilean accession to NAFTA officially began in Mexico City.

06/07/95 — Trade ministers from the United States, Mexico, Canada, and Chile announce the structure and work schedule for the negotiation of Chile's accession to the North American Free Trade Agreement.

12/9-11/94 — Summit of the Americas held in Miami. Political commitment was made to negotiate a "Free Trade Area of the Americas" by the year 2005. In a separate action, the United States, Canada, and Mexico invited Chile to enter into negotiations to join NAFTA.

01/01/94 — The North American Free Trade Agreement entered into force.

For Additional Reading

CRS Issue Briefs

CRS Issue Brief IB95050. *Caribbean Basin Interim Trade Program (NAFTA/CBI PARITY)*, by Vladimir N. Pregelj.

CRS Reports

CRS Report 95-1138. *Andean Pact—U.S. Trade Relations: Evolution and Prospects*, by Raymond J. Ahearn.

CRS Report 97-56. *Chilean Trade and Economic Reform: Implications for NAFTA Accession*, by J.F. Hornbeck.

CRS Report 97-876, Fast-Track Authority: Debate Over the President's Proposal, by George Holliday.

CRS Report 97-762. *A Free Trade Area of the Americas: Toward Integrating Regional Trade Policies*, by J.F. Hornbeck.

CRS Report 97-514. *Hemispheric Free Trade: Status, Hurdles, and Opposition*, by Raymond J. Ahcarn.

CRS Report 95-940. *MERCOSUR-U.S. Trade Relations: Evolution and Prospects*, by Raymond J. Ahearn.

CRS Report 97-811. *NAFTA, Mexican Trade Policy, and U.S.-Mexico Trade: A Longer Term Perspective*, by J.F. Hornbeck.

CRS Report 98-330. *Summit of the Americas II, April 18-19, 1998: Background, Objectives, and Expectations*, by K. Larry Storrs.

ANDEAN PACT - U.S. TRADE RELATIONS: EVOLUTION AND PROSPECTS

Raymond J. Ahearn and Shelley Wallace

INTRODUCTION

The Andean Pact (*Pacto Andino*),[1] consisting of Bolivia, Colombia, Ecuador, Peru, and Venezuela, was created in 1969 to facilitate economic development through regional economic integration. With an internal market of over 97 million people, a combined GDP of $181 billion, and an average per capita GDP of $1,856, the Pact is currently the third largest preferential trade bloc in the Western Hemisphere (The North American Free Trade Agreement consisting of Canada, Mexico and the United States is the largest, and the MERCOSUR consisting of Argentina, Brazil, Paraguay and Uruguay is the second largest).

Acting unilaterally as well as under the auspices of the Pact, the Andean countries have significantly liberalized their trade and investment regimes. Free trade in a limited number of products has been in effect among several of the Andean countries since the early 1980s. In 1992, Colombia and Venezuela implemented a bilateral free trade area (FTA), and they were joined by Bolivia and Ecuador in early 1993. Moving beyond an FTA, Colombia, Ecuador, and Venezuela adopted a common (but with exceptions) external tariff (CET) in 1995, thereby forming a partial customs union. The degree of integration achieved to date, in turn, has had favorable impact on economic activity in the region and on U.S. trade and investment flows.

At the same time, the Andean Pact today must address some fundamental challenges bearing on the group's unity and direction. Colombia and Venezuela, the dominant countries of the Pact, have negotiated a free trade agreement with Mexico, thereby undermining the preferences of Ecuador and Bolivia. Colombian and Venezuela are also confronting difficult economic and political problems. The recent war between Ecuador and Peru also has done little to enhance the ability of the Pact members to achieve common policies. Peru, furthermore, remains undecided about re-joining the Pact.

This report explores the formation, accomplishments, and prospects of the Andean Pact, including trade relations with the United States. Background information providing an economic profile of each Andean country and its trade relationship with the United States is provided in an Appendix.

---

[1] It is also known as the Andean Group (*Grupo Andino* - GRAN) as well as the Andean Common Market (ANCOM).

Figure 1

TABLE 1. Andean Countries: Basic Statistics 1994

Data	Total	Bolivia	Colombia	Ecuador	Peru	Venezuela
Population (millions)	97.4	7.2	34.5	11.2	23.4	21.1
GDP (U.S.$ millions)	180,793	9,042	55,926	14,513	50,347	50,965
Growth (%)	3.8	4.2	5.7	4.0	12.7	-3.3
GDP per capita (U.S.$)	1,856	1,256	1,621	1,296	2,152	2,415
Exports (U.S.$ millions)	33,471	985	8,572	3,717	4,502	15,695
Growth (%)	17.3	38.7	15.4	28.0	30.0	12.0
Imports (U.S.$ millions)	28,615	1,122	10,901	3,272	5,611	7,709
Growth (%)	3.5	5.1	20.0	40.7	38.8	-30.7
Trade Balance (U.S.$ mil.)	4,856	-137	-2,329	445	-1,109	7,986

Source: Inter-American Development Bank.

FORMATION OF THE ANDEAN PACT

The Andean Pact, created by the Cartagena Agreement of 1969, is one of the oldest attempts at regional economic integration in the Western Hemisphere. The original membership included Bolivia, Chile, Colombia, Ecuador, and Peru. Venezuela joined in 1973, and Chile withdrew in 1976. Peru suspended its participation in 1992, but may rejoin by January 1996.

The Andean Pact initially aimed to promote economic development by relying on an inward-looking and protectionist industrialization strategy. The key principles of the Cartagena Agreement included the primacy of the state as the leading agent in the economic development effort, protection of member state's infant industries from non-member imports, and a subsidiary role for foreign direct investment.[2]

Despite good intentions and some success in the early 1970s, the integration process slowed down in the late 1970s and early 1980s as the policy of shunning foreign goods and multinationals resulted in Andean consumers paying higher prices for lower-quality regional products.[3] By 1983, trade among the Andean Pact countries was actually declining, due to the Pact's protectionist policies, conflicting macroeconomic policies of member countries, and worsening economic conditions.[4]

In an effort to reinvigorate the integration process, the presidents of the five Andean countries in the late 1980s issued a number of directives that profoundly modified and redefined the Cartagena Agreement. New principles and priorities were established. Most importantly, the private sector and open markets were recognized as leading forces in economic development, an export-oriented strategy of industrialization was embraced, and a greater role for foreign capital was established. In the process, Andean economic integration came to be seen as a way to find new markets and economies necessary to become competitive internationally.[5]

In subsequent meetings, the Presidents of Bolivia, Colombia, Ecuador, Peru, and Venezuela agreed to create a regional free trade area by January 1992 and to establish a customs union -- that would link members with a four-level

---

[2] Cahn-Sanchez, Julio J. "Economic Integration in Latin America: The Andean Group in the 1990s," Paper delivered at the 1995 meeting of the Latin American Studies Association, Washington, D.C. September 28-30, 1995.

[3] "NAFTA Is Not Alone," *The Economist*, June 18, 1994, pp. 47-8.

[4] O'Keefe, Thomas Andrew. "Recent Developments in Andean Economic Integration and the Opportunities It Provides for Foreign Investors," *Focus Americas*, Volume 3, No.7, July/August 1995.

[5] Jatar, Ana Julia. "Two Steps Forward, One Step Back," *Hemisfile*, Vol 6, No. 4, July/August 1995, p. 6.

Common External Tariff (CET) -- by 1995. The Presidents also emphasized the need for closer economic ties with other Latin American countries and established the creation of a common market as the Andean Group's new long-term objective.[6]

In March 1992, Colombia and Venezuela launched the process by eliminating tariffs on all goods, except automobiles and some agricultural products, produced by the two countries. The other members, however, did not follow suit immediately. Ecuador, acting out of concern for increased import competition primarily from Colombia, demanded a slower liberalization pace. Peru, handicapped by an overvalued currency, insisted on being granted special concessions previously reserved for Ecuador and Bolivia, the Pact's less developed members.[7] And Bolivia, somewhat isolated at the end of the continent and more dependent on trade with Argentina and Brazil than with the other Andean countries, began entertaining thoughts of joining MERCOSUR.[8]

STATUS OF ANDEAN INTEGRATION

Since its formation, the Andean Pact's ultimate goal has been to create a common market. A sequential process to establish the common market was envisioned, with a free trade area and then a customs union to be achieved initially. A free trade area, such as NAFTA, eliminates tariffs on intra-regional or intra-group trade. A customs union entails free trade among its members and a common external tariff, but it does not involve the free movement of capital and labor among member countries. To achieve a common market, not only are free movement of labor and capital required, but coordination of macroeconomic and industrial policies are also necessary.

Free Trade Area

Overcoming the initial conflicts and exemptions, free trade among Ecuador, Colombia, Bolivia, and Venezuela has been in effect since February 1993 when virtually all tariffs on products manufactured and traded among member countries were eliminated. Colombia and Venezuela, the dominant Pact countries that account for 80 percent of all intra-regional trade, eliminated their tariffs for other Andean countries first. Bolivia, after being unsuccessful in

---

[6] Pasco-Font, Alberto and Sylvia Saboria. "U.S.-Andean Pact Free Trade," In Saboria, Sylvia. *The Premise and the Promise: Free Trade in the Americas.* Overseas Development Council, Washington, D.C. p. 235.

[7] In the aftermath of Peruvian President Fujimori's April 1992 self-inflicted coup, Colombia and Venezuela suspended negotiations with Peru.

[8] O'Keefe, "Recent Developments in Andean Economic Integration and the Opportunities It Provides for Foreign Investors," p. 3; For background on MERCOSUR, see: Ahearn, Raymond J. MERCOSUR - U.S. Trade Relations: Evolution and Prospects, CRS Report 95-940 F. August 28, 1995. 25p.

pursuing membership in MERCOSUR, joined the free trade area next. Ecuador, after overcoming the reservations of its private sector, followed Bolivia. Peru, which suspended its participation in the Andean Pact in 1992 due to President Fujimori's self-coup, must decide by January 1996 whether to join the free trade area.[9]

As is the case in other free trade areas, the Pact devised rules of origin to accompany intra-regional trade liberalization. Most generally, all goods traded among the five Andean countries must be accompanied by a certificate of origin certifying that they have at least 50 percent regional content. This requirement is intended to prevent non-member goods from being imported into the Andean country with the lowest external tariff and then re-exported to another Andean country duty-free. Such rules are necessary as long as all products imported from non-member countries are not covered by a common external tariff.[10]

Customs Union

In November 1994, the trade and integration ministers of the five Andean Pact countries approved the introduction of a CET. The CET went into effect on February 1, 1995, for Colombian, Venezuelan, and Ecuadorian imports from non-Andean Group countries. The tariff applies to 90 percent of the member-countries' imports and is based on the degree foreign goods have been processed or transformed. A four-tier schedule establishes a tariff of 5 percent for raw materials, 10 percent for semi-processed materials, 15 percent for manufactured goods, and 20 percent for highly manufactured goods. Goods not produced by any Andean Pact member are charged the lower import tariff of 5 percent.[11]

Each country also negotiated a list of products to be exempted from the CET for four years. Some 400 products were excluded by Ecuador and slightly over 200 by Colombia and Venezuela. Under a separate agreement, Colombia Ecuador, and Venezuela adopted a harmonized automotive policy with tariff rates of 35 percent for passenger vehicles, 15 percent for mass transit and cargo vehicles, and 3 percent for assembly kits.[12]

Bolivia and Peru have not yet joined the CET. Bolivia is less exposed to international trade than the other members, and currently applies a lower two-tier tariff schedule -- 5 percent and 10 percent. Peru applies a uniform tariff of 15 percent, with a few exceptions at 25 percent. Despite these disparities in the

---

[9] Ibid.

[10] Ibid.

[11] "Andean Group Sets External Tariffs," *Latin American Weekly Report,* December 8, 1994, p. 3.

[12] Office of the United States Trade Representative, *1995 Trade Estimates Report,* p. 67.

tariff rates among the Andean countries, they all are very low compared to the rates that prevailed in the region in the 1980s.[13]

Since February 1, 1995, the Andean Group has been applying a price band system for selected agricultural products. The purpose of the system is to moderate the prices of agricultural imports through tariff adjustments. Tariffs on products such as palm oil, soybean oil, rice, sugar, barley, milk, corn, soybeans, wheat, chicken, and pork are raised when international prices fall below a pre-determined minimum level and lowered when international prices rise above a pre-established ceiling.[14]

Common Market

As recently as 1991, Pact members reaffirmed their commitment to achieve a common market by calling for the development of common policies in areas such as industrial development, agricultural development, infrastructure development, exchange rate, monetary, financial and fiscal policies, and treatment of foreign investment.[15]

Nevertheless, the formation of a common market is not currently an issue under active consideration. Inability to fully achieve lesser forms of integration (i.e., a free trade area and customs union) explains why this is the case. Although the Andean members have developed some common policies in the areas of foreign direct investment, intellectual property protection, and air transportation that could facilitate the eventual formation of a common market, lack of cooperation and tensions within and between countries all but makes the free movement of people and capital an academic question at this point in time.

TRADE AND INVESTMENT EFFECTS

The economic integration achieved to date -- an almost complete free trade area among four members and a partial customs union among three members-- has helped boost trade among the Andean countries in recent years. Trade among members of the group (so-called intra-regional trade) grew by 27 percent in real terms between 1990 and 1994. Venezuela and Colombia, the dominant members of the group, have experienced the greatest increases in their trade shares. In 1994, Venezuela accounted for 48 percent of the Andean Group's intra-regional exports, and Colombia accounted for 32 percent.[16]

---

[13] O'Keefe, "Recent Developments in Andean Economic Integration and the Opportunities It Provides for Foreign Investors," p. 3.

[14] Inter-American Development Bank, *Economic Integration in the Americas,* Periodic Note, July 1995, p. 18.

[15] Ibid., footnote #37, p. 10.

[16] Ibid., p. 19.

At the same time that Andean intra-regional trade rose rapidly, Andean exports to countries outside the Pact grew by only 5 percent per year. As a result, the relative importance of intra-regional trade for these countries rose from 4 percent in 1990 to over 9 percent in 1994.[17] While this increase is notable, trade with the rest of the world remains of much greater importance for members of the Group.

The United States, which purchased 40 percent of Andean Group exports in 1994, is the main market for these countries. Trade with the rest of Latin America and with the European Union each represented about 13 percent of its total exports.

Figure 2.
Andean Pact -- Exports by Destination
(total US$35 billion: 1994)

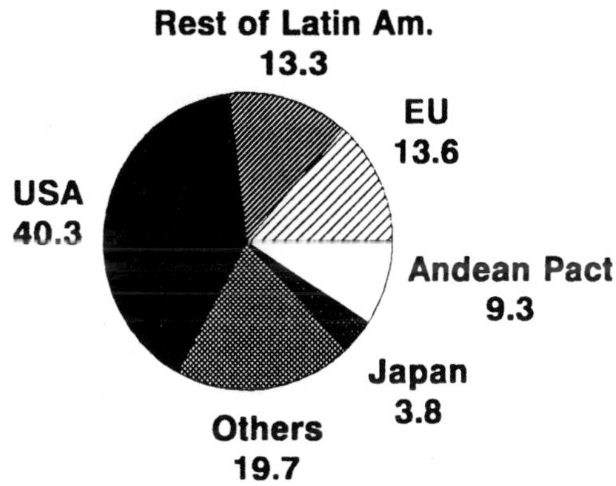

Source: Inter-American Development Bank.

Andean exports to the United States have been encouraged by the Andean Trade Preference Act (APTA), passed by Congress in 1991. The program arose out of U.S. concern over drug exports from four Andean countries (Bolivia, Colombia, Ecuador, and Peru) and is designed to encourage alternatives to coca cultivation and production by offering broader access to the U.S. market. Under the APTA, which went into effect in 1991 and expires in 2001, goods that have at least 35-percent content from any of the four countries may enter the United States duty free. More than 6,000 products are eligible to benefit from this

[17] Ibid., p. 18.

program including cut flowers and tropical fruits, timber and wood products, seafood and precious metals.[18]

For the United States, integration has coincided with expanding export and investment flows. U.S. exports to the region have increased by 37 percent, from $6.7 billion in 1990 to $10.8 billion in 1994. During this same period, U.S. imports have declined by 5 percent, falling from $15.1 billion in 1990 to $14.3 billion in 1994. As a result of these developments, the U.S. trade deficit with the Andean Group has declined from $8.4 billion in 1990 to $3.5 billion in 1994.

TABLE 2. U.S.-Andean Group Trade, 1990-1994 ($US billions)

	1990	1991	1992	1993	1994
U.S. Exports	6.7	8.6	10.9	10.2	10.8
U.S. Imports	15.1	13.2	13.2	13.5	14.3
Balance	-8.4	-4.6	-2.3	-3.3	-3.5

Source: U.S. Department of Commerce merchandise trade statistics.

The commodity composition of U.S.- Andean Group trade remains highly complementary and congruent with the varied resource endowments of the two regions. U.S. imports from the Andean Group are comprised overwhelmingly of energy products (nearly 70 percent of total imports are crude oil, coal, or oil) and natural resource-based products such as bananas, coffee, fish and minerals (tin, tungsten, and iron ores). Conversely, the main U.S. exports are manufactured goods such as parts for machinery and engines, computers, automobiles, trucks, and aircraft. In addition, the United States exports a substantial amount of wheat and corn.

In terms of foreign investment, the United States is the largest source of capital for the region. In Colombia and Venezuela, the region's dominant economies, the United States accounts for over 60 and 50 percent, respectively, of the total stock of foreign direct investment.

The U.S. direct investment position in the Andean countries more than doubled over the last five years, rising from an accumulated stock valued at $3.8 billion in 1990 to $8.3 billion in 1994, according to U.S. historical cost data. The bulk of the increase took place in Venezuela, up from $1.1 billion in 1990 to $2.3 billion in 1993 and in Colombia, where the stock of U.S. investment increased from $1.6 billion to $2.5 billion over the same period.

[18] O'Keefe, "Recent Developments in Andean Economic Integration and the Opportunities It Provides for Foreign Investors," p. 5.

TABLE 3. U.S. Direct Investment Position in Andean Group
($US millions)

	1990	1991	1992	1993	1994
Colombia	1,647	1,876	2,436	2,542	3,442
Ecuador	278	321	294	511	728
Peru	594	492	620	631	836
Venezuela	1,063	1,427	1,977	2,295	2,978
Bolivia	196	185	122	196	269
Totals	3,778	4,301	5,449	6,175	8,253

Source: Historical-cost data based on various editions of Survey of Current Business.

As in other regions that have become larger and more open due to successful economic integration schemes and unilateral liberalization programs, the Andean Pact may be providing U.S. investors with some new opportunities for setting up manufacturing, distribution, and marketing operations with an eye to greater rationalization and streamlining of operations. Much of the new investment in the Andean region has also been spurred by the rapid privatization of state enterprises. Bolivia, Colombia and Peru, which have been pursuing ambitious privatization plans, are particularly favored. Ecuador has been slow to privatize while Venezuela has temporarily frozen its program due to financial problems.[19]

IMPACT ON TRADE RELATIONS

In recent years, the Andean countries have entered into negotiations for reciprocal reductions of trade barriers both as a regional entity and as individual countries. The regional approach has been directed at a possible broader free trade area between the Andean Group and MERCOSUR. There is also a possibility that the Andean Group at some future date could negotiate as a regional entity for accession to NAFTA.

Since 1994, representatives of the Andean Group and MERCOSUR have held a number of meetings to explore the possibility of merging the two trading blocs. Such a merger would be a major step towards creating a South American Free Trade Area (SAFTA), a proposal that has considerable support in Brazil. At these meetings, however, differences have surfaced over the best way to

[19] Thurston, Charles W. "Struggling to Survive," *International Business*, October 1994, pp. 38-42.

achieve a free trade area between the two blocs and the process appears to be moving slowly.[20]

Outside the Andean Pact framework, Venezuela and Colombia negotiated a trade liberalizing agreement with Mexico on June 13, 1994. This agreement, which took effect on January, 1, 1995, seeks to establish a free trade area by 2005. This so-called Group of Three (G-3) Accord includes nearly all of the same chapters as NAFTA (only the energy chapter is missing). Obligations are included for areas such as rules of origin, safeguards, government procurement, financial services, and telecommunications. Adoption of NAFTA-equivalent obligation by Colombia and Venezuela in these areas could facilitate the eventual accession of these countries to NAFTA.[21]

Overlap between the G-3 and the CET of the Andean Group, however, has sparked protests from Colombian and Venezuelan manufacturers. The concern is that because G-3-partner Mexico imports most of its capital goods duty-free from the United States pursuant to NAFTA, Colombian and Venezuelan manufacturers are disadvantaged since they are subject to a tariff floor at least 5 percent under the terms of the Andean CET.[22]

Colombia and Venezuela have also signed free trade agreements with Chile and with the Caribbean Common Market (CARICOM). In addition, they are discussing free trade agreements with the Central American Common Market. As is the case with the G-3 accord, these separate agreements erode the preferences of Bolivia and Ecuador and have the potential to undermine Andean Pact unity.[23]

The other members of the Andean Group have also negotiated free trade agreements separately. Bolivia has signed free-trade agreements with Uruguay (1991), Argentina (1992), Chile (1993), Brazil (1994), Mexico (1994), and Paraguay (1994). Peru signed a free trade agreement with Brazil (1993), and Ecuador signed one with Chile (1994). What effect these agreements are having on the preferences built into the Andean Pact, as well as on Andean unity, remain largely unknown.[24]

---

[20] Latin American Regional Reports: *Andean Group Report*, "Trade Integration Faces Setbacks," April 13, 1995, pp. 4-5.

[21] O'Keefe, "Recent Developments in Andean Economic Integration and the Opportunities It Provides for Foreign Investors," p. 4.

[22] O'Keefe, Thomas Andrew. "Operating Under the Group of Three (G-3) Trade Accord," *Latin American Law and Business Report,* January 31, 1995, footnote #3, p. 32.

[23] Inter-American Development Bank, *Economic Integration in the Americas,* pp. 4-5.

[24] Ibid., p.5.

PROSPECTS

The future of the Andean Pact is difficult to predict. Entering the latter half of the 1990s, will it consolidate and deepen earlier gains achieved from integration by formally completing the formation of the free trade area and the customs union? Will a deeper level of integration translate into a stronger commitment to play a active role as a sub-regional entity in negotiating free trade arrangements with either NAFTA or the MERCOSUR? Or is the Pact more likely to weaken or break-up as a result of conflict within and among its members?

It is clear that the future challenges the Pact must address are formidable. Two members, Peru and Ecuador, engaged this year in a costly war and tensions between the two countries remain high. Peru and Bolivia remain outside the customs union, refusing to adopt the common external tariff. Peru, moreover, wants some form of compensatory duties as a price for joining the free trade area. Bolivia and Ecuador, the two poorest members of the Pact, remain in a position to demand exceptions and exemptions to the common policies of the Pact. Colombia and Venezuela, the key countries of the Pact, are coping with difficult economic and political problems. While both countries were both designated by the Bush Administration as potential candidates for accession to NAFTA, consideration of this possibility has abated.

In Colombia, the Administration of President Ernesto Samper, which has been in power for just over one year, has demonstrated very little interest in accelerating domestic economic reforms or in consolidating the Andean integration process. Although the country's trade and investment interests lie predominantly with North America, the government has shown a greater inclination in pursuing negotiations with Brazil and the MERCOSUR. The lack of linkage with drug and human rights issues that such negotiations present perhaps plays a role in this calculation of the Samper Administration.

The situation in Venezuela is even more difficult. The Administration of President Rafael Caldera, which took office in February 1994, has reversed the free market reforms instituted by the Perez Administration in 1989. Under Caldera, banks have been rescued through a government bail-out, exchange controls have been reinstituted, and price controls on a large number of consumer goods have been reintroduced. These actions have done little to revive a sinking economy or to curb one of the world's highest inflation rates. The Caldera Administration may next impose import restrictions and devalue the currency in an effort to deal with a growing trade deficit. If that happens, the competitive effects of making Venezuela's exports cheaper and its imports more expensive could severely test Andean Pact unity.

Despite these problems and pressures, there are good reasons for the countries to continue integrating economically. A decision to deviate from Pact commitments or to formally dissolve the Pact, for example, could send a very negative signal to foreign investors that the economic climate in these countries has deteriorated. Without foreign capital, the efforts of these countries to stabilize their economies and deal with their socio-economic problems would be much more difficult. Moreover, a case can be made that scope for future trade gains through integration and liberalization is greatest with the United States -- the main trade partner of each member country -- and that such integration will not take place on a bilateral basis between each country and the United States, but rather between a regional entity, such as the Andean Pact, and the United States.

Nevertheless, for now, U.S. trade relations with the Andean countries are conducted largely on a bilateral basis. All the Andean Pact countries individually have signed trade and investment agreements with the United States. These agreements provide a framework for detecting, monitoring, and resolving bilateral trade and investment problems. Unless and until the Andean Group as a regional entity forges a trade relationship with the United States, U.S. trade relations and negotiations with these countries will continue to have a heavy bilateral component for the indefinite future.

APPENDIX

BOLIVIA - U.S. TRADE RELATIONS

Bolivia, a landlocked country covering over 424,000 square miles in the middle of South America, is one of the poorest countries in the western hemisphere. Per capita income in 1994 was an estimated $1,000, lower than all other Latin American countries except Haiti. Seventy percent of the population lives in poverty and the average life expectancy is 60 years. In a country of 7.7 million, fewer than 1 million have formal jobs, only 350,000 have bank accounts, and 45,000 depositors own 85 percent of the assets. Although Spanish is the official language, the majority consists primarily of indigenous Aymara- and Quechua-speaking peoples of the "highlands" who remain tied to subsistence agriculture and primitive commerce.

Mine owners and landowners dominated Bolivia's economy until a 1952 revolution nationalized the mines and opened the countryside to land reform. But the revolution, followed by military dictatorships and political instability, led to a decade of economic turmoil, hyperinflation and capital flight.

Soon after the return of civilian government in 1982, Bolivia became one the first Latin American countries to attempt to dismantle its state-dominated and heavily protected economy and expose itself to greater international competition. Market-oriented reforms including introduction of a freely floating exchange rate, elimination of import and investment liberalization permits, reduction of government spending, and greater freedom for companies to operate in areas formerly reserved for government enterprises were instituted in 1985.

The results of these and other reforms have been a dramatic drop in inflation (to less than 15 percent since the astronomical 23,000 percent in 1986), steady economic growth (between 2.5 and 4.1 percent annually starting in 1987), and growing amounts of private investment and savings.[25] Moreover, the nation sits on vast, if underdeveloped, natural resources, including fertile farm lands and mineral, oil, and gas deposits.

This overall positive record and future potential, however, has not been sufficient to significantly improve the lives of the poor majority. Faster economic growth, the current government believes, is required to achieve this objective. To this end, the government is seeking to promote a sharp increase in the private investment rate.[26]

---

[25] U.S. Department of State, "Country Reports on Economic And Trade Practices," February 1995, p. 329.

[26] Fidler, Steve. *The Financial Times*, "Economic Growth Is the Key," November 9, 1994, p. I.

The Administration of President Gonzalo Sanchez de Lozado, which took office in August 1993, hopes to increase private investment from the current level of 14 percent of GDP to 20 percent by 1996. At the heart of the Sanchez plan is an effort to privatize six state-owned industries -- oil, electricity, telecommunications, airlines, railroads, and tin smelting -- that account for over half of the country's economic activity.

Under Bolivia's "capitalization" program, state companies are being sold differently than under most other privatization schemes. New investors can bid on half the companies' shares and full management control in return for investing millions of new capital (equivalent to the value of each company's underlying assets) in each of the public companies. The remaining shares will be divided among adult Bolivians and will be held in retirement accounts in a new private pension system. By turning over the government's half-ownership in the companies to the Bolivian people, the government hopes to increase the incomes of poor Bolivians through private-sector ownership and establish a pool of domestic savings to fuel investment within the country.[27]

Trade and Investment Flows

Bolivia was one of the first countries in Latin America to follow Chile's lead and adopt market-oriented reforms designed to promote trade and investment flows. Tariffs are the lowest in the region: 5 percent for capital goods and 10 percent for all other imports. Capital is allowed to freely flow into and out of Bolivia. Nearly ten years after these reforms were initiated, Bolivia's economy is much more diversified and integrated with foreign economies.

Exports of tin, zinc, gold ore, and natural gas -- so-called traditional exports derived from mining or hydrocarbons -- still account for over half of all export revenue. But growing non-traditional exports such as soybeans, timber, Amazon nuts, refined gold jewelry, and textiles now account for close to half of all export revenues.[28]

Approximately 40 percent of Bolivia's trade is with other Latin American countries, and Argentina, Brazil, and Chile are its major regional trading partners. The European Union accounts for 28 percent of Bolivia's trade and imports mostly traditional mineral-based products. The United States accounts for 24 percent of Bolivia's trade and is Bolivia's main market for non-traditional exports.

In 1994, U.S. imports from Bolivia totalled $260 million, a 27-percent increase over 1993. The main categories of U.S. imports were jewelry and parts

---

[27] Hendrix, Steve. "A Capital Idea in Bolivia", *Wall Street Journal,* September 22, 1995, p A15.

[28] Bowen, Sally. "A Healthier Footing," *Financial Times*, November 9, 1994, p. II.

($104 million), tin ($51 million), wood ($29 million), cane or beet sugar ($11 million), and lead ores ($9 million).

U.S. exports to Bolivia have been uneven over the last four years: the U.S. exported $190 million in 1991, $222 million in 1992, $216 million in 1993, and $186 million in 1994. The principal U.S. export commodities to Bolivia in 1994 were wheat and flour ($23 million), parts for machinery ($8 million), cyanide ($8 million), computer equipment ($7 million), and machinery for sorting and screening minerals ($6 million).

The U.S. merchandise trade balance with Bolivia has shown considerable variation in recent years. As shown in table 4, U.S. trade with Bolivia was in deficit in 1990, 1991, and 1994 and in surplus in 1992 and 1993.

TABLE 4. U.S.-Bolivia Trade, 1990-1994 ($US millions)

	1990	1991	1992	1993	1994
U.S. Exports	138	192	222	218	185
U.S. Imports	203	208	162	191	260
Balance	-65	-16	+60	+27	-75

Source: U.S. Department of Commerce merchandise trade statistics.

The United States is the largest foreign investor in Bolivia. The stock of U.S. investment, which grew by over 25 percent between 1990 and 1994 (rising from $196 million to $269 million), is concentrated in the petroleum, energy, and jewelry industries.

U.S. investment in Bolivia is likely to grow as a result of the capitalization program. To date, Bolivia has selected three U.S. companies as owners of a 50 percent stake in three electricity-generating companies. Within a year, the telecommunications and airline industries are scheduled to be offered up for sale.

Major Bilateral Issues

Bolivia is seldom the target of U.S. complaints about trade and investment barriers. According to the U.S. Department of State, Bolivia does not impose significant barriers to U.S. exporters or investors. As the world's third largest producer of coca leaf, however, Bolivia's relations with the United States are dominated by U.S. counter-narcotics efforts.

In its March 1995 international narcotics control certification to Congress, the Clinton Administration could not completely certify that Bolivia was fully cooperating on counter-narcotics efforts, but waived the requirement to cut off U.S. aid on national security grounds. The Clinton Administration warned

Bolivia that it would face a funding cutoff if it did not sign a new extradition treaty, develop a coca eradication plan, and eradicate 1,750 hectares by June 30, 1995. While Bolivia met the eradication goals and signed a new extradition treaty in June, U.S. eradication efforts remain a politically volatile issue in Bolivia.[29]

U.S. officials express some concerns about Bolivia's intellectual property rights protection and the conclusion of a bilateral investment treaty. On intellectual property, the United States is seeking improvements in Bolivia's legislation to prevent piracy of books, software, and movies. Bolivia's continuing reluctance to allow for binding arbitration in the hydrocarbons sector has been a major obstacle to concluding a bilateral investment treaty.

COLOMBIA - U.S. TRADE RELATIONS

Colombia is the most populous Andean Pact country with over 35 million inhabitants. It has the second largest economy within the Pact in terms of both GDP and per capita GDP (Venezuela is the largest). And it also is the only South American country with coastlines on both the Pacific Ocean and the Caribbean Sea.

For most of its history, Colombia has been dependent on exports of a few traditional commodities such as petroleum, coffee, and coal. During the past decade, a more diversified economy has evolved that includes a large number of retail and financial services industries and a broad array of manufacturing industries. Trade in contraband goods, including cocaine and consumer goods, continues to thrive despite the concerted efforts by the Colombian government to curtail it.[30]

Since 1958, Colombia has been governed by freely elected civilian presidents, every one of whom completed his term in office. Nevertheless, weak and elite-based political institutions are viewed as important contributing causes to the country's widespread criminal violence, perpetuated by the drug cartels, rightist paramilitary groups, the military, and leftist guerrillas. Corruption, public and private, is also widespread.[31]

Despite the persistence of political and drug-related violence and corruption, Colombia's economic performance has been one of the strongest of any Latin

---

[29] Serafino, Nina M. *Bolivia: Briefing Paper,* CRS Report No. 95-680 F, June 2, 1995. 2 p.

[30] U.S. International Trade Commission. *U.S. Market Access in Latin America: Recent Liberalizing Measures and Remaining Barriers,* USITC Publication 2521, June 1992, pp. 6-8 and 6-9.

[31] Serafino, Nina M. *Colombia: Briefing Paper,* CRS Report No. 95-588 F. May 12, 1995. 2 p.

American country over the past two decades. During the 1980s, Colombia achieved moderate and stable economic growth rates averaging 3.5 percent and avoided the sharp downturn and foreign debt problems that most countries in Latin America experienced. More recently, Colombia escaped any fall-out from Mexico's financial crisis, another tribute to prudent economic management policies.[32]

In 1990, Colombia initiated a 5-year plan of economic reforms known as "apertura" (opening). The plan, which is designed to encourage foreign investment and the development of globally competitive industries, included liberalization of trade and investment policies, deregulation of the exchange rate, privatization of state enterprises, and reform of labor and tax laws.[33]

Since Colombia's new trade and investment policies were launched, Colombia's economy has produced real growth increases in excess of 5 percent and attracted growing amounts of foreign investment.[34]

The administration of Ernesto Samper, which assumed office in August 1994, has promised to continue the main thrust of the liberalization policies. President Semper, however, has indicated a preference for increasing spending on social development, particularly education and housing, and for slowing down the pace of the privatization program. The new administration is also committed to reducing unemployment, which has risen to nearly 9 percent, and the gap between rich and poor. Billions of dollars in revenues from recently discovered oil finds are counted on by the Samper government to pay for the new programs.[35]

Trade and Investment Flows

Colombia's "apertura" policies, begun under the leadership of former President Cesar Gaviria (1990-1994), have made great strides in making the Colombian economy more open to international trade and investment. The rapid opening of Colombia's economy, combined with faster economic growth, has led to a significant increase in imports.

From 1990-1994, imports rose $5.6 billion to $12 billion, a 53-percent increase. During this same period, Colombia's exports have increased by 23

---

[32] Hakim, Peter. "Colombia, the Gem and Bane of the Hemisphere," *Christian Science Monitor,* August 24, 1995, p. 19.

[33] U.S. International Trade Commission. *U.S. Market Access in Latin America: Recent Liberalization Measures and Remaining Barriers,* p. 6-8.

[34] U.S. Department of Commerce, "Colombia: Business Fact Sheet," Document #2102 available on OLAC Facts.

[35] Serafino, Nina M. *Colombia: Briefing Paper,* p. 2.

percent, rising from $6.8 billion to $8.9 billion. As a result of the more rapid increase in imports, Colombia is experiencing growing trade deficits.

Colombia's major exports continue to be fuel and natural resource-based products. In 1994, Colombia's major exports were petroleum and petroleum products (accounting for around 18 percent of export earnings), coffee (accounting for around 15 percent of export earnings), coal (accounting for around 7 percent of export earnings) and gold (accounting for around 4 percent of export earnings). The United States purchased over one-third of Colombia's total exports in 1994 and is Colombia's top market. Colombia's next most important country markets are Venezuela, Japan, Germany, and Brazil, respectively.

Nearly 90 percent of U.S. exports to Colombia are manufactured goods. Principal U.S. exports include aircraft, computers, motor vehicles, parts of machinery, plastics and cereals, and organic chemicals. In Latin America, only Mexico, Brazil, Venezuela, and Argentina are larger markets for U.S. exports.

Since posting small balance of trade deficits with Colombia in 1990 and 1991, the United States has recorded trade surpluses. In 1994, the U.S. trade surplus grew to $0.89 billion.

TABLE 5. U.S.-Colombia Trade, 1990-1994 ($billions)

	1990	1991	1992	1993	1994
U.S. Exports	2.03	1.95	3.28	3.24	4.06
U.S. Imports	3.17	2.74	2.84	3.03	3.17
Balance	-1.14	-0.79	+0.44	+0.21	+0.89

Source: U.S. Department of Commerce merchandise trade statistics.

The United States is the largest foreign investor in Colombia, accounting for an estimated 64 percent of the accumulated stock. U.S. investment is concentrated in petroleum (51 percent), mining (18 percent), manufacturing (21 percent) and financial institutions (6 percent).

U.S. investments have grown by 50 percent over the past four years, rising from $1.7 billion in 1990 to $3.4 billion in 1994. These substantial new U.S. investments have been spurred by Colombian's rich energy and mineral resources and by Colombia's vigorous privatization program. Seaports, airports, highways, telecommunications, energy projects and financial institutions are among the government assets that have been privatized. The government is also moving forward on the privatization of the nation's railroads, utilities, and telecommunications sectors. Continued growth can be expected as more and more U.S. companies choose to set up their headquarters for the Andean region in Colombia.[36]

Major Bilateral Issues

Colombia has made major progress in opening its economy to foreign trade in the 1990s. Tariffs have been reduced from 35-40 percent to an average of roughly 12 percent, import licensing requirements have been mostly eliminated, and investment screening and most prohibitions have been ended. Foreign investors, for example, can own up to 100 percent of financial institutions and virtually all other sectors of the Colombian economy except for those dealing with national security or disposal of hazardous waste products.[37]

Despite the progress made, Colombia still imposes some trade and investment barriers. The agricultural sector remains heavily protected through import licensing, variable levies, and outright bans. Colombia's compliance with the European Union's import licensing regime for bananas has invited U.S. threats of trade sanctions. Discriminatory government procurement measures, foreign television programming requirements, and weak intellectual property protection are some key remaining obstacles to foreign trade and investment.[38]

As in the case with Bolivia, bilateral trade and investment issues continue to be overshadowed by counter-narcotics efforts. In February 1995, the Clinton Administration could not certify to Congress that Colombia was cooperating fully on counter-narcotics efforts, but waived the requirement to cut off U.S. aid on national interest grounds.[39]

ECUADOR - U.S. TRADE RELATIONS

Ecuador, which is about the size of Colorado, is the smallest Andean country in terms of land area and, with 11 million inhabitants, the second smallest in terms of population. Based on per capita income, Ecuador ranks with Peru as being the poorest Andean country.

Ecuador is a constitutional republic with a president and a 77-member unicameral legislature chosen in free elections. The 1994 midterm elections left President Sixto Duran Ballen's governing coalition with only nine seats in the National Assembly. The Assembly has used its extensive powers to censure and

---

[36] U.S. Department of Commerce, "Colombia: Commercial Overview", OLAC Facts, Document #2112.

[37] U.S. Department of State. "Country Reports on Economic Policy and Trade Practices, 1995, p.349.

[38] Ibid., p. 351.

[39] Serafino, Nina M. *Colombia: Briefing Paper,* p. 2.

remove dozens of cabinet ministers over the past few years. The judiciary is constitutionally independent, but it has a history of being susceptible to outside pressures.[40] Ecuador's Vice President recently resigned and fled the country following a decision by the Supreme Court to issue an arrest warrant for him on charges of corruption.[41]

The Ecuadorian economy has long been dependent on natural resource-based products. Oil generates over 40 percent of the country's export earnings and nearly half of the central government's revenue. Ecuador is the world's largest exporter of bananas and a major producer of shrimp, which together account for a third of the country's exports. Ecuador's farmers also produce a variety of crops for domestic consumption. Manufacturing is largely oriented to producing for the domestic market, but regional economic integration is creating more export opportunities for manufacturers. The services sector -- including wholesale and retail trade, transport and communications, and financial services -- accounts for one-half of Ecuador's GDP and is responsible for much of Ecuador's growth during the past decade.[42]

During the 1970s, Ecuador experienced annual growth rates that averaged almost 9 percent, making it one of Latin America's fastest growing economies. This expansion was driven primarily by growing revenues associated with sharply rising prices for petroleum exports. During the oil boom years of the 1970s, the government borrowed heavily from foreign banks, increased spending on consumers and producers, and expanded the government's role in the economy. When oil prices began to decline in the 1980s, however, the economy began to slow dramatically and fiscal deficits began to escalate to the point where in 1987 Ecuador stopped paying debt service to foreign commercial banks.[43]

Ecuador implemented an IMF-backed macroeconomic stabilization program beginning in 1988 and began partial repayments of its debt in 1989. In 1992, a conservative advocate of economic liberalization, Sixto Duran Ballen, was elected president over social democratic and populist opposition. Since his election,

---

[40] U.S. Department of State. Annual Report on Human Rights Practices, 1994.

[41] Culitt, Raymond. "Ecuador in Crisis as Vice-President Flees," *Financial Times*, October 13, 1995, p. 7.

[42] U.S. International Trade Commission. Annual Report on the Impact of the Andean Trade Preference Act on U.S. Industries and Consumers and On Drug Crop Eradication and Crop Substitution, USITC Publication 2814, September 1994, p. 15.

[43] Ibid.

President Duran has attempted to stabilize the economy, reduce the large public sector deficit, and expand the role of the free market.[44]

During the early 1990s, Ecuador also initiated a major liberalization of its trade and investment regimes. A highly protectionist tariff schedule was overhauled, reducing tariffs for most products to the 5 to 20 percent range. Import surcharges were eliminated for most products and customs procedures were streamlined. Foreign investors were provided full national treatment and investment screening and approval requirements were largely eliminated.[45]

Trade and Investment Flows

The United States provides Ecuador with its largest foreign market. In 1994, U.S. purchases of $1.8 billion of goods accounted for 44 percent of Ecuador's total exports. Leading Ecuadorian exports to the United States in 1993 included oil ($532 million), fish ($455 million), bananas ($212 million) and coffee ($186 million). Germany, which accounts for around 6 percent, and Chile and Peru, which each account for around 4 percent, are Ecuador's next largest country markets.[46]

The United States is also Ecuador's leading supplier of imports. In 1994, the United States accounted for 35 percent of Ecuador's total imports of $3.8 billion. The leading U.S. exports to Ecuador (1993 data) were parts for machinery ($112 million), paper and paperboard ($64 million), computers ($40 million), chemicals ($32 million), bulldozers ($32 million), and cars ($31 million). Japan (12 percent) and Colombia (9 percent) were the next leading suppliers of Ecuador's import needs.

In recent years, the United States has posted small trade deficits with Ecuador. The largest deficit of $698 million was registered in 1990.

TABLE 6. U.S.-Ecuador Trade, 1990-1994 ($millions)

	1990	1991	1992	1993	1994
U.S. Exports	678	948	999	1,100	1,195
U.S. Imports	1,376	1,327	1,344	1,399	1,726
Balance	-698	-379	-345	-299	-531

Source: U.S. Department of Commerce merchandise trade statistics.

---

[44] U.S. Department of State. "Country Reports on Economic and Trade Practices," February 1995, p. 367.

[45] Ibid., p. 369.

[46] International Monetary Fund. *Directions of Trade Statistics Yearbook: 1988-94.*

In the area of foreign direct investment, the United States is the largest investor in Ecuador. Most of the U.S. investment is concentrated in petroleum ($355 out of a total stock of $511 million in 1993), but a significant amount ($97 million) is in manufacturing.

While remaining between $184 and $240 million from 1989 - 1992, U.S. foreign direct investment increased rapidly in 1993 to $511 million and again in 1994 to $728 million. Some of the additional investment may have been stimulated by economic and investment reforms implemented and some may have been attracted by Ecuador's privatization program. To date, a number of state-owned businesses, including cement plants and hotels have been divested and sold. Privatization of the telecommunications, transportation and utility sectors is also being planned.[47]

Major Bilateral Issues

Although Ecuador has not opened up its economy as rapidly as a number of other Latin American countries, the trend has clearly been toward substantial liberalization of its trade and investment regimes. Ecuador's acceptance by the World Trade Organization (WTO) for membership in 1995 is a confirmation of the progress made.

Ecuador's remaining trade and investment barriers are relatively minor problems. On the trade front, aspects of Ecuador's customs procedures, price bands for agricultural products, procedures for bidding on government contracts, and enforcement of intellectual property rights remain problems for some U.S. exporters. In terms of investment issues, some remaining limitations on foreign investment in petroleum, mining, fishing, electricity, telecommunications, and the media could be raised in the future.[48]

PERU - U.S. TRADE RELATIONS

Peru is situated on the western coast of South America between Ecuador and Chile. The terrain of Peru varies widely, encompassing the western coastal plain, rugged Andes, and the eastern lowland jungle of the Amazon Basin. With a population of close to 24 million inhabitants, Peru is the second largest Andean country next to Colombia and with a GDP of $50 billion, it is the third largest Andean economy.

Despite its abundant silver, copper, tin, lead, gold, and zinc reserves, Peru experienced one of the worst economic performances of any Latin American

---

[47] Yolen, Steve.- "A Master Juggler of Modernization," *Wall Street Journal,* September 26, 1995, p. B15.

[48] *Wall Street Journal.* "Ecuador: An Improved Investment Climate," September 9, 1994, p. A6.

country during the 1980s. The economy contracted on average by a little over 1 percent annually during this period. Foreign debt obligations grew dramatically and Peru's ability to service those payments declined commensurately. Inflation also rose dramatically, reaching over 7,000 percent in 1990.[49]

A number of reasons may account for Peru's dismal economic performance in the 1980s. Protectionist and interventionist state policies aimed at controlling economic activity were one major cause. A second was the economic dislocations caused by violent anti-business and anti-government guerilla movements, primarily associated with activities of the *Sendero Luminoso* (Shining Path).[50] The terrorist activities of this group and others inflicted millions of dollars of damage on Peru's transportation and power systems and sharply discouraged foreign investment.[51]

Since the first election of Alberto Fujimori as President in 1990, Peru has taken dramatic steps to convert its economy from one dominated by a protectionist and interventionist state to a liberal economy dominated by the private sector and market forces.[52] Price controls and subsidies have been greatly reduced or eliminated and trade, investment, and foreign exchange restrictions have been lifted. The Fujimori Administration also adopted one of Latin America's most extensive privatization programs with plans to sell 75 state-owned companies, two-thirds of which have already been sold for over $3 billion.[53]

President Fujimori coupled his market-oriented economic reforms with a direct offensive against the Shining Path guerrillas. While constitutional rule was suspended during most of 1992, the government captured and jailed key guerilla leaders, including Shining Path founder Abimael Guzman in September 1992. Since his capture, terrorist attacks have declined significantly.[54]

---

[49] U.S. International Trade Commission. Annual Report on the Impact of the Andean Trade Preference Act on U.S. Industries and Consumers, p. 16.

[50] For background on the Shining Path see: *Peru's Shining Path: Background on the Movement, Counterinsurgency Strategy, and U.S. Policy.* CRS Report No. 93-295 F. March 1, 1993. 35 p. By Larry A. Niksch and Mark P. Sullivan.

[51] Ibid.

[52] U.S. Department of State. "Country Reports on Economic Policy and Trade Practices," February 1995, p. 416.

[53] Brooke, James. "Peru: On the Very Fast Track," *New York Times*, January 31, 1995. pp. D1, D19.

[54] U.S. International Trade Commission. Annual Report on the Impact of the Andean Trade Preference Act on U.S. Industries and Consumers, p. 16.

Fujimori's economic reforms and the lessening of guerilla violence helped facilitate a dramatic turnaround in Peru's economy. The GDP recovered from a downward spiral and grew at 6.5 percent in 1993 and by almost 13 percent in 1994 -- the world's fastest growth rate. Peru's economic growth is expected to be around 8.5 percent in 1995. Annual inflation has dropped to a little over 10 percent from the 7,000 percent level when Fujimori entered office in 1990. In addition, the more stable and open economy has attracted an upsurge in foreign investment.[55]

Trade and Investment Flows

Peru's trade began to expand in the 1990s as the economy became more stable and open. Exports rose from $3.2 billion in 1990 to $4.5 billion in 1994, a 28-percent increase. Peru's traditional exports -- copper, fishmeal, zinc, gold, petroleum, and lead -- accounted for over 60 percent of total export revenues. Non-traditional exports including textiles, apparel, and metallic minerals accounted for around 40 percent of the total revenue.

The United States is the top market for Peruvian exports, purchasing 28 percent of Peru's exports in 1994. Japan and the United Kingdom are Peru's second and third best customers respectively. Peru's principal exports to the United States include jewelry, oil, silver, lead, flour, and coffee.

The United States is also Peru's leading supplier of imports. In 1994 the United States also supplied 28 percent of total Peruvian imports. Principal U.S. products purchased by Peru include non-crude oil, machinery parts, computer equipment, wheat, and fertilizers.[56]

U.S. exports to Peru increased at a faster rate than U.S. imports from Peru during 1990 to 1994. As a result, the U.S. merchandise trade balance with Peru improved from a $30 million deficit in 1990 to a $560 million surplus in 1994.

TABLE 7. U.S.-Peru Trade, 1990-1994 (millions US dollars)

	1990	1991	1992	1993	1994
U.S. Exports	772	840	1,005	1,072	1,408
U.S. Imports	802	776	738	754	841
Balance	-30	+64	+267	+318	+567

Source: U.S. Department of Commerce merchandise trade statistics.

[55] Serafino, Nina M. *Peru: Briefing Paper.* CRS Report No. 94-797 F, May 31, 1995, 2 p.

[56] U.S. Department of Commerce trade data.

In the area of foreign investment, the United States is the largest direct investor in Peru. On an historical cost basis, the stock of U.S. investment has increased from $594 million in 1990 to $836 million in 1994, a 29-percent increase. This large increase owes much to both Peru's improved economic outlook and its extensive privatization program. Reportedly, U.S. petroleum and mining companies are increasing drilling and digging activities and a wide range of firms are participating in Peruvian sales of state-owned enterprises.

Major Bilateral Issues

Over the past five years, Peru has eliminated almost all import and investment barriers. There are no remaining quantitative or qualitative limits on imports, and Peru's investment regime is now among the most liberal in the world. A few exceptions to this trend of greater openness, however, exist. Import surcharges remain on a number of agricultural products (covering wheat, rice, corn, sugar, and milk products), but they are scheduled to be phased out by the end of 1996 as a condition for disbursement of an Inter-American Development Bank trade-sector loan. Peru's intellectual property treatment also still falls short of international standards.[57]

Bilateral relations continue to be predominantly focused on counter-narcotics cooperation as Peru is the world's largest producer of coca leaf. In 1994 and 1995, President Clinton certified Peru eligible for continuing assistance on national interest grounds, even though it judged that the country was not fully cooperating on counter-narcotics efforts.[58]

VENEZUELA - U.S. TRADE RELATIONS

Located in the northernmost part of South America, Venezuela borders the Caribbean Sea between Colombia and Guyana. It covers an area that is slightly more than twice the size of California. With a population of 21 million, Venezuela's economy generates a GDP of roughly $51 billion and a per capita income level of $2415.

Petroleum is the backbone of the Venezuelan economy. The nationalized petroleum industry is a major source of domestic production, government revenue and foreign exchange earnings, accounting for 23 percent of GDP, and over 75 percent of export earnings and government revenue in recent years. Government-owned companies also dominate industrial sectors such as

---

[57] U.S. Department of State. *Peru: 1994 Country Report on Economic Policy and Trade Practices*, February 1995, p. 417.

[58] Serafino, Nina M. *Peru: Briefing Paper*, p. 2.

hydrocarbons, basic petrochemicals, steel, aluminum, iron and bauxite mining, and utilities.[59]

Venezuela's rich natural resources base, particularly oil, enabled the country to achieve one of the highest standards of living in the region during the 1970s. But the collapse in oil prices during the 1980s, combined with heavy government foreign borrowing to support unproductive state companies, led to severe inflationary pressures and a balance-of-payments crisis in 1989.

The financial crisis prompted President Carlos Andres Perez (1989-1993) to initiate major "market-oriented" reforms. These included a liberalization of exchange rate, trade and investment controls, elimination of most price controls, a reduction in public spending, privatization of state companies, and a major tax reform designed to lower individual rates.[60]

The Perez free market program, which was intended to move Venezuela away from a petroleum-based, statist economy, were described by the World Bank "as one of the most forward-looking in Latin America." In strictly economic terms, the reforms proved successful as the economy grew at an average annual rate of 7 percent from 1990 through 1992 and foreign capital began to accelerate, with more money invested in 1990 alone than in the 1980s altogether.

But the program, which included deep budget cuts that reduced the purchasing power of most Venezuelans and exacerbated already high levels of unemployment, was politically unpopular. Bloody riots erupted in 1989 when the reform measures were introduced, and these riots were followed by two military coup attempts in 1992. Then, in May 1993, the program's unpopularity contributed to the ouster of President Perez on corruption charges, who was replaced by a provisional president.[61]

By the time a new elected President, Rafael Caldera, took office in February 1994, the Venezuelan economy was in the midst of a banking and foreign exchange crisis, as well as a recession. President Caldera reacted to Venezuela's deteriorating economic situation by reversing the free market reforms instituted in 1989 by Perez. Under President Caldera, the banks were rescued through a huge and inflationary infusion of government funds, exchange controls were reinstituted, and price controls on an extensive range of consumer goods were

---

[59] U.S. International Trade Commission. *U.S. Market Access in Latin America: Recent Trade Liberalization Measures and Remaining Barriers*, USITC Publication 2521, June 1992. p. 6-15.

[60] Sucre, Alejandro J. "Mexican Beware! What IMF Austerity Did for Venezuelans," *Wall Street Journal,* February 24, 1995, p. A11.

[61] Sullivan, Mark. *Venezuela: Political and Economic Situation and U.S.-Venezuelan Relations,* CRS Report No. 94-362 F, April 25, 1994. p. 8.

reintroduced. Privatization of state-owned enterprises and other cuts in the public sector work force were put on hold.[62]

To date, the Caldera controls have done little to revive economic activity. The economy is shrinking for the third consecutive year, inflation is running at around 70 percent -- among the world's highest rates -- and private investment is continuing to decline. Although the Caldera Administration initially touted the controls as temporary, it has not yet outlined a coherent plan for tackling the country's increasingly difficult economic woes.[63]

Trade and Investment Flows

The United States is Venezuela's largest trading partner, accounting for 50 percent of its exports and 43 percent of its imports in 1994. Venezuela's other major trading partners are Germany, Japan, Italy, Brazil, and Colombia.[64]

U.S. imports from Venezuela have experienced consistent and steady increases over the past seven years, rising from $5.2 billion in 1988 to $8.4 billion in 1994. The vast bulk of U.S. imports (90 percent) consist of crude oil and petroleum. Remaining significant categories of imports include iron ores and concentrates, bitumen and asphalt, eithers and ether-alcohols, spongy ferrous products and iron, and unwrought aluminum.

U.S. exports to Venezuela, over 80 percent of which are manufactured goods, have been affected by that country's economic reforms and conditions. Following initiation of Venezuela's reform program in 1989, U.S. exports declined by almost 40 percent, falling from $4.9 billion in 1988 to the $3.0 billion level in 1989 and 1990. U.S. exports then rebounded in 1992 to $5.4 billion, an increase of 80 percent over the 1989 level. But Venezuela's political and economic difficulties over the past three years (1993-1995) have contributed to another sharp decline in U.S. exports.

The contraction in U.S. exports over the past three years, combined with steady or constant U.S. imports from Venezuela, has led to a rise in the U.S. trade deficit with Venezuela from $2.8 billion in 1992 to $4.4 billion in 1994. This trend is unlikely to change unless Venezuela is able to create a more stable and productive economy.

---

[62] Moffett, Matt. "Venezuela Is Suffering, Its Economy Strangled by Too Many Controls," *Wall Street Journal,* August 16, 1995. pp. A1, A6.

[63] Ibid.

[64] U.S. Department of Commerce data.

TABLE 8. U.S.-Venezuela Trade, 1988-1994 ($US billions)

	1988	1989	1990	1991	1992	1993	1994
U.S. Exports	4.9	3.0	3.1	4.7	5.4	4.6	4.0
U.S. Imports	5.2	6.8	9.5	8.2	8.2	8.1	8.4
Balance	-0.3	-3.8	-6.4	-3.5	-2.8	-3.5	-4.4

Source: U.S. Department of Commerce merchandise trade statistics.

With regards to foreign investment, the United States is the largest source in Venezuela, supplying a little over 50 percent of total foreign direct investment in recent years. The Netherlands, which supplies about 10 percent of Venezuela's direct investment, is the second largest supplier.

In 1994, U.S. foreign direct investment totalled $3.0 billion, twice the amount registered in 1989 when the reform program began to create a more hospitable environment for foreign direct investment. Most of the U.S. investment is concentrated in manufacturing ($1.5 billion) and petroleum ($0.2 billion). However, as a result of recent exchange and price controls, a number of foreign companies have curtailed their expansion plans, while international interest in Venezuela's privatization plan has dropped off significantly. For foreign investment to pick up again, the Caldera Government may have to reestablish credibility that the controls will be ended soon.[65]

Major Bilateral Issues

Venezuela liberalized its trade and investment regimes with the implementation of major free market reforms in 1989 and with its 1990 accession to the General Agreement on Tariffs and Trade. Significant trade and investment barriers, however, still exist and the Venezuelan market has become less attractive and hospitable since the Caldera Administration reversed course by implementing controversial and interventionist economic policies. In addition, Venezuelan exports of gasoline have raised an environmental controversy that has involved numerous legal battles.[66]

The Venezuelan tariff schedule has been substantially liberalized, and quantitative restrictions have been almost completely removed with the exception of used cars, used clothing and used tires. Venezuela's average tariff is roughly 10 percent, but higher rates apply to products of particular U.S.

---

[65] Fidler, Stephen. "Reaching For New Credibility," *Financial Times*, January 2, 1995, p. 3.

[66] For background on this issue, see: *Implementation of the Reformulated Gasoline Program*, CRS Report 95-850 ENR, August 1, 1995. 26p. [By Susan Mayer, Lawrence Kumins, and Migdon Segal]

concern, including chemicals, wines, breakfast cereals, and canned soups.[67] Although Venezuela no longer has an import licensing regime, it still effectively bans U.S. poultry and pork imports by denying the necessary sanitation certificates. Venezuela also does not provide an adequate and effective level of intellectual property protection, leading USTR to place it on the "watch list" under "special 301" provision of the 1988 Trade Act.

With respect to foreign investment, the Perez Administration greatly liberalized the Venezuelan regime by according national treatment in most sectors, allowing foreign investment in many sectors previously reserved for national companies, and by authorizing free transfer of capital, profits, and dividends. An approval or screening process was also eliminated. These changes, combined with an ambitious privatization program to sell off several state companies, greatly improved the environment for foreign direct investment.

These reforms notwithstanding, Venezuela still maintains restrictions on foreign investment in petroleum, basic industries, insurance, and professional services sectors. In addition, unclear procedures governing repatriation and remittances profits, as part of the Caldera Administration's recently established exchange controls, represents a significant obstacle and disincentive to foreign investment at this time.[68]

---

[67] Office of the United States Trade Representative. "Trade Estimates Report:1995," p. 314.

[68] U.S. Department of Commerce, "Venezuela: Economic Overview," OLAC Facts #2405.

A FREE TRADE AREA OF THE AMERICAS: TOWARD INTEGRATING REGIONAL TRADE POLICIES

J.F. Hornbeck

The spirit of free trade has swept through Latin America over the past decade and although broadly embraced as a much-needed improvement to longstanding closed economic policies, it has produced a confusing patchwork of hemispheric free trade agreements (FTAs). Currently, Western Hemisphere countries have either signed or are negotiating over 50 subregional trade pacts. Looming over all these efforts is the promise of creating by 2005 the Free Trade Area of the Americas (FTAA), an agreement covering 34 nations that would stretch from northern Canada to the southern tip of Chile and, many hope, would also tie together these disparate and sometimes overlapping trade arrangements (see appendix 1 for a list of regional trade agreements).

These developments place U.S. trade policy squarely at the crossroads of whether or how to proceed formally with an FTAA. Trade policy debates have been contentious in the aftermath of NAFTA and the turbulent fallout from Mexico's 1994 peso devaluation. Also, issues raised by labor, environmental groups, and import competing industries, which were central to the NAFTA debate, continue to be concerns in the FTAA context.

Within the free trade debate are complicated issues surrounding the possible inefficiencies of multiple regional trade agreements and whether moving toward an FTAA is better -- the focus of this report. The Clinton Administration has embraced the FTAA as central to achieving closer ties with Latin America. The President emphasized the potential for significant gains for all participating countries and much of the business community supports the FTAA with equal vigor.[1] U.S. interests are varied and involve: 1) enhancing U.S. trade and investment opportunities; 2) replacing the existing myriad trade pacts with a more consistent regional understanding; and 3) supporting growth, stability, and modernization of Latin America's economic and political systems. In short, the FTAA is seen by many as an important part of building "an enduring framework of political and economic cooperation" in the region.[2]

---

[1] See: U.S. Department of State. *Dispatch Supplement*. May 1995, pp. 1-2, Davidow, Jeffrey. Testimony before the Trade Subcommittee of the House Ways and Means Committee, July 22, 1997, and U.S. Chamber of Commerce and Council of the Americas. *Belo Horizonte: Building the FTAA*. Washington, DC, April 1997.

[2] Inter-American Dialogue. *The Americas in 1997: Making Cooperation Work*. Washington, D.C., 1997. p. 1. See also: U.S. Library of Congress. Congressional Research Service. *Trade and the Americas*. CRS Issue Brief 95017, by Raymond J. Ahearn. Updated Regularly. 14p.

Congress plays a central role in defining how U.S. interests are realized in the trade policy process. Specifically, Congress is responsible for authorizing trade negotiating authority (fast track) under which the Administration will operate and secondly, eventually passing the implementing legislation that will allow the trade agreement to become operational. The 105th Congress is currently engaged in this process as it debates the merits of President Clinton's fast-track proposal, which he submitted September 16, 1997.[3]

The FTAA is a central focus of the fast-track debate and congressional hearings have already begun to explore many of the critical economic questions related to expanding hemispheric trade that this report addresses. First, what has changed that now makes Western Hemisphere trade relations a vital issue? Second, how important is Latin American trade? Third, how has the cobweb of free trade agreements evolved in the region? Fourth, what are the economic implications for the United States and Latin America of pursuing an FTAA? Fifth, what is the status of the FTAA and does it matter how it is achieved?

Moving Toward an FTAA

Interest in a regional trade agreement did not materialize over night. It evolved, to a great extent, as the Latin American governments radically altered their economic policies to lift themselves out of the 1980s debt crisis. As part of this wholesale reform, Latin America embraced export-led growth and reduced restrictions on imports. Impetus to pursue the FTAA would not exist without these developments.

Trade and Economic Reform in Latin America

Over the past two decades, Latin America has embraced progressively more open trade policies intra-regionally and with the world as part of its overall economic reform. The larger economies of Latin America, once known for their collective indebtedness, are in the 1990s considered among the more promising emerging markets for trade and investment opportunities. Three economic policy shifts in Latin America paved the way for this new perspective: 1) reduced roles for government in managing the economies, with greater reliance placed on markets, private ownership, and deregulation; 2) use of conventional and generally restrictive macroeconomic policies to promote economic growth and stability; and 3) the movement away from protectionism, often by way of unilateral reductions in tariffs and other trade barriers.

These policies were implemented to promote economic efficiency in an international market setting, guided by the belief that long-term real growth in output, productivity, and income could no longer be held hostage to elite-

---

[3] See: U.S. Library of Congress. Congressional Research Service. *Trade Agreements: Renewing the Negotiating and Fast-Track Implementing Authority*. Issue brief 97016, by Vladimir N. Pregelj. Updated Regularly and Holliday, George. *Fast-Track Authority: Debate Over the President's Proposal*. Report No. 97-876 E, September 23, 1997.

controlled, closed economic systems. Trade policy played an important part in this story and the myriad trade pacts currently in effect are the tangible evidence of such reformed thinking. Sustaining reform, however, is far from a certainty and in many cases economic progress has fallen short of expectations. Long-term average annual growth of Latin American economies, for example, has hovered around 3%, a rate inadequate to alleviate poverty and far below levels seen in the Asian developing economies. Also, real wages have stagnated and social conditions of the poor remain little changed.[4]

Attention is now turning to a "second generation" of reforms needed to consolidate economic stability and build on it to address distributional issues. They emphasize developing autonomous public institutions (independent central banks and judiciaries), investing long term in human and physical capital (education and infrastructure), and doing so by improving domestic savings rates and attracting foreign direct investment. Success depends on Latin America creating a stable social and political environment and spurring strong export-led growth through open trade.[5]

Without broader economic participation, progress could fall victim to social and political instability in some cases. Yet, implementing these new reforms may also prove politically difficult. The FTAA is seen by many as a stabilizing force in this picture. Much as Mexico held firm under NAFTA on its commitment to open trade and other economic policies when it faced recent financial disaster, so too is the FTAA expected to support broader economic reforms in Latin America. An evaluation of the FTAA, therefore, will likely need to go beyond looking at strictly short-term trade effects.

The FTAA Process So Far

Latin America was enthusiastic about an FTAA and procedural negotiations began after the Miami Summit of the Americas in December 1994. Progress has been slow, but deliberate. The process began with the first Western Hemisphere Trade Ministerial in Denver held in June 1995 and proceeded to a second in Cartagena, Colombia (March 1996) and a third recently completed in Belo Horizonte, Brazil (May 1997).

The Denver ministerial established some basic principles under which an FTAA will be negotiated. First, it will be a balanced and comprehensive "single undertaking," requiring each country to accept all obligations. Second, the FTAA is to be compatible with the World Trade Organization (WTO) and build

---

[4] On the limitations of a closed economy (import substitution) approach to development, see: Krueger, Anne O. *Trade Policies and Developing Nations*. Washington, D.C., The Brookings Institution, 1995. pp. 33-36.

[5] Edwards, Sebastian. *The Disturbing Underperformance of the Latin American Economies*. The Inter-American Dialogue. Washington, D.C. January 1997 and Burki, Shahid Javed and Guillermo E. Perry. *The Long March: A Reform Agenda for Latin America and the Caribbean in the Next Decade - Executive Summary*. Washington, D.C., The World Bank, 1997.

on progress made in existing regional agreements. Third, participants are to work toward maximizing market openness and not raising barriers against non-FTAA countries. Fourth, the FTAA will take into consideration the adjustment concerns of smaller economies, a difficult hurdle for many countries. Finally, seven working groups were formed to evaluate alternative negotiation strategies and also to establish, in their respective areas, comprehensive data bases on the trade regimes for each country.[6]

The second ministerial in Cartagena called for further preparatory work, but directed that existing recommendations be formally reassessed so that a "launch date" for formal negotiations could be set at the Belo Horizonte meeting, a goal that was later postponed until 1998. Other developments included: identifying certain early action items; deciding to consider environmental and workers' rights issues; and receiving recommendations on 13 topics developed by the Americas Business Forum, a group representing private sector interests. Importantly, four more ministerial working groups were also created.[7]

The third ministerial in Belo Horizonte established a twelfth and final working group and set the stage for deliberating differences over how to proceed with formal negotiations. It was agreed to craft formal procedures at the fourth ministerial scheduled for February 1998 in San Jose, Costa Rica. This would allow negotiations to begin in April 1998 at the second Summit of the Americas in Santiago, Chile. The Joint Declaration calls for creation of a Preparatory Committee in the intervening year to "build consensus and to complete recommendations," a signal to be taken that all parties are seriously committed to moving ahead. Other significant developments included allowing an expanded role for labor and other "non-business interests."[8]

The most important issue to resolve in the near future is how to proceed with these negotiations. In April 1997, the United States dropped its objection to proceeding with all working groups simultaneously. Previously, the United States had preferred a two-phase negotiation strategy that diverged from both a Brazilian three-phase proposal and Canada's stand for simultaneous negotiations, also embraced by many Latin American countries.[9] Brazil has expressed concern that it is not ready to take on the full economic adjustment process inherent in trade liberalization and effectively blocked establishing formal negotiation procedures in the latest round of talks. This was done by adhering to its position that non-tariff barriers be negotiated first, with tariff

---

[6] Summit of the Americas. *Joint Declaration of the Denver Trade Ministerial*. June 30, 1995. p. 1.

[7] Summit of the Americas. *Joint Declaration of the Cartegena Trade Ministerial*. March 21, 1996. p. 1.

[8] Summit of the Americas. *Joint Declaration of the Belo Horizonte Ministerial*. May 16, 1997. p. 1 and *Americas Trade*, May 20, 1997, p. 3 and 6.

[9] U.S. Drops Demand for Two-Stage FTAA Talks, Isolating MERCOSUR. *Inside NAFTA*. April 17, 1997. p. 1. and Hemisphere Nationals Delay Key FTAA Decisions Until Feb. 98 Ministerial. *Inside NAFTA*. April 22, 1997. p. 1.

and market access issues put off until 2003. The issue was left to be resolved by the next ministerial in Costa Rica and Brazil has already indicated a possible softening of its position toward simultaneous talks.[10]

In total, the 12 ministerial working groups have responsibilities for the following areas of negotiation: market access; customs procedures and rules of origin; investment; product standards and technical barriers; sanitary and phytosanitary practices; subsidies, antidumping, and countervailing duties (CVDs); smaller economies; services; intellectual property rights (IPRs); government procurement; competition policy; and dispute resolution. They are proceeding at different paces in meeting their obligations set out above.

Patterns of Trade in the Western Hemisphere

One measure of U.S. interest in the FTAA may be seen in how the trade relationship with Latin America has changed over time. Although historically relegated to being a minor trading partner, developments in Latin America have led to considerable growth in U.S. trade with the region. U.S. trade with Canada also has grown briskly, suggesting that the Western Hemisphere as a whole is a significant trade area and logically a major focus for trade policy.

U.S. Direction of Trade

U.S. trade with the world has evolved in recent years away from longstanding partners, such as Western Europe, toward emerging markets in Asia and Latin America. Nonetheless, trade data show that Latin America still represents a relatively small portion of total U.S. trade. Figure 1 illustrates that as a proportion of total trade or trade turnover (exports plus imports), trade with Mexico grew from 6.6% of the total in 1990 to 9.2% in 1996 (data appear in appendix 2). Trade with the rest of Latin America and the Caribbean grew as a percentage of total trade from 6.6% to 7.1% so that Latin America as a whole accounts for about 16% of total U.S. trade. The Western Hemisphere, including the NAFTA countries, accounts for nearly 37% of all U.S. trade.

U.S. trade with Latin America, however, is growing faster than any other region. Small changes in Latin America's proportion of total trade with the United States between 1990 and 1996 actually reflect a doubling of trade turnover with Mexico and a 70% increase with the rest of Latin America (see appendix 2). Latin America's relative gain is offset by smaller growth rates in U.S. trade with Western Europe, Africa, and even some parts of Asia.

Latin America and Mexico stand out even more as export markets. U.S. exports worldwide grew by 58% from 1990 to 1996, with Asia growing at a higher than average rate of 71%. U.S. exports to Mexico and the rest Latin America, however, doubled, reflective of both U.S. economic interests and lower

---

[10] *Americas Trade*, July 24, 1997, p. 1.

FIGURE 1. U.S. Direction of Trade
(Exports plus Imports) 1990 and 1996
LAC = Latin America/Caribbean, except Mexico

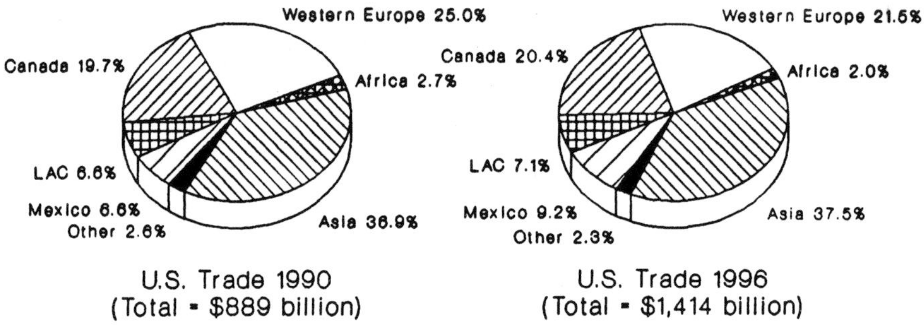

barriers to trade in the region. This trend may also be seen in table 1, which shows U.S. trade with selected Latin American countries. Export growth from 1990 to 1996 more than doubled in Argentina, Honduras, Brazil, Chile, Colombia, Peru, and Guatemala and exceeded, by far, growth in imports. The United States has run a regular trade surplus with the region.

U.S.-Latin American merchandise trade also supports U.S. technology-enhanced industrial exports such as motor vehicles and parts, computers, and electronic, telecommunications, electrical, and power generation equipment. These are products that the United States produces relatively efficiently, and so as pointed out in one study, are the ones that the United States gains most from exporting. They are also the products with which the United States competes "most vigorously" with Japan and East Asia for third market access.[11] By comparison, the United States imports semi-manufactured goods (especially from Mexico), natural resource goods, and petroleum products from Latin America.

The strong growth in U.S.-Mexico trade reflects, to a great extent, the large trade volume in intermediate goods, or those that are further processed for additional export.[12] The *maquiladora* trade, which by definition involves joint production facilities in both countries, actually expanded in 1995 whereas total U.S. exports to Mexico fell following the 1994 peso devaluation. This highlights the significance of efficiency gains from intra-industry trade, an important dynamic of U.S.-Mexico economic integration.[13]

---

[11] Rich, Patricia Gray. Latin America and Present US Trade Policy. *The World Economy*, v. 20, January 1997. pp. 91-94.

[12] For a discussion of the U.S.-Mexican trade relationship, see: U.S. Library of Congress. Congressional Research Service. *NAFTA, Mexican Trade Policy, and U.S-Mexico Trade: A Longer-Term Perspective*. Report No. 96-225 E, by J. F. Hornbeck.

[13] United States International Trade Commission. The Maquiladora Industry Thrives Since the Peso's Devaluation. *International Economic Review*. February/March 1996. p. 17.

Table 1. U.S. Merchandise Trade with Selected Latin American Countries, 1990-1996 ($ billions)

Country	1990	1992	1994	1996	% Change 90-96
		U.S. Exports			
Brazil	5.1	5.8	8.1	12.7	149.0%
Venezuela	3.1	5.4	4.0	4.7	51.6%
Colombia	2.0	3.3	4.1	4.7	135.0%
Argentina	1.2	3.2	4.5	4.5	275.0%
Chile	1.7	2.5	2.8	4.1	141.2%
Dominican Republic	1.7	2.1	2.8	3.2	88.2%
Costa Rica	1.0	1.4	1.9	1.8	80.0%
Peru	0.8	1.0	1.4	1.8	125.0%
Honduras	0.6	0.8	1.0	1.6	166.7%
Guatemala	0.8	1.2	1.4	1.6	100.0%
Jamaica	1.0	1.0	1.1	1.5	50.0%
Panama	0.9	1.1	1.3	1.4	55.6%
Ecuador	0.7	1.0	1.2	1.3	85.7%
El Salvador	0.6	0.7	0.9	1.1	83.3%
Other	4.5	4.6	5.5	6.2	37.8%
Total LAC*	25.7	35.1	42.0	52.2	103.1%
Mexico	28.3	40.6	50.8	56.8	100.7%
Total Latin America	54.0	75.7	92.8	109.0	101.9%
		U.S. Imports			
Brazil	7.9	7.6	8.7	8.8	11.4%
Venezuela	9.5	8.2	8.4	12.9	35.8%
Colombia	3.2	2.8	3.2	4.3	34.4%
Argentina	1.5	1.3	1.7	2.3	53.3%
Chile	1.3	1.4	1.8	2.3	76.9%
Dominican Republic	1.8	2.4	3.1	3.6	100.0%
Costa Rica	1.0	1.4	1.7	2.0	100.0%
Peru	0.8	0.7	0.8	1.3	62.5%
Honduras	0.5	0.8	1.1	1.8	260.0%
Guatemala	0.8	1.1	1.3	1.7	112.5%
Jamaica	0.6	0.6	0.9	0.8	33.3%
Panama	0.2	0.3	0.3	0.4	100.0%
Ecuador	1.4	1.4	1.7	1.9	35.7%
El Salvador	0.2	0.4	0.6	1.1	450.0%
Other	3.1	3.2	3.2	3.5	12.9%
Total LAC*	33.8	33.6	38.5	48.7	44.1%
Mexico	30.2	35.2	49.5	73.0	141.7%
Total Latin America	64.0	68.8	88.0	121.7	90.2%

Source: U.S. Department of Commerce.
* LAC = Latin America and the Caribbean, except Mexico.

Regional Trade Patterns

U.S.-Latin American trade is but one part of the regional trade story. The United States is the largest, but not the only market in the region. Canada and Latin America are pursuing trade agreements on a subregional basis and have developed their own trade agendas independently of ties with the United States (see appendix 1). Brazil, Argentina, Paraguay, and Uruguay, in forming the Southern Cone Common Market (Mercado Comun del Sur -- MERCOSUR), have become the major competing hemispheric trade block to NAFTA. The data in table 2 suggest a number of points regarding to intra-regional trade in the Western Hemisphere, particularly with respect to MERCOSUR and NAFTA.

First, *trade within the hemisphere, although not huge, is growing and becoming relatively more important.* In 1996:

- 54% of the hemisphere's exports stayed in the hemisphere;

- 69% of Latin America's exports stayed in the hemisphere and;

- intra-hemispheric exports grew by 9.4%, but hemispheric exports to the world grew at a slower rate of 7.4%.[14]

Second, based on export volume and growth, NAFTA countries are the largest trade bloc of the hemisphere, not surprising given that they constitute 90% of the region's GDP. For 1996:

- 83% of the intra-hemispheric exports went to NAFTA countries;

- 74% of Latin America's exports to the Western Hemisphere were sent to NAFTA countries;

- 88% of NAFTA's exports to the hemisphere went to NAFTA countries and;

- NAFTA world exports grew by 7%, but NAFTA export growth to regional groups was higher: G-3 (Mexico, Colombia, Venezuela) (16%), NAFTA (10%), and the hemisphere (9%).

Third, MERCOSUR still depends heavily on world and regional markets, despite being the largest trade bloc in South America. In 1996:

- 48% of MERCOSUR's total exports stayed in the hemisphere;

---

[14] This trend is also seen earlier in the 1990s, but was not evident during the integration efforts that took place in Latin America during the 1960s. See: Wolff, Jason R. Putting the Cart Before the Horse: Assessing Opportunities for Regional Integration in Latin America and the Caribbean. *Fletcher Forum of World Affairs*, v. 20, Winter/Spring 1996. p. 114.

Table 2. 1996 Western Hemisphere Exports by Destination[1]							
	Exporting Regions						
Destination	MERCOSUR	Andean Community	G-3	CACM	Latin America	NAFTA	Hemisphere
	U.S. $ billions						
MERCOSUR	16.1	1.5	2.4	---	20.7	20.7	40.0
Andean Com	3.2	4.7	5.0	0.2	10.3	14.8	23.8
CACM	0.2	0.7	1.5	1.5	3.4	7.2	9.7
CARICOM	0.2	1.3	1.5	---	1.7	4.3	5.8
NAFTA	13.0	20.1	98.8	2.9	121.0	435.4	475.2
G-3	1.9	3.1	3.2	0.2	6.5	67.0	72.6
Latin Amer	23.7	8.9	11.4	2.1	42.5	109.1	146.9
Hemisphere	35.9	30.0	111.2	4.9	163.5	492.7	570.1
World	75.1	43.0	125.6	7.7	237.2	920.4	1,063.6
	Percent Change 1995-1996						
MERCOSUR	12.2	0.3	6.1	-2.9	9.7	6.8	8.1
Andean Com	-8.5	-0.6	0.5	5.3	-2.7	-0.7	-2.0
CACM	-13.5	10.7	11.8	4.6	8.0	5.1	4.8
CARICOM	-4.9	5.0	6.4	46.8	5.5	5.9	5.5
NAFTA	9.7	19.5	20.2	12.8	17.9	10.0	10.4
G-3	-17.4	-2.4	-2.8	37.1	-6.2	15.5	13.2
Latin Amer	9.0	1.4	6.8	8.9	7.2	11.3	9.9
Hemisphere	8.4	13.6	18.5	10.4	14.7	9.3	9.4
World	6.6	10.3	16.4	5.7	11.2	7.4	7.4
	Percent Share of Total						
MERCOSUR	21.5	3.5	1.9	0.2	8.7	2.2	3.8
Andean Com	4.2	10.8	3.9	2.0	4.3	1.6	2.2
CACM	0.3	1.7	1.2	19.9	1.4	0.8	0.9
CARICOM	0.3	3.0	1.2	0.6	0.7	0.5	0.5
NAFTA	17.3	46.7	78.7	38.1	51.0	47.3	44.7
G-3	2.5	7.3	2.6	3.2	2.8	7.3	6.8
Latin Amer	31.6	20.7	9.1	27.9	17.9	11.8	13.8
Hemisphere	47.8	69.8	88.6	64.2	68.9	53.5	53.6
World	100.0	100.0	100.0	100.0	100.0	100.0	100.0

Source: Inter-American Development Bank. *Integration and Trade in the Americas: A Preliminary Estimate of 1996 Trade*. December 1996. p. 3.
[1] Estimated from data available through November 1996.
CACM = Central American Common Market; CARICOM = Caribbean Community and Common Market; G-3 = Group of Three. See appendix 1 for details.

- but only 22% remained within MERCOSUR and;
- 17% went to NAFTA countries;
- 66% of MERCOSUR's exports to the hemisphere went to Latin American countries, 45% to MERCOSUR countries, and 36% to NAFTA countries, and finally;

- MERCOSUR's exports to various regional groups grew at the following rates: MERCOSUR (12%); NAFTA (10%); Western Hemisphere (8%); and the world (7%).

To summarize, Western Hemisphere intra-regional trade is growing and NAFTA countries, especially the United States, may be in a position to lead the way toward an FTAA based on their relatively large economies. MERCOSUR, under Brazil's leadership, presents a counterbalancing force in the southern part of the hemisphere. Its trade is much less dependent on NAFTA countries than many other countries of the region, but NAFTA markets also show promise of being potentially more important to the MERCOSUR countries. The data highlight that MERCOSUR and NAFTA could increase their trade with each other in an FTAA, but that there may be no compelling need to do so. Given so many trade pacts in the region and the apparent lack of impetus to create stronger ties between two of the largest Western Hemisphere economies, questions arise about the economic effects of maintaining the status quo compared to various options leading to an FTAA.

The FTAA and Economic Issues of Regionalism

The movement toward "free trade" in Latin America raises questions about who may actually benefit from the expanding cobweb of agreements. At issue is the prospect that the economic gains associated with free trade may be quite different under regional trade agreements (RTAs) compared to the multilateral context. Distinguishing between the two and how they might apply in the case of Latin America is important to understanding the current trade situation and how the FTAA might change the status quo.

Regional Versus Multilateral Free Trade

The general case for free trade based on *comparative advantage* argues that through global competition, a country can improve its economic welfare by producing those goods at which it is relatively more efficient, while trading for the rest. Economic benefits come about first through so-called *static gains* or "the one-time increment to the nation's economic welfare that arise from the more efficient allocation of resources afforded by free trade."[15] For example, lower-priced imports replace higher-priced domestically produced goods, lowering costs throughout the region. Second, *dynamic gains*, or those associated with additional long-term growth from the trade-induced restructured economy, are also important.

Economic theory assumes nondiscrimination among trading partners, a tenet that was institutionalized in 1947 by the international community when

---

[15] For a more in-depth discussion of the "gains from trade," see: U.S. Library of Congress. Congressional Research Service. *Trade Policy in an Economic Perspective.* Report No. 95-529 E, by Craig K. Elwell. March 9, 1995. p. 4.

it adopted the General Agreement on Tariffs and Trade (GATT), now assumed under the World Trade Organization (WTO). The GATT established the rules governing the multilateral trading system that has led, slowly but surely, to liberalization of world trade over the past five decades. At the heart of GATT/WTO is the concept that all participants should be treated in a *nondiscriminatory* fashion with respect to tariffs and other barriers to trade. This is known as the *most-favored-nation* principle and in practice, all participating members are subject to a country's same lower trade barriers, which presumably leads to fairness in treatment and efficiency in resource allocation.[16]

The WTO allows for exceptions to the MFN rule under three different provisions. Under Article XXIV of GATT, countries may form RTAs or customs unions provided barriers are eliminated on "substantially all" trade, the agreement is put fully into place over "a reasonable period of time," and trade barriers are not made more restrictive on third party countries than prior to the agreement. This is the primary rule used to establish regional unions.[17]

Many of the Latin American RTAs fall under the Enabling Clause, which allows developing countries to form agreements outside of Article XXIV rules provided "the arrangement be designed to facilitate and promote the trade of developing countries, and not to raise barriers to or create undue difficulties for the trade of other contracting parties."[18] Among Latin American trade agreements that fall under the Enabling Clause are the LAIA, the G-3, and many of the bilaterals.

Finally, a non-reciprocal trade agreement (see appendix 1), such as the U.S. Caribbean Basin Initiative (CBI), can be granted a waiver from WTO rules under Article XXV. Because of the slow pace at which multilateral agreements have proceeded, their limited achievements in some nontariff areas, and the rather loose enforcement of RTA rules, many countries have pursued their free trade agenda via regional trade agreements, producing a lively economic debate.

Regional Trade Agreements: Economic Concerns

RTAs complicate the general economic case for free trade; in fact, they stand in contrast to the MFN principle, giving rise to two fundamental issues.

---

[16] See: U.S. Library of Congress. Congressional Research Service. *Most-Favored-Nation Policy of the United States*. Issue brief No. 93107, by Vladimir N. Pregelj. Updated regularly. p. 1.

[17] World Trade Organization. *Regionalism and the World Trading System*. Geneva, WTO, 1995. pp. 8-9. For a recent list of agreements and how they are covered under the GATT/WTO, see: Bhagwati, Jagdish and Arvind Panagariya. Preferential Trading Areas and Multilateralism - Strangers, Friends, or Foes? In Bhagwati, Jagdish and Arvind Panagariya, eds. *The Economics of Preferential Trade Agreements*. Washington, D.C., The AEI Press, 1996. pp. 55-73.

[18] World Trade Organization, ibid, pp. 18-19.

First, do regional agreements distort trade patterns, thereby diminishing the anticipated gains from freer trade under a multilateral arrangement, and second, do RTAs tend to encourage or hinder the creation of multilateral trade agreements? Interestingly, the response by economists to these questions has been prolific and varied.

Static Effects: Trade Diversion and Trade Creation

A fundamental debate over RTAs is whether the static (one-time) welfare effects of trade liberalization are, on balance, positive or negative. Regional pacts can result in *trade creation*, when trade flows cause production shifts from higher cost domestic producers to lower cost producers of trading partners. Ideally, this should occur in multiple directions so there are numerous opportunities for trade creation within a regional group.[19]

Because regional trade agreements are inherently discriminatory (favoring some partners over others), however, they can also cause *trade diversion* and risk leaving some countries worse off, including those within the agreement.[20] Trade diversion occurs if the RTA causes a shift in a country's imports away from low-cost producers outside the agreement to higher cost producers within it. Economists generally consider an RTA to improve the welfare of countries to the extent that trade creation outweighs trade diversion.

Both trade creation and diversion can occur, so each case must be analyzed individually, a particularly vexing problem in a region like Latin America that has so many trade agreements. In attempting to evaluate the effects of regional integration, a number of general guidelines apply that suggest when trade creation and positive welfare effects dominate:[21]

- high initial tariffs suggest both a greater chance of trade creation and a lesser chance of trade diversion;

---

[19] In a simple bilateral agreement, for example, there should be production shifts in both countries so that there is a two-way path for trade creation to occur.

[20] See: Corden, W. Max. A Western Hemisphere Free Trade Area: Implications for Latin America. In *Trade Liberalization in the Western Hemisphere*. Washington, D.C., Inter-American Development Bank and United Nations Economic Commission on Latin America and the Caribbean, 1995. p. 15. There is another theoretical issue of *trade contraction*, which occurs if regional trade agreements raise tariffs on nonparticipating countries. This is not allowed under WTO and addressed in the FTAA's first trade ministerial declaration with a firm commitment not to do so.

[21] This is not an exhaustive list, see: Michaely, Michael. *Trade Preferential Agreements in Latin America: An Ex-Ante Assessment*. Washington, D.C., The World Bank, Policy Research Working Paper No. 1583, March 1996. pp. 4-6; Brown, Wilson P. and Jan S. Hogendorn. *International Economics: Theory and Context*. Reading, Addison-Wesley Publishing Company, 1994. pp. 324-26; Lawrence, Robert Z. *Regionalism, Multilateralism, and Deeper Integration*. Washington, D.C., The Brookings Institution, 1996. pp. 26-27; and Appleyard, Dennis R. and Alfred J. Field, Jr. *International Economics, Second Edition*. Chicago, Richard D. Irwin, 1995. pp. 324-28.

- lower external tariffs for non-members reduces trade diversion;
- the larger the union (number of countries and economic size), the better chance for trade creation because it will be more diversified, exclude fewer countries (from which trade could be diverted), and improve chances of capturing the low-cost producer; however, this will also increase possible harm for those not included;
- if the agreement includes countries that already do a large percentage of trade with each other compared to countries outside the agreement, there is less opportunity for trade diversion.[22]

Assessments of RTAs, based on the above criteria, vary. Many proponents of regional agreements note the limitations to the GATT/WTO and that RTAs are responsible for much of global trade liberalization, perhaps covering more than 50% of world trade.[23] Further, many argue that trade diversion is either small, nonexistent, or inadequately measured, suggesting that the detrimental static effects are overstated and can possibly be mitigated if the above conditions are largely met.[24] It also has been argued that those agreements that go beyond existing WTO provisions may have positive effects that would support export growth even for countries that are not part of an RTA.[25]

Still, others point out that any deviation from multilateralism is suboptimal for both the trading partners and the world trading system. Trade diversion may be underestimated. For example, having initially high trade levels may not be indicative of a "natural" trade relationship, but rather of earlier "artificial" trade preferences that are being used to support the case for an extended regional arrangement. With U.S.-Mexico trade, existing high trade volume was considered a basis for making the "natural trade partner" argument for NAFTA, when in fact it was at least partially the result of earlier preferential treatment provided under the *maquiladora* program.[26]

Outsiders can be hurt by an RTA despite WTO provisions designed to prevent such an outcome. Mexico's tariff increases on goods from non-NAFTA trading partners following the peso crisis is one example, although the tariff

---

[22] There are other broad economic forces to consider such as the higher the level of demand for other country's goods or the higher the price sensitivity of supply and demand markets, the higher expected positive response to an RTA. Further, if countries are experiencing high growth, they can adjust more easily to changing trade rules.

[23] WTO, *Regionalism and the World Trading System*, p. 39.

[24] Lawrence, *Regionalism, Multilateralism, and Deeper Integration*, pp. 24-26, 96, and 99-100.

[25] Ibid, p. 32.

[26] Bhagwati and Panagariya, *The Economics of Preferential Trade Agreements*, pp. xiv-xvii and 34-35. Further, the authors argue that there are only two exceptions that would justify an RTA: 1) the agreement accomplishes "truly deep integration" a la the European Union or 2) multilateral negotiations come to a standstill.

increases were not directly related to NAFTA. Finally, the proliferation of FTAs in Latin America has made navigating international commercial relations exceedingly complicated and potentially inefficient, particularly if numerous overlapping agreements materialize, sometimes referred to as the "hub and spoke" pattern.[27]

A frequently cited case in point is NAFTA's effects on the Caribbean economies, which are heavily dependent on the U.S. market. Prior to NAFTA implementation, most of the Caribbean countries enjoyed preferential treatment for their exports to the United States under the Caribbean Basin Economic Recovery Act (CBERA), also called the Caribbean Basin Initiative (CBI). With passage of NAFTA, the Caribbean countries' duty preference diminished relative to Mexico's "adversely affecting the competitiveness of CBERA countries with Mexico in the U.S. market."[28]

NAFTA affected key Caribbean export sectors and goods, particularly textiles and apparel. To the extent that tariff differentials led to trade diversion, Mexico's welfare has been improved at the expense of the Caribbean countries and the United States also has been purchasing goods from relatively higher-cost producers in Mexico. Hence, the Caribbean parity debate, in which Congress is weighing the possibility of passing legislation that would extend NAFTA-equivalent trade preferences to the CBI countries. Importantly, from a trade policy perspective, this issue also points to the prospect for correcting trade diversion created by an RTA by implementing tariff reductions outside the regional agreement.[29]

There is also some concern over possible trade diversion effects of MERCOSUR, with a World Bank study using export data to argue that it has been pervasive. This study was criticized, however, with an Inter-American Development Bank (IDB) paper using import data to counter that "substantial trade diversion" was not evident, but that trade in petroleum and perhaps a few other industries might be subject to some trade diversion. This issue has not been fully resolved, but these studies point to the prospect that sectoral and industry trade diversion probably exists, and that careful analysis is needed to determine if, on balance, RTA costs exceed benefits.[30]

---

[27] Wonnacott, Paul. Beyond NAFTA - The Design of A Free Trade Agreement of the Americas. In Bhagwati and Panagariya, eds, *The Economics of Preferential Trade Agreements*, pp. 87-90.

[28] U.S. Library of Congress. Congressional Research Service. *Caribbean Basin Interim Trade Program (NAFTA/CBI Parity*. Issue brief 95050, by Vladimir N. Pregelj. Updated regularly. p. 5.

[29] On compensation for trade diversion, see: Lawrence, *Regionalism, Multilateralism, and Deeper Integration*, pp. 26 and 99.

[30] See, Inter-American Development Bank, *Integration and Trade in the Americas*, Annex 1 and U.S. International Trade Commission. A Closer Look at MERCOSUR. *International Economic Review*, February/March 1997. pp. 9-11.

Trade diversion may also be occurring with many of the Western Hemisphere trade agreements. The Chile-Canada 1997 bilateral agreement reduced Chile's 11-percent tariff on many items imported from Canada. This lowered the cost to Canadian companies relative to U.S. firms, a disadvantage the United States Trade Representative (USTR) cites as one reason why U.S. firms lost a $200 million telecommunications equipment bid in Chile. Negotiating for equal access to Chilean and other markets is one argument for the United States pursuing the FTAA.[31] In another direction, concern over the FTAA is even broader: that more efficient producers outside the agreement (e.g. Asia, Europe) might lose trade (particularly in the U.S. market) to less competitive members in the FTAA.

As a third possible outcome, some RTAs may have little trade or economic significance, particularly smaller bilateral agreements. A preliminary World Bank study asserts that the prospect for significant welfare improvements from Latin American intra-regional pacts is unlikely. Because of unilateral trade liberalization, tariff levels have already fallen significantly and intra-regional trade, although growing, is not large. Trade agreements, particularly the smaller bilaterals, should have relatively little economic effect given the modest volume of trade involved. The possible exceptions are those agreements including the largest economies such as Argentina, Brazil, and the United States.[32]

Static Effects: Tariff Revenue Losses

In addition to the potential for inefficient trade patterns to develop, one analysis suggests that another static effect can be significant for the country that liberalizes the most under an RTA, even if the agreement results in welfare enhancing trade creation for the union. The issue is lost tariff revenue, which can be an adjustment problem for developing countries highly dependent on tariffs for public revenue. This issue is well known and is part of the structural fiscal reform that must accompany trade liberalization.[33]

The additional problem, explored in one study, is that the country reducing its tariffs the most could also be made worse off because it reduces that country's terms of trade (the purchasing power of its exports relative to its imports) compared to countries that already had low tariffs. The net effect is a redistribution of income from the country with a "high degree of protection" to the more open country. The Mexico-United States relationship under NAFTA

---

[31] Testimony of Ambassador Charlene Barshefsky, United States Trade Representative before the Senate Finance Committee. June 3, 1997. p. 10. This issue is disputed.

[32] Michaely, *Trade Preferential Agreements in Latin America*, pp. 29, 44-45.

[33] The case of Argentina is clearly made in: Mondino, Guillermo and Alejandro Reca. Toward a Hemispheric Free Trade Area: The Case of Argentina. In Jatar, Ana Julia and Sidney Weintraub. *Integrating the Hemisphere: Perspectives from Latin America and the Caribbean*. Washington, D.C., Inter-American Dialoge, 1997. pp. 186-87.

is cited as a case in point. The difference in initial tariff rates provided a greater benefit to the United States because Mexico had to reduce its tariffs significantly more than did the United States. The United States not only gained relatively greater access to Mexican markets, but did so on better relative price terms.[34]

The significance of this revenue effect, however, can vary, particularly if the RTA is part of a broader trade liberalization program. For example, to the extent that Mexico liberalizes trade with the world, the tariff differential under NAFTA becomes less of an issue. Even the author of this argument recognizes this by noting that the best solution to addressing this potential tariff revenue problem is for countries in regional agreements to "liberalise externally as they liberalise within an RTA framework."[35] Most economists would agree that minimizing the magnitude of preference in an RTA is the most efficient way to proceed. In cases where countries have unilaterally reduced tariffs, the issue is far less worrisome.

Such static losses by themselves, however, may not be a compelling deterrent. It was clear from the beginning that Mexico had farther to go than the United States in terms of tariff reductions to meet NAFTA provisions. Mexico, however, was well on the way to opening its economy by the time it negotiated NAFTA, which must be seen as only a part of Mexico's broad economic reform program. In this light, Mexico was looking to the long-term future, and certainly beyond short-term tariff revenue effects, in weighing the costs and benefits of entering into an RTA. In fact, it was Mexico that approached the United States about NAFTA.[36] Much of Latin America may well follow suit, particularly if it is making an attempt to liberalize trade unilaterally. As average tariffs fall, the obligations of a regional agreement become less "traumatic," which will serve to encourage formation of an FTAA.[37]

Dynamic Effects: Economic Growth

Economists look beyond static effects to the dynamic effects when evaluating regional trade agreements. These refer to how economies may evolve differently than if they had not entered into a freer trade arrangement. Factors such as foreign investment, technology transfer, heightened competition and greater opportunity for realizing scale economies in an enlarged market can generate higher levels of economic growth than would have been possible in the

---

[34] Bhagwati and Panagariya, *Preferential Trading Areas and Multilateralism - Strangers, Friends, or Foes?*, p. 7, and Panagariya, Arvind. The Free Trade Area of the Americas: Good for Latin America? *World Economy*, v. 19, Sept. 1996. pp. 486 and 496.

[35] Panagariya, ibid, p. 511.

[36] Feinberg, Richard E. *Summitry in the Americas: A Progress Report*, Washington, D.C., Institute for International Economics, 1997. p. 7.

[37] Weintraub, Sidney. Western Hemisphere Free Trade: Getting From Here to There. In *Trade Liberalization in the Western Hemisphere*, p. 338.

absence of an RTA. Dynamic gains from such growth are generally thought to be significantly more important than any static welfare effects mentioned above. Although difficult to measure, if dynamic gains lead to even small increases in national economic growth, as widely believed even for preferential arrangements, they could overpower any static losses.[38]

These gains may vary depending on country circumstances. For example, scale economies potentially may be an important factor for smaller economies where growth in production has been restricted because of domestic market size. At the same time, given technological and other constraints, it may take time for smaller countries to fully realize these gains. As a case in point, the absence of dynamic gains may be a key to why intra-Latin America trade agreements signed in the 1960s and 1970s effectively failed. Recognizing the potential for such gains in an RTA that includes the United States' larger economy may be a reason for Latin American countries supporting the FTAA negotiations.[39]

Nontraditional Effects

Many economists look beyond both static and dynamic effects in evaluating RTAs. So-called "nontraditional gains from trade" in a more orthodox framework, however, might be considered a subgroup of dynamic effects that are characteristic of agreements between *developing* countries and their *developed* partners. They fall into three main categories: 1) guaranteed market access; 2) WTO-plus arrangements; and 3) locked-in economic reforms. There is some disagreement over the implications of these benefits, but they may encourage trade and more importantly foreign investment, which is an important link to all three nontraditional gains because it generally is considered a dynamic force that can lead to faster economic growth.

Guaranteed Market Access. Sometimes referred to as reciprocity, it is viewed by some as the most important reason for smaller countries to go beyond unilateral trade liberalization and push for regional agreements with their larger trading partners. In effect, the RTA acts, albeit in a limited fashion, as "insurance" against possible future negative policy decisions and so may explain why countries enter into agreements when the short-term static effects are either small or even negative. Guaranteed markets also encourage investment and other longer-term effects.[40]

---

[38] Lawrence, *Regionalism, Multilateralism, and Deeper Integration*, pp. 28 and 74, McCulloch, Rachel. The Optimality of Free Trade: Science or Religion? *American Economic Review*, v. 83, May 1993. p. 369, and Appleyard and Field, *International Economics*, pp. 329-30.

[39] For a technical discussion of the benefits of scale economies compared to static effects and the FTAA see: Chichilnisky, Graciela. Strategies for Trade Liberalization in the Americas. In *Trade Liberalization in the Western Hemisphere*, pp. 165-88.

[40] Fernandez, Raquel. *Returns to Regionalism: An Evaluation of Non-Traditional Gains from RTAs*. Cambridge, National Bureau of Economic Research, Inc., March 1997.

(continued...)

NAFTA provides one example of an agreement that integrated a developing economy with two larger developed economies. In so doing, Mexico was guaranteed preferential treatment by its largest foreign market, reducing possible future trade restrictions resulting from negative U.S. sentiment against free trade in general, or Mexico in particular. In fact, if NAFTA in any way provided incentive for the United States to assist Mexico during its financial crisis, and this is not clear, it provided a very real, but perhaps unintended, insurance policy for Mexico.[41]

Some dispute that the United States would ever take a more protectionist stand against Mexico.[42] Concerns over unbridled trade liberalization, however, can be strong in any country and in the United States are fueled by special interests, a general distrust of NAFTA, and unease over the U.S. trade deficit. Mexico, aware of these sentiments, would seem to be acting rationally by securing its largest export market.[43] This is a position that other countries in Latin America may well consider in deciding to push for the FTAA or even certain subregional agreements. Further, for countries that compete in the U.S. market with Mexico and Canada, such as Chile, equalizing and guaranteeing access to that market can be an important trade policy goal.[44]

WTO-Plus Arrangements. RTAs that go beyond WTO standards can provide deeper integration and potentially, additional welfare effects. NAFTA expanded coverage compared to the Canada-U.S. Free Trade Agreement and went beyond Uruguay Round provisions of GATT in some areas: services; intellectual property rights (IPRs); investment; and to some extent, labor and environmental standards as embodied in the side agreements. Other areas, such as protection against antidumping and countervailing duties, were changed little, yet an RTA may still be seen as another avenue to pursue these issues. It has been pointed out that the trade effects of such deepening are not always mutually beneficial. For example, intellectual property rights tend to favor developed countries, with developing economies incurring most of the costs.[45]

---

[40](...continued)
pp. 16-17, Dornbusch, Rudiger. North-South Trade Relations in the Americas: The Case for Free Trade, in *Trade Liberalization in the Western Hemisphere*, p. 45, and Corden, W. Max, A Western Hemisphere Free Trade Area: Implications for Latin America, in *Trade Liberalization in the Western Hemisphere*, p. 17.

[41] Fernandez, ibid, pp. 16-18 and 23-24.

[42] Panagariya, *The Free Trade Area of the Americas*, p. 498 suggests this guarantee comes at some cost to Mexico in terms of static losses and in any event is unnecessary because U.S. trade policy would simply be unlikely to restrict ties with Mexico.

[43] Lawrence, *Regionalism, Multilateralism, and Deeper Integration*, p. 29 and Feinberg, *Summitry in the Americas*, p. 51.

[44] Butelmann, Andrea and Patricio Meller. Evaluation of a Chile-U.S. Free Trade Agreement, in *Trade Liberalization in the Western Hemisphere*, p. 362.

[45] Lawrence, *Regionalism, Multilateralism, and Deeper Integration*, pp. 31-32 and 70-72. This issue is also more fully developed in: U.S. Library of Congress.
(continued...)

Locking-In Reforms. Finally, broader economic reforms in Latin America were a driving force of trade opening and it is argued that once in place, trade policy can serve to discipline broader macroeconomic and microeconomic policy decisions. Mexico during the peso crisis, for example, tightened monetary and fiscal policy as a way to turn around the large current account deficit. In previous financial crises, Mexico relied heavily on restrictive trade policies, effectively closing the economy to imports. NAFTA is widely regarded as influencing Mexico's policy choice in 1995, which has bolstered the argument that RTAs can lend a sense of "credibility and permanence" to policy reform.[46]

Although a trade agreement may support broader economic policy reform, it is no guarantee against macroeconomic instability, nor that a certain policy will necessarily be implemented or maintained.[47] Nonetheless, once some level of credibility is achieved, longer term commitments, such as foreign investment, may well provide additional incentive to maintain stability and consistency in policy, if at all possible. The value of such stability may be evident in the quick return of investment capital to Mexico following the 1994-95 financial crisis which, given the sensitive issue of Mexico's indebtedness to the United States, was a mutually beneficial outcome for both countries.

RTAs and the Multilateral Trading System

Another major concern is the possibility that RTAs will compromise the multilateral trading system by encouraging the formation of competitive regional trading blocs that would hinder the overreaching goal of a unified freer trade system worldwide. One article summarizing the literature on this subject points out that such a result depends on the nature of the trade agreement and whether it is intended as a vehicle for creating a protectionist trade bloc or, alternatively, for promoting a regional trade system committed to openness.[48]

Latin American regionalism is still being evaluated. Opponents continue to argue that benefits are distributed more equally in a multilateral system.[49] Supporters of RTAs, while recognizing that multilateral agreements are the most efficient choice, view regionalism as potentially compatible with the multilateral approach and downplay the negative aspects raised by dissenters of

---

[45](...continued)
Congressional Research Service. *Intellectual Property Rights and U.S. Foreign Trade*. CRS Report 96-847 E, by Glennon J. Harrison.

[46] Krueger, *Trade Policies and Developing Nations*, pp. 72-73 and Feinberg, *Summitry in the Americas*, p. 51.

[47] Fernandez, *Returns to Regionalism*, pp. 11-13 and Panagariya, *Free Trade Area of the Americas*, pp. 499-500.

[48] Sager, Michelle A. Regional Trade Agreements: Their Role and the Economic Impact on Trade Flows. *World Economy*, v. 20, March 1997. pp. 247-51.

[49] Barfield, Claude E. Regionalism and U.S. Trade Policy. In Bhagwati, Jagdish and Arvind Panagariya, eds. *The Economics of Preferential Trade Agreements*. Washington, D.C., AEI Press, 1996. pp. 136 and 142-43.

RTAs. Trade diversion may occur, but often it is considered small, restricted to only a few industries, can be offset by other trade policies, or may be overwhelmed by other benefits. Further, if RTAs are "WTO-plus" agreements and tend to emphasize openness rather than protectionism, many see them as a potential path to further multilateralism.[50]

In between the two cases lies the prospect that Latin American RTAs may result in something other than large trading blocs. Some suggest that if large regional trading blocs are welfare-reducing compared to an open multilateral system, multiple RTAs may fall in between the two cases with respect to global welfare and may have a long-term positive effect, particularly if they have rules encouraging their own expansion. Finally, if the proliferation of RTAs is eventually viewed as threatening by many countries, they may actually pursue multilateral negotiations more vigorously as a defensive response.[51]

Rules of Origin and Other Concerns

Because RTAs allow each member country to set external tariffs with the outside world, rules of origin are required to ensure that the lowest-tariff country is not used as a transshipment point for goods manufactured outside the trade agreement.[52] Such rules define content and value added that must take place to have a good considered domestically produced within the trade agreement area. Rules of origin are a frequently cited problem of RTAs. They are cumbersome to administer and can be designed to be a protectionist tool within an agreement, particularly at the sectoral or industry level. As more RTAs are created, additional rules of origin further confuse the trading process.

Another commonly cited "rules issue" regards antidumping actions, which have become an increasingly used form of protectionism as tariff rates have declined. These concerns, raised by many, suggest that as the world moves toward greater use of regional agreements, WTO rules governing their formation need to be rethought and perhaps enforced more strictly to make RTAs more compatible with the WTO.[53]

---

[50] Lawrence, *Regionalism, Multilateralism, and Deeper Integration*, pp. 26-27 and Hufbauer, Gary Clyde and Jeffrey J. Schott. *Western Hemisphere Economic Integration*. Washington, D.C., Institute for International Economics, 1994. pp. 162-64 and 173-77.

[51] Lawrence, *Regionalism, Multilateralism, and Deeper Integration*, p. 37 and Sager, *Regional Trade Agreements*, p. 250-51. For more on RTA effects on the multilateral trading system, see also: U.S. Library of Congress. Congressional Research Service, *Regional Trade Agreements: Implications for U.S. Trade Policy*. CRS Report 97-663 E, by George Holliday, June 25, 1997. pp. 13-15 and Carnegie Endowment for International Peace. *Reflections on Regionalism: Report of the Study Group on International Trade*. Washington, D.C., 1997.

[52] Moving to a customs union with a common external tariff solves this problem.

[53] This report will not venture in the this area in detail. On evaluating WTO rules governing RTAs, which many agree need revamping, see: Lawrence, Robert Z. (continued...)

The FTAA: A Preliminary Assessment

The economics of free trade become much more complicated when the discussion moves from a multilateral to a regional focus, an important issue for a hemisphere navigating over 50 regional trade agreements. There is near unanimous agreement that nondiscriminatory multilateralism is preferable. In the absence of this "first best" solution, regional trade agreements must be evaluated on their own merits, but most agree that the current situation in the Western Hemisphere is confusing and inefficient.

Opponents of RTAs argue that static (one-time) losses, such as trade diversion and diminished tariff revenue, can be serious for some countries. For this argument to be the decisive factor in deciding against an FTAA, the static losses would have to overpower the combined weight of any static, dynamic (growth-inducing), and nontraditional (guaranteed market access) gains. Such pessimism is not broadly embraced. Also, static losses tend to diminish the larger and more inclusive an agreement becomes; intuitively, one trade agreement should be more efficient than fifty.

Latin American Issues

In the case of Latin America, these lessons are evident in the early integration failures that occurred thirty years ago. Small unions based on relatively closed economies and limited participation were unable to generate significant gains. Under such circumstances, discipline of RTA rules became difficult and the agreements proved unenforceable. Similarly, many of Latin America's current small trade agreements may prove insignificant in terms of measurable economic effects. Nonetheless, they are forming in a much different policy atmosphere than before, one embracing unilateral trade liberalization as the cornerstone of broader economic reform.[54] The term "open regionalism" conveys the dominant perspective in Latin America (and perhaps the United States) that unilateral, regional, and multilateral trade opening can be mutually supportive within the context of the WTO.

The larger RTAs (NAFTA, MERCOSUR, and FTAA) increase the potential for real gains and if the Latin American and Caribbean countries continue to liberalize trade policy unilaterally, the potential for negative effects will decline. Latin American countries appear cautiously committed to further trade opening,

---

[53](...continued)
Regionalism and the WTO: Should the Rules be Changed? In Schott, Jeffrey J., ed. *The World Trading System: Challenges Ahead*. Washington, D.C. Institute for International Economics, 1996. p. 52, and Holliday, *Regional Trade Agreements*, pp. 20-22.

[54] The World Bank states firmly in its recent analysis of the Latin American economies that, "*Trade liberalization*, or the reduction in the average level and dispersion of tariff and para-tariff charges and the sharp reduction in nontariff barriers, is the reform that has been the deepest and most generalized in the region." Burki and Perry, *The Long March*, p. 5.

convinced that it will be an important part of long-term growth in investment, output, and income levels. Opening and "guaranteeing" long-term access to the U.S. market is a key goal of this strategy for most countries, even if it involves short-term costs. Stated differently, with the formation of RTAs in Latin America, it is generally considered a distinct disadvantage to be the country that is excluded from a closer trade relationship with the largest market in the hemisphere.[55]

Such a conclusion argues, from a Latin American perspective, for pursuing an FTAA with U.S. participation, consolidating smaller arrangements, and avoiding creation of dueling blocs (MERCOSUR versus NAFTA). Because the United States has so far deferred passage of trade negotiating authority, many Latin American countries are no longer waiting to consider NAFTA expansion as an avenue for regional trade integration. Chile, for example, has moved forward with unilateral trade liberalization and bilateral agreements; other countries have done the same or simply put trade policy on hold.[56] For the region as a whole, the FTAA is viewed as the best promise for consolidating trade policies and pursuing freer trade.

This is not to say that all Latin American countries will easily embrace an FTAA should formal negotiations begin in 1998. It is a region of diverse economies and adjustment problems, which could slow the integration process. Brazil, the largest Latin American economy, has only recently made strides toward broad economic reform and will likely seek to keep the integration process in check as long as possible to allow internal adjustments to catch up. Very small economies, such as those composing CARICOM and the Andean Community, face different problems. They already enjoy significant preferential treatment under existing non-reciprocal agreements (e.g. CBI) and face regional integration on equal terms understandably with some trepidation. All countries face some uncertainty over how key industries will fare in a more competitive environment. These are some of the critical issues that will have to be addressed as the FTAA process moves forward.[57]

U.S. Issues

For the United States, although trade with Latin America is growing, the benefits of an FTAA may have to be evaluated by other than short-term trade effects because they will simply be too small. Latin America is a relatively poor region and excluding Mexico, makes up only 7% of U.S. trade. Over the long-run, however, Latin America shows promise for faster economic growth, and if incomes rise in tandem, for becoming a more significant U.S. export market.

---

[55] Meller, Patricio. An Overview of Chilean Trade Strategy. In Jatar and Weintraub, eds., *Integrating the Hemisphere*, pp. 146-50.

[56] Edwards, Sebastian. NAFTA Offers Latins Little They Can't Have Now. *The Wall Street Journal*, April 18, 1997, p. A19.

[57] See relevant country chapters in Jatar and Weintraub, eds., *Integrating the Hemisphere*.

U.S. interests extend to supporting long-term merchandise trade goals, improving trade in services (financial services, telecommunications), harmonizing rules governing key trade issues (intellectual property rights, antidumping), opening foreign investment markets, and even supporting stability and growth in Latin America. The debate over fast-track and the FTAA will likely involve evaluating all these issues to determine if a regional agreement is the best option for pursuing these goals given that most observers consider the status quo confusing and inefficient.[58]

A key to making hemispheric trade integration successful is to keep the process open and see that it conforms to WTO rules. In this light, there has been a broad outcry to clarify, strengthen, and better enforce these rules. In the meantime, for Latin America the starting point for evaluating trade agreements has shifted. No longer is the issue one of moving from a closed economic position to an open one. Trade liberalization has arrived and the Western Hemisphere is now facing consolidation of uneven arrangements one way or another.

Open regionalism can be beneficial if it serves to pull together the myriad and confusing array of trade pacts. In addition to providing more uniform trade rules, merging the hemisphere's RTAs may lead to broader regional and perhaps even global trade understandings, as well as lend support for continuing economic, political, and social reform in Latin America. All are stated goals of U.S. business and the Clinton Administration. In the meantime, despite the call by some for a return to multilateralism, it seems that reversing the trend toward regional trade agreements in Latin America is unlikely, even if it is an imperfect substitute for a global approach.

There is no economic evidence to suggest that U.S. interests are best served by the status quo of multiple subregional trade agreements. The FTAA process provides some promise that for the region, a mutually beneficial solution may eventually emerge. This, however, is not the only possible outcome. Much attention is still focused on MERCOSUR's outreach as an alternative in South America to either NAFTA or an FTAA. A North-South face off is another possibility, which could become even more complicated if Mexico and Canada sign trade agreements with MERCOSUR. This would seem to promote a more disorderly, in not outright contentious, situation, imperiling the integration process that an FTAA seeks to promote. The United States is faced with the question of whether its interests can be served best by leading the formal process toward an FTAA or by standing on the sidelines.

---

[58] For a broader discussion of U.S. interests and policy goals see: U.S. Library of Congress. Congressional Research Service. *Hemispheric Free Trade: Status, Hurdles, and Opposition*. CRS Report 97-514 F, by Raymond J. Ahearn. June 3, 1997.

Appendix 1. Western Hemisphere Trade and Economic Cooperation Agreements

The FTAA involves negotiations among 34 nations of the Western Hemisphere: Antigua & Barbuda; Argentina; Bahamas; Barbados; Belize; Bolivia; Brazil; Canada; Chile; Colombia; Costa Rica; Dominica; Dominican Republic; Ecuador; El Salvador; Grenada; Guatemala; Guyana; Haiti; Honduras; Jamaica; Mexico; Nicaragua; Panama; Paraguay; Peru; St. Kitts & Nevis; St. Lucia; St. Vincent; Suriname; Trinidad & Tobago; United States; Uruguay; and Venezuela. All are members of other regional trade agreements (see table 3 and list and the end of this appendix).

Table 3. Major Western Hemisphere Regional Trade Agreements

Agreement	Members	Total Intra-Group Trade (1995 $ bil)	Year Effective
Free Trade Area of the Americas (FTAA)	34 countries		Negotiating
North American Free Trade Agreement (NAFTA)	Canada, Mexico, United States	$362.0	1994
Caribbean Community and Common Market (CARICOM)	Antigua & Barbuda, Bahamas, Barbados, Belize, Dominica, Grenada, Guyana, Haiti, Jamaica, Montserrat, St. Kitts & Nevis, St. Lucia, St. Vincent, and Surinam, Trinidad & Tobago.	0.7	1973
Southern Cone Common Market (MERCOSUR)	Argentina, Brazil, Paraguay, Uruguay.	14.3	1991 and 1995 (CET)
Andean Community (formerly Pact)	Bolivia, Colombia, Ecuador, Peru* Venezuela.	3.6	1969
Central American Common Market (CACM)	Costa Rica, El Salvador, Guatemala, Honduras, Nicaragua.	1.5	1961-62

* Peru's membership was suspended in 1992 and is still considering formal withdrawal.
CET = common external tariff.
Source: *Western Hemisphere Trade Agreements*. U.S. Department of Commerce. Office of Latin America and the Caribbean. June 1996 and Organization of Americans States, see their web page at: www.sice.oas.org.

The road to the FTAA has a long, but until recently, discouraging history. Following in the footsteps of economic cooperation efforts made in Europe, Latin America attempted to achieve some level of economic integration in the 1960s, forming many trade alliances such as the Latin American Free Trade Association (now the Latin American Integration Association, see below) and a couple of the groups listed in table 3. These early attempts, however, went largely unrealized for decades. The remnants of these agreements plus new initiatives in the post-debt crisis reform era are what constitute the new wave of trade agreements breaking out in the region.[59]

At last count there were over 50 trade and economic cooperation agreements either signed or being negotiated in the Western Hemisphere; they may be arranged into five basic categories. For the purposes of this report they are grouped more according to how they function rather than by their intended goals or formal titles. Because many of these agreements are works in progress, it could be argued that any one of them might actually fall into one or another category. This exercise in trade agreement taxonomy, therefore, is admittedly only one approach to simplifying a complicated and murky situation.

The most prevalent arrangement is the *free trade agreement* (FTA) characterized by elimination of tariffs on trade among member countries. NAFTA is the largest. Others include: the Group of Three (Colombia, Mexico, Venezuela); Colombia-Venezuela-Central America; Mexico-Central America; Colombia-Caribbean Community, and the Central American Free Trade Agreement (CAFTA). There are also bilateral FTAs that have either been signed or are under negotiation. Although all agreements have a common goal of tariff elimination, some are not yet fully implemented. For example, CAFTA is a subgroup of Central American Common Market members (see below) encouraging, but not yet achieving, more rapid movement toward an FTA between Central America and Mexico, and eventually the United States. Should Costa Rica join, CAFTA would effectively become part of the CACM.

The second type of pact is the *non-reciprocal preferential trade agreement*, where one country lowers tariffs on certain goods for selected countries without receiving similar treatment in return. This arrangement is less comprehensive than an FTA and usually motivated heavily by political as well as economic reasons. Included in this group are the Caribbean Basin Initiative (CBI) and the U.S.-Andean Trade Preference Act (ATPA). The United States Congress passed ATPA in 1991 to "promote the development of sustainable economic alternatives to drug crop production....by offering alternative Andean products broader access to the U.S. market."[60] The CBI provides tariff relief expressly to assist the small Caribbean countries with economic reform and development, in part, as a way to promote political stability and cooperation. Other regional trade preference agreements include the Caribbean-Canadian Common Market (CARIBCAN) and Venezuela-CARICOM trade agreement.

Third is the *customs union*, noted for the common external tariff (CET) imposed by member countries on all imported goods from non-members. The most well-known in Latin America is the Southern Cone Common Market

---

[59] For background on the earlier agreements, see: Wolff, Jason R. Putting the Cart Before the Horse: Assessing Opportunities for Regional Integration in Latin America and the Caribbean. *Fletcher Forum of World Affairs*, v. 20, Winter/Spring 1996. pp. 106-12.

[60] See: United States International Trade Commission. *Andean Trade Preference Act: Impact on U.S. Industries and Consumers and on Drug Crop Eradication and Crop Substitution*. USITC Publication 2995. Washington, D.C. September 1996. p. vii.

(Mercado Comun del Sur -- MERCOSUR) comprising Brazil, Argentina, Paraguay, and Uruguay. MERCOSUR and its individual members also have separate FTAs with individual countries. Many view these numerous MERCOSUR initiatives as a serious building block to a larger South American Free Trade Area (SAFTA), particularly if it succeeds in linking with other groups such as the Andean Community. In addition, other pacts that technically fall within this category are: the Caribbean Community/Common Market (CARICOM), which has a CET, but is not uniformly applied; the Andean Community; and the Organization of East Caribbean States (OECS), a subregional group of smaller CARICOM members.

In addition, the Central America Common Market (CACM) qualifies as a customs union, but in some analyses, also as a fourth category, the *common market*, which is a customs union with the free movement of capital and labor. Although the CACM has made progress toward loosening controls on the movement of capital and labor, it has not yet even achieved a uniform CET for all members, and has some nontariff barriers in place for agricultural products, further clouding its definition as a trade pact. Deeper economic integration agreements (economic and monetary unions) are not in place, nor envisioned.

A fifth type of agreement extends beyond trade to include political, cultural, and economic cooperation such as: 1) the Rio Group comprising Argentina, Bolivia, Brazil, Chile, Colombia, Ecuador, Mexico, Panama, Paraguay, Peru, Uruguay, and Venezuela; and 2) the Association of Caribbean States (ACS) constituting Belize, Colombia, Cuba, Mexico, Guyana, Venezuela, and the Central American and Caribbean states. The Latin American Integration Association (LAIA) is an altogether different arrangement. It operates as an "umbrella organization" that encourages the formation of preferential trade pacts among its members, provided they are open to all and are consistent with the WTO, among other constraints.

FTAs continue to evolve in the Western Hemisphere, circumventing U.S. participation, in part encouraged by the lack of movement towards passage of fast-track trade negotiation legislation. Chile and Mexico, for example, are considering deepening their "goods-only" trade agreement, including exploring areas very sensitive to the United States, such as antidumping policy. Canada, which also has an FTA with Chile, has expressed a strong interest in consummating one with MERCOSUR outside the NAFTA expansion process. Peru has also asked to begin talks on joining MERCOSUR and may yet withdraw from the Andean Community. Mexico has initiated preliminary bilateral talks to implement trade agreements with virtually all countries in Latin America, including MERCOSUR.[61]

As of July 1997, there were at least 56 trade or economic cooperation agreements in the Western Hemisphere, including those under negotiation. Many are bilateral agreements. They are listed below with all the members

---

[61] *Americas Trade*. May 1, 1997. p. 2 and *The Journal of Commerce*. May 16, 1997. p. 4 and discussion with Embassy of Mexico, July 3, 1997.

included and the date that the agreement was signed. Given the quick evolution of these agreements, this list should be considered a "moving target."[62]

Hemispheric Trade Agreements

1. *Free Trade Area of the Americas* (FTAA) - Under negotiation.
   Members: 34 nations of the Western Hemisphere: Antigua & Barbuda; Argentina; Bahamas; Barbados; Belize; Bolivia; Brazil; Canada; Chile; Colombia; Costa Rica; Dominica; Dominican Republic; Ecuador; El Salvador; Grenada; Guatemala; Guyana; Haiti; Honduras; Jamaica; Mexico; Nicaragua; Panama; Paraguay; Peru; St. Kitts & Nevis; St. Lucia; St. Vincent; Suriname; Trinidad & Tobago; United States; Uruguay; and Venezuela.

2. *North American Free Trade Agreement* (NAFTA) - 1992 (ratified by United States in 1993 and implemented January 1, 1994).
   Members: United States, Canada, Mexico.

3. *Southern Cone Common Market* (Mercado Comun del Sur - MERCOSUR) - 1991. (Common external tariff established in 1995).
   Members: Argentina, Brazil, Paraguay, Uruguay.
   Note: there are numerous bilateral agreements between members of MERCOSUR and various other Latin American countries separate from any agreement they may have with MERCOSUR proper (see below).

4. *Caribbean Community and Common Market* (CARICOM) - 1973.
   Members: Antigua & Barbuda, Bahamas, Barbados, Belize, Dominica, Grenada, Guyana, Jamaica, Montserrat, St. Kitts & Nevis, St. Lucia, St. Vincent, Surinam, and Trinidad & Tobago.

5. *Andean Community* (formerly Pact) - 1969 (revised 1989; renamed 1996).
   Members: Bolivia, Colombia, Ecuador, Peru, Venezuela.
   Note: Peru's membership was suspended in 1992 and it formally withdrew in April 1997 and made known its interest in joining MERCOSUR.

6. *Central American Common Market* (CACM) - 1960 (revised 1991).
   Members: Costa Rica, El Salvador, Guatemala, Honduras, Nicaragua.

7. *Latin American Integration Association* (LAIA) - 1980 (formerly Latin American Free Trade Association - 1960).
   Members: Argentina, Bolivia, Brazil, Chile, Colombia, Ecuador, Mexico, Paraguay, Peru, Uruguay, Venezuela.

---

[62] Compiled from: *Latin Trade*, June 1997, pp. 4A-6A, U.S. Department of Commerce. *Western Hemisphere Trade Agreements*, June 1, 1996, and discussions with staff of the Inter-American Development Bank, Organization of American States, and Embassy of Mexico. See also: U.S. Library of Congress. Congressional Research Service. *Western Hemisphere Trade Developments*. CRS Report No. 96-541 F, by Raymond J. Ahearn. 6 p.

8. *Organization of East Caribbean States* (OECS) - 1981.
Members: Antigua and Barbuda, Dominica, Grenada, Montserrat, St. Kitts and Nevis. St. Lucia, and St. Vincent and the Grenadines.
Note: this is a subregional group of CARICOM.

9. *Rio Group* - 1989. (formerly Group of Eight.)
Members: Argentina, Bolivia, Brazil, Chile, Colombia, Ecuador, Mexico, Panama, Paraguay, Peru, Uruguay, Venezuela with Jamaica representing Caribbean countries and Central American representation done on a rotating basis.

10. *Association of Caribbean States* (ACS) - 1994.
Members: Belize, Colombia, Cuba, Mexico, Guyana, Venezuela, and the Central American and Caribbean states.

11. *Group of Three* (G-3) - 1994.
Members: Colombia, Mexico, Venezuela.

12. *Caribbean Basin Initiative* (CBI) - 1984 (provisional status with passage of Caribbean Basin Economic Recovery Act (CBERA); permanent status 1990).
Members: Antigua & Barbuda, Bahamas, Barbados, Belize, British Virgin Islands, Costa Rica, Dominica, Dominican Republic, El Salvador, Grenada, Guatemala, Guyana, Haiti, Honduras, Jamaica, Montserrat, Netherlands Antilles, Nicaragua, Panama, St. Kitts/Nevis, St. Lucia, St. Vincent, Trinidad & Tobago, United States.

13. *Andean Trade Preference Act* (ATPA) - 1991.
Members: Bolivia, Colombia, Ecuador, Peru, United States.

14. *Colombia-Venezuela-Central America* - 1993 (not implemented)

15. *Central American Free Trade Agreement* (CAFTA) - 1992 (proposed, only partial implementation).
Members: Guatemala, El Salvador, Honduras, Nicaragua.
Note: CAFTA is a subgroup of Central American Common Market members encouraging more rapid movement toward an FTA between Central America and Mexico, and eventually the United States. Should Costa Rica join, CAFTA would effectively become part of the CACM.

16. *Caribbean-Canadian Common Market* (CARIBCAN) - 1986.
Members: Antigua and Barbuda, the Bahamas, Barbados, Belize, Canada, Dominica, Grenada, Guyana, Jamaica, St. Kitts and Nevis, St. Lucia, St. Vincent and the Grenadines, Trinidad and Tobago, and the British Caribbean Dependencies.

Bilateral Agreements

17. *Mexico-Central America* - 1992 (framework agreement only).

18. *Colombia-Caribbean Community* - 1994
Members: Antigua & Barbuda, Barbados, Belize, Colombia, Dominica, Grenada, Guyana, Jamaica, Montserrat, St. Kitts/Nevis, St. Lucia, St. Vincent, Suriname, and Trinidad and Tobago.

19. *CARICOM-Venezuela* - 1992.

20. *CARICOM-Colombia* - 1994.

21. *CARICOM-Mexico* - 1993.

22. *MERCOSUR-Chile* - 1996.

23. *MERCOSUR-Bolivia* - 1995.

24. *Argentina-Brazil* - 1990.

25. *Argentina-Chile* - 1991.

26. *Argentina-Colombia* - 1991.

27. *Argentina-Bolivia* - 1992.

28. *Argentina-Venezuela* - 1992.

29. *Argentina-Ecuador* - 1993.

30. *Bolivia-Paraguay* - 1994.

31. *Bolivia-Peru* - 1992.

32. *Bolivia-Uruguay* - 1991.

33. *Bolivia-Brazil* - 1994.

34. *Brazil-Venezuela* - 1994.

35. *Chile-Canada* - 1996.

36. *Chile-Bolivia* - 1993.

37. *Chile-Mexico* - 1991.

38. *Chile-Ecuador* - 1994.

39. *Chile-Colombia* - 1993.

40. *Chile-Venezuela* - 1993.

41. *Mexico-Costa Rica* - 1994.

42. *Mexico-Bolivia* - 1994.

43. *Mexico-Nicaragua* - 1997

Agreements Under Negotiation

44. *Andean Pact-MERCOSUR*

45. *Chile-Central America*

46. *Chile-Panama*

47. *Chile-Peru*

48. *Colombia-Central America*

49. *Mexico-Ecuador*

50. *Mexico-El Salvador*

51. *Mexico-Guatemala*

52. *Mexico-Honduras*

53. *Mexico-Panama*

54. *Mexico-Peru*

55. *Mexico-MERCOSUR*

56. *Venezuela-Central America*

Appendix 2. U.S. Direction of Trade, 1990 and 1996 ($ billions)

U.S. Exports	1990	1996	% Change 90-96
Western Europe	113.1	141.3	24.9%
Canada	83.7	132.6	58.4%
Mexico	28.3	56.8	100.7%
LAC	25.7	52.2	103.1%
Asia	120.3	205.2	70.6%
Africa	8.0	11.0	37.5%
Other	14.5	23.7	63.4%
World Total	393.6	622.8	58.2%

U.S. Imports	1990	1996	% Change 90-96
Western Europe	109.0	163.4	49.9%
Canada	91.4	156.5	71.2%
Mexico	30.2	73.0	141.7%
LAC	33.7	48.6	44.2%
Asia	207.3	324.5	56.5%
Africa	15.8	17.7	12.0%
Other	7.9	7.6	-3.8%
World Total	495.3	791.3	59.8%

Trade Turnover	1990	1996	% Change 90-96
Western Europe	222.1	304.7	37.2%
Canada	175.1	289.1	65.1%
Mexico	58.5	129.8	121.9%
LAC	59.4	100.8	69.7%
Asia	327.6	529.7	61.7%
Africa	23.8	28.7	20.6%
Other	22.4	31.3	39.7%
World Total	888.9	1,414.1	59.1%

U.S. Trade Balance	1990	1996
Western Europe	4.1	-22.1
Canada	-7.7	-23.9
Mexico	-1.9	-16.2
LAC	-8.0	3.6
Asia	-87.0	-119.3
Africa	-7.8	-6.7
Other	6.6	16.1
World Total	-101.7	-168.5

Source: U.S. Department of Commerce.

COLOMBIA: CONDITIONS AND U.S. POLICY OPTIONS

Nina M. Serafino

Introduction

Difficult new circumstances face U.S. policy towards Colombia, a country of 39 million people. That policy has focused for almost two decades on joint efforts to destroy drug-trafficking organizations and decrease the flow of cocaine from Colombia, which, according to U.S. officials, has produced some 75-80% of the world's supply. Now, however, Colombians are cultivating new areas with coca leaf, and a multitude of small, independent trafficking organizations has replaced the two major cartels of the 1980s and early 1990s, complicating those efforts. In addition, within the past few years Colombia's political and economic stability has been threatened by high levels of violence and conflict stemming from the increased strength and illegal activities of leftist guerrilla groups and rightist paramilitary organizations. The efforts of Colombian President Andres Pastrana, who took office in August 1998, to end Colombia's 30-year conflict by making peace with the country's two major guerrilla groups have added a new dimension to the debate about U.S. policy toward Colombia.

Within the last year, the United States has substantially increased U.S. assistance for counternarcotics efforts, most of which currently goes to activities of the Colombian National Police. This year, some policymakers and analysts are arguing for still greater assistance, although with disparate purposes — some believe more aid is needed for greater military participation in counternarcotics efforts, others believe the United States should consider counterinsurgency aid to counter the threat from the guerrillas, and others would broaden U.S. assistance to provide support for economic and political reforms in Colombia.

This report first discusses U.S. interests in Colombia. It then provides information on Colombia's current conflict, with sections on the guerrillas, the paramilitaries, and President Pastrana's efforts to deal with the conflict through the peace process, and the reform and rehabilitation of the Colombian military. The last section describes congressional concerns, and possible policy options.

U.S. Interests in Colombia

The United States' longstanding and, thus far, dominant interest in curbing the production and shipment of illegal narcotics from Colombia has been joined, and some would argue supplanted, by other important U.S. interests in the new situation in Colombia. Developing a coherent U.S. policy to further these interests — strengthening counternarcotics efforts, supporting Colombia's weak democracy and eroded economy, maintaining U.S. economic ties, and preventing regional instability — has proven to be a difficult task. In part, the difficulty is due to the problem of addressing sometimes conflicting interests simultaneously, and to the lack of agreement on priorities among these interests, as reflected in the section on U.S. Options, below.

Combat Illegal Narcotics Production and Trafficking. The continuing metamorphosis of Colombia's drug problem presents new counternarcotics challenges for Colombia and the United States. From the early 1980s, Colombia and the United States cooperated in a campaign to deal with the cocaine trafficking of the Medellin and Cali cartels.[1] With the demise of these cartels by the mid-1990s, there was hope that Colombia's drug trafficking problem would be ameliorated. Instead, the problem has, many argue, become more difficult to deal with than before.

For one, the large Medellin and Cali cartels have been replaced by smaller, independent traffickers and splinters from the Cali cartel. As of mid-1998, the Colombian police had counted some 43 independent trafficking groups, about half of them based in the Antioquia Department, of which Medellin is the capital, and the others in the northern Cauca Valley, around Cali. Several groups of independent cocaine traffickers from the northern Cauca Valley have expanded their activities through the sale of cheap, high quality heroin. (Heroin became a significant export from Colombia after 1990, when substantial opium poppy cultivation in Colombia was first reported, and Colombian traffickers are now the largest suppliers of heroin to the eastern United States.) The rise of independent traffickers has complicated efforts to reduce trafficking, according to some analysts. Because they adopt conservative lifestyles, and work in groups of 10 to 20, using small legitimate businesses as fronts, independent traffickers are hard to identify.

In addition, since the mid-1990s, coca leaf production has expanded in Colombia. Less than a decade ago, Colombian traffickers flew semi-processed coca base from Bolivia and Peru into Colombia, where laboratories processed it into cocaine, which was then exported by the trafficking cartels. In 1999, however, according to the General Accounting Office (GAO), as coca cultivation decreased in Bolivia and Peru, Colombia surpassed both countries in acreage under cultivation, dedicating 50% more to such cultivation than in 1998, despite eradication spraying.

---

[1] The Medellin cartel became prominent in the early 1980s, as cocaine replaced marijuana as Colombia's primary illegal export and Colombia became the source of most of the world's supply. It attempted to force the government to desist from counternarcotics efforts, largely through assassinations and bombings. In the 1980s and early 1990s, hundreds of policemen, judges, and journalists, as well as four presidential candidates were killed, and the Medellin cartel was believed responsible for many of the killings. The cartel's leader, Pablo Escobar, was killed by security forces after escaping from jail in December 1993. Other cartel leaders were arrested; in 1996, Escobar's No. 2 man, Jorge Luis Ochoa, and Ochoa's two brothers, Juan David and Fabio, were released.

The Cali cartel operated differently, insinuating itself into elite social and political circles, and depending largely on corruption rather than violence to achieve its ends. Much more sophisticated than the Medellin cartel, Cali cartel shipped large quantities of cocaine to the United States and invented sophisticated money-laundering schemes. At the height of its power earlier in the 1990s, the Cali cartel earned annual revenues of $7 billion, according to the U.S. Drug Enforcement Administration (DEA). The cartel's activity reportedly declined after the June 1995 arrest of cartel leader Gilberto Rodriquez Orejuela, and the subsequent arrest of the remaining top leaders by September 1996.

Figures from the State Department's International Narcotics Control Strategy Report, 1999, of March 2000, show Colombian coca cultivation had grown from over 126,000 acres in 1995 to 251,000 acres in 1998, to 302,600 acres in 1999. The estimated potential cocaine production reportedly increased from 230 to 520 metric tons over the same period.[2] The expansion of coca leaf cultivation in Colombia is viewed as particularly troublesome, as Colombian coca leaf has proved to be of a higher quality (i.e., more cocaine can be extracted from a given amount of coca leaf) than previously believed.

Support Colombia's Democracy and Human Rights. For much of this century, the United States has had close relations with Colombia, and often looked to Colombia for diplomatic support in international affairs. In the interest of sustaining this relationship, the United States has played an activist, some would say interventionist, role in buttressing Colombia's political institutions in the face of drug corruption. Although differences over the appropriate methods to deal with Colombia's drug problem have soured or impeded relations with recent Colombian administrations, most notably with that of President Pastrana's predecessor, Ernesto Samper, relations under the Pastrana Administration have returned to the traditional, close mode. Some analysts argue that the United States should now help sustain Colombia's friendly democracy by providing aid to confront its new challenge: the recent intensification of the guerrilla conflict which erodes the Colombian government's legitimacy by bringing into question its ability to provide security to its citizens. A few analysts also argue that the government's survival itself is in jeopardy, as the guerrilla groups are relatively much stronger than the Colombian military and may be able to topple the government if the imbalance persists. Many are concerned, however, that assistance to support the Colombian government only be provided if it will support, rather than undermine, respect for human rights. Some also fear that the problems of Colombian democracy are so complex that U.S. aid will at best provide a palliative, and do little to resolve them. (See section on Congressional Concerns, below.) Drug corruption within the Colombian government is also a continuing source of concern.

Support Colombia's Economy. The Pastrana Administration's political problems are compounded by an economic crisis unprecedented in Colombia in recent decades. For several decades, Colombia's economy was consistently one of the most successful in the hemisphere, with sustained annual growth rates averaging just under 5%, and a negligible public sector deficit. President Pastrana, however, inherited an economy that was deteriorating by most major indices. In 1999, Colombia's Gross Domestic Product (GDP) contracted for the first time in over 50 years. (As of early 2000, the economy's decline has been calculated differently by different sources: one source indicated a decline of about 1%, another of 5%.). The country's foreign debt jumped in 1999 to $36 billion, some 41.3% of GDP, up from 34% of GDP in 1998. (Some 57% of this is owed by the public sector.) Unemployment in Colombia's seven major metropolitan areas has risen sharply from lows under 10% in the early 1990s, to about 18 percent at the end of 1999. (The year end rate, however, was a drop

---

[2] U.S. Department of State. Bureau for International Narcotics and Law Enforcement Affairs. International Narcotics Control Strategy Report, 1999. Released March 2000. [http://www.state.gov/www/global/narcotics_law/1999_narc_report/samer99_part3.html].

from a peak of 20% in the third quarter.) State spending expanded beginning in the early to mid-1990s, with a corresponding increase in the public sector deficit. On the other hand, inflation rates have improved, showing a continuous decline over the 1990s, running under 10% at the end of 1999, according to private sector estimates. Declining prices in the late 1990s for coffee and oil, two of Colombia's major imports, exacerbated the country's economic problems, as has the guerrilla insurgency. Colombian experts have estimated that the conflict costs the country 3% of growth per year.[3]

Many analysts believe that the troubled legal economy not only deprives the government of the funds needed for rural development programs to attract rural inhabitants away from coca cultivation and the insurgency, but also drives many desperate Colombians into the cultivation and trafficking of illegal narcotics.[4] Among these Colombians are the increasing number of unemployed, and the million or so internally displaced persons.[5] Some fear that it may increase the significance of the drug trade to Colombia's economy. According to recent estimates, income from illegal narcotics provides as much as $4 billion to Colombia, or some 5% of the country's $80 billion Gross Domestic Product (GDP).[6]

Some GDP growth is expected in 2000, however. Improving petroleum and coffee prices in 2000 may, however, contribute to a marginally improved outlook.

Maintain U.S. Trade and Investment. Economic problems and the continuing guerrilla conflict have economic effects on foreign businessmen trading with Colombia and on foreign investors. Colombia is the United States' eighth largest oil supplier, and its fifth largest market in Latin America.[7] U.S. firms have provided 40% of Colombia's foreign direct investment, of which petroleum investments are an

---

[3] Congressional testimony of Deputy Assistant Secretary of State for Western Hemisphere Affairs, John P. Leonard, before the Senate Subcommittee on the Western Hemisphere, Peace Corps, Narcotics, and Terrorism, March 24, 1999.

[4] As of 1997, 54% of Colombia's rural inhabitants lived in poverty, and more than half of those inhabitants (29% of all rural inhabitants) lived in extreme poverty. In urban areas, 39% of the inhabitants lived in poverty, and 15% lived in extreme poverty. United Nations. Economic Commission for Latin America and the Caribbean. *Panorama Social: 1998.* LC/G.2050-P. April 1999. p. 19.

[5] For more information on the displaced persons in Colombia, see CRS Report RL30314, *Colombia: Human Rights Conditions and U.S. Concerns.*

[6] This was a very preliminary figure for 1998, from estimates being prepared by the Colombian government. Larry Rohter. Colombia Adjusts Economic Figures to Include Its Drug Crops. *The New York Times.* June 27, 1999. p. 3.

[7] Colombia is the United States' twenty-sixth largest export market (in 1997 and 1998) and its fifth largest trading partner in Latin America after Mexico, Brazil, Venezuela and Argentina. The United States is Colombia's major trading partner, with $11 billion in two-way trade in 1998. (U.S. exports to Colombia constituted 41.5% of all Colombian imports in 1997, and Colombian exports to the United States were 38% of all Colombian exports.) U.S. exports to Colombia include vehicles, agricultural products, electrical power generators and other machinery, chemicals and plastics. U.S. imports of Colombian goods include petroleum, coffee, cut flowers, semiprecious stones, sugar, and tropical fruits.

important part. Within the past decade, oil companies have discovered and begun exploitation of significant petroleum reserves in Colombia; estimates of potential reserves suggest that the country may be an important source of petroleum for the United States in the future. The partnership of British Petroleum and Amoco has the largest foreign petroleum investment in Colombia. Another U.S. firm, Occidental Petroleum, has the second largest investment. (U.S. environmental and indigenous rights groups have protested proposed drilling by Occidental Petroleum on lands claimed by the U'wa Colombian indigenous group as their ancestral territory.[8] Foreign traders and investors claim that the need to provide additional security on their own significantly increases the cost of doing business in Colombia. Although profits are large enough for many companies to absorb these costs, the lack of security is viewed as discouraging further trade and investment. According to some reports, Colombia received very little foreign investment in 1999.

Prevent Regional Instability. The spillover effects of the continued insurgency on Colombia's five neighbors is transforming Colombia's internal conflict into a regional problem. Colombian guerrillas have regularly crossed the borders into Panama and Venezuela, using adjacent areas as safehavens and to conduct criminal activities. Guerrillas reportedly have attacked Venezuelan security forces.[9] In 1995, guerrillas attacked Ecuadoran military and police units; more recently they have harassed Ecuadoran truck drivers in Colombia. In addition, U.S. officials blamed the FARC for the September 1999 kidnapping of 12 foreigners in Ecuador.[10] Paramilitary forces reportedly have pursued guerrillas across the border into Panama and Venezuela; in September 1999 paramilitary leader Carlos Castaño declared that Panamanian National Guardsmen who supported Colombian guerrillas were "military targets" and accused Venezuelan President Hugo Chavez of backing the guerrillas. Refugees from Colombia's conflict have also crossed the borders into Panama and Venezuela, seeking safety. (Although many apparently return, some reportedly do so unwillingly.) Such incidents and statements have led to growing concerns about the threats to Colombia's neighbors from growing instability and lawlessness in border areas. Because much of Colombia's borders with Brazil, Ecuador, Peru and Venezuela lies in the largely unpopulated Amazon Basin, some analysts also anticipate an increase in drug trafficking and arms smuggling, as well as an increase in border crossings by groups of people fleeing conflict.

Defense of U.S. Citizens. The United States has an interest in clarifying the status of three disappeared Americans and in bringing to justice their kidnappers and the killers of three other Americans. The United States has information that the FARC was responsible for the kidnapping of three American missionaries from the New Tribes Mission — David Mankins, Mark Rich, and Richard Tennenoff — on

---

[8] John Otis. Death in a Hot Zone: How three American activists were killed in Colombian Drama of Rebels, Oil, Indians. *The Houston Chronicle.* October 3, 1999. p. A!.

[9] Gabriel Marcella and Donald Schulz. *Colombia's Three Wars: U.S. Strategy at the Crossroads.* Carlisle Barracks, Pa.: U.S. Army War College Strategic Studies Institute, March 5, 1999, pp. 19-20. [http://carlisle-.army.mil/usassi/ssipubs/pubs99/3wars/3wars.htm].

[10] For more on the effects of the Colombia situation on Ecuador, see: CRS Report RS20494, Ecuador: International Narcotics Control Issues.

January 31, 1993.[11] (Their current whereabouts is unknown.) The FARC has admitted that on March 4, 1999, one of its members killed three American environmental and indigenous rights workers — Terence Freitas, Ingrid Washinawatok, and Laheenae Gay — who had been visiting the U'wa indigenous group in Colombia. U.S. policymakers doubt that responsibility ends with the soldier that FARC leaders identified as the killer. In mid-February, 2000, President Pastrana reportedly stated that the Colombian government would not extradite to the United States a captured FARC regional commander, German Briceño, whom the United States accuses of ordering the three killed.

Colombian Democracy and the Current Conflict

Many observers have viewed Colombian democracy as a paradox. Because of its stable two-party system and regular elections, Colombia was long considered one of Latin America's model democracies. Yet, for decades, it has been rent by almost continuous violence.

Since the 1960s, Colombia's two political parties — the Conservatives and the Liberals—have peacefully transferred power to one another through elections. This two-party system evolved from the political settlement of a widespread, armed civil conflict, which began in the 1940s, that pitted adherents of the Liberal Party against those of the Conservative Party. In 1957, the two political parties agreed to form a coalition "National Front" government, which shared power and regularly alternated the presidency from 1958 through 1974. That political settlement established peace, at least in the urban areas, putting an end to the period known as "*La Violencia*," in which an estimated 200,000 partisans and others died.

Yet, conflict continued in the rural areas, where peasant armies joined with leftist guerrillas to gain or retain possession of land. Colombia's counterinsurgency campaign of the 1960s destroyed the nine "independent republics" established by the peasants, several of which were controlled by the Communist Party, but never entirely defeated the guerrillas. Another unfortunate legacy, according to some analysts, was a climate of political intolerance throughout the country.

In subsequent decades, violence remained a prominent feature of Colombian life. The rise of the Medellín cocaine cartel in the 1980s brought high levels of drug-related violence until its demise in the early 1990s. Since then, Colombia continues to have a high rate of murder committed in the context of criminal acts, and political violence carried out by paramilitary groups and the leftist guerrillas, largely in rural areas.[12] Until the guerrillas began operating close to Bogatá in the last two years, however, the conflict between the paramilitary groups and the guerrillas went largely unnoticed in Colombia's urban centers, where some 75% of Colombians live.

---

[11] Jacobs, Andrew. 3 Kidnapped Americans Killed: Colombian Rebels Are Suspected. *The New York Times*. March 6, 1999.

[12] For analysis and theories of the possible causes of Colombian violence, see the Berquist, Chernick, and Thoumi works cited in the Bibliography.

Even as he campaigned as the Conservative party candidate for the March 1998 election, President Pastrana decided that he must not only curb drug trafficking, but, like other Presidents before him, make an attempt to end political violence by bringing the guerrillas into the political system through negotiations. This task requires him not only to meet the military and political challenges presented by the guerrillas, but also to deal with the paramilitary presence.

The Guerrilla Challenge

While Colombia's guerrilla groups have operated almost continuously and generally unimpeded in rural areas for over 50 years, they have not, in recent decades, controlled and operated in the expanse of territory that they now do, nor fought with such intensity. The two main groups—The Revolutionary Armed Forces of Colombia (*Fuerzas Armadas Revolucionarias de Colombia*, or FARC) and the National Liberation Army (*Ejército de Liberación Nacional*, or ELN)—now reportedly control or influence local governments in 40% to 50% of Colombian territory, all of it in rural areas. They not only attack police and military forces, but regularly attack civilian populations, commit massacres and extrajudicial killings, collect war taxes, compel citizens into their ranks, force farmers to grow illicit crops, and regulate travel, commerce, and other activities. The ELN routinely bombs oil pipelines. During 1998, some two-thirds of all kidnappings in Colombia were committed by guerrilla groups, with 667 cases attributed to the FARC, 566 to the ELN, and 152 to other groups.[13]

Current Strengths and Actions. The guerrillas have gained great strength in recent years. Since the early 1990s, their numbers reportedly have increased substantially (some analysts calculate as much as fourfold) and they have dramatically increased their revenues from kidnapping and involvement in drug trafficking. The larger of the two forces, the FARC, has 10,000-15,000 regular troops according to U.S. estimates, and apparently can also activate other supporters for military actions when desired. This is a substantial increase from 1998, when U.S. officials estimated FARC strength at 7,000-10,000 troops. At 3,000-6,000, the estimated size of the ELN has not changed since 1998.

Guerrilla troops are well clothed and equipped (even better than Colombian soldiers), and paid salaries and pensions, according to U.S. officials and other analysts. Most analysts argue that the FARC and ELN guerrillas have been highly disciplined soldiers, although some believe that their discipline is attributable to fear of punishment rather than loyalty to their organization. There are some recent indications, however, that traditional discipline has broken down. According to Colombian intelligence reports, the FARC, in mid-1999, was equipped with five

---

[13] The information on guerrilla human rights violations in this paragraph is from U.S. Department of State. Bureau of Democracy, Human Rights, and Labor. *Colombia Country Report for Human Rights Practices for 1998*, February 26, 1999. [http://www.state.gov/www/global/human_rights/1998_hrp_report/colombia.html]. For more information on guerrilla violations, as well as those of the paramilitary and the security forces, see CRS Report RL30314, *Colombia: Human Rights Conditions and U.S. Concerns*.

Cessna aircraft, four reconnaissance helicopters, and one medical evacuation helicopter.[14]

The degree to which the guerrillas enjoy popular support among the inhabitants of the areas in which they operate, is a matter of debate. In the areas that they control or where their influence is strong, the guerrillas provide many of the public services of a government, or negotiate with the elected government to undertake certain projects. This may earn them loyalty and active support. (According to one report, the FARC has created a clandestine political party, the Bolivarian Movement for a New Colombia, "which actively co-governs in areas of guerrilla influence."[15]) On the other hand, observers report that the inhabitants have no alternative but to render the obedience that the guerrillas demand. Reports from the "demilitarized zone" created by the Pastrana Administration in November 1998 at the outset of the peace talks and controlled by the guerrillas indicate that at least some inhabitants resent the guerrillas' arbitrary and at times brutal rule. As part of the peace process, the Pastrana Administration has recognized the FARC as a legitimate political force, although a Colombian involved in the previous administration's peace efforts described the guerrillas as "quite weak in political terms."[16]

The Military Situation. Over 1998 and 1999, the guerrillas launched extensive attacks, persuading many analysts that they are a more capable armed force than the Colombian military. In the days before President Pastrana's August 1998 inauguration, they launched a nationwide offensive, in which at least 130 people were killed and dozens of policemen and soldiers were taken prisoner. They also destroyed a major military base, Miraflores, in the Guaviare province. In addition, they attacked 40 other installations, including police stations and oil facilities, in over half the country's 32 provinces.[17] Since then, the guerrillas have carried out several other attacks on significant military targets. On July 8, 1999, the FARC attacked an army camp of some 70 soldiers near the village of Gutierrez, 27 miles southeast of Bogotá, and then, over the next three days, carried out at least 24 attacks in nine states. Although over 60 military troops and policemen were killed, the Colombian army claimed to have halted the offensive by killing more than 200 guerrillas in several areas.[18] (This, for some analysts, marked a turning point in the army's capacity to counter the guerrillas.) The guerrillas have not yet, however, launched attacks in

---

[14] Jineth Bedoya Lima. *The Air Power of the Guerrillas and "Paras"*. From Semana, July 5, 1999, as translated by the Foreign Broadcast Information Service (FBIS), Document # FTS19990707000040.

[15] Arturo Alape. *The Possibilities for Peace*, in NACLA Report on the Americas, March/April 1998. p. 36.

[16] Remarks by Daniel Garcia-Peña during a May 1998 conference organized by the Latin American Program of the Woodrow Wilson Center, as published by the center in Peace and Human Rights in Colombia in Comparative Perspective, a Special Edition of Noticias, December 1998. Garcia-Peña was at that time Colombia's High Commissioner for Peace.

[17] Laura Brooks. Debacle in Colombia Shows Rebel Strength. *The Washington Post*. August 6, 1998.

[18] Tim Johnson. Colombia says it halted guerrillas, killing 200. *The Miami Herald*. July 12, 1999.

urban areas, although one Colombian government agency claims that the guerrillas have formed urban militias in the country's main cities which create public disturbances, kidnap people, and extort money.[19] Guerrilla activities have increasingly affected urban life, however, as ELN sabotage of the electrical power system in late 1999 and early 2000 has caused numerous blackouts in highly populated areas, including the cities of Bogotá and Medellín.

Guerrilla Participation in the Illegal Drug Industry. Both the FARC and the ELN fund their operations, at least in part, from income generated by their involvement in the illegal drug industry. (The FARC, at least, has been involved since the early part of the cocaine boom in the late 1970s and early 1980s.[20]) U.S. officials estimate that some two-thirds of the FARC fronts and one-third of the ELN fronts have some involvement with illegal narcotics.[21] Their major involvement includes protecting crops, laboratories, storage facilities, and airfields from government anti-narcotics efforts, and collecting "taxes" from those who benefit from that protection. According to some sources, some guerrilla fronts are also increasingly engaged in marijuana, cocaine, and heroin production and sales,[22] although Administration analysts state that such production is small. Part of the expansion of the coca cultivation reported in June 1999 by the GAO has appeared in two areas, the San Lucas mountains and the department ofNorte de Santander, which are under ELN control, indicating a possible rise in ELN involvement in drug trafficking.[23] The guerrillas deny any involvement in drug trafficking.

Estimates of annual guerrilla income from drug trafficking have varied widely. A 1997 report of the Institute for National Strategic Studies (INSS) covered the higher end of the range. It stated that the guerrillas had gained half of their estimated $500 million to $1.5 billion annual income from involvement in the drug trade. Of this income, the INSS report estimated that $20 million was used to purchase weapons

---

[19] Security Agency Says Urban Militias Gaining Strength. El Espectador (Internet Version), May 14, 1999, as translated by the Foreign Broadcast Information Service (FBIS), Document # FTS10009515001028. A July 1999 poll conducted in four Colombian cities (Bogotá, Cali, Medellín, and Barranquilla) found, however, that many urban dwellers have negative views of the guerrillas, with 79% believing they aid and abet narcotraffickers, 93% believing they violate human rights, and 78% believing the FARC is not committed to reaching a peace agreement (79% in the case of the ELN). From a summary "Colombians Voice Overwhelming Pessimism," prepared by USIA's Office of Research and Media Reaction (M-150-99), August 4, 1999, of a Gallup poll. There was no information on opinions concerning the guerrillas' political, social, and economic positions.

[20] Alfredo Molano, "Violence and Land Colonization," in Charles Bergquist, Ricardo Peñaranda, and Gonzalo Sánchez, eds. Violence in Colombia: the Contemporary Crisis in Historical Perspective. Wilmington, DE: SR Books, 1992. pp. 210-216.

[21] Department of Defense briefing, August 1998.

[22] James L. Zackrison and Eileen Bailey. Colombian Sovereignty Under Seige. National Defense University Strategic Forum, No. 112, May 1997. p. 3. (From the web version at [http://www.ndu.edu/inss/strforum/forum112.html].

[23] Juanita Darling. U.S. Is Losing War on Drugs in Colombia. Los Angeles Times. August 8, 1999. p. 1.

and other military equipment and the rest was "invested in land, transportation businesses, and a well-managed portfolio."[24] More recent accounts have generally quoted a range of $400 -$600 million. (This is about 10%-15% of Colombia's total annual estimated $4 billion income from illegal narcotics activities.) However, a September 1999 news report cited a "secret assessment by American intelligence" which estimated a range of only $30 to $100 million.[25] Income from drug trafficking may not be the guerrilla's greatest source of income, however; recent Colombian government estimates indicate that, in 1997 and 1998, the FARC and ELN earned twice as much from kidnapping and "robbery" [i.e., presumably meaning extortion] as they did from drugs, and a little less from kidnapping than from drugs.[26]

The "Paramilitary" Presence [27]

The many illegal privately armed rightist groups involved in political violence — including killings, abductions, and intimidation — have come to be regarded as a sizeable military presence in Colombia. Known in the United States as "paramilitary" groups and in Colombia also as "self-defense" groups, their primary targets are guerrillas, and suspected guerrilla supporters and sympathizers. In addition, they target those suspected of helping the guerrillas, however unwillingly. They have been responsible, according to human rights groups, for the greatest number of extrajudicial killings and forced disappearances since 1995. They also demand "war taxes" from individuals, and threaten with death those who refuse to pay.

These groups — which range in size from small, rural self-defense groups to large forces — evolved from two types of anti-guerrilla organizations. One was the civilian "self-defense" groups originally organized by the Colombian military. Although the latest of these were the "*Convivir*" civilian rural defense organizations, created in 1994, the Colombian military had earlier organized such groups as part of its 1960s counterinsurgency campaign.[28] Other private armed forces were organized

---

[24] Colombian Sovereignty Under Seige, op.cit. p. 1.

[25] Tim Golden and Steven Lee Myers. U.S. Plans Big Aid Package to Rally a Reeling Colombia. *The New York Times*. September 15, 1999. p. A12.

[26] *Joint Study Sums Up FARC, ELN Earnings*. From El Tiempo, May 17, 1999, as translated by FBIS, Document # FTS19990517001601. The study was prepared by Colombia's National Planning Department and the Colombian Army.

[27] Sources for this section include: Human Rights Watch. *Colombia's Killer Networks: The Military-Paramilitary Partnership and the United States.* New York: Human Rights Watch, November 1996; Amnesty International. Colombia: Paramilitaries, "Disappearance" and Impunity. Document No. AMR 23/39/1998, June 1998. [http://www.amnesty.org/ailib/aipub/1998/AMR/22303998.htm]; Guy Gugliotta and Jeff Leen. *Kings of Cocaine: Inside the Medellin Cartel.* New York: Simon and Schuster, 1989; and Human Rights Watch. *War without Quarter: Colombia and International Humanitarian Law, 1998.* [http://www.hrw.org/reports98/colombia].

[28] See: Human Rights Watch, November 1996, op. cit., pp. 10-16. Human Rights Watch describes the use of civilians for counterinsurgency tasks as consistent with "a well-developed U.S. cold war strategy." The U.S. military provided advice and training for the Colombian

(continued...)

by drug traffickers. In 1981, over 200 drug traffickers contributed funds and men to form the "Death to Kidnappers" (*Muerte a Secuestradores* or MAS) group which vowed to end ransom kidnappings by killing guerrillas. Illegally armed groups subsequently proliferated, with funding from drug traffickers and large landowners, and the participation of small landowners. All have sought to protect themselves against the kidnappings for ransom and extortion of "war taxes" by the guerrillas, to destroy the guerrilla base, and to silence political figures who opposed them. By one account, as of mid-1999, the paramilitary groups controled over 15% of Colombian territory.[29] In 1999, U.S. officials estimated their numbers at 5,000 - 7,000; however in March 2000, the head of the largest organization (see next paragraph) said his force numbers 11,200.[30]

The largest organization is the United Self-Defense Groups of Colombia (*Autodefensas Unidas de Colombia* or AUC). It was created in 1995 to consolidate at least seven "self-defense" groups operating in northern and central Colombia under one organizational structure, with the goal of gaining both military strength and political recognition. (The term "paramilitary groups" is now most often used to refer to illegal forces carrying out active anti-guerrilla campaigns, the most important of which is the AUC.) The largest AUC group is the Peasant Self-Defense Groups of Cordobá and Urabá (*Autodefensas Campesinas de Cordobá and Urabá*/ACCU), with more than 2,000 members trained and armed, and other supporters who will engage in specific actions.[31] The founder and head of the AUC (also a leader of the ACCU), Carlos Castaño, has stated that the AUC's purpose is to force the guerrillas to negotiate.[32] His forces reportedly are well-paid. (According to some analysts, they have been able to attract fighters away from both the Colombian military and the guerrillas.) As of mid-1999, the AUC/ACCU forces reportedly possessed "over 30"

---

[28] (...continued)
counterinsurgency campaign in the 1960s. For information on the legal basis for paramilitary groups in the 1960s see: Washington Office On Latin America. i pp. 78-83; for information on the Convivir groups, see: Organization of American States, Inter-American Commission on Human Rights. Third Report of the Human Rights Situation in Colombia. OEA/Ser.L/V/II.102, Doc. 9, rev.1, February 26, 1999. pp. 22-23, 27; and War Without Quarter, op.cit. pp 88-99. The Colombian government ceased authorizing the creation of new groups in July 1998; as of December 28, 1999, of the 414 licensed groups, 20 still had licenses in force. The others, according to information provided by Colombian government, no longer had licenses and had ceased operations.

[29] Doug Farah. U.S. Ready to Boost Aid to Troubled Colombia. *Washington Post*. August 24, 1999. p. A12.

[30] Tim Johnson. Paramilitary Chief Hopeful about Colombian Peace Talks. *Miami Herald*. March 3, 1999.

[31] *War without Quarter*, op.cit. p. 108.

[32] Interview with Carlos Castaño by Maria Cristina Caballero, Cambio 16, December 15, 22, and 29, 1997, as translated and posted on the International Consortium of Investigative Journalists (ICIJ) website. Entitled "This War Can't Go On Any Longer," the interview can be accessed at [http://www.icij.org] under "Investigative Reports."

aircraft, including 11 Cessnas, four cargo planes, and "an entire fleet of reconnaissance helicopters."[33]

Castaño's political standing among the population in the areas where his forces are strong is a topic of debate. He told one human rights observer that he has hired sociologists, anthropologists, and agronomists "to come up with solutions to Colombia's problems" and that the ACCU "sponsors grade schools, cooperatives, land reform, and agricultural credits."[34] Castaño has acknowledged ordering killings of those he believes are guerrilla sympathizers, and his forces are feared in many towns. Yet, reportedly he has gained a popular following in some areas, such as *Norte de Santander*, where "people tend to believe that with their arrival the paramilitaries are not only going to restore peace to the region, but will bolster it economically."[35]

Relationship with Drug Trafficking. Some of these paramilitary groups are believed to have continued links to or involvement in drug trafficking, but there are no official estimates on the amount of income they receive from the drug industry, nor the type or extent of their participation in it. In 1999, the Inter-American Commission on Human Rights opined that "In general, these groups have moved away from their connection with the drug trade, although paramilitary attacks against judicial officials investigating drug crimes demonstrates that a connection still exists in at least some cases."[36] In April 1998, a Colombian government agency identified Castaño, as a leading drug boss in the Medellin area,[37] a judgment shared by the U.S. Drug Enforcement Administration.

Castaño has acknowledged that the AUC collects substantial taxes from coca producers, and funding from traffickers. (He has cited the amount of the tax on coca producers as 40% of proceeds in one interview, 60% in another.) In an interview reproduced on the AUC website, he denies that the AUC exports cocaine, stating that "we are not narcotraffickers." At the same time, however, he states that the AUC finances about 70% of its operations from "narcotrafficking and narcotraffickers."[38]

Human Rights Controversy

Although all parties to the Colombian conflict have been guilty of gross violations of human rights over the past several years, it is generally agree that the incidence of human rights abuses committed by members of the Colombia military has decreased to a few percentage points of total violations. The current controversy

---

[33] *The Air Power of the Guerrillas and "Paras,"* op.cit.

[34] Robin Kirk. A meeting with Paramilitary Leader Carlos Castaño, in NACLA Report on the Americas, March/April 1998. p. 31.

[35] Maria Jimenez Duzan. Castaño, the Liberator. From *El Espectador*, June 17, 1999, as translated by FBIS, Document # FTS199063001514.

[36] *Third Report of the Human Rights Situation in Colombia*, op.cit., p. 23.

[37] Latin American Regional Reports—Andean Group. June 23, 1998.

[38] [Http://www.colombialibre.org/entrivis.htm], page 15 of 28.

over human rights focuses on the degree to which the paramilitaries have become the principal violators of human rights and the degree to which the Colombian army is complicit in its violations. Human rights organizations that keep statistics have documented increases over the past five years in extrajudicial killings and massacres committed by paramilitary groups, as well as a rise in kidnappings committed by the guerrillas.[39]

Colombia's military forces have a long record of human rights abuse, including extrajudicial killings, forced disappearances, and torture. However, their record has improved somewhat in recent years. The State Department noted in its three most recent reports on the status of human rights in Colombia (covering 1997,1998, and 1999)[40] that the number of violations committed by the Colombian security forces appears to have decreased. In the first nine months of 1997 all 80 of the politically-motivated extrajudicial killings committed by Colombian security forces were committed by members of the Army, particularly of the 20th Intelligence Brigade. The brigade was disbanded in May 1998, and the army prohibited its successor, the Army Military Intelligence Center, from directly undertaking armed operations. The State Department cited figures attributing 21 of the extrajudicial killings in the first nine months of 1998 to security forces, a substantial decrease, and 24 of those in the same period in 1999 to security forces .

Some 2,000 - 3,000 politically-motivated murders and extrajudicial killings were believed to be committed in most of those years, although the perpetrator in most cases are never identified. The paramilitaries are widely believed to be responsible for most of such killings over the past few years, although the Colombian security forces have recently disputed that belief. Of those where perpetrator were identified during the first 9 months of 1999, the State Department human rights report cites figures from a Colombian non-governmental organization, CINEP, attributing, besides the 24 committed by security forces, some 814 to paramilitary forces and 269 to guerrillas. It also cites different figures from the Colombian Defense Ministry, which lists the paramilitaries as responsible for 743 of these killings, and the guerillas for 908.

---

[39] Statistics, however, are not comprehensive, and year-to-year comparisons are not highly reliable. The numbers of human rights violations for which perpetrators were not identified tends to be high, and was even higher in the mid-1990s. Also the methods and sources used to gather statistics are not uniform among the groups that collect them, and have changed somewhat over the years. There are several groups which keep statistics on human rights violations. Official Colombian sources include the Colombian government's own Human Rights Ombudsman, and as of late the Colombian military itself. Non-governmental organizations include the Colombian Commission of Jurists (CCJ), the Free Country Foundation (Fundación País Libre), and the CINEP (the Spanish acronym of the organization whose statistics are used in the annual State Department reports on human rights, translated by State Department as the Center for Investigations and Popular Research).

[40] Colombia Country Report for Human Rights Practices for 1997, 1998, and 1999. The 1999 report, issued on February 25, 2000, is available at [http://wwww.state/gov/www/global/human_rights/1999_hrp_report/colombia.html]. Previous editions are also available through the State Department website.

The guerrillas are cited as responsible for most of the kidnappings which take place in Colombia. Figures collected by País Libre, and cited in the State Department human rights report for 1999, show that of 2,945 kidnappings committed during 1999, some 1,645 were committed by the FARC (728), the ELN (695), and a number of other guerrilla groups (122). These figures include 136 cases of police and military troops captured in combat, and about 50 mayors. País Libre attributes 103 kidnappings in 1999 to paramilitary forces, 300 to common criminals, and 6 to family members. It has not been able to identify the perpetrators of some 891 cases.

While the military's gross human rights violations, such as extrajudicial killings, have declined, the continued ties of military officers, particularly army officers, to paramilitary groups have been a source of concern. Many international organizations and human rights groups have found evidence of widespread and continuing links between security forces and paramilitary groups. They have accused members of the military of tolerating the activities of paramilitary groups where they do not actively support them. [41]

The most recent report of the human rights community concerning such links, by Human Rights Watch, cites incidents of collaboration between security forces and three Colombian Army brigades (the Third, based in Calí, the Fourth, based in Medellín, and the Thirteenth, based in Bogotá). Most saliently, it accuses members of the Third Brigade of organizing the "Calima Front" with active duty, retired, and reserve Third Brigade personnel and members of the ACCU, and providing it with weapons and intelligence, in response to the May 1999 seizure of 140 people attending mass at a Calí church. It cited Colombian government investigators investigations listing "hundreds of cellular telephone and beeper communications between known paramilitaries and Fourth Brigade officers," including two lieutenant colonels, three majors, and one lieutenant. In discussing human rights abuses committed by members of the Thirteenth Brigade, particularly intimidation of human rights workers, the report cites the intimidation and killings of government investigators looking into paramilitary activities. At least some of the later is believed to be carried out by contract killers hired by Carlos Castaño working with their own intelligence and intelligence provided by Thirteenth brigade intelligence personnel..

---

[41] In a 1999 report, the United Nations Commissioner for Human Rights stated that the security forces' action against paramilitary groups was "occasional and not in proportion to the participation of these groups in serious violations of human rights." She also noted that the Prosecutor General's office could not take action against the paramilitaries based on its knowledge of the location of many paramilitary meeting and training sites because it lacked the support of the police and army. United Nations. Economic and Social Council. Report of the United Nations High Commissioner for Human Rights on the Office in Colombia. E/CN.4/1998/8. March 16, 1999. Point. 36. The report states that many of the members of the prosecutor general's office who were murdered in 1998 were investigating paramilitary groups, and that several other prosecutors investigating paramilitary groups or security forces were forced to quit their jobs or flee the country. See point 58. [http://www.unhchr.ch/Huridocda/Huridoca.nsf/TestFrame/ff030ceede968d518025675900 303d8b?Opendocument].

These threats and killings were cited as insurmountable impediments to continuing government investigations. [42]

In response, the Commander of the Colombian Military Forces, Fernando Tapias Stahelin, stated that the Human Rights Watch report "fails to speak the truth, because it is inexact" and accused it of being politically motivated in order to block or obstruct U.S. assistance. It cited the fact that the report relied on data provided by Colombian government investigators as evidence that "investigations on alleged human rights violations are being conducted" and of "an effective action of the State." He also provided data that the military forces had arrested 289 members of paramilitary groups since 1997, 116 of them in 1999 and 38 in 2000, and killed 87 in the same time frame, 26 in 1999 and y in 2000. (The data indicated that police forces had arrested 403 paramilitaries since 1997, 170 in 1999 and 48 in 2000, and killed 53, 7 in 1999 and 25 in 2000.)[43] General Tapias' response repeated earlier statements made by the Colombia Vice President Gustavo Bell.

(For background on the human rights situation in Colombia and further references through mid-1999, see CRS Report RL30314, *Colombia: Human Rights Conditions and U.S. Concerns*, of September 21, 1999.)

The Pastrana Administration's Response

Since he assumed office in August 1998, President Pastrana has continued efforts to deal with drug trafficking, has asked for increased U.S. counternarcotics assistance, and has pursued efforts to make peace. Although all his predecessors since 1982 have attempted to negotiate an end to the guerrilla war, President Pastrana perceived that the possibility of success was much greater in 1998 because of a widespread popular demand for peace, and the new involvement of Colombian business and civic groups in the peace process. His peace efforts are three-pronged: (1) to pursue peace talks with the guerrilla groups, (2) to make the army a more effective force, and (3) to secure international economic support, military assistance, and aid for a program of social and political reform.

Initiation of the Peace Process with the FARC.[44] As a first step in the peace process, President Pastrana responded to FARC's request to create a demilitarized zone and ordered the withdrawal of security forces from five municipalities for 90 days, commencing November 6, 1998. (The five municipalities, which cover some 16,000-17,000 square miles — somewhat over twice the size of Massachusetts — are Mesetas, Vista Hermosa, La Uribe, La Macarena, and San Vicente del Caguán, primarily in the departments of Meta and Caquetá. Some 80,000-90,000 people live

---

[42] Human Rights Watch. Americas Division. "The Ties That Bind: Colombia and Military-Paramilitary Links." February 2000, Vol. 12, No. 1 (B). [Http://www.hrw.org/reports/2000/colombia/].

[43] Copy of a letter of March 1, 2000, provided by the Embassy of Colombia.

[44] See Appendix B for background on the FARC and ELN, and on their negotiations with previous Colombian administrations.

in the area.) His stated intent was to create a climate of trust in which guerrilla leaders and government representatives could establish a negotiating agenda.

On January 7, 1999, President Pastrana traveled to the demilitarized zone to meet with guerrilla leaders as talks began. Talks over an agenda soon broke down, however, when the guerrillas accused the government of breaking its agreement to remove all security forces from the demilitarized zone by leaving a small 130-man caretaker military guard at the base in San Vicente del Caguán. They also asked that the government dismantle the paramilitary groups. Subsequently, the Pastrana Administration removed the caretaker contingent and, in February, extended the "demilitarized" status for the five municipalities through May 7. Government and FARC negotiators resumed talks on the agenda on April 21.

President Pastrana has stated that his objective is to incorporate the guerrillas into Colombia's current political system with appropriate social and institutional reforms to ensure "peace with social justice" and to eradicate the roots of the conflict. In his Administration's 10-point proposal for an agenda at the start of the January talks, the government called for unconditional respect for human rights (with specific mention of an end to kidnappings), an analysis of Colombia's social and economic structure to achieve reforms aimed at reducing poverty and income disparities, political and state reforms to deepen democracy and build a new legal state, and the eradication of drug trafficking accomplished through crop substitution and legal and institutional reforms.[45] The FARC's agenda proposal called for far ranging political, economic, and military reforms. (See Appendix C for a synopsis of the FARC proposal.) On May 6, 1999, the Colombian government and the FARC agreed upon a 12-point agenda for negotiations. Negotiations were initially scheduled to begin in July 1999, but were delayed over issues involving a verification commission In November 1999, government and FARC negotiations began discussions on procedural issues.

Progress of the Peace Process in 2000. On January 8, 2000, government and FARC negotiators agreed on the procedures for negotiations. They also agreed to begin talks with the topics of economic and social structures, the development of a coherent agrarian policy, and the exploitation and conservation of natural resources, and to devote six months to these topics. In February 2000, FARC and government negotiators traveled together to meet for 25 days with European leaders and experts in six countries and the Vatican as a prelude to negotiations.[46] Public hearings related to economic and social structures began April 9 in the village of Los Pozos, in the demilitarized zone, which appears to have been extended indefinitely. As of early May, the FARC appeared ready to discuss a possible cease-fire as negotiations progressed. FARC also announced that it was prepared to institute its own judicial system in San Vincente de Caguán, a major town in the demilitarized zone, and that it would force all individuals and corporations worth more than one million dollars to pay it a "peace tax." According to some reports, FARC is also seeking belligerent status.

---

[45] These points were summarized from the document as it appeared in *El Espectador* (Internet Version), on January 12, 1999, and translated by FBIS, Document #FTS19990112001695.

[46] The countries were Norway, Sweden, Italy, Spain, Switzerland and France.

Progress in Peace Talks with the ELN. The Pastrana Administration's continued efforts to initiate negotiations with the ELN within in the context of tripartite talks among the ELN, and representatives from the government and from civil society appeared to be coming to fruition in late April 2000. Progress to that point had been halting. In May 1999, after the ELN kidnapped parishioners attending church in Calí, the Pastrana Administration had announced that it was breaking off all contacts with the ELN, but subsequently contacts resumed. The government has refused, however, various ELN requests to demilitarize areas in northern Colombia as a site for civil society consultations and talks. The latest refusal came when the ELN asked at the end of 1999 for the demilitarization of an area where, reportedly, followers of Carlos Castaño have weakened the ELN. News reports indicated that objections from military officers and from the mayors of the municipalities in the area prompted the Pastrana Administration's refusal.[47] In late 1999, the ELN commenced an active campaign to blow up electric facilities.

On April 24, 2000, President Pastrana announced that the government and the ELN had reached an agreement in principle concerning the demilitarization of three municipalities – San Pablo, Cantagallo, and Yondo – in the oil production region of central Colombia along the Magdalena River to facilitate talks with the ELN. Although details of the agreement appear to be still worked out, Colombian government officials indicated that security forces would not relinquish total control of the areas along the river. Reportedly, some residents of the area, where paramilitary forces also operate, have protested the planned withdrawal of security forces.

Criticisms of and Prospects for a Negotiated Settlement. President Pastrana has been criticized by many Colombians for the slowness with which the peace process has proceeded and the concessions that he has made to the guerrillas. In May 1999, Colombian Defense Minister Rodrigo Lloreda resigned and 16 army generals offered their resignations, criticizing Pastrana for excessive concessions to the guerrillas and the continued extension of the demilitarized zone. President Pastrana defends his efforts to secure "not peace at any price, but a genuine peace which will strengthen our democracy, maintain territorial integrity, and offer to each Colombian a fair place in our future."[48]

Many analysts foresee a lengthy negotiation process that may not be concluded during the Pastrana Administration. Colombian analysts acknowledge that Colombians themselves do not understand the varied and complicated local and regional relationships among drug traffickers, guerrillas, paramilitaries, local elites, public officials, military officers and troops, and local populations, including coca growers, that may well make an agreement difficult to conclude, and subsequently to implement. However, the procedures adopted in January 2000 for negotiations with the FARC allow for the implementation of agreements on individual topics as they occur.

---

[47] El Otro Despeje. Semana.com. January 14, 2000. [http://www.216.35.197.109/923/actualidad/ZZZUIBGI63C.asp].

[48] Statements before the U.N. General Assembly, September 30, 1999. Text supplied by the Colombian Embassy in Washington, D.C.

Military Reform and Rehabilitation. The Pastrana Administration has attempted to improve the poor performance of Colombia's military (a 121,000-man Army, 15,000-man Navy, and 7,500-man Air Force) on the battlefield. It also has dismissed several army officers who are believed to have supported or tolerated human rights abuses by paramilitary forces.

Efforts to Improve Military Performance. Analysts have advanced several explanations for the military's failure to confront the guerrillas during the last several years, and its general inability to perform effectively when it has tried to engage in combat. Some analysts have perceived the problem as a lack of will and desire to engage the guerrillas. Others have viewed it as a lack of certain basic military tools, such as good intelligence and a coherent military strategy, and still others have believed that officers and troops lack the training, skills, and equipment to do the job. Some also have argued that the military is stretched too thin because it devotes a large number of soldiers to guarding installations[49] and performing administrative duties, and it exempts (by law) conscripts with a high school education from combat. The military is also seen as seriously underfunded by some analysts who have criticized the government for failing to provide the military with adequate training and resources to conduct an effective counterinsurgency campaign. As of 1999, the Colombian government was spending about $3 billion annually on its security forces, according to U.S. officials, an amount some analysts judged to be insufficient to pursue a successful counterinsurgency campaign.

General Fernando Tapias Stahelin, the commander-in-chief of the armed forces since the beginning of the Pastrana Administration, has undertaken reforms to correct the army's weaknesses. Among them are a reorganization of the armed forces to replace conscripts with professional soldiers and to make more soldiers available for fighting, an improvement of intelligence services, the development of a military strategy, and coordination of the activities of the three armed service branches. The military's effective response to the July 1999 guerrilla offensive and its August 1999 seizure of two FARC encampments 60 miles from Bogotá has raised some hopes that its performance may continue to improve. Some analysts attribute such improvements in the army's performance to a reorganization of the Colombian intelligence apparatus, and to a U.S. decision, as of March 1999, to share more intelligence with a police and military counternarcotics task force. (See Appendix A for more information on U.S. assistance and restrictions on assistance.)

Efforts to Improve Respect for Human Rights. The Pastrana Administration has taken several steps to foster respect for human rights within the military. Upon taking office, the Administration installed a new military leadership that seemed more

---

[49] The Heritage Foundation, in an early 1999 publication, stated that 55,000 Army soldiers "are committed to protecting urban centers, oil fields, and other key installations," while 30,000 are being used for counter-insurgency operations. "Because it is stretched so thin, the army has established small company and platoon-sized posts wherever possible, but this has enabled the rebels to achieve local numerical superiority, a situation that is exacerbated by the lack of equipment for small Colombian units." *Tread Cautiously in Colombia's Civil War,* by John P. Sweeney. The Heritage Foundation Backgrounder, No. 1264, March 25, 1999. [http://www.heritage.org/library/backgrounder/bg1264es.html].

sensitive to human rights concerns, according to State Department officials. On April 10, 1999, President Pastrana retired two of the army generals, Rito Alejo del Rio and Fernando Millan Perez, who had been under investigation by the Prosecutor General's office, apparently for involvement with paramilitary groups. Eleven days later, the former commander of the 20th Brigade, retired Col. Bernardo Ruiz, was arrested and charged with arranging the 1995 assassination of Alvaro Gomez Hurtado, a former Ambassador to the United States who had been prominent in Conservative party politics. In August 1999, Colombia's attorney general, whose office has investigated numerous cases of alleged support for paramilitary groups, ordered dishonorable discharges for an army captain and two lieutenants, who had failed to halt a May 1998 paramilitary massacre in Barrancabermeja. On September 2, President Pastrana retired Gen. Alberto Bravo Silva, commander of the Army's 5th Brigade. Although no reason was given for Bravo's forced retirement, soldiers of his command had done nothing to stop paramilitary groups who had killed at least 36 people.

Securing International Assistance. Since he announced his peace initiative, President Pastrana has sought domestic and international funding to support it. Initially, he sought to create a development fund, to be administered by business and civic representatives, that would provide financing for economic infrastructure and jobs in guerrilla areas once a peace agreement was concluded. Little was forthcoming, however. On September 17, 1999, he outlined a new $7.5 billion three-year plan to bring peace to Colombia. Of this, Pastrana seeks $3.5 billion in international assistance, about half to be used to strengthen and restructure the military and to combat drug trafficking. The Colombian government has previously budgeted $4 billion for the effort, and has received $750 million from international financial institutions for social programs.[50]

According to a synopsis from the Colombian Embassy in Washington, D.C., in the counternarcotics area, President Pastrana's "Plan Colombia" calls for (1) reducing by 50% the cultivation, processing, and distribution of illegal drugs over the next six years, (2) the increased interdiction of illegal drugs in the air, on land and on Colombian waterways, (3) the expansion of eradication and fumigation programs; (4) seizure of resources used in the production and distribution of illegal drugs, and (5) cooperation with other governments to halt the import into Colombia of illegal arms and chemicals used in processing.

Other measures include: (1) the promotion of alternative agricultural and economic activities in rural areas, and other rural development projects; (2) the improvement of health care, education, and social services for the "most vulnerable" Colombians, (3) military reform; (4) economic reform; and (5) reforms to improve the judicial system and protect human rights.

---

[50] Larry Rohter. Plan to Strengthen Colombia Nudges U.S. for $3.5 Billion. *The New York Times.* September 18, 1999. p. A5.

Congressional Concerns and Policy Opinions

For the past several years, congressional opinion on Colombia has been sharply divided. In 1997, 1998, and 1999, Congress approved increasing funding for counternarcotics support to the Colombian police forces and to the military. In 1999, it approved considerably more funding, primarily for the police forces, than had been requested by the Administration. Congress, however, also imposed restrictions on that assistance to prevent it from supporting units that included human rights abusers, and it has shied away from consideration of any direct involvement in Colombia's counterinsurgency.

Congressional Concerns

Human Rights Concerns. Because of concerns about the human rights abuses by the Colombian military, Congress has increasingly restricted U.S. assistance to Colombia through the "Leahy Amendment" restrictions.[51] As contained in FY2000 legislation, these prohibit U.S. military assistance supported by funding contained in Foreign Operations appropriations and training from funds in the Department of Defense appropriations, to units of foreign security forces where there is credible evidence that a member of the unit has committed a gross violation of human rights. Because of those restrictions, the Administration provides assistance to the Colombian police,[52] air force and navy, and a number of battalion-sized and smaller Army units. It has denied assistance to other units, and constantly reviews the status of units currently receiving assistance for continued compliance.

Additional concerns about the connections between members of the Colombian armed forces and the illegal paramilitary groups have led some Members of Congress to consider additional restrictions on aid. In October 1999 legislation (S. 1758), Senators Coverdall, DeWine, and Grassley, the sponsors, included not only the Leahy Amendment restrictions on funding in the bill, but also proposed that the Leahy amendment restrictions should apply "with respect to the availability of funds for a unit of the security forces of Colombia if the Secretary of State reports to Congress

---

[51] For more details on the Leahy Amendments, and the their texts as included in the FY2000 legislation, see Appendix A.

[52] U.S. counternarcotics assistance has been largely provided thus far to a special counternarcotics unit of the Colombian National Police. Human rights groups have reported only one case of possible human rights abuse by the counternarcotics unit, i.e., they have charged the unit stationed at the Miraflores anti-narcotics base in the department of Guaviare with complicity, along with army and navy units, in the October 18-20, 1997 paramilitary killings. In a letter to the Secretary of State, human rights observers asserted that these forces "actively supported a paramilitary massacre" because they failed to apprehend paramilitary hit men from the "Southern Self-Defense Group" as the killings were carried out over three days. Defenders of the counternarcotics unit claim that the unit was involved in a counternarcotics operation at the time, and state that, in any case, the unit only has jurisdiction over antidrug issues. (According to officials of the Colombian Embassy, however, any member of the Colombian police or military can arrest a person caught in the act of committing a crime.) See Congressional debate of September 16, 1998, Congressional Record, pp. H7848 -H7852.

that credible evidence exists that a member of that unit has provided material support to irregular forces in Colombia or to any criminal narcotics trafficking syndicate that operates in Colombia."

Displacement of Civilians. A growing humanitarian concern has been the large number of persons displaced by the violence in Colombia. As the guerrilla and paramilitary offensives have extended throughout the country, increasing numbers of civilians, mostly poor peasant farmers from remote rural areas, have been forced to flee to escape the rising tide of violence. Entire towns with thousands of citizens have been abandoned by a populace terrified by massacres or threats of massacres. Over one million people are estimated to have been displaced since 1985, according to refugee organizations. In the last few years, more and more cases of massive displacements have occurred: 130,000 Colombians were displaced in 1995, 180,000 in 1996, and 250,000 in 1997, and 350,000 in 1998.[53]

According to a Colombian non-governmental organization that maintains a data bank on the displaced, 33 percent of those displaced between 1995 and 1997 blamed paramilitaries for their displacement, 28 percent held the guerrillas responsible, and 10 percent blamed the armed forces. The rest blamed more than one party or did not know whom to blame for their displacement.[54]

Some communities have expressed their neutrality in the conflict and declared themselves to be "peace communities." Nevertheless, throughout 1998, there were reports that paramilitaries and the FARC had killed members of these communities, according to Amnesty International.[55]

Possible Increase of Drug Trafficking in Demilitarized Zone. Many U.S. policymakers have been concerned that President Pastrana's decision to remove security forces from the five demilitarized municipalities would run counter to U.S. efforts to eradicate coca cultivation and control drug trafficking, and could lead to an increase in cultivation in those areas.[56] In early 1999, Administration officials stated

---

[53] Gallón, Gustavo. The Challenge of Avoiding Colombia's Extinction. *Colombia Update*. Spring/Summer 1998, p. 3. Gallón is the director of the Colombia Commission of Jurists.

[54] *Country Report: Colombia* .U.S. Committee on Refugees. [No date given.] www.refugees.org/world/countryrpt/amer_carib/colombia.htm. A massive displacement of civilians occurred in early 1998 in the Choco department, near the Panamanian border, which illustrates how the interaction of all parties has interacted to displace rural populations. There, civilians were subjected to sustained attacks by the ACCU paramilitary organizations, aerial bombardments by the army, and reprisal killings by the FARC.

[55] *Amnesty International Report 1998: Colombia. op. cit.*

[56] The Western Hemisphere Drug Elimination Act, passed by Congress October 1998 as part of the Omnibus Consolidated and Emergency Supplemental Appropriations for FY1999 (P.L.105-277) stated that assistance should not be provided if the Colombian government permits the establishment of any demilitarized zone where the eradication of drug production by the security forces is prohibited, with a 90-day waiver permitted if the President determines such assistance is in the U.S. national interest. Administration officials have stated that this

(continued...)

that some 3% of Colombia's coca cultivation takes place in the demilitarized zone, and some coca processing labs are located in the demilitarized area. Some suspect the amount has grown: as of February 2000, some U.S. officials state that the guerrillas are forcing peasants to grow coca crops in the zone. According to a State Department official, the "demilitarized" status did not disrupt planned eradication efforts, as those were concentrated on higher priority areas. In addition, the Colombian National Police (CNP) raided a lab in the demilitarized zone in late 1998. Still, the United States capacity to monitor cultivation in the area has fluctuated as surveillance aircraft have been called to other missions.

Policymakers are concerned that the zone may become particularly attractive to traffickers if it becomes a feature of prolonged negotiations, leading to much increased use of the area for production and trafficking. Further, some analysts fear that, in the long run, the weak Colombian military may not provide President Pastrana with the military muscle to negotiate a settlement that would firmly establish government control over the demilitarized zone. They also worry that President Pastrana, or a successor government, might even cede some control to the guerrillas, although Colombian officials deny that they would negotiate such an outcome. This so-called "Balkanization" of Colombia could have adverse affects on perceptions of the Colombian government's legitimacy and even its stability over the long run, and could facilitate the activities of drug traffickers in Colombia.

U.S. Policy Options

As presented to Congress, initially on January 11 and then with the annual budget request on February 7, 2000, the Clinton Administration aid proposal to support the Colombian government's "Plan Colombia" contains over $954 million in supplemental FY2000 funding and over $318 million for FY2001 spending. (This is in addition to about $150 million allocated and planned for existing programs in each fiscal year.) The proposal's centerpiece is the "Push into Southern Colombia" program, which would enable the Colombian government to extend CN activities throughout southern Colombia. The core of the Southern Colombia program would include training and equipping two new army CN battalions, and purchasing Black Hawk and Huey helicopters to transport them. Total funding for the Southern Colombia (SC) program is set at $512 million in FY2000 and $88 million in FY2001. Of this, AID would receive $31 million ($12 million in FY2000 and $19 million in FY2001) to resettle and fund alternative economic opportunities for peasants who would be deprived of their livelihood by operations in Southern Colombia.

The remaining proposed assistance, to be administered by six agencies, is divided into five other categories. These are: (1) drug trafficking interdiction, (2) improving CNP eradication capabilities, (3) economic development, (4) "boosting government capacity," i.e., funding to support human rights monitors and improve the justice

---

[56] (...continued)
prohibition would only apply if the establishment of the demilitarized zone were to interfere with counternarcotics efforts. Those officials have stated that the provision has not been triggered , as no eradication efforts were planned for the current demilitarized area.

system and the rule of law; and (5) other economic assistance and assistance for the peace process.

(CRS Report RL30541 provides details on the Administration proposal, and compares it with other legislation. At the time of this update, the comparison is with the H.R. 3908, the emergency supplemental appropriations bill as passed by the House on March 30. The bill allocates some $1.4 billion for FY2000 and FY2001 emergency spending for the same purposes as the Administration proposal.)

Colombia's current dilemmas have led to a wide range of opinion about the desirability of altering current U.S. policy and the uses of further aid. Many see the Pastrana peace initiative, which seeks to incorporate the guerrillas into an improved version of Colombia's current democratic system, as providing a needed context for the discussion about Colombia's future; they believe it should be supported whether or not it produces an agreement with the guerrillas in the short run. Virtually all analysts, from a wide range of political perspectives, argue that the United States should be concerned with the problem presented by the paramilitary groups. Differences arise over specific approaches to dealing with drug trafficking and the leftist guerrillas, however. This has led to an active debate over U.S. options, particularly regarding the levels, purposes, and circumstances of U.S. assistance. One unknown factor, which may cause opinion to change over time, is the possible reaction of drug traffickers to alterations in U.S. policy.

Increase Military Aid. Some policymakers and analysts have argued that the United States should increase military aid, some in line with the amount proposed by the Administration. Many would continue to limit that assistance to just counternarcotics purposes, such as greater support and equipment for interdiction and eradication. They believe substantially more assistance, particularly helicopters that can operate at higher altitudes to eradicate opium poppies, are needed by the Colombian army to enable it to provide protection for police operations and to keep the Colombian police from losing ground in their counternarcotics efforts. Others, however, argue that the Administration package provides too much aid to the Colombian military while shortchanging the CNP, which has already proved itself effective in the kinds of operations that aid to the military is designed to allow the army to assist in.[57]

Some also believe that the United States should allow assistance of the sort that is currently provided for counternarcotics efforts, such as intelligence and training, to be provided for both counternarcotics and counterinsurgency purposes. Those who argue for dual purpose aid draw the line at direct U.S. battlefield involvement, however: one such analyst urged Congress to place limits on any military assistance

[57] In an op-ed piece, Representative Ben Gilman criticized the Clinton Administration for the slow delivery of currently funded helicopters to the Colombian National Police, and stated that the CNP needs 100 helicopters [of which the U.S. has promised about 40] to conduct effective counternarcotics operations. He also urges the Administration to provide "fast-track processing of Colombian army and police aid from U.S. stockpiles." Choppers to Colombia. *The Washington Post*. September 22, 1999. p. A33.

to ensure that U.S. soldiers do not "participate in battles between the Colombian army and drug-trafficking rebels."[58]

Many policymakers and analysts argue that increased counternarcotics aid, provided to the military, is necessary to provide an incentive for the guerrillas to negotiate. They believe that the primary obstacle to the peace process is the guerrillas' ability to bring in substantial funds from their participation in the illegal narcotics trade. This, they argue, might force the Colombian government to accept a peace accord which would allow the guerrillas a large degree of autonomy over areas where they now have control and where they would continue to grow and process coca unimpeded. In addition, some note that a major reason for the creation and growth of the paramilitaries is that Colombian police and military forces cannot provide protection throughout large parts of Colombia. If the paramilitaries are to be dismantled, they argue, the United States will need to provide the assistance necessary to expand substantially the areas in which police and military troops operate.

In addition, some argue that increased aid would enable the police and military not only to mount more effective counternarcotics efforts, but also, with greater training, intelligence, and other types of support applicable to counterinsurgency, to perform more effectively in strictly counterinsurgency operations. They worry that without substantially more assistance, the Colombian military might at best remain on the defensive against guerrilla attacks and may, within the next few years, suffer significant defeats However, some analysts who favor increased military aid, even extending to counterinsurgency purposes, caution that it may well be a few years before the military could take the offensive against the guerrillas.[59] Others also believe that pressures to dismantle the paramilitaries before the military becomes more effective and can operate over a larger area may relieve any existing pressures on the guerrillas to negotiate.

Some analysts warn that any increase in military aid for eradication efforts may have unintended consequences, some of which it may be possible to guard against by funding a timely program to provide alternative employment for those whose crops are destroyed. For instance, some claim that, in the current economic conditions, many peasants without such alternatives would take up arms offered by guerrillas to defend their crops. The guerrillas could portray the deaths of such peasants as a result of *yanqui* imperialism, and claim that as a rationale for stalling or pulling out of peace talks.[60] (According to a news report of February 2000, the Colombian Defense Minister fear that there will be violent protests when the U.S. trained Colombian Army Counternarcotics Battalion begins operations this year in the southern state of Putumayo, where guerrillas are active. At least six protesters were killed in 1996, when tens of thousands of coca growers marched to protest

---

[58] *Tread Cautiously in Colombia's Civil War*, op.cit.

[59] Retired Special Forces Major F. Andy Messing Jr. (Director of the National Defense Council Foundation, Alexandria, Va.) and Dillon Twombly. Will Narco-Guerrillas Become the Rulers? *Los Angeles Times/Washington Edition*, August 3, 1998.

[60] Conversation with Maria Cristina Caballero, Colombian journalist and Research Fellow of the Joan Shorenstein Center on the Press, Politics, and Public Policy of Harvard University. September 24, 1999.

eradication policies.[61]) Alternatively, some coca growers in guerrilla areas might decide simply to move elsewhere to work in areas where drug traffickers run coca plantations or even where paramilitaries provide protection, thus increasing the revenues and power of traffickers and paramilitaries. There does not appear to be sufficient information on the structure of coca and heroin production to evaluate possible effects.

Continue Aid at Current Levels. Other analysts argue that assistance might best be kept at FY1998 or FY1999 levels, or lower. Some view the increase in U.S. assistance in FY1998 (up about $50 million over 1997) as a factor bringing the guerrillas to agree to peace talks with the Pastrana government, and believe that continued assistance at some level will provide an incentive for guerrillas to continue negotiating. However, they fear that increasing aid, particularly if it were focused more on the military than on police forces, would provide the guerrillas with a rationale for breaking off peace talks and placing the blame on the United States. This, they argue, could create an emotional reaction among Colombians that would heighten anti-American sentiments and serve to legitimize the guerrillas and the drug trade. Continuing some aid, these analysts argue, would provide the Colombian government the assistance necessary for continued counternarcotics operations and sufficient leverage on the military to reform and to cut ties with paramilitary groups, but would not give the guerrillas a propaganda tool.

Condition Military Aid More Stringently. Among those who favor continued aid, whether at reduced, current, or increased levels, many believe that the United States should impose new conditions on the Colombian military and government. These conditions would serve several purposes.

In addition to retaining current conditions that assistance only be provided to security forces which respect human rights, many policymakers and analysts believe that the United States must devise conditions that will halt paramilitary activities. The paramilitary groups, many argue, present not only an obstacle to the peace process, as their continued existence discourages guerrillas from negotiating, establishing a cease-fire, and ultimately laying down their arms, but also a threat to the government, as their activities undermine the legitimacy of the state. (On the other hand, paramilitaries and their supporters would argue that their actions provide an incentive for the guerrillas to negotiate, and that the paramilitaries themselves, as groups with political ideas and a popular following in some areas, should be part of the negotiation.) Possible conditions could refuse aid to military and police forces that provide support to paramilitary groups (see proposed language of S. 1748, in the section on Congressional concerns, above), have links to paramilitary groups, or even those that are found to have tolerated paramilitary activities. Some would argue further that the United States should also seek the dismantling of the paramilitary groups as a condition for continued military aid, on the grounds that the military could influence the major groups to disarm.[62]

---

[61] Article from CNN-Interactivo, "Colombia Expects Peasants to Fight Cocaine-Crop Removal," February 4, 2000.

[62] Proposing this course, Carlos Salinas, Advocacy Director for Latin America and the (continued...)

Some would impose greater conditions on the military, providing assistance only if the military evidences good faith in supporting a negotiated solution to the guerrilla conflict. Those who argue for conditions of this sort believe that guerrilla leaders are sincere in seeking peace, and that neither their ideology nor their income from the drug trade is an obstacle to a settlement. They argue that the leaders are pragmatists rather than ideologues, that their recent political statements have sought reform rather than revolution, and that the guerrillas' income from illegal activities is spent to maintain their fighting force, and will no longer be needed when the conflict ends.[63] They also note that the Colombian military has hindered previous peace efforts, most recently in the Samper Administration (1994-1998).

Other analysts argue that the United States should not provide greater assistance unless the Colombian people, particularly the business class, are willing to bear a greater part of the burden. In particular, they argue that Colombians must pay more taxes to support the security forces and to fund a good part of the potential costs of post-war reconstruction. Some also believe that the government should lift restrictions on military service, which provide that no one with a high-school diploma or higher will be sent into combat. This not only protects the middle classes and elite from danger when called under Colombia's universal conscription, but also reduces the potential of the Colombian military, depriving it of needed brainpower in combat and lessening the urgency for many voters of providing the military with the resources to fight efficiently.

Terminate Aid to the Military. Two schools of thought underlie arguments that the United States should terminate all assistance to the military (although not necessarily to the police forces.) Some analysts argue that such aid only undermines the peace process by strengthening an abusive, inept and insubordinate army that has no desire to reform or negotiate peace with the guerrillas, and will only block any attempts to reach a reasonable settlement. Other analysts fear that continued U.S. military assistance will allow the guerrillas to convincingly blame the United States if they pull out of talks. Some also argue that the United States may not be able to function as an "honest broker" in the search for an acceptable peace settlement if it is providing military aid, especially if that aid is used for or linked to counterinsurgency purposes.

Broaden U.S. Policy to Provide Multi-faceted Aid, and Deemphasize Counternarcotics Efforts. Many analysts argue that the United States should substantially broaden the scope of funding that it provides to include support for economic, social and political reform, and encourage international donors to contribute aid. These analysts attribute Colombian production of illegal narcotics and the armed violence in large part to institutional and socioeconomic weaknesses, which

---

[62] (...continued)
Carribean at the Washington Office of Amnesty International, USA, also suggests that cattle ranchers and other rural land owners supporting the paramilitaries should be denied visas for travel to the United States. In Foreign Policy in Focus: Colombia: Volume 2, Number 49, November 1997. [http://www.foreignpolicy-infocus.org/briefs/vol2/v2n49col.html].

[63] Testimony of Mark Chernick before the House Subcommittee on Western Hemisphere Affairs, August 5, 1998.

they argue must be addressed, and note that substantial U.S. assistance for interdiction and eradication has not lead to a decrease in supply.[64] While those who agree with this conclusion have different views on the desirability of aid to the police and military and on its appropriate levels, many view the current U.S. policy emphasis – and that of the Clinton Adminstration 2000 proposal – on counternarcotics as an impediment to a resolution of the Colombian crisis, arguing that the continued emphasis on counternarcotics may well exacerbate the guerrilla conflict. The central dilemma of U.S. policy they identify is that increasing counternarcotics efforts "will push more campesinos into the arms of anyone who can help them," including paramilitary groups and the insurgents.[65] Thus, many suggest that counternarcotics may have to take second place in promoting peace.[66]

Instead, they argue that the United States should support the Colombian government in devising and implementing agrarian reform and rural development programs which will provide peasants with land and the ability to work it profitably. These could include zones of development established during the conflict in areas where the guerrillas do not currently operate. Such zones, they argue, would not only provide a buffer against further guerrilla expansion, but demonstrate to rebel fighters that (1) the government is willing to make significant socioeconomic reforms, and (2) they would be capable of earning a livelihood if they demobilized. In the long run, these analysts argue, a peace settlement and rural development will do more to curb the production and trafficking of illegal narcotics than will continuing current eradication and other police and military counternarcotics efforts that deprive rural inhabitants of their livelihoods. Others who favor alternative development argue, however, that it must be carried out in conjunction with eradication efforts, because coca profits are so high that growers must be offered both incentives and disincentives if they are to replace coca plants.

Assistance is also required in other areas, according to these analysts. These areas include: humanitarian aid for displaced persons, increased funding for judicial reform, and assistance that would promote social and political reforms, including funding for the growing movement of non-governmental organizations that seek to broaden the political system. Some analysts also recommend that the United States help strengthen Colombia's economy by extending the Andean Trade Preference Initiative, which provides duty-free access to U.S. markets for many Colombian products. Currently, it will expire in 2001.

---

[64] According to two analysts from the U.S. Army War College, "While military power is essential, it is not sufficient. Indeed, militarizing the effort may be a good indicator of continued failure." Donald Shultz and Gabriel Marcella, *Colombia's Three Wars: U.S. Strategy at the Crossroads*, op.cit.

[65] Many Colombian peasants who were earning a subsistence living undertook coca cultivation, beginning in the 1970s, as a means to avoid ruin, according to some analysts, and perhaps even to accumulate the capital necessary to enter more lucrative legitimate agricultural enterprises, such as cattle raising and commercial farming. See: *Violence and Colombia,* op.cit.

[66] See not only Shultz and Marcella, op.cit., but also Michael Shifter, *Colombia's Security Predicament and Opportunities for Peace: Guidelines for U.S. Policy*, Inter-American Dialogue Policy Brief. [http://www.iadialog.org].

To secure economic and social assistance of the magnitude that President Pastrana requested in September 1999, international financial institutions and many other countries would have to contribute. Some analysts suggest that an international coalition to provide such assistance "can be assembled only with the leadership of the United States."[67]

Some policymakers and analysts argue, however, that U.S. and other international assistance is unlikely to wean Colombia from the drug economy, and improve the political system, without broad social and political changes. These include both those who would argue that such aid would be of little use without a prior demonstration from the Colombian elite of its commitment to carry out necessary reforms, and others who argue that substantial international funding could provide the cushion necessary to make such reforms palatable. Some Colombian analysts have viewed the rise of drug trafficking in Colombia as the result of many intangible factors, including "weakening of religious values, secularisation [sic], the desire for enrichment, the toleration of corruption, the use of violence and the absence of penal sanctions" as both contributing to the development of the drug trade and its corruption of state institutions, and as a result of its existence.[68] In addition, many link the current political violence to the 1957 "National Front" political settlement, which resolved the country's political problems at the elite level, but did virtually nothing to address the country's widespread social problems or to bring the majority of the population into the political system. Many also blame the intransigence of economic interests and a lack of political will in several successive governments for the failure of subsequent attempts at agrarian reform and other rural improvements.

---

[67] Bernard Aronson. War in Colombia: The U.S. Role. *Washington Post*, August 5, 1999. p. A23.

[68] Jorge Orlando Melo. *The Drug Trade, Politics and the Economy: The Colombian Experience*, in Elizabeth Joyce and Carlos Malamud, eds., Latin America and the Multinational Drug Trade. New York: St. Martin's Press, 1998. p. 65.

Appendix A. Scope of and Restrictions on Current U.S. Assistance to Colombia

U.S. assistance to Colombia, virtually all of it related to counternarcotics efforts, has increased steadily over the last five years. (See Table A at the end of this section.) The United States provides equipment, supplies, and other aid for the counternarcotics efforts, largely for the Colombian National Police, with some assistance to the Colombian military. Most of the funding supports the tracking, interdiction and arrest of traffickers, the destruction of laboratories, and eradication efforts. A small amount supports reforms to the judicial system, and alternative development.

The State Department has been the primary agency in counternarcotics efforts, providing most of the funding for the efforts of the other civilian agencies involved. These agencies include the Drug Enforcement Administration, the Federal Bureau of Investigation, and the Agency for International Development. They work with Colombia's judicial system to improve law enforcement capabilities, criminal justice procedures, and the accessibility and fairness of the justice system. They also assist Colombia's eradication and interdiction efforts, providing training, equipment, and spare parts. The State Department runs an air wing which supplies aircraft for the eradication program.

The Department of Defense (DOD) is also a major, and increasingly controversial, source of funding for Colombian counternarcotics efforts. It has provided support for Colombian efforts to detect and monitor illicit narcotics operations, principally the maintenance of five radar sites in Colombia. DOD has also conducted surveillance overflights from locations outside Colombia.[69] DOD has also worked with Colombian Naval units to build a riverine patroling and interdiction capability. Through Section 506 (a) of the Foreign Assistance Act of 1961, as amended, DOD has provided substantial amounts of equipment to the Colombian military and police. In 1999, DOD began to assist in establishing and training a special counternarcotics battalion of some 950 members, which commenced operations late in 1999. It will conduct its own counternarcotics missions and assist the CNP in its operations.[70] U.S. uniformed military personnel stationed in Colombia numbered about 80 as of early February 2000. In addition, the number of U.S. military trainers on rotation in Colombia at any one time generally has fluctuated between 175 and 250.

In addition, the United States is funding the construction of the Joint Intelligence Center (JIC) at *Tres Esquinas* in southwest Colombia. U.S. officials

---

[69] On July 23, 1999, five U.S. soldiers and two Colombians on a surveillance mission were killed when their De Havilland RC-7 reconnaissance plane crashed while flying over the Putamayo Department in southern Colombia.

[70] *Drug Control: Narcotics Threat from Colombia Continues to Grow*. op. cit. According to GAO, the battalion will require some $70 million in equipment and training, including $60 million to provide helicopters.

expect the JIC to strengthen police and military intelligence gathering and analysis capabilities, and encourage the sharing of intelligence between the police and military. (According to U.S. officials, currently the police are reluctant to share intelligence with corresponding military units because of suspicions that they are corrupted by narcotraffickers.)

Many critics of military assistance argue that although provided for counternarcotics purposes, it can often be used to further counterinsurgency efforts. News reports in the summer of 1998 alleged that the United States had provided covert assistance to the Colombian military for counternarcotics and counterinsurgency operations, including the participation of active duty military personnel and private contractors.[71] At the same time, the press reported the presence of U.S. special operations forces who were training with Colombian military units under the Joint Combined Exchange Training program (U.S.C. Title 10, Section 2011), [72] which some interpreted as providing de facto counterinsurgency aid. Although the Clinton Administration denies that the United States provides counterinsurgency assistance, analysts acknowledge that some types of U.S. counternarcotics training provide lessons that can also be applied to counterinsurgency operations. The Clinton Administration has also held that assistance provided to police and military forces in operations targeted at guerrilla drug production or protection activities fits within the definition of counternarcotics aid. In March 1999, the Administration expanded the conditions under which it provides intelligence to Colombian security forces, routinely providing a Colombian police-military Joint Task Force with intelligence information related to the guerrillas, whether or not that information is strictly related to their narcotics activities. Although the United States provides the information to assist with counternarcotics operations, the General Accounting Office reported that the U.S. Embassy in Colombia "does not have a system to ensure that it is not being used for other than counternarcotics purposes."[73]

Human Rights Concerns and the "Leahy Amendment" Restrictions

In 1996, Congress adopted the first "Leahy Amendment" provisions in the FY1997 Foreign Operations Appropriations Act (as contained in the Omnibus Appropriations Act, 1997, P.L. 104-208). These provisions prohibited the use of FY1997 International Narcotics funds appropriated by the act for assistance to any unit of foreign security forces "if the Secretary of State has credible evidence that such unit has committed gross violations of human rights, unless the Secretary determines and reports to the Committees on Appropriations that the government of

---

[71] Tod Robberson. U.S. Launches Covert Program To Aid Colombia. *Dallas Morning News*. August 19, 1998. p 1.

[72] Dana Priest and Douglas Farah. U.S. Force Training Troops in Colombia. *The Washington Post*. May 25, 1998, p A1; Diana Jean Schemo and Tim Golden. U.S. To Increase Support for Colombian Army Unites. The New York Times. June 2, 1998, p. 1. Also see CRS Report RL30034, *Joint Combined Exchange Training (JCET) and Human Rights: Background and Issues for Congress*, January 26, 1999.

[73] *Drug Control: Narcotics Threat from Colombia Continues to Grow*, op.cit., p. 21.

such country is taking effective measures to bring the responsible members of the security forces unit to justice..." In FY1998 (P.L. 105-118, Section 570) and subsequent foreign operations appropriations, this restriction was extended to all other funds made available by the act, including IMET (International Military Education and Training funds), and FMF (Foreign Military Financing).[74]

In addition, Congress attached another "Leahy Amendment" restriction to the Department of Defense FY1999 Appropriations Act (P.L. 105-262).[75] As a result of reports that the United States military was providing training to Colombian troops with funds exempt from previous Leahy restrictions, Congress decided to prohibit the use of any funds appropriated by the act "to support any training program involving a unit of the security forces of a foreign country if the Secretary of Defense has received credible information from the Department of State that a member of such unit has committed a gross violation of human rights, unless all necessary corrective steps have been taken." There are provisions for a waiver in extraordinary circumstances. A related provision in the FY1999 Foreign Operations appropriations as included in the omnibus appropriations, required the Secretary of State and Secretary of Defense to provide jointly to Congress, by January 31, 1999, a report on all overseas military training provided to foreign military personnel under programs administered by DOD and the State Department, including the foreign policy justification and purpose for the training activity, the number of foreign students trained and their unit of operation, the location of the training, and the operational benefit to U.S. military forces and units.

FY2000 Human Rights Restrictions: Texts of the Leahy Amendments

FY1999 restrictions on funding or training of human rights abusers — the so-called **Leahy Amendments** — are continued in FY2000 legislation.

- The conference report version of the Foreign Operations, Export Financing and Related Programs Appropriations Act, 2000 (H.R. 2606, H.Rept. 106-339) contains the "Leahy Amendment" prohibition on providing funds in the act (which include International Narcotics funds, IMET, and FMF) to any unit of foreign security forces found to have committed gross violations of human rights. The language is as follows:

> None of the funds made available by this Act may be provided to any unit of the security forces of a foreign country if the Secretary of State has credible evidence to believe such unit has committed gross violations of human rights, unless the Secretary determines and reports to the Committees on Appropriations that the government of such country is taking effective measures to bring the responsible members of the security forces unit to justice: Provided, That nothing in this section shall be construed to withhold funds made available by this Act from any unit of the security forces of a foreign country not credibly alleged to

---

[74] There apparently was debate within the executive branch over whether funds extended by the Export-Import Bank were also restricted by the provision; the Bank finally decided that they were.

[75] It was added by a voice vote during Senate Floor consideration of the DOD Appropriations bill for FY1999 (S. 2132, as incorporated in H.R. 4103) and retained in conference. (Conference Report 105-746, Sec. 8130)

be involved in gross violations of human rights: Provided further, That in the event that funds are withheld from any unit pursuant to this section, the Secretary of State shall promptly inform the foreign government of the basis for such action and shall, to the maximum extent practicable, assist the foreign government in taking effective measures to bring the responsible members of the security forces to justice.

- The Department of Defense Appropriations Act, 2000, (P.L. 106-79, H.R. 2561) contains the following human rights restrictions on DOD training:

SEC. 8100. TRAINING AND OTHER PROGRAMS. (a) PROHIBITION- None of the funds made available by this Act may be used to support any training program involving a unit of the security forces of a foreign country if the Secretary of Defense has received credible information from the Department of State that the unit has committed a gross violation of human rights, unless all necessary corrective steps have been taken. (b) MONITORING- The Secretary of Defense, in consultation with the Secretary of State, shall ensure that prior to a decision to conduct any training program referred to in subsection (a), full consideration is given to all credible information available to the Department of State relating to human rights violations by foreign security forces. (c) WAIVER- The Secretary of Defense, after consultation with the Secretary of State, may waive the prohibition in subsection (a) if he determines that such waiver is required by extraordinary circumstances.

(d) REPORT- Not more than 15 days after the exercise of any waiver under subsection (c), the Secretary of Defense shall submit a report to the congressional defense committees describing the extraordinary circumstances, the purpose and duration of the training program, the United States forces and the foreign security forces involved in the training program, and the information relating to human rights violations that necessitates the waiver.

Table 1. U.S. Assistance to Colombia, FY1995-FY1999
(Obligations and authorizations, $ millions)

Category of Foreign Aid or Other Assistance	**FY1995**	**FY1996**	**FY1997**	**FY1998**	**FY1999**	**FY2000[a]**
State Dept./International Narcotics and Law (INL)	*16.4*	*16.3*	*38.2*	*43.0*	*32.7*	*50.0*
INL Air Wing	*2.5*	*5.9*	*19.0*	*24.0*	*30.0*	*35.0*
INL Huey Upgrades	*0*	*0*	*3.2*	*14.0*	*40.0[b]*	—
Other:[b] *UH-60 Helicopters:* *Other police aid:* *A-37 upgrades and radar:*	—	—	—	—	 *96.0* *23.2* *14.0*	—
Agency for International Development (AID)[c]	*0.1*	*0.12*	*0.05*	*0.02*	—	—
International Military Education and Training (IMET)	*0.6*	*0.1*	*0.1*	*0.7*	*0.9*	*0.9*
Foreign Military Financing[c]	*10.0*	*0*	—	—	—	—
Administration of Justice (AOJ)	0	0	1.8	2.0	1.8	—
Department of Defense (DOD) Sec.1004/124	NA	NA	42.8	39.7	51.8	60.9
DOD Sec. 1033	NA	NA	NA	2.0	13.3	17.2
DOD Sec. 506 Drawdown	0	40.0	14.2	41.2	58.1	—
Other Section 506 Drawdown (Departs. of Transportation, Justice, State and Treasury)					14.5	
Totals:	29.6	62.42	119.35	166.62	375.4	164.0

Sources: Department of State (December 14, 1999 for FY1999, January 27 for FY2000); Department of Defense, January 5, 2000 for revised 1999 and FY2000. DEA, Sept. 14, 1999. This chart includes direct U.S. foreign assistance (i.e., the categories usually counted as U.S. foreign aid, which are in italics) plus the costs of goods and services provided to Colombia from other U.S. government programs supporting counternarcotics efforts in Colombia. The United States also provides a small amount of DOD Excess Defense Articles (EDA) to Colombia. Other funds are spent in Colombia on counternarcotics and other activities that are considered part of U.S. programs: for instance, the Drug Enforcement Administration (DEA) spends its own funds on joint operations in Colombia, and U.S. special forces train Colombian military personnel under the Joint Combined Exercise Training (JCET) program whose primary purpose is to train U.S. troops.

[a] These allocations are from funds appropriated during 1999. The DOD Section 1004/124 and Section 1033 amounts are expected to change, the INL Air Wing figure may change.

[b] From FY1999 Supplemental Appropriations funding.

[c] AID pipeline funding of $5.0 million authorized in previous years was expended in FY1999; AID also provided some earthquake disaster relief in FY1999. FMF pipeline funding of $13 million authorized prior to FY1995 and funding available from the FY1995 FMF authorization was intended to be expended from mid-FY1997 through FY1999.

NOTE: This chart also appears in CRS Report RS20451. That report will be more frequently updated than this one, therefore more recent aid figures may be available in that report.

Appendix B. Overview of the FARC and the ELN[76]

The Revolutionary Armed Forces of Colombia (*Fuerzas Armadas Revolucionarias de Colombia*, or FARC) and the National Liberation Army (*Ejército de Liberación Nacional*, or ELN) both trace their roots back to the warfare of the late 1940s, and were formally organized in the mid-1960s. They are the last of several leftist guerrilla groups which have challenged the Colombian government. The others have largely withered or have joined the political process through peace accords. [A third group, the Popular Liberation Army (*Ejército de Liberación Popular*, or ELP), is much smaller and apparently largely inactive.]

The harshness and limitations of life in rural areas are often cited as the contributing greatly to the decisions of peasants and other rural dwellers to join the guerrillas. For generations, political conflict in the rural areas has been fed by high levels of poverty among peasants who have been deprived of their land or adequate resources to farm it. In the 1950s, peasants developed armed movements to defend their land against members of the elite who sought to acquire large estates; some subsequently were incorporated into guerrilla groups during and after the 1960s. Even where peasants managed to retain their land initially, they often were forced to sell and move elsewhere because the soil was depleted and when they could no longer afford or because it became increasingly unprofitable to compete with large-scale agriculture.

The FARC was organized in 1966 among peasants living in the remote, isolated mountainous areas largely between Bogota and Cali. There, the Communist Party had organized communities, later dubbed "independent republics," during the early years of *la violencia* in the late 1940s and the 1950s. The independent republics existed in areas where the national government either had no presence, or its local authorities conceded control to the "republican" leadership. FARC founders, including current leader, Manuel Marulanda Vélez (nicknamed *Tirofijo*, i.e., Sure Shot), of a peasant background, were members of Colombia's Communist Party Central Committee, and identified with a Soviet Marxist-Leninist ideology. Until the mid-1960s, the Communist Party had advocated "mass struggle" using the constitutional, electoral system rather than armed opposition to gain power. It organized an armed movement, however, in response to the army's counterinsurgency efforts beginning in 1961, which destroyed the independent republics, and the National Liberation Army's initiation of armed struggle. Although powerful in its first two years, the FARC was debilitated by 1968, but revitalized during the late 1970s.

The ELN launched operations in early 1965. Its leader was a student who had taken part in the Workers', Students' and Peasants' Movement (MOEC). MOEC militants thought they could bring about armed struggle by rearming and organizing

---

[76] This summary draws on several sources, most importantly the Chernick, Eisenstadt, Gott, Hanratty, and Pereyra works cited in the Bibliography, and War Without Quarter, op. cit.. See these sources for a fuller account of the complex history of negotiations during the 1980s and 1990s, including the effects on negotiations of drug violence, the opposition of military leaders, and the activities of the M-19 and other guerrilla groups.

peasant guerrillas. In 1984, the ELN began to take action against international petroleum companies operating in Colombia, including the kidnapping of executives, engineers, and other workers, sabotage of pipelines, and extortion of funds. It continues these activities. Unlike all other Colombian guerrilla groups, the ELN has never negotiated independently with the Colombian government; it has only engaged in peace negotiations as part of an alliance with the FARC.

Previous Negotiation Attempts

During the 1980s, the FARC engaged in peace negotiations with successive Colombian administrations, and attempted to join the political process. In March 1984, FARC signed the La Uribe cease-fire agreement in exchange for promises from then-President Belisario Betancour (1982-1986) that his government would present legislation to Congress to improve living conditions for the poor. The accord took effect in May. Although most of the FARC members at that time apparently abandoned armed struggle, some fronts refused to participate. In 1985, those FARC adherents pursuing the political path created the *Union Patriótica* (Patriotic Union or UP), which won 1.4% of the vote in March 1986 congressional elections and 4% in the May 1986 presidential elections. Although the UP distanced itself from the FARC fighting force, its candidates and followers became targets for assassination. (In late 1987, UP leader and its 1986 presidential candidate, Jaime Pardo Leal, was murdered; by 1989, the UP counted several hundred murdered members, and by 1985, some 2,000.) In July 1987, the main FARC organization resumed armed struggle, joining the ELN and four other guerrilla groups in September 1987 in the Simón Bolívar Guerrilla Coordinating Group (CGSB)

Less than two years later, the FARC again attempted to negotiate with the government, but mainly, according to some analysts, because it feared losing political ground to another major CGSB member, the M-19, which had begun to negotiate with the government of Virgilio Barco (1986-1990). In early 1989, the FARC declared a unilateral cease-fire and organized a "commission of notables" which included two former Colombian presidents (one of them Misael Pastrana Borrero, father of the current president) to mediate negotiations with the Barco government. The M-19 laid down its arms in March 1990, forming a political party. During the 1990 presidential election, two former guerrilla candidates were killed: UP candidate Bernardo Jaramillo in March and, in April, Carlos Pizarro, the M-19 guerrilla commander who ran for president on the leftist banner after Jaramillo's death. Despite their deaths, and those of other guerrillas who had joined the political process, the M-19 gained almost 27% of the vote in December 1990 constituent assembly elections. (The killers were not identified in most cases, but they were presumed to be linked to drug interests and paramilitary groups.)

For the next decade, no progress was made in talks between the government and the FARC and ELN, despite continuing initiatives by both sides. In the early 1990s, President Barco's attempts at negotiations with the FARC, ELN, and smaller CGSB groups floundered because, according to some analysts, the FARC and ELN leadership continued to believe that a military victory was possible. This conviction, and the continuing murders of demobilized guerrillas, left the FARC and the ELN as the two major holdouts in peace negotiations with the administration of President César Gaviria (1990-1994), during which several smaller guerrilla groups joined the political process through negotiations. By late 1991, the FARC and ELN had begun a crusade to undermine elections, starting with the municipal elections in October. (It has carried out such tactics in several elections since then.) FARC also began that year to kill demobilized EPL (Ejército Popular de Liberación) guerrillas and its supporters who had formed a political party. Attempts at negotiation by Gaviria's successor, Ernesto Samper (1994-1998), failed to prosper. Among the reasons for the failure, according to some analysts, was that the guerrillas distrusted Samper, who, under pressure from the military, had reneged on promises to create a demilitarized zone to pursue talks. In addition, guerrillas saw no advantage in dealing with a political figure discredited by his acceptance of campaign contributions from drug traffickers.

Appendix C. Current FARC Position

The FARC's "10-point" negotiating agenda,[77] presented to the government when talks commenced in January 1999 calls for far-reaching political, economic, and military reforms. Statements by FARC leader Manuel Marulanda Vélez ("Tirofijo") in January 1998 concerning that agenda suggested that the guerrillas were still intent on seeking broad change of a socialist nature, which would incorporate the lessons learned from the Soviet, Chinese, Vietnamese and Cuban experiences.[78] The agenda first called for a political solution to the country's conflict. The other points included:

- Political reforms, with a reorganization of various state institutions, including the legislature, the court system, and the attorney general's office, in order to provide "democratic participation at the national, regional, and municipal levels in the decisions that commit the future of society."

- Economic reforms, including state investment in "strategic areas of national industry," 50% of the national budget invested in social welfare, a reorganization of the tax system to redistribute wealth, an agrarian reform to redistribute land and agricultural policies which would provide ample credit, technical and marketing assistance to producers.

- Changes regarding the security forces, including a revision of military doctrine to base it on defending Colombia's borders rather than on internal control, reduction of the size of the military and its budget, and the separation of the police from the military hierarchy.

- Changes in international relations, including a review of military agreements, measures to protect the Colombian economy against international competition, renegotiation of the foreign debt to secure a 10-year moratorium, and "a solution to the phenomenon of production, marketing, and consumption of narcotics and hallucinogens" that would involve "international communities and the commitment of the large powers..."

- Renegotiation of "detrimental" contracts signed with multinational companies to exploit natural resources such as petroleum, gas, coal, gold, nickel and emeralds "for the benefit of the regions and the country."

---

[77] These points were summarized from the document as it appeared in *El Espectador* (Internet Version), January 12, 1999, and translated by FBIS, Document #FTS19990112001695.

[78] 'Tirofijo' se destapa. Semana. January 18, 1999. [http://www.semana.com.co/users/semana/semana99/ene18/nacion.htm]

Bibliography[79]

Bergquist, Charles, Ricardo Peñaranda, and Gonzalo Sánchez, eds. *Violence in Colombia: the Contemporary Crisis in Historical Perspective.* Wilmington, DE: SR Books, 1992.

Crandall, Russell. The End of Conflict in Colombia: The Military, Paramilitaries, and a New Role for the United States. *SAIS Review.* Vol 19, No. 1. 1999.

Chernick, Mark. *Negotiating Peace Amid Multiple Forms of Violence: The Protracted Search for a Settlement to the Armed Conflict in Colombia*, in Comparative Peace Processes in Latin America, edited by Cynthia Arnson. Stanford, CA: Stanford University Press, 1999.

Eisenstadt, Todd, and Daniel Garcia. *Colombia: Negotiations in a Shifting Pattern of Insurgency*, in Elusive Peace: Negotiating an End to Civil Wars, edited by I. William Zartman. Washington, D.C.: The Brookings Institution, 1995.

Gott, Richard. *Guerrilla Movements in Latin America.* London: Thomas Nelson and Sons, Ltd., 1970.

Hanratty, Dennis M. and Sandra W. Meditz, eds. *Colombia: A Country Study.* Washington, D.C.: Headquarters, Department of the Army, 1990.

Marcella, Gabriel, and Donald E. Schulz. War and Peace in Colombia. *The Washington Quarterly*. Summer 1999.

Martz, John D. *The Politics of Clientelism: Democracy and the State in Colombia*. New Brunswick, NJ: Transaction Publishers, 1997.

Melo, Jorge Orlando. "The Drug Trade, Politics and the Economy: The Colombian Experience," in *Latin America and the Multinational Drug Trade*, Elizabeth Joyce and Carlos Malamud, eds. New York: St. Martin's Press: 1998.

Pereyra, Daniel. *Del Moncada a Chiapas: Historia de la Lucha Armada en America Latina (1950-1990)*. Madrid: Los Libros de la Catarata, 1994.

Richani, Nazih. The Political Economy of Violence: The War System in Colombia. *Journal of Interamerican Studies & World Affairs*. Summer 1997.

Shifter, Michael. Colombia on the Brink. *Foreign Affairs*. July/August 1999.
—. Colombia at War. *Current History*. March 1999.

Thoumi, Francisco. *Political Economy and Illegal Drugs in Colombia*. Boulder, CO: Lynn Rienner Publishers, 1995.

---

[79] Sources consulted in addition to those cited in detailed footnotes.

Figure 1. Colombia: Departments and Larger Cities

Map adapted by CRS from Magellan Geographix. Used with permission. Data source: Dennis M. Hanratty and Sandra W. Meditz, eds. Colombia: A Country Study, Washington, D.C.: Department of the Army, 1990, p. xxii.

Figure 2. Areas of Colombian Insurgent, Paramilitary, and Drug-trafficking Activities

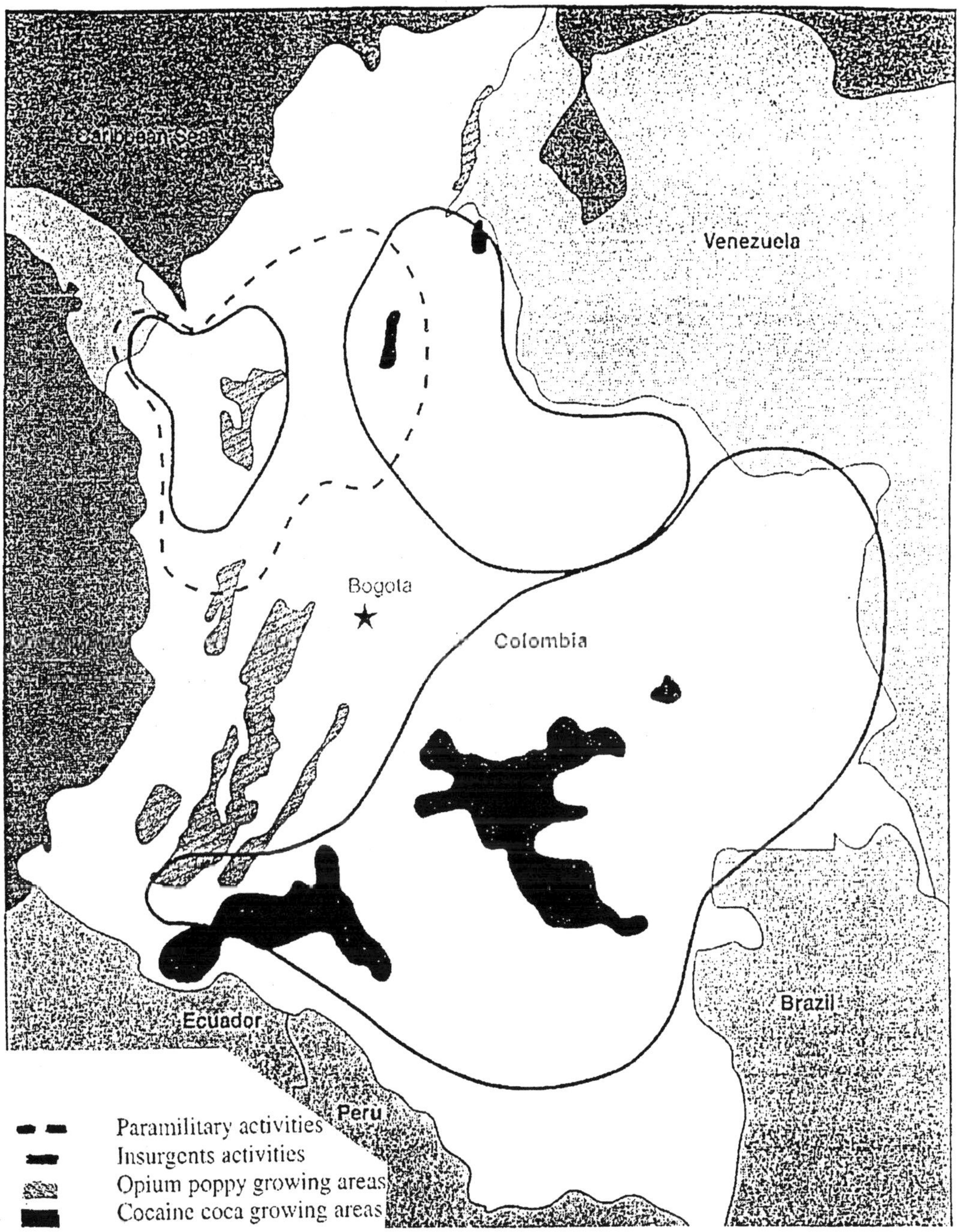

Source: U.S. agencies, as published by the General Accounting Office in: *Drug Control: Narcotics Threat from Colombia Continues to Grow*. GAO/NSIAD-99-136, June 1999, p. 8.

VENEZUELA: POLITICAL/ECONOMIC SITUATION AND U.S. RELATIONS, 1997

Mark P. Sullivan

Summary

Venezuela, which has had a history of democratic elections since 1958, has experienced significant economic and political challenges in the 1990s. The election of Rafael Caldera as President in December 1993 brought a measure of political and economic stability to the country, but the standard of living for many Venezuelans has declined over the past several years. U.S. relations with Venezuela remain strong and are characterized by an important trade relationship. In 1995, Venezuela became, and remains, the largest foreign supplier of petroleum for the United States accounting for almost 17% of U.S. oil imports. President Clinton is scheduled to visit Venezuela October 12-13, 1997. Press reports maintain that several agreements will be signed on customs, energy, the environment, and cooperation against drug trafficking.

Political and Economic Situation

Although Venezuela has experienced significant political and economic difficulties in the 1990s, the current government of President Rafael Caldera, inaugurated in February 1994 for a five-year term, has brought a measure of political and economic stability to the country. Nevertheless, while the macroeconomy began to improve in 1996 as the Caldera government implemented an economic reform program, the standard of living for many Venezuelans has not. In addition, high crime levels and notable human rights problems persist. As the country begins to look ahead to presidential and legislative elections scheduled for December 1998, the traditional political parties remain unpopular. There are also periodic fears about the 81-year old President's health, with some Venezuelans calling for the presidential election to be moved ahead.

Upon taking office in 1994, the Caldera government was faced with a severe banking crisis in which the nation's second largest bank collapsed, triggering a series of runs on other banks. Resolving the crisis -- which occurred because of years of mismanagement of the financial system -- cost the government more than $10 billion. President Caldera reversed some of the free market reforms begun under the government of Carlos Andres Perez (1989-1993). He also imposed price and foreign exchange controls in 1994. Nevertheless, economic performance under the Caldera government continued to deteriorate. In 1995, inflation was

Location:	Northern South America, bordering the Caribbean Sea, Colombia, Brazil, and Guyana
Area:	352,143 sq. miles, slightly more than twice the size of California
Population:	21.98 million (July 1996 est.)
Ethnic Groups:	Mestizo (mixed ethnic background) 67%; European 21%; African 10%; Amerindian 2%
Life Expectancy:	71 years (1995)
Literacy:	91% (1995)
GDP:	$69.4 billion (1995)
GNP per capita:	$3,020 (1995)
U.S. Aid:	FY1996: $928,000 FY1997: $950,000 (est.) FY1998: $1 million (req.)

Sources: CIA's World Factbook 1996; World Bank's World Development Report 1997; and U.S. Agency for International Development's FY1998 Congressional Presentation.

over 50%, the highest in the region. In response to considerable pressure, the government devalued the bolívar by 40% in December 1995, but it kept foreign exchange and price controls in place. Living conditions deteriorated considerably with the country's middle class shrinking and poverty increasing.

In order to combat the nation's economic decline, President Caldera announced a package of austerity measures in April 1996 that included price hikes in gasoline, an increase in luxury taxes, and a lifting of currency controls. The measures were significant because they represented a sharp economic policy turnaround for President Caldera, who had sharply criticized the free-market policies of the Perez government. As a result of the measures, Venezuela signed an agreement with the International Monetary Fund (IMF) in early June 1996 that would make available $3 billion over three years, of which $1.4 billion would be available in the first year.

Caldera's economic policy shift, welcomed by economists, initially led to increased inflation and negative economic growth in 1996, but by 1997 had begun to reap rewards. Inflation, which reached a record rate of 103% in 1996, is projected to decline to around 30% for 1997, and economic growth, which fell 1.6% in 1996, is projected to be at least 3% in 1997. According to the Department of State, the economy is making a comeback, largely because of the opening of the petroleum sector to foreign investment, a broad privatization program, and plans to reform public sector operations.[1] In particular, the opening to foreign investment in the petroleum sector has pumped several billion dollars into the economy and estimates are that investments over the next decade will reach $60 billion.[2]

In the sphere of politics, Caldera's election in December 1993 was notable because it restored a limited measure of stability to Venezuela's political system. The system had withstood the strains of two military coup attempts in 1992 and the ouster of President Perez on corruption charges in 1993.[3] In the 1993 election, Caldera's disparate National Convergence (CN) coalition defeated Venezuela's two traditional parties -- the Democratic Action Party (AD) and the Social Christian Party (COPEI). Caldera's supporters only gained one-fifth of the seats in the Chamber of Deputies, but received legislative support from the left-of-center Movement to Socialism (MAS) -- which had backed Caldera's presidential race — and the AD. In March 1996, however, MAS announced that it was withdrawing from an official coalition with the CN to form an alliance with COPEI and the populist Radical Cause Party

---

[1] U.S. Department of State. Background Notes: Venezuela, September 1997.

[2] Bussey, Jane. Oil Auction Windfall Just the Beginning for Venezuela, Global Investments Could Pump up to $60B into Economy. *Miami Herald*, June 15, 1997.

[3] Perez was convicted by the Supreme Court in May 1996 of misusing public funds. After more than two years under house arrest, he was freed on September 19, 1996.

(CAUSA R). As the December 1998 elections get closer, it could become increasingly difficult for the government to gain backing for its legislative proposals as parties jockey to position themselves for the campaign.

In President Caldera's first year of office, his popularity among Venezuelans remained solid, over 70%, but that support eroded significantly in 1995 and 1996 amidst economic recession and a decline in living standards. Labor strikes and civil unrest have challenged the government at times and the government's austerity measures have further exacerbated social tensions. In a June 1997 public opinion poll, 71% thought the government was doing a poor job and 51% thought that their economic situation had grown worse over the last six months (despite the government's success in bringing down inflation).[4]

Looking ahead to the December 1998 presidential elections, at this point the leader in the polls is Irene Saez, mayor of the Caracas district of Chacao and a former Miss Universe. Saez received 33.7% in a September 1997 presidential preference poll, while Claudio Fermin, a likely candidate of the AD placed a distant second with 10.5%. Saez does not belong to a political party, but some elements of COPEI are reportedly interested in Saez as the party's presidential candidate.[5]

As governments before, the Caldera Administration faces the challenge of improving the nation's difficult human rights problem. According to the State Department's 1996 human rights report, the Venezuelan government's human rights record is poor in several areas. These include: extrajudicial killings by the police and military; torture and abuse of detainees; failure to punish police and security officers accused of abuse; arbitrary and lengthy detentions; corruption and inefficiency in the judicial and law enforcement systems; deplorable prison conditions; and a lack of respect for the rights of indigenous peoples. In March 1997, Human Rights Watch issued a report describing the appalling conditions in Venezuela's prisons, and called on the government to take measures to reform the prison system.[6] The Caldera government demolished the infamous Reten de Catia prison in March 1997, but abysmal conditions persist in many of the country's remaining prisons. In late August 1997, 29 inmates died in a prison riot at El Dorado prison, a facility described by a human rights monitor as not being fit to hold anyone because of its filthy conditions.[7]

U.S. Relations

U.S. relations with Venezuela remain strong and are characterized by an important trade relationship. In 1995, Venezuela became, and remains, the largest foreign supplier of petroleum for the United States accounting for almost 17% of U.S. oil imports. The U.S. trade deficit with Venezuela has grown in recent years in large part because of the increase in petroleum imports. In 1996, the U.S. trade deficit with Venezuela was almost $8.2 billion, with Venezuela exporting $12.9 billion in goods to the United States (petroleum imports accounted for almost $11.3 billion alone) and importing $4.7 billion in goods from the United States.

---

[4] Prospects None Too Rosy. *Latin American Weekly Report*, July 8, 1997, p. 323.

[5] Colitt, Raymond. Saez Heads Venezuelan Political Polls. *Financial Times*, September 30, 1997, p. 6.

[6] Punishment Before Trial: Prison Conditions in Venezuela. Human Rights Watch/ Americas. March 1997.

[7] At Least 29 Dead in Venezuela Prison Riot, *Miami Herald*, August 29, 1997.

The United States is by far Venezuela's most important trading partner, in both exports and imports, and is also the largest foreign investor in Venezuela. In 1995, Venezuela exported 55% of the value of its total exports to the United States, with the lion's share of that, 83%, in oil. In the same year, Venezuela imported almost 55% of its total imports from the United States, with major products being a wide range of industrial equipment and consumer goods. U.S. foreign investment in Venezuela, which amounted to almost $3.4 billion in 1994, accounts for about half of all foreign investment in the country. Almost half of U.S. investment in Venezuela is concentrated in the manufacturing sector, and U.S. investment in the petroleum sector has been increasing over the past few years.

While Venezuela has liberalized its trade and investment regimes in recent years, barriers still exist. According to the Office of the U.S. Trade Representative (USTR), in its *1997 National Trade Estimate*, Venezuela's average tariff is about 10%, but it maintains higher tariffs on some products of interest to U.S. exporters. USTR also maintains that Venezuela's denial of certain sanitary and phytosanitary certificates to U.S. exporters lacks a scientific basis and is discriminatory. In foreign investment, the government continues to control key sectors of the economy, although as noted above, the government has opened up the petroleum sector significantly to investment through joint ventures and equity associations. For example, in July 1997, a subsidiary of the Venezuelan state oil company concluded an agreement with three U.S. companies — Arco, Phillips, and Texaco — to produce, upgrade, and market 200,000 barrels per day of crude oil from the Orinoco Belt region beginning in 1999.[8]

The USTR report also cited Venezuela for not providing adequate or effective intellectual property rights protection. USTR did acknowledge that Venezuela's enforcement of copyright law improved in 1996 because of the creation of an anti-piracy policy unit. Overall, however, USTR maintained that enforcement remains inadequate, with widespread piracy of well-known trademarks, videos, satellite signals, and other protected works.

In the 1990s, counternarcotics cooperation has become an important issue in U.S.-Venezuelan relations. Venezuela is a major transit country for cocaine, marijuana, and heroin to the United States, and has become a minor source country for illicit drugs, with opium poppy, coca, and cannabis cultivated in the border region with Colombia. With its large financial sector, Venezuela is also a major center for drug money laundering. Although the President certified Venezuela in February 1997 as cooperating with the United States fully on counternarcotics efforts, the Administration's statement of explanation noted a number of serious problems. With regard to maritime interdiction, the statement noted that in 1996 Venezuela denied four U.S. government requests from third country vessels to board suspected Venezuelan vessels suspected of narcotics trafficking. The Administration's statement also called on Venezuela to reform its judicial branch swiftly because corruption threatens the country's ability to combat its drug problem. Weak banking supervision and regulatory authority were also cited as reasons for money laundering in Venezuela.

President Clinton is scheduled to visit Venezuela October 12-13, 1997, on the first stop on a trip that will also take him to Brazil and Argentina. According to Assistant Secretary of State for Inter-American Affairs Jeffrey Davidow, the trip to Venezuela "will highlight our close partnership in developing clean and reliable energy supplies, our close cooperation against drugs and crime, and the durability of the Venezuelan people's commitment to

---

[8] Orinoco Belt Projects to Take Off, *Latin American Regional Reports — Andean Group*, July 22, 1997, p. 6.

democracy." [9] Additionally, the Assistant Secretary said: "the President will continue to broaden our relationship to include renewable energy, energy efficiency, natural gas development and integration of energy resources."[10] Press reports maintain that Venezuela and the United States will sign several agreements during the President's trip, including cooperation agreements on customs, energy, and the environment, and an agreement strengthening cooperation against drug trafficking. Talks reportedly are also ongoing for an investment agreement and an agreement on intellectual property rights protection, although it is unclear if bilateral negotiations will be completed before the President's visit.[11]

Another issue that could be discussed during the visit is U.S. interest in an open skies agreement with Venezuela, whereby each countries' airlines would enjoy freedom in the other country regarding destinations and routes.[12] Venezuela reportedly has opposed such an agreement as long as the country remains in a conditional category under the U.S. Federal Aviation Administration's International Aviation Safety program. Venezuela was placed in that category in 1995, a measure that allows Venezuelan air carriers to fly to the United States under heightened surveillance while Venezuela works to correct safety deficiencies. In August 1996, after rigorous U.S. inspections of Venezuelan aircraft resulted in flight delays and suspensions, the Venezuelan government took retaliatory action by blocking U.S. carriers from leaving Caracas for two days. The United States and Venezuela subsequently agreed to continue air service between the two countries while Venezuela works to improve its international aviation safety standards.[13]

---

[9]Statement of Ambassador Jeffrey Davidow, Assistant Secretary of State for Inter-American Affairs, House International Relations Committee, Subcommittee on the Western Hemisphere, South America Overview Hearing, October 8, 1997.

[10] Ibid.

[11] Venezuelan Foreign Ministry on U.S. President's Agenda, *Foreign Broadcast Information Service*, September 30, 1997.

[12] Open Skies Policy to be Discussed During Clinton's Visit, *Foreign Broadcast Information Service*, August 14, 1997.

[13] U.S. Department of Transportation. U.S.-Venezuela Reach 30-day Agreement on Continued Air Service. Press Release, August 10, 1996.

PANAMA - U.S. RELATIONS

Mark P. Sullivan

MOST RECENT DEVELOPMENTS

On December 31, 1999, the United States officially transferred control of the Panama Canal to Panama in accordance with the 1977 Canal treaties. Thousands of Panamanians celebrated as the Panamanian flag was raised at the former Panama Canal Commission administration building. Because of the conflict with millennium celebrations, a more elaborate transition ceremony was held December 14, 1999. President Clinton and Secretary of State Albright declined invitations to attend that ceremony, which led to some resentment in Panama. In addition to the Canal turnover, all U.S. troops in Panama have been withdrawn in accordance with the Canal treaties.

On January 15, 2000, Secretary of State Albright visited Panama and met with Panamanian President Mireya Moscoso. She noted that the Canal transfer marked a new era in U.S.-Panamanian relations in which "discredited patterns of paternalism and resentment have been supplanted by partnership and resolve."

BACKGROUND AND ANALYSIS

Political and Economic Situation

The December 1989 U.S. military intervention was the culmination of two and a half years of strong U.S. pressure against the de facto political rule of General Manuel Antonio Noriega, commander of the Panama Defense Forces (PDF.). President Bush ordered U.S. forces into combat on December 20, 1989 for four reasons: "to safeguard the lives of Americans, to defend democracy in Panama, to combat drug trafficking, and to protect the integrity of the Panama Canal Treaty." A new Panamanian government was installed headed by Guillermo Endara, who was widely believed to have won the May 1989 elections by a 3-1 margin. On January 3, 1990, General Noriega, who had taken refuge at the Vatican Embassy, turned himself over to U.S. officials, whereupon he was arrested by members of the U.S. Drug Enforcement Administration and brought to the United States to stand trial on drug trafficking charges. After this, President Bush announced that all four objectives of the U.S. intervention had been accomplished. (After a seven-month trial, on April 9, 1992, Noriega was convicted on 8 out of 10 drug trafficking counts in U.S. federal court in Miami, and on July 10, 1992, he was sentenced to 40 years in prison. On March 4, 1999, a federal judge reduced Noriega's prison term to 30 years because of disparity between his sentence and his co-conspirators. The reduction makes Noriega eligible for parole in 2007.)

A decade after the U.S. military intervention, Panama has made notable economic and political progress, with abundant U.S. assistance and cooperation, but the country still faces notable challenges. The economy has rebounded, but critics maintain that the recovery has not trickled down to the nation's poorer classes. Under the Endara government (December 1989 - August 1994), a new civilian Public Force replaced Noriega's Panama Defense Forces (PDF), but the demilitarization process was difficult, with some police and former PDF members at times plotting to destabilize, if not overthrow, the government. Panama cooperates closely with the United States on counter-narcotics measures, but the nation remains a major narcotics money laundering and illicit drug transshipment center. The government generally respects human rights, but, as noted by the State Department in its human rights report for 1998, serious human rights problems include excessive force against detainees by police and prison guards; poor prison conditions; prolonged pretrial detention; an inefficient and often corrupt criminal justice system; and instances of illegal searches and political pressure on the media.

Election of Perez Balladares

On May 8, 1994, Panamanians went to the polls to vote in presidential and legislative elections that observers called the freest in almost three decades. The results of the presidential race confirmed what opinion polls had been saying in the months leading up to the elections. Ernesto Perez Balladares, candidate of the former pro-Noriega Democratic Revolutionary Party (PRD) who led a coalition known as "United People" won the election with 33% of the vote. Then Secretary of State Warren Christopher expressed satisfaction that the elections were conducted freely and fairly. Perez Balladares was inaugurated on September 1, 1994.

Placing a surprisingly strong second, with 29% of the vote, was Arnulfist Party (PA) candidate Mireya Moscoso de Gruber (widow of former president Arnulfo Arias) who headed a coalition known as the "Democratic Alliance." Internationally known salsa singer Ruben Blades, candidate of the Papa Egoro party, placed a disappointing third, with just over 17% of the vote. In 1993, Blades had topped public opinion polls of presidential hopefuls, but had dropped to second in 1994 polls. In fourth place, with between 16-17% of the vote, was former Controller General Ruben Dario Carles, candidate of an electoral coalition dubbed "Change 94." Three other candidates each received 2% or less of the total vote.

In the electoral race, Perez Balladares campaigned as a populist and advocated greater social spending and attention to the poor. He stressed the need for addressing unemployment, which he termed Panama's fundamental problem. Perez Balladares severely criticized the Endara government for corruption, while weathering attempts to portray him as having been closely associated to General Noriega. (Perez Balladares served as campaign manager during the 1989 elections for candidate Carlos Duque, which the Noriega regime had tried to impose through fraud.) Instead, Perez Balladares focused on the PRD's ties to the populist policies of Gen. Omar Torrijos, Panama's military leader who died in a plane crash in 1981.

Although Panama's constitution does not allow for direct presidential reelection, President Perez Balladares had been actively seeking a second term in 1999 and sought approval in a national referendum to amend the constitution to allow for direct election. In 1997, the President's PRD began studying the possibility of amending it in time for the country's May 1999 elections. Panama's Legislative Assembly approved a bill in May 1998, and a national referendum was scheduled for August 30, 1998. Leading up to the vote, polls had shown that those opposed were ahead of those in favor. But the overwhelming defeat of the constitutional amendment, by a vote of 64% to 34%, surprised many observers.

President Moscoso

In her second bid for the presidency, Arnulfist Party (PA) candidate Mireya Moscoso was victorious in the May 2, 1999 elections. Moscoso, who was inaugurated September 1,

1999, for a 5-year term, captured almost 45% of the vote and soundly defeated the ruling PRD's candidate Martin Torrijos (son of former populist leader Omar Torrijos), who received almost 38% of the vote. Until March 1999, Torrijos had been leading in opinion polls, but as the election neared the two candidates were in a dead heat. A third candidate, Alberto Vallarino, heading a coalition known as Opposition Action, received about 17% of the vote.

While Moscoso took the presidency, the PRD-led New Nation coalition won a majority of 41 seats in the 71-member unicameral Legislative Assembly. Just days before her inauguration, however, Moscoso was able to cobble together a People's Bloc coalition that gave her government 36 seats in the Assembly compared to 35 for the opposition. In the newly formed coalition, the Solidarity Party, the Christian Democratic Party (PDC), and the National Liberal Party threw its support behind Moscoso.

President-elect Moscoso, a coffee plantation owner and Panama's first female president, ran as a populist during the campaign, promising to end government corruption, curb the pace of privatizing state enterprises, and reduce poverty. She also promised to ensure that politics and corruption do not interfere with the administration of the Canal. The memory of her husband Arnulfo Arias, who was elected three times as president, but overthrown each time, was a factor in the campaign, particularly since Arias was last overthrown in 1968 by General Omar Torrijos, the father of the PRD's 1999 presidential candidate.

Economic Conditions and Outlook

Before the December 1989 U.S. intervention, the Panamanian economy had been severely damaged by two years of strong U.S. economic sanctions and economic disruption caused by the political crisis. Gross Domestic Product (GDP) had declined some 25% between 1987 and 1989. Since that time, the service-based economy has made considerable progress. Under the 1990-1994 Endara government, real economic growth averaged almost 6.6%. Under Perez Balladares, economic growth was sluggish in 1995 (1.9%) and 1996 (1.5%), but rebounded in 1997 (4.7%) and 1998 (4.6%). Economic growth for 1999 was estimated at 3.4%. Despite Panama's substantial economic recovery in the 1990s, the government estimates that more than 40% of the population live in poverty.

The Perez Balladares government implemented an economic reform program that included liberalization of the trade regime, privatization of state-owned enterprises, the institution of fiscal reform, and labor code reform. In 1997, Panama lowered its tariff rates to a range of 10-15% (with the exception of rice, milk products, and automobiles) in preparation for joining the World Trade Organization. To date, privatizations have included two ports, electrical distribution companies, electrical power plants, the Panama Canal Railway, the state telecommunications company, two sugar companies, and a cement company. However, privatization of the state water company was canceled after strong opposition by labor and political groups, and President-elect Moscoso has vowed not to privatize it. The Perez Balladares government also postponed the public bid for Panama's Tocumen International Airport until October 1999, after the Moscoso government is in place.

Given the populist rhetoric of Moscoso's electoral campaign, some observers have expressed concern about the President-elect's economic policy direction, but most observers do not believe that she will pursue anti-market economic policies. During the campaign, she promised to raise import tariffs temporarily in order to give local producers time, especially in the agriculture sector, to adjust to global competition. Moscoso also promised to slow the pace of privatizing state enterprises in Panama. Looking ahead, Moscoso will face the challenge of finding viable investments and projects for the reverted U.S. military facilities.

Policy Issues and Concerns

Over the past several years, U.S.-Panamanian relations centered on the continued implementation of the Panama Canal treaties and the possibility of a continued U.S. military presence in Panama into the next century. Talks on a U.S. military contribution for a new Multinational Counternarcotics Center (MCC) began in 1996 and led to a draft U.S.-Panamanian agreement in December 1997. But on September 25, 1998, both countries announced that they were ending the talks through mutual agreement. Some believe that Panama's internal politics, where President Perez Balladares was actively seeking a constitutional change for a second term of office, appear to have influenced the MCC negotiations. While Panamanian opinion polls overwhelmingly favored a continued U.S. military presence, President Perez Balladares appeared concerned about vocal opposition to the center. Some U.S. and Panamanian politicians believe that there is still an opportunity for the United States to negotiate the use of facilities in Panama for counternarcotics missions. This could consist of the establishment of a Forward Operating Location (FOL) in Panama for anti-drug operations in the region, similar to FOLs negotiated for a U.S. presence in Ecuador, Aruba, and Curacao.

Other U.S. interests or concerns in Panama include controversy over the extent to which the United States will clean up three firing ranges in Panama; continued Panamanian cooperation on antidrug efforts; and a 1999 scandal involving a Chinese immigrant smuggling ring, with the alleged involvement of Panamanian government officials. In addition, another issue that has been raised by some are allegations that China could threaten the operation of the Panama Canal because of its links to a Hong Kong company operating ports at both ends of the Canal. These and other issues are discussed in more detail below.

Future of U.S. Military Presence in Panama

Under the terms of the Panama Canal Treaty, all U.S. military forces withdrew from Panama by December 31, 1999, since no mutual agreement was reached to continue their presence. At that time, Panama assumed responsibility for defending as well as operating the Canal. Nevertheless, under the terms of the Treaty on the Permanent Neutrality and Operation of the Canal, often referred to as the Neutrality Treaty, the United States will have the right to use military force to reopen the canal or restore its operations. (Also see discussion of treaties in the "Operation of the Panama Canal" section below.)

Role and Presence of U.S. Troops. Over the years, U.S. military forces in Panama had several functions. The primary purpose of the troops was to provide for the defense of the Panama Canal, as set forth in the Panama Canal Treaties, until December 31, 1999. Another function served by the presence of the U.S. military in Panama stemmed from its activities throughout Latin America. Until late September 1997, Panama served as the headquarters of the U.S. Southern Command (SOUTHCOM), a unified command responsible for all U.S. military operations south of Mexico. In March 1995, President Clinton announced that

SOUTHCOM headquarters, located at Quarry Heights in Panama, would be moved to Miami. The move began in June 1997 and was completed by the end of September 1997. U.S. bases in Panama also supported assistance to Latin American nations combating drug trafficking, such as aerial reconnaissance and counter-narcotics training. Howard Air Force Base provided secure staging for detection, monitoring, and intelligence collecting assets. Panama also provided unique opportunities and facilities for military training, including the Jungle Operations Training Center (which was deactivated on April 1, 1999) at Fort Sherman.

At this juncture, all U.S. forces have withdrawn from Panama, and all of the U.S. bases and facilities have reverted to Panamanian control. Ten major installations were returned to Panama over a 4-year period: Fort Davis and Fort Espinar in early September 1995; Fort Amador, at the Pacific entrance to the Canal, on October 1, 1996; Albrook Air Force Station on October 1, 1997; Galeta Island on March 1, 1999; Rodman Naval Station on March 11, 1999; Fort Sherman, on the Atlantic side, on June 30, 1999; Howard Air Force Base, which ceased air operations in May 1999, was officially turned over to Panama on November 1, 1999, along with Fort Kobbe; and Fort Clayton and was turned over on November 30, 1999.

Failed Negotiations for a Multinational Counternarcotics Center (MCC). In September 1995, President Clinton and President Perez Balladares met in Washington and announced that the two countries would begin informal discussions to determine if there was mutual interest in the United States maintaining a military presence in Panama beyond the end of 1999. Those talks never materialized, but instead there were a series of bilateral talks regarding a U.S. contribution to a Multinational Counternarcotics Center (MCC). President Perez Balladares had announced in July 1996 that Panama would be willing to allow the United States to use Howard Air Force Base, at no cost, as a international drug interdiction center. He stated that Panama would "provide the facility free of charge as part of our contribution to the drug war."

Talks on a potential MCC began in late November 1996 and ultimately led to a tentative agreement, announced December 24, 1997, on the establishment of a MCC with the United States contributing troops for the center. Despite the tentative accord, progress on a final agreement was stymied during 1998, and on September 25, 1998, both countries announced that they were ending the MCC talks without a final accord.

As described in the press, the MCC would have involved about 2,000 U.S. troops operating at Howard Air Force Base, Rodman Naval Station, and Fort Kobbe on the Pacific side of the Canal. Other facilities reportedly to be utilized would have been communication facilities at Galeta Island and Corozal. Panama would have provided free use of the bases, while the United States would have been expected to pay for such facilities as housing. The MCC reportedly would have been established for a 12-year period, renewable for additional five-year periods, with the potential participation of participation of other Latin American nations. Reportedly the MCC would have had a Directors' Council made up of the foreign ministers of participating countries and presided over by Panama's foreign minister. If the United States and Panama had agreed on the MCC, the next step would have been for Panama's Legislative Assembly to approve the agreement, and then would have been subject to a national referendum in Panama.

As early as April 1998, the Clinton Administration had expressed concern that negotiations would have to be concluded soon, or the United States would be forced to locate the U.S. antidrug operations elsewhere. Although the text of the draft MCC accord was not made public, press reports indicated that one problem in the negotiations was a provision that would permit U.S. soldiers to engage in other missions beyond counter-narcotics. Panama and several Latin American nations expected to join the MCC expressed reservations about this aspect of the accord, with concerns centered on the potential for U.S. military intervention in the region. U.S. officials, however, maintained that U.S. military activities beyond antinarcotics work would consist of such benign activities as search and rescue and disaster relief. Another reported problem in the negotiations was U.S. rejection of Panama's call for a change in the agreement, whereby the center could be dissolved after 3 years if the drug trafficking problem diminished.

Some, including former Ambassador Thomas McNamara, the lead negotiator in the talks with Panama, believe that the main reason that an agreement was not reached was Panama's internal politics. While Panamanian opinion polls overwhelmingly favored a continued U.S. military presence, the President appeared concerned about vocal opposition, even from within his own party, to the proposed center. Moreover, President Perez Balladares was actively seeking a constitutional change for a second term of office, and this appeared to have influenced the MCC negotiations.

Possibility of Panama as a Forward Operating Location (FOL). In early December 1998, U.S. officials announced that they had begun talks with several Latin American countries to find new bases of operation in Central and South America to replace the antidrug mission of the U.S. presence in Panama. Short-term interim agreements were concluded in April 1999 to have Forward Operating Locations (FOLs) in Ecuador, Aruba, and Curacao for U.S. aerial counternarcotics missions. Subsequently, the United States concluded longer-term 10-year agreements with Ecuador and the Netherlands (for Aruba and Curacao) for the anti-drug FOLs. An additional FOL site also was being sought in Central America, and on March 31, 2000, and a 10-year agreement was signed with El Salvador, although the Salvadoran legislature still has to vote on the agreement.

In 1999, some Members of the U.S. Congress and politicians in Panama suggested that there was still an opportunity for the United States to negotiate the use of facilities in Panama for U.S. antidrug flights, similar to the FOLs negotiated with arrangements with Ecuador, Aruba, and Curacao. Press reports suggested that President-elect Moscoso was interested in allowing the U.S. military to use Panama as a staging area for anti-drug flights (e.g. see "A Panama Site for U.S. Anti-Drug Planes," *Miami Herald*, August 5, 1999.) However, the FOL agreement with El Salvador signed in March 2000 appears to make any potential U.S. consideration of an FOL in Panama unlikely.

Congressional Views. In previous sessions, Congress has gone on record twice favoring negotiations to consider a continued U.S. presence in Panama beyond the end of 1999, and in the 104th Congress the Senate approved a nonbinding resolution on the issue. In 1991, Congress enacted legislation (P.L. 102-190, Section 3505) expressing the sense of Congress that the President should begin negotiations with Panama to consider whether the two nations should allow the permanent stationing of U.S. forces in Panama past 1999. Twelve years earlier, Congress had approved the Panama Canal Act of 1979 (P.L. 96-70, Section 1111) which states that "it is the sense of the Congress that the best interests of the United States require that the President enter into negotiations" with Panama "for the purpose of arranging for the stationing of United States military forces after the termination of the

Panama Canal Treaty." And on September 5, 1996, the Senate approved S.Con.Res. 14, expressing the sense of Congress that the President should negotiate a new base rights agreement with Panama, while consulting with Congress regarding any bilateral negotiations that take place.

In the 106th Congress, numerous measures have been introduced relating to a continued U.S. military presence in Panama, many introduced late in the first session as the Canal turnover approached. No legislative action has been taken on these measures. Three resolutions – S.Con.Res. 59 (Smith), S.J.Res. 37 (Smith), and H.Con.Res. 233 (Myrick) – urge the President to negotiate a new base rights agreement with Panama to permit U.S. troops beyond December 31, 1999. H.Con.Res. 186 (Rohrabacher)/S.Con.Res. 61 (Sessions), among other provisions, express the sense of Congress that the United States should negotiate security arrangements with Panama to protect the Canal and ensure Panama's territorial integrity. S.Res. 257 (Craig), expresses the sense of the Senate that the President should negotiate security arrangements with Panama regarding the protection of the Canal, and that any attack on or against the Canal would be considered an act of war against the United States. H.R. 2244 (Hunter), among other provisions, authorizes and directs the President to confer with Panama to renegotiate the terms of the Panama Canal Treaties or to negotiate a new agreement for the purpose of providing for the security of the Canal. H.R. 3452 (Baker) provides that unpaid balances of the Panama Canal Commission shall be payable to Panama only upon completion of an agreement that leases half of Howard Air Force Base to the United States. (Also see LEGISLATION section for broader initiatives related to the overall implementation of the Panama Canal Treaties.)

Introduce in the second session, H.R. 3673 (Gilman) would provide Panama with certain benefits if Panama agreed to permit the United States to maintain a presence there sufficient to carry out counternarcotics and related missions in Panama. The benefits would be preferential trade access to the U.S. market similar to that enjoyed by Canada and Mexico; a scholarship program for Panamanians to study in the United States; assistance in preparing for construction of a new bridge across the Canal; and assistance in preparing for construction of a new sewage treatment plan for Panama City.

Panamanian Views. Over the past several years, public opinion polls in Panama have cited overwhelming support for a continued U.S. military presence. Nevertheless, while public opinion polls have consistently shown that a majority of Panamanians would like some U.S. military presence after the end of 1999, Panamanian opponents to the MCC were vocal and staged protests at various times. After formal talks with the United States on the MCC were announced in 1997, there were several protests by student, human rights, and labor groups who oppose a continued U.S. presence. In 1997, an umbrella organization was formed known as the Organizations Against Military Bases, which included some 30 labor, peasant, and student groups, and in early 1998 another umbrella organization opposed to the MCC was formed, the National Movement for the Defense of Sovereignty, consisting of labor, student, and professional organizations.

Some observers point out that President Perez Balladares seemed more concerned with his reelection bid than actually attaining an agreement with the United States for the MCC. They believe that President Perez Balladares, cognizant that his PRD receives much its support from the left, ratcheted up the political rhetoric on the MCC, that is, criticizing the United States, in order to quell his critics from the left and advance his reelection chances.

Some Panamanians oppose a U.S. military presence beyond the end of 1999, arguing that only with the U.S. military out of the country will Panama be able to break the dependent relationship it has with the United States and recover its own national identity. Some Panamanian politicians opposed the MCC because they believe it would have been a disguised way of perpetuating U.S. military bases beyond 1999. Others maintain that their country's use of the bases and their extensive infrastructure could be a great economic boom that could overcome the loss of income from the departure of U.S. forces. On the other side, some have focused on the importance of continuing a U.S. military presence to help conduct counternarcotics operations in Panama and in the region. They point with concern to incursions of Colombian narco-traffickers into the Darien jungle region of Panama.

Contamination of Defense Sites. A controversial bilateral issue that has arisen is the extent to which the United States will clean up three ranges (Empire, Pina, Balboa West) that were used for testing ground explosives. U.S. officials acknowledge that some 7,500 acres being returned to Panama will be not available for unrestricted use because "the technology is not available to do the job safely while protecting the environment." (New York Times, October 14, 1998, "U.S. Balks at Cleanup of Hazardous Canal Zone Sites") They assert that it is not possible to remove the unexploded ordinance without tearing down the rain forest and threatening the Canal's watershed. They point to a Canal treaty provision (Agreement in Implementation of Article IV of the Panama Canal Treaty, Article IV) which states that the United States is obligated to take all measures, "insofar as may be practicable," in order to ensure that hazards to human life, health and safety are removed from the defense sites reverting to Panama. Officials of the Perez Balladares government believed that the United States was reneging on its treaty commitment and wanted to press the United States to clean up the firing ranges regardless of economic cost. The Pina range was turned over to Panama in June 1999, while the Empire and Balboa West ranges were turned over in July 1999. Some 60,000 Panamanians live in areas surrounding the ranges, and reportedly at least 21 Panamanians have been killed in the last two decades by coming into contact with the explosives ("No Home on Panama's Range, U.S. Munitions Scattered Over Canal Training Zones," *Washington Post*, January 10, 2000).

In September 1999, the new Moscoso government announced plans for an independent study to determine the level of danger posed by the unexploded ordnance. In October 1999, President Moscoso appointed Juan Mendez to head a Task Force on the cleanup of the bases. She also raised the issue during her October 19, 1999, meeting with President Clinton in Washington. President Clinton stated that the United States had met its treaty obligations to clean up the ranges to the extent practicable, but did say that the United States wanted to stay engaged and work with Panama on the issue. The issue also came up during Secretary of State Albright's visit to Panama on January 15, 2000, in which she reportedly promised to send a mission to Panama to investigate the situation at the ranges. In mid-February, a group of 10 U.S. experts traveled to Panama to visit the ranges.

Operation of the Panama Canal

When Panama proclaimed its independence from Colombia in 1903, it concluded a treaty with the United States for U.S. rights to build, administer, and defend a canal cutting across the country and linking the Pacific and Atlantic oceans. The treaty gave the United States rights in the so-called Canal Zone (about 10 miles wide and 50 miles long) "as if it were sovereign" and "in perpetuity." Construction of the canal was completed in 1914. In the

1960s, growing resentment in Panama over the extent of U.S. rights in the country led to pressure to negotiate a new treaty arrangement for the operation of the Canal. Draft treaties were completed in 1967 but ultimately rejected by Panama in 1970.

New negotiations ultimately led to the September 1977 signing of the two Panama Canal Treaties by President Jimmy Carter and Panamanian head of government General Omar Torrijos. Under the Panama Canal Treaty, the United States was given primary responsibility for operating and defending the Canal until December 31, 1999. (Subsequent U.S. implementing legislation established the Panama Canal Commission to operate the Canal.) Under the Treaty on the Permanent Neutrality and Operation of the Panama Canal, or simply the Neutrality Treaty, the two countries agreed to maintain a regime of neutrality, whereby the Canal would be open to ships of all nations. The U.S. Senate gave its advice and consent to the Neutrality Treaty on March 16, 1978, and to the Panama Canal Treaty on April 18, 1978, both by a vote of 68-32, with various amendments, conditions, understandings, and reservations. Panama and the United States exchanged instruments of ratification for the two treaties on June 16, 1978, and the two treaties entered into force on October 1, 1979.

Some treaty critics have argued that Panama did not accept the amendments, conditions, reservations, and understandings of the U.S. Senate, including the DeConcini condition to the Neutrality Treaty. That condition states: "if the Canal is closed, or its operations are interfered with, the United States of America and the Republic of Panama shall each independently have the right to take such steps as each deems necessary, in accordance with its constitutional processes, including the use of military force in the Republic of Panama, to reopen the Canal or restore the operations of the Canal, as the case may be." However, as the State Department has asserted, Panama expressly accepted all U.S. Senate amendments, conditions, and understandings to the two treaties, including the DeConcini condition. All the Senate provisions were incorporated into the U.S. and Panamanian instruments of ratification for the two treaties.

Over the years, U.S. officials consistently affirmed a commitment to follow through with the Panama Canal Treaty and turn the Canal over to Panama at the end of 1999. That transition occurred smoothly on December 31, 1999. The Panama Canal Treaty terminated on that date, and the Panama Canal Commission (PCC), the U.S. agency operating the Canal, was succeeded by the Panama Canal Authority, a Panamanian government agency established in 1997. Panamanian Alberto Aleman Zubieta, who served as Administrator of the PCC since 1996, also is serving as Administrator of the Panama Canal Authority.

Under the terms of the Neutrality Treaty, which has no termination date, Panama will have responsibility for operating and defending the Canal after 1999. As noted above, both Panama and the United States, however, in exercising their responsibilities to maintain the regime of neutrality (keeping the Canal secure and open to all nations on equal terms) will each independently have the right to use military force to reopen the Canal or restore its operations. This is delineated in condition (1) of the Neutrality Treaty.

Congressional Action. In April 1994, the Clinton Administration, submitted recommendations to Congress (House Document 103-233) for changes to the Panama Canal Commission in order to facilitate and encourage the operation of the Canal through an autonomous entity under the government of Panama when Panama assumes control of the Canal in the year 2000. Most significantly, the Administration recommended that the PCC be designated a government corporation with "an organizational structure that allows market responsiveness and operational flexibility." On February 10, 1996, the President signed into law the FY1996 defense authorization measure (P.L. 104-106, S. 1124), that includes a provision amending the Panama Canal Act of 1979 in line with many of the President's recommendations.

Authorizations for Panama Canal Commission expenditures are usually included in defense authorization measures. For FY2000, PCC expenditures are included in P.L. 106-65 (Title XXXV). The law authorize expenditures until December 31, 1999, when the Canal is transferred to Panamanian control according to the Panama Canal Treaty of 1977, and authorizes an Office of Transition Administration to expend funds until October 1, 2004 (see LEGISLATION section).

As the Canal turnover approached, several Members introduced resolutions regarding the implementation of the Panama Canal Treaties, but no action was taken on these measures. H.R. 2244 (Hunter), among other provisions, authorizes and directs the President to confer with Panama to renegotiate the terms of the Panama Canal Treaties or to negotiate a new agreement for the purpose of providing for the security of the Canal. H.J.Res. 77 (Chenoweth) nullifies the Canal treaties and recognizes the validity of the 1903 treaty regarding U.S. control of the Canal. H.Con.Res. 231 (Paul) expresses the sense of Congress that the Panama Canal is and ought to remain U.S. property. H.R. 3452 (Baker) provides that unpaid balances of the Panama Canal Commission shall be payable to Panama only upon completion of an agreement that leases half of Howard Air Force Base to the United States. H.R. 3231 authorizes the transfer to Panama of certain U.S. properties as set forth in the Panama Canal Treaties. Another resolution introduced in the second session of the 106th Congress, S.Res. 257 (Craig), expresses the sense of the Senate that any attack against the Canal by any country will be considered an act of war against the United States; the resolution also called for the President to negotiate security arrangements with Panama regarding the protection of the Canal.

Privatization of Two Panamanian Ports and the China Issue. A controversy that arose in U.S.- Panamanian relations in 1996 relates to the privatization of two Panamanian ports at either end of the Panama Canal, Balboa on the Pacific and Cristobal on the Atlantic. In July 1996, the Panamanian government awarded the concession to the Hong Kong company, Hutchison International Port Holdings (one of the world's largest container port operators and a subsidiary of the Hutchison Whampoa Limited Group) which operates the concession in Panama as the Panama Ports Company, S.A. Then U.S. Ambassador to Panama William Hughes complained about the lack of transparency in the bidding process in which several U.S. companies competed. The Panamanian government responded with a communique describing the process by which Hutchison was awarded the 25-year concession. Panamanian officials maintain that Hutchison had the highest bid, agreeing to pay Panama $22.2 million annually over the life of the concession. In May 1997, six U.S. Senators charged in a letter to the Federal Maritime Commission that there were irregularities in the bidding process that denied U.S. companies an equal right to develop and operate terminals in Panama. After a review of the issue, the Commission responded that while the port award processes were unorthodox and irregular by U.S. standards, it saw no evidence that U.S. companies were subjected to discriminatory treatment. A May 1997 Senate Foreign Relations Committee staff report on the issue also concluded that while the bidding process was unorthodox, U.S. officials found no evidence of illegality.

In addition to the privatization process, some press reports in March 1997 raised the issue of Hutchison's relationship with the Chinese government and the China Ocean Shipping Company (COSCO) and suggested that China would gain control of the Panama Canal. (Also see CRS Report 97-476, *Long Beach: Proposed Lease by China Ocean Shipping Company (COSCO) at Former Naval Base*.) The same May 1997 Senate Foreign Relations Committee staff report mentioned above concluded that Hutchison's operations of the ports does not constitute a threat to the Panama Canal. It noted that there are legal safeguards in the Panama Canal Treaties and Panamanian law that guarantee the continued operation of the Canal and ensures its access to all nations.

In early August 1999, Senator Trent Lott raised questions about Chinese influence over the Canal in a letter to Defense Secretary William Cohen. Subsequently, both the State Department and the Department of Defense made statements responding to the concerns raised about potential Chinese influence in Panama. In an August 12, 1999 press briefing, the Department of Defense noted that it does not consider Hutchison's ownership of two port facilities as a threat to U.S. security. DOD asserted that "the company does not have any ability to stop or impede traffic through the Canal," and noted that under the Neutrality Treaty, "the United States has a unilateral right to maintain the neutrality of the Canal and reopen it if there should be any military threat." The State Department, in an August 12, 1999, press briefing, noted that it has seen "no capability or interest on the part of the People's Republic of China, a major user of the Canal, to disrupt is operations."

According to September 29, 1999 congressional testimony by Peter Romero, Acting Assistant Secretary of State for Western Hemisphere Affairs (before the House International Relations Committee, Subcommittee on the Western Hemisphere), the U.S. intelligence community also studied the question of the influence of China in Panama as a result of the concession. Romero testified that, after reviewing the study, the State Department concluded that the Hutchison concession "does not represent a threat to canal operations or other U.S. interests in Panama."

On October 22, 1999, the Senate Armed Services Committee held a hearing on Canal security. Officials from the Department of Defense, the Panama Canal Commission, the SOUTHCOM, and the Department of State testified, and all concluded that the Hutchison's port operations did not constitute a threat to the Canal. Ambassador Lino Gutierrez, Principal Deputy Assistant Secretary of State for Western Hemisphere Affairs, stated that the Department found no information to substantiate the allegation that Hutchison is a front for the People's Republic of China. He noted that Panama's contract with Hutchison (Law 5) does not give China any role in determining which ships will pass through the Canal or in which order they will travel, and it does not give Hutchison any control over Canal pilots. Alberto Aleman Zubieta, Administrator of the Panama Canal Commission, stated that "Hutchison has no authority whatsoever to interfere with, dictate or influence the operation of the Canal, nor will it ever be allowed to do so." Gen. Charles Wilhelm, SOUTHCOM Commander in Chief, stated: "We are not aware of any current internal or external threats to the Panama Canal, and we have no evidence that it has been targeted by terrorists or foreign governments." In contrast, two Member of Congress, Representatives Bob Barr and Dana Rohrabacher, testified before the Committee, arguing that Hutchison, because of its alleged close associations with China and the Chinese military, poses a future threat to Canal operations. In addition, former Secretary of Defense Casper Weinberger testified that the

United States should work out details with Panama about how the United States will have the right to defend the Canal in the future once Panama takes over its operation.

On November 30, 1999, President Clinton dismissed concerns that the security of the Canal would be threatened by the operation of the two ports by Hutchison. But in doing so, the President misspoke and implied that China would be operating the Canal. The State Department subsequently corrected the record and indicated that the President was referring to the operation of the two ports by Hutchison.

In the 106th Congress, three measures have been introduced related to the port concession issue. H.R. 2244 (Hunter), among several other provisions, requires a report from the President describing how Hutchison was selected to manage the two ports. The bill also prohibits U.S. assistance to Panama if a defense site or military installation built or formerly operated by the United States has been conveyed to any foreign government-owned entity. Identical concurrent resolutions H.Con.Res. 186 (Rohrabacher) and S.Con.Res. 61 (Sessions) express the sense of Congress that the United States should request Panama to nullify the lease agreements for the two ports and to investigate charges of corruption related to the granting of the concession. (See LEGISLATION section.)

Drug Trafficking and Money Laundering

An important concern for U.S. policymakers has been securing Panamanian cooperation in anti-drug-trafficking and anti-money-laundering measures. Panama is an important drug money laundering center and a drug transhipment point from South America to the U.S. market. The county is also a small-scale producer of coca leaf in the remote Darien province area bordering Colombia.

On June 22, 1996, President Perez Balladares acknowledged that accused Cali cartel drug trafficker Jose Castrillon had contributed $51,000 to his 1994 presidential campaign, although the President maintained that he was unaware of where the money came from. Castrillon was arrested in Panama on drug charges in April 1996. The President's acknowledgment, which tarnished his government's image, sparked a broad investigation into the contributions of drug money launderers to a number of politicians. Castrillon was subsequently flown to the United States in May 1998 to face justice on drug trafficking charges in Tampa, Florida. A *Washington Post* investigative article ("In Panama, Drug Money's Clout Outlives Noriega, November 19, 1998) maintained that Castrillon had high-level contacts in the Perez Balladares government and quoted sources stating that Castrillon had provided hundreds of thousands of dollars to the Perez Balladares 1994 campaign.

For 1995-1999, the Clinton Administration certified Panama as fully cooperating with the United States on counter-narcotics measures. The State Department's March 1999 International Narcotics Control Strategy Report stated that Panama's law enforcement agencies have maintained excellent relations with their U.S. counterparts. It noted that Panama seized near-record amounts of illicit narcotics in 1998, demonstrated its political commitment to cooperate with the United States on major drug trafficking cases, and enacted a major banking reform bringing Panama into compliance with international standards. The report also noted that Panama is continuing to implement its own 5-year master plan (1996-2001) emphasizing prevention and treatment as well as law enforcement. Looking to what further efforts Panama should take, the 1999 drug strategy report noted that major U.S. goals include the conclusion of a maritime interdiction agreement; refinement of Panamanian banking reforms announced in 1998; and enactment of legislation to extend the existing law against drug money laundering to include the proceeds from all serious crimes.

Security Concerns

In testimony before the Senate Foreign Relations Committee on June 22, 1999, SOUTHCOM commander-in-chief Gen. Charles Wilhelm expressed concern about the incursion of Colombian guerrillas into Panama and about the ability of Panama's security forces to deal with the threat. He asserted that the Panamanian Public Forces (PPF) were neither organized nor equipped to deal with incursions by Colombian insurgents. In late May 1999, several hundred guerrillas of the Colombian Revolutionary Armed Forces (FARC), in flight from Colombian paramilitaries, crossed into the dense jungle Darien province region of Panama. President Moscoso has vowed to equip the National Police with weapons, helicopters, and other equipment to bolster surveillance on the border. Concerns about the spillover of violence from Colombia heightened in early November 1999 when two tourist helicopters were hijacked near Panama City by armed men claiming to be FARC guerrillas

Chinese Immigrant Scandal

A scandal involving a Chinese immigrant smuggling ring resulted in President Perez Balladares' firing several officials in June 1999, including Samantha Smith, the head of Panama's intelligence agency. Press reports allege that the scandal also prompted a dispute between U.S. Ambassador Simon Ferro and the U.S. Department of Justice, where officials claim the Ambassador jeopardized the secrecy of a U.S. investigation when he canceled the U.S. visa of Samantha Smith ("U.S. Immigrant-Smuggling Probe Jars Panama," *Miami Herald*, August 8, 1999).The scandal allegedly involved the sale of Panamanian visas for as much as $15,000 to Chinese citizens who would fly from Hong Kong to Panama, then travel to Central America or Mexico, and then into the United States. Other high-ranking Panamanian officials reportedly were involved in the scheme. In October 1999, the U.S. Embassy in Panama revoked the visas of three other Panamanian officials, including the Controller General, Gabriel Castro ("3 Panamanians' Visas Revoked; Smuggling Probe Intensifies," *Miami Herald*, October 22, 1999).

Democratization

Panama has made great progress in restoring functioning political institutions after 21 years of military-controlled government. A critical challenge for the government is the administration of justice. According to the U.S. Department of State's human rights report for 1999, Panama's principal human rights problems include a judicial system subject to corruption and political manipulation; the use of excessive force by police and prison guards against detainees and prisoners; poor prison conditions; prisoners subject to prolonged pretrial detention.

Under the Perez Balladares government, there was some controversy over the pardoning of military and government officials for abuses under military rule. When the President took office in September 1994, he pardoned 222 former government officials and military members, and in September 1995, Vice President Tomas Duque pardoned 130 officials when the President was out of the country. In 1996, the Legislative Assembly began considering a general amnesty that would pardon over 951 people. The amnesty was criticized by Panamanian human rights groups and Amnesty International and sparked street protests in Panama. As a result of the opposition, the Legislative Assembly postponed debate on the amnesty indefinitely. In September 1999, President Moscoso rescinded pardons granted by President Balladares to 33 individuals for abuses committed under military rule.

Considerable criticism was prompted by the November 1, 1997 acquittal of Pedro Miguel Gonzalez, the son of a prominent Panamanian politician (PRD president Gerardo Gonzalez) for the shooting of a U.S. soldier, Sgt. Zak Hernandez, killed in June 1992. U.S. officials expressed deep disappointment with the verdict and maintained that it was inconsistent with persuasive testimony and physical evidence. Pedro Gonzalez was elected to National Assembly on the PRD ticket in the May 2, 1999 elections.

Another controversy that arose under the Perez Balladares government related to freedom of the press. In mid-August 1997, the government announced that it would not renew the work permit of a Peruvian investigative journalist, Gustavo Gorriti, who serves as associate editor of the Panamanian daily newspaper La Prensa. Gorriti had reported recently on corruption and political scandals. Human rights organizations criticized the government's action and the U.S. Embassy asserted that the action raised questions about Panama's commitment to a free press. In September the government took further action by serving Gorriti with a deportation order. After considerable U.S. and international criticism, the Panamanian government reversed itself on October 15, 1997, by renewing Gorriti's work permit for another year. Panamanian newspapers and human rights groups praised the government for its reversal, and claimed a victory for freedom of the press.

In 1999, the Panamanian government was again criticized for violations of freedom of the press. In March 1999, the New York-based Committee to Protect Journalists condemned Panama for its use of gag laws to limit press freedom and punish journalists. The Organization of American States also issued a June 1999 report criticizing the use of laws by public officials to stifle criticism against the government. After her inauguration in September 1999, President Moscoso said that she wanted to get rid of such press restriction laws, and by December, the President ratified the National Assembly's decision to eliminate the gag laws.

LEGISLATION

P.L. 106-65 (S. 1059/H.R. 1401)

FY2000 Defense Authorization bill. Authorizes expenditures for the Panama Canal Commission. S. 1059 reported by Senate Committee on Armed Services (S.Rept. 106-50) May 17, 1999; Senate passed, amended, 92-3, May 27, 1999. H.R. 1401 reported by House Committee on Armed Services (H.Rept. 106-162) May 24, 1999; House passed amended, 365-58, June 10, 1999. House passed S. 1059 June 14, substituting the language of H.R. 1401. Conference report (H.Rept. 106-301) filed August 6, 1999. House agreed to conference report September 15. Senate agreed to conference report September 22. Presented to the President September 23. As approved, Title XXXV authorizes expenditures for the Panama Canal Commission from a revolving fund for the operation, maintenance, improvement, and administration of the Canal until the termination of the Panama Canal Treaty of 1977 on December 31, 1999. Not more than $75,000 can be expended for official reception and representation expenses. An Office of Transition Administration is authorized to expend funds until October 1, 2004.

H.R. 2244 (Hunter)

United States-Panama Security Act of 1999. Prohibits U.S. assistance to Panama if a defense site or military installation built or formerly operated by the United States has been conveyed by Panama to any foreign government-owned entity, and for other purposes. Requires several reports from the Administration, including a report from the President describing how Hutchison Whampoa was selected to manage the ports of Balboa and Cristobal. Authorizes and directs the President to confer with Panama to renegotiate the terms of the Panama Canal Treaties or to negotiate a new agreement to supersede the treaties for the purpose of providing for the security of the Canal into the 21st century. Introduced June 16, 1999; referred to the Committee on International Relations and to the Committees on Banking and Financial Services, Armed Services, and Intelligence (Permanent Select).

H.R. 3231 (Crane)

Authorizes the transfer to Panama of certain U.S. properties as set forth in the Panama Canal Treaties. Introduced Nov. 4, 1999; referred to the Committee on Armed Services.

H.R. 3452 (Baker)

Provides that unpaid balances of the Panama Canal Commission shall be payable only upon completion of an agreement that leases to the United States not less than 50% of Howard Air Force Base; and grants to the United States the continuing authority to ensure the proper disbursement and use of the balance paid.

H.J.Res. 77 (Chenoweth)

Notifies Panama of the nullity of the Carter-Torrijos treaties and recognizes the validity of the Hay-Bunau-Varilla Treaty with respect to control of the Panama Canal Treaty. Introduced November 9, 1999; referred to the Committee on Armed Services.

H.R. 3673 (Gilman)

Provides certain benefits to Panama (preferential trade access, a scholarship program, and assistance in preparing for construction of a new bridge across the Canal and a new sewage treatment plant for Panama City) if Panama agrees to permit the United States to maintain a presence there sufficient to carry out counternarcotics and related missions. Introduced Feb. 16, 2000; referred to Committee on International Relations and Committee on Ways and Means.

H.Con.Res. 186 (Rohrabacher)/ S.Con.Res. 61 (Sessions)

Identical concurrent resolutions expressing the sense of Congress that the United States should request Panama to nullify the lease agreements for the Balboa and Cristobal port facilities and to investigate charges of corruption related to the granting of the lease; and that the United States should negotiate security arrangements with Panama to protect the canal and ensure the territorial integrity of Panama. H.Con.Res. 186 introduced Sept. 17, 1999; referred to the Committee on International Relations. S.Con.Res. 61 introduced Oct. 19, 1999; referred to Committee on Foreign Relations.

H.Con.Res. 231 (Paul)

Expresses the sense of Congress that the Panama Canal and the Panama Canal Zone should be considered to be the sovereign territory of the United States. Introduced November 16, 1999; referred to the Committee on Armed Services.

H.Res. 160 (Gallegly)

Congratulates the government and people of Panama on free and democratic elections held May 2, 1999. Introduced May 5, 1999; referred to the Committee on International Relations.

S.Con.Res. 59 (Smith)/ S.J.Res. 37 (Smith)/H.Con.Res. 233 (Myrick)

Similar resolutions expressing the sense of Congress that the President should negotiate a new base rights agreement with Panama to permit the stationing of U.S. troops in Panama beyond December 31, 1999. S.Con.Res. 59 introduced Oct. 14, 1999; referred to Senate Committee on Foreign Relations. S.J.Res. 37 introduced November 4; placed on Senate Legislative Calendar under General Orders November 5, 1999. H.Con.Res. 233 introduced November 17, 1999; referred to House Committee on International Relations and to the House Committee on Armed Services.

S.Res. 257 (Craig)

Expresses the sense of the Senate that any attack on or against the Panama Canal by any other country will be considered an act of war against the United States, and that the President should, prior to June 1, 2001, negotiate security arrangements with Panama regarding the protection of the Canal. Introduced Feb. 10, 2000; referred to Committee on Foreign Relations.

Congressional Hearings, Reports, and Documents

U.S. Congress. House. Committee on National Security. Special Oversight Panel on the Merchant Marine. *Annual Authorization of the Panama Canal Commission and the Annual Authorization for the United States Maritime Administration.* Hearing, March 10, 1999, H.N.S.C. No. 105-34. Washington, U.S. Govt. Print. Off. 1998. 100 p.

U.S. Congress. Senate. Committee on Foreign Relations. *Future of U.S. Military in Panama.* Staff Report, Committee Print. May 1997. S. Prt. 105-22. Washington. U.S. Govt. Print Off. 1997. 47 p.

—— *The Panama Canal and United States Interests.* Hearing, June 16, 1998, S. Prt. 105-672. Washington. U.S. Govt. Print Off. 1998. 61 p.

—— *Staff Report on the Privatization of Panamanian Ports.* May 1997. Available from the Committee. 40 p.

INDEX